Capturing Long-Distance Travel

RESEARCH STUDIES IN TRAFFIC ENGINEERING SERIES

Series Editor: **Professor M. G. H. Bell**
Imperial College London,, UK

Capturing Long-Distance Travel

Edited by

K. W. Axhausen, J.-L. Madre, J. W. Polak *and* Ph. Toint

RESEARCH STUDIES PRESS LTD.
Baldock, Hertfordshire, England

RESEARCH STUDIES PRESS LTD.
16 Coach House Cloisters, 10 Hitchin Street, Baldock, Hertfordshire, SG7 6AE, England
http://www.research-studies-press.co.uk/

and

Institute *of* Physics PUBLISHING, Suite 929, The Public Ledger Building,

150 South Independence Mall West, Philadelphia, PA 19106, USA

Marketing:

Institute *of* Physics PUBLISHING, Dirac House, Temple Back, Bristol, BS1 6BE, England
www.bookmarkphysics.iop.org

Distribution:

NORTH AMERICA

AIDC, 50 Winter Sport Lane, PO Box 20, Williston, VT 05495-0020, USA
Tel: 1-800 632 0880 or outside USA 1-802 862 0095, Fax: 802 864 7626, E-mail: orders@aidcvt.com

UK AND THE REST OF WORLD

Marston Book Services Ltd, P.O. Box 269, Abingdon, Oxfordshire, OX14 4YN, England
Tel: + 44 (0)1235 465500 Fax: + 44 (0)1235 465555 E-mail: direct.order@marston.co.uk

Library of Congress Cataloging-in-Publication Data

Capturing long distance travel / edited by K.W. Axhausen ... [et al.].
    p. cm -- (Research studies in traffic engineering series ; 3)
  Includes bibliographical references and index.
  ISBN 0-86380-257-5
  1. Tourism—Europe--Statistical methods. 2. Travel--Europe--Statistical methods. 3.
Tourism--Statistical methods. 4. Travel--Statistical methods. I. Axhausen, K. W., 1958-
II. Series.

G155.E8 C26 2001
910'.7'27--dc21

                                                                2001019347

British Library Cataloguing in Publication Data
A catalogue record for this book is available from the British Library.

ISBN 0 86380 257 5

Printed in Great Britain by SRP Ltd., Exeter

Editorial Foreword

If the catch phrase "evidence-based policy" is not to be entirely vacuous, there is a growing demand for good data. Although the amount of data, particularly concerning long-distance travel, grows exponentially with the spread of web-based booking, e-tickets and smartcards, this does not necessarily constitute "good data" in the sense of useful information. To be useful, there must be a common understanding of the terminology and concepts behind the data, not a simple matter given the diversity of language and culture across Europe. Nowhere is this more true than for the development of policy for the Trans-European Network (TEN), which, as the authors say, requires "coherence of vision and cooperation between member states".

This book shows that the measurement of travel behaviour is not a simple matter. Firstly, there needs to be harmonisation of terminology and concepts, as already mentioned. Secondly, there are tricky issues associated with non-response and missing values. Are those who respond typical examples of those who don't, and if not, what should be done about it? For instance, frequent travellers are less likely to be at home to answer a questionnaire. On the other hand, frequent travellers may be more motivated to respond. Should these biases be corrected for, and if so, how? The curious (or desperate) reader will find useful ideas and suggestions, if not definitive answers, to these and other vexed questions in the following chapters.

New technologies are providing exciting ways of unlocking data about travel behaviour. Personal Digital Assistants (PDAs) open up the possibility of greater interaction between the interviewer and the interviewee. Geographic Information Systems (GIS) make the provision of geographical data ever easier. However, with new technologies come new biases. For example, the oft cited "digital divide" may discourage certain sections of society from responding to a computer-aided survey. These and related issues are addressed in the cLosing chapters. I commend this book to you.

M.H.G. Bell (Series Editor)

Preface and acknowledgements

This book documents the collaboration of a large number of researchers, administrators, support staff and of the institutions for which they worked and work. The bulk of the work reported here was made possible by two grants of the 4th Framework Programme of the European Union: Methods for European Surveys of Travel Behaviour (MEST) (1996–1999) and Technologies for European Surveys of Travel Behaviour (TEST) (1997–1999), which were co-ordinated by the Fakultät für Bauingenieurwesen und Architektur at the Leopold-Franzens Universität, Innsbruck.

The consortium consisted out of the following institutions and firms:

Transportes, Inovação e Sistemas (TIS)
Rua Vilhena Barbosa 11
P - 1000 Lisboa

Socialdata
Hans-Grässel-Weg 1
D - 81375 München

Büro Dr. Herry
Argentinierstr. 21
A - 1040 Wien

TOI
Box 6110 Etterstad
N - 0602 Oslo

Statistics Sweden (SCB)
Box 24300
S - 10451 Stockholm

DEST
INRETS
2 Ave Général Malleret Joinville
F - 94110 Arcueil

Statistics Netherlands (CBS)
Department of Transport Statistics
P.O. Box 4481
NL - 6401 CZ Heerlen

Deutsche Forschungsanstalt für Luft-
und Raumfahrt (DLR)
Linder Höhe
D - 51147 Köln

Centre for Transport Studies (CTS)
Department of Civil Engineering
Imperial College
UK - London SW7 2BU

TRAIL
TU Delft
Berlageweg 1
NL – 2628 CR Delft

Transportation Research Group (GRT)
Facultés Universitaires ND de la Paix
61, rue de Bruxelles
B - 5000 Namur

Their support is gratefully acknowledged.

There were two projects, with two official project numbers, but they were conducted as one project, which was funded in two phases: project partners and project organisation were the same; the project meetings addressed issues of both projects. At Innsbruck two researchers drew the short straw and had to add project administration to their other tasks: Maria Youssefzadeh (MEST) and Ines Haubold (TEST), both acquitted themselves very well in both roles and the consortium and its guests at various workshops benefited from their skill. Maria Youssefzadeh also undertook the final formatting of this book. This is very gratefully acknowledged.

These guests were too numerous to mention here, but they generously gave their time to discuss our progress with us and thus helped to shape our work.

A project on survey methods depends on the fieldwork of the firms conducting the surveys. Their enthusiasm, commitment and skill are indispensable. We would like to thank all the firms involved, but would like to highlight those whose contribution went beyond the call of duty: STRS (Twickenham, now Isle-of-Wight), Metris (Lisbon), SCB (Örebrö) and IPSOS Region (Lyon).

Central to the success of European Union-funded collaborative research is the on-going support and interest of the staff of the responsible Directorate General. We have been lucky, in both respects, with the research officers supervising our work: Keith Keen, Richard Butchart, Anna Panagopoulou, Alexander Tsiotras, José Elias de Freitas, but in particular Leonidas Kioussis, who accompanied us for most of the project duration.

While the authors of the following chapters have been involved with the project, not all project participants had the time and resources to write a chapter. We want to acknowledge their important contributions to the success of our work: Cristina Elvas, TIS; Erhard Erl, Socialdata; Amie Lindeberg, SCB; Ger Moritz, CBS; Hans-Georg Nüsser, DLR; John Plaxton, IC; Mart Tacken, TRAIL and Jose Viegas, TIS.

It is satisfying for a project to see that its efforts are translated into further action. We are pleased to see this happening, as the European Union is funding, for the first time, a major survey of long-distance travel (see http://www.ncl.ac.uk/dateline/), for which our results prepared the ground. We hope that this book, which documents our theoretical and empirical results, will help this and other related surveys to achieve better quality results through improved survey protocols and designs and through improved sampling, coding and data analysis strategies.

Kay Axhausen, Jean-Loup Madre, John Polak and Philippe Toint
April 2003

Table of Contents

List of Figures

List of Tables

Chapter 1
Introduction

K. W. Axhausen, J.-L. Madre, J. W. Polak and Ph. L. Toint

1.   Introduction[1]

K. W. Axhausen	J.-L. Madre	J. W. Polak	Ph. L. Toint
IVT	DEST	CTS	GRT
ETH	INRETS	Imperial College	FUNDP
CH – 8093 Zürich	F – 94110 Arcueil	UK – London, SW7 2BU	B – 5000 Namur

1.1   STARTING POSITION

In the last ten years, the improving standards and rising expectations in the domain of transport policies have made understanding long-distance travel an important topic, both from the academic research and pragmatic infrastructure planning points of view. At the European level, the progressive construction of the Trans-European Network (TEN) has been an additional powerful motivation to pursue this subject in a manner that would enforce coherence of vision and cooperation between the member states. The research which is reported in this volume is, largely, the result of these trends and, as we optimistically believe, a basis for further progress in this increasingly crucial field.

In 1994, with the publication of the European Union 4th Framework Research Program workplan, the need for a coherent view of the travel patterns of Europeans across the continent had become obvious to the European transport research community. With the contribution of several European consultancies, public sector agencies and research institutions, a project was then set up, with the ambition of exploring how to reach such a view. In particular, it wanted to progress in three complementary directions: The measure of long-distance travel through specifically designed travel surveys, the methodological issues involved in setting up and analysing such surveys, and the technologies, both proven or promising, that could be used to support them. This comprehensive project was then submitted to the European Union 4th Framework Research Program and was finally accepted in this context in the form of two distinct research contracts. The first, named "Methods for European Surveys of Travel behaviour" (MEST), principally focussed on the first two domains – design and piloting of coherent long-distance travel surveys across Europe and the associated methodological questions. The second, entitled "Technologies for European Surveys of Travel

---

[1] Preferred citation: K. W. Axhausen, J.-L. Madre, J. W. Polak and Ph. L. Toint (2003) Introduction, in K. W. Axhausen, J.-L. Madre, J. W. Polak and Ph. L. Toint (eds.) *Capturing Long-Distance Travel*, 1-6, Research Studies Press, Baldock.

behaviour" (TEST), emphasised the contribution of a number of supporting technologies. This book is primarily designed not only as a means to disseminate the conclusions of these research projects, but also to foster further progress in this area by including contributions which relate to the subject of long-distance travel without being direct products of the MEST and TEST work.

Summarising these contributions is a difficult exercise, given the scope of the objectives and diversity of approaches. But it is probably useful, at this stage, to indicate broadly what were the main questions posed in the three chosen directions of investigation, and what are the main lessons that we have learnt after three years of active and enthusiastic research.

1.2   THE SURVEYS

If we start by considering the domain of travel data collection itself, with an emphasis on long-distance displacements, the picture of 1994 was that of a rising interest, but also of a very fragmented approach, differing substantially both in extent and methodology across the member states. This situation is reviewed in more depth by Youssefzadeh in Chapter 3, but we do not disclose too much here by saying that it revealed the need, not so much for a standard travel survey design that could be applied everywhere in the Union (a goal whose compatibility with the necessary efficiency of a large pan-European survey remains in doubt), but rather for a benchmarking tool, to which specifically designed data collection campaigns could then be compared for coherency and consistency. In particular, the uncertainty and confusion on the concepts and terminology used to describe long-distance travel appeared as a major obstacle to comparability. A number of questions were also unanswered concerning the best survey protocol to use (prospective versus retrospective, telephone-based versus mail-based, etc.). Of course, these questions had already been considered in previous work, such as, at the European level, the COST 305 concerted action (Fabre, Klose and Somer, 1988) and the Eurostat initiative to pilot surveys in several member states (Axhausen, 1998). Although this earlier work provided an important motivation and reference point for the members of the MEST/TEST consortium, it was far from resolving all these issues, leaving open a large field of investigation. Besides these design and methodological problems, an organisational challenge also quickly became obvious for the consortium: the detailed knowledge about how to follow and control the local field contractors who would, in each member state, be in charge of conducting the survey and contacting the respondents, was largely missing and needed to be resolved in a way that would nevertheless allow firm and meaningful recommendations for practice.

A first benefit of the MEST research work was to clarify the notion and vocabulary that are relevant to long-distance travel surveys, including the notion of "long distance" itself. This clarification proved to be essential for the rest of the work, even though it was the subject of an ongoing debate. The conclusions are presented by Axhausen in Chapter 2. Several conclusions were also drawn from the MEST survey work itself (reviewed by Axhausen and Youssefzadeh in Chapter 6), and by its analysis (analysed by Axhausen in Chapter 9), and were supported by the experience of consortium members in related domains, such as the Austrian National Travel Survey (discussed by Herry in Chapter 5). The first of these conclusions is that, somewhat unsurprisingly, survey techniques that are appropriate for measuring travel at the urban level do not scale well to the specific context of long-distance travel. The second important conclusion is that the strength and importance of cultural differences across Europe, and their impact on the response to a travel survey, is even larger than we had anticipated. This provided *a posteriori* further justification for our choice to work on a benchmarking tool rather than a standard survey. In terms of survey design, the overarching conclusion is that no single design is likely to be most efficient in every member state, but that a mix of techniques (which, in our case, was influenced by the Eurostat pilots) is a better alternative[2].

Finally, the organisation of a co-ordinated survey with different field contractors in different member states and different cultures underlined the importance of specifying the details of the contracts and emphasised the overall complexity of managing multinational data collection. The resulting recommendations in terms of organisation and quality control may be found, along with other important recommendations, in Chapter 18.

1.3   METHODOLOGICAL ISSUES

On the methodological front, the main question posed was how to handle non-response, a problem all too common in travel surveys. In particular, in the context of long-distance travel (possibly implying long absences from home), the fact that a respondent does not provide any response may be due as much to the fact that response is not possible because the respondent could not be found at home as to his or her lack of willingness to respond. On the other hand, frequent travellers may be more interested in answering the survey. These examples merely illustrate that non-response might be correlated to specific travel behaviour, therefore introducing a potential bias in the analysis if not properly handled. Various techniques were available for this purpose, such as weighting and data imputation, but it was not clear, at the start of the project, whether they were really adequate, nor what was their potential contributions or pragmatic applicability. Furthermore, although important, non-response as such was not the only question that the consortium wanted to face: Questionnaire design, the cost-efficiency of different protocols and techniques, and sample selection issues were also on the agenda.

The reader will find the consortium contributions on the non-response issue in Chapter 8, where Denstadli and Lian provide some empirical evidence of the correlation between the type of survey conducted (combined travel or long-distance only) and response rate, while special emphasis is put on data yield (including response rate) in Chapter 9, where Axhausen describes an in-depth

---

[2] It is, of course, fair to say that the MEST research did not investigate all possible protocols and their combinations. For instance, a pure computer-assisted telephone interview (CATI) protocol could not be tried because of budget limitations.

analysis of MEST and other related surveys. The diagnostic and early treatment of non-response is also investigated by Midenet and Fessant in Chapter 12, where they show the very encouraging potential of self-organising maps (SOM) for these tasks. Correction of non-response is also investigated by Armoogum and Madre (in Chapter 10), who discuss the potential of weighting and data imputation methods, and by Han and Polak (in Chapter 11) who investigate statistical techniques for the imputation of non-ignorable items. Survey design questions are reported on in Chapter 7 by Denstadli and Lian in the context of the Norwegian Air Travel Survey. Finally, sampling issues are addressed by Armoogum and Madre in Chapter 13, who indicate that the global survey purpose is central for a good choice of the corresponding sampling scheme.

Globally speaking, the MEST research work supports the intuitive idea of a linkage between mobility and non-response and shows that the effect of this phenomenon may be reduced by a careful survey design that takes the non-ignorability of the non-response into account.

1.4   SUPPORTING TECHNOLOGIES

The impact of technological advances on long-distance travel surveys may not seem obvious at first glance, but practice reveals that it is highly significant. Indeed, both the collection and the dissemination of travel data can take substantial advantage of new communication techniques and media. The internet, with the associated emergence of websites dedicated to various aspects of transportation, is probably the most obvious of such media and, amongst other issues, the consortium was interested in asserting its potential in this domain. The progress of miniaturisation, with the wider availability of small handheld computers, also raised the question of whether they could be exploited for data collection purposes. Finally, improvements and enrichments of the travel data itself seemed possible by the use of large databases, and supporting techniques like geographical information systems (GIS) and intelligent software tools; however, further work was needed to assess their true potential.

One of the major conclusions of this part of the research is that the fast-changing standards in hardware and software – a phenomenon that we might call the "technological volatility" – is in strong opposition to the relative stability of data, as the latter typically remains significant and useful over long periods. Servicing the data with the technology therefore requires careful technical choices: The chosen technologies should be applied quickly (in order to avoid early obsolescence) and, most importantly, clear preference should be given to open technical standards since they have shown a much greater durability in the past. However, and although we regret after the fact not having investigated in more depth the impact of techniques like GSM and GPS, the research conducted by the consortium provides evidence that the use of technology, such as web-based data collection, the use of advanced software tools (see the papers by Lothaire and Toint in Chapter 15, and by Hubert in Chapter 17) and web-based dissemination of results (Reginster and Toint in Chapter 18), will remain an important topic for the foreseeable future. Technology was shown to influence survey design rather strongly, but also raises the unresolved question of the potential impact and bias of the "digital divide", that is the differentiated capability of the population to use modern techniques. In particular, we believe that the analysis of the process of bringing people to "talk" to small technological devices (see the contribution of Haubold in Chapter 14) is an important subject for the future of continuous data collection and should be pursued. Finally, we remain convinced of the importance of data weighting, data imputation and data servicing for data dissemination. This social and scientific importance of this latter task is growing, which justifies some efforts to develop suitable interfaces with a broad public (again, see Chapter 18).

1.5   CONCLUSION

As the reader may have realised by now, the field of long-distance travel analysis is very rich and complex, and its importance for the medium- and long-term future of our societies is more obvious every year. If the research work presented here, either conducted in the context of the MEST and TEST projects or outside this context by members of the consortium, does not permanently settle the questions raised, it is hoped that it will be of interest to practitioners, public authorities and researchers alike. This hope is supported by the knowledge that the work reported in this book has already been influential in the design of other travel surveys in Europe, such as the Belgian National Mobility Survey (www.mobel.be) or the Dateline survey of the European Union.[3] It is a manifest understatement to say that, besides the technical, practical and scientific results of the projects, the MEST and TEST work has reinforced the links, understanding and co-operation between a number of European decision makers, consultants and scientists. The editors of this volume feel that the best way to capitalise on the success of these projects is to share their findings with a community as large as possible. This is the purpose of the book you have in your hands, a book which, we hope, will support a lasting interest and help future investigations in this captivating research area.

1.6   REFERENCES

Axhausen, K.W. (1998) - The EUROSTAT pilots of long distance travel diaries. *Report to the Österreichischem Statistischen Zentralamt, Wien and Eurostat*, Luxembourg, Innsbruck.

Fabre, F., A. Klose and G. Somer (Eds) (1988) - Data system for the study of demand for interregional passenger transport, final report. *COST*, **305**, Commission of the European Communities, Brussels.

---

[3] See http://www.ncl.ac.uk/dateline/ for further information.

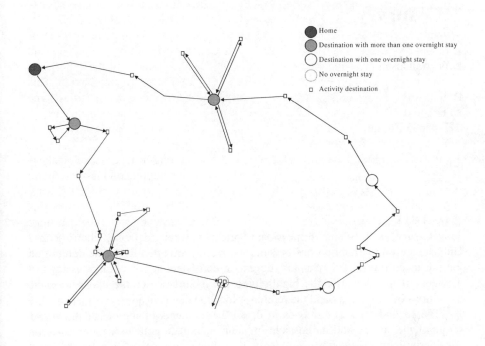

Chapter 2
Defining the scope of a long-distance travel survey

K.W. Axhausen

2. Defining the scope of a long-distance travel survey[1]

K.W. Axhausen

IVT
ETH
CH – 8093 Zürich

Abstract

Travel surveys rely on professional practice when defining their scope. Unfortunately this tradition has become imprecise, in particular in the context of long-distance travel. This chapter suggests a consistent set of definitions for the elements of movement, while highlighting the importance of the two associated definitions of the activity and the reference location.

The second section discusses in detail the elements of the definition of the scope of the survey and its possible implementation. In conclusion, examples of such definitions are given.

Keywords

Long-distance survey, travel survey, definitions, movement, activity, scope of survey.

---

1 Preferred citation: Axhausen, K.W. (2003) Defining the scope of a long-distance survey, in K.W. Axhausen, J.-L. Madre, J.W. Polak and Ph.L. Toint (eds.) *Capturing Long-Distance Travel*, 7-26, Research Studies Press, Baldock.

2.1 INTRODUCTION

The universe of journeys to and from home can be classified according to a number of criteria, each reflecting a particular policy interest. The most important ones are distance, duration and purpose. Unfortunately, there are different ways of defining these criteria, e.g.:

- Distance
  - Distance travelled (the kilometres walked, cycled, driven, ridden or flown)
  - Crow-fly distance from home to furthest point of the journey
- Duration
  - Days absent from home
  - Overnight stays away from home
- Purpose
  - Usual activity types, such as work, leisure etc.
  - Move to a new home, or better reference location (see below)

Different mixtures of these definitions in different policy areas result in overlaps between the categories derived, which often make comparisons between results difficult. It is clear that any survey has to clarify the definition of its object of interest before it can start formulating questions and designing its protocol and instruments. Unfortunately, professional habits and standards cannot replace a careful definition. When long usage has started to blur any original definition, it is worthwhile to reconstruct and reconsider this definition. The purpose of this chapter is to discuss these definitional issues and the associated measurement problems with the aim of developing a workable definition of the subject of long-distance travel surveys. This work was an important element of the MEST project work (Axhausen, 1996), but this chapter will also include results of the author's on-going work on this issue (Axhausen, 2000).

The duration of a journey is the primary criterion used to categorise it, daily mobility, tourism, including business trips and residential moves. Surveys of daily mobility (see Richardson, Ampt and Meyburg, 1995 or Axhausen, 1995) ask for (nearly) all movements which begin and/or finish on the reporting day. This approach is maintained for local surveys when they are extended to cover multiple reporting days.

Tourism statistics (Eurostat, 1995, 1998) are mainly interested in all journeys involving an overnight stay away from the usual living environment.[2] They also define a journey which is followed by more than 365 overnight stays away from the original home as a move, and therefore outside their scope. The tourism definition has grey areas at either end of the spectrum, as it is unclear how: a) journeys involving an overnight movement are to be classified (travelling through the night by car or bus, railway sleeping cars or overnight flights or ferries); and b)

---

[2] More recent definitions include the same-day visitor to locations outside the normal environment for non-work purposes, but the EU tourism statistics directive does not require data collection for this type of tourist.

how moves shorter than 365 days to a second, but familiar, environment are to be treated – students going to college, a visit to a second home or the weekly commute to the weekend or family home. Most tourism surveys overcome these ambiguities by adding a distance criterion, which, strictly speaking, might or might not capture the idea of the familiar environment.

The use of distance as a criterion to classify journeys is motivated by the different market structures of the different distance bands, as the preferred mode moves from walking, through cycling, to the car or local and regional public transport, and finally to long-distance public transport modes. Regulators, planners and service providers with an interest in the last category want to concentrate their survey resources on those journeys of interest to them. The simplest way to capture those from their point of view is a minimum distance criterion, such as 100 km crow-fly distance between home and the furthest destination of the journey (see Figure 2.1, which delimits the scope of these classifications in the space of distance away from home and duration of absence from home).

Figure 2.1 Classification of travel by distance and absence from home

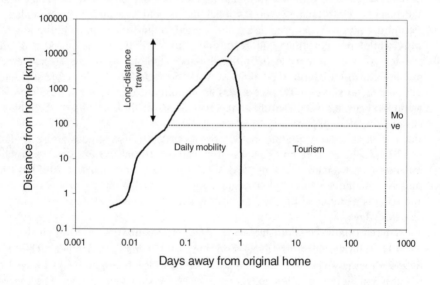

From a survey implementation point of view, this censoring is both helpful and problematic. While some surveys are content to provide just the number of movements, most want to provide, in addition, information about the characteristics of those movements for modelling or more detailed analysis; purpose, timing, duration, origin, destination, modes used, size of party, expenditures for movement and the activity at the destination to name the most important ones. While a null response is perfectly acceptable when the first objective dominates, it is a waste of survey resources when the second dominates, as the costs of establishing the contact with respondent and gaining their co-operation are substantial in comparison with the other costs involved.[3]

To reduce this wastage, it is necessary to increase the probability that the respondent has at least one journey to report. This improves the survey performance by assuring that the respondent has something to report, which increases the likelihood of a response by the respondent (reduction of sample unit non-response) and also yields reported journeys. In surveys of daily mobility it is enough to increase the duration of the reporting period from one to two or three days to achieve a near 100% probability of at least one journey. For long-distance mobility the reporting period has to be more substantially increased: Assume for the moment that the average person undertakes six journeys a year to destinations more than 100 km away from home. This would require a two-month reporting period under the second assumption that these journeys are equally distributed over the year.

In most survey situations it is unfeasible to ask respondents to keep a diary of all movements for such an extensive period of time (see Axhausen, Zimmermann, Schönfelder, Rindsfüser and Haupt, 2000, for an exception). It is necessary to ask the respondents to report only a subset of all movements, but for an extended period of time. Both the censoring and the duration of the reporting period create problems; communication of the selection rule and recall problems.

It is obvious that the accuracy with which people can recall events easily, or can recall them at all after some effort, depends on the interval between the event and the survey. In addition, depending on the level of detail requested, the willingness of the respondent to reconstruct the event for the survey might change, independently of whether the respondent reconstructs it from memory or from a diary or some combination of records (credit card bills, invoices etc.).

The designer of a retrospective long-distance travel survey has therefore to balance the duration of the survey period, the position of the cut-off point [km] and the amount of detail requested in a way, which maximises both the response rate, so as to reduce the likely non-response bias, and the data yield, i.e. the number of journeys described accurately in full by the respondents. Unfortunately, these trade-offs are complicated by the uneven distribution of long-distance trip-making in the population. The bulk of such trips is made by a small share of all travellers who travel either for business or because home and work/school location are separated (weekly or monthly commuters, students, drafted soldiers and conscientious objectors during their service, owners of second homes, etc.). For these frequent travellers a level of detail, cut-off point and duration of recall period

---

[3] There is unfortunately very little information about the shares of the three main elements of the total social survey costs: Successful distribution of the survey material including contact and gaining confidence; time spent by the respondent in answering the questions and coding, verification and correction of the answers.

chosen for the median traveller might be wholly inappropriate, which is an important problem as such travellers contribute many journeys to the data yield.

The following sections present approaches which try to address these dilemmas. Before we can report these results, it is necessary to discuss the basic definitions used to describe movements throughout the book (next section) and then to define the study object, i.e. to delimit those movements which are inside the scope of a long-distance travel survey (section on measurement problems). The conclusion summarise the main results of this chapter.

2.2   DEFINITIONS

Any survey of travel requires definitions to divide the observable stream of acts into a sequence of distinct elements which can be counted and characterised for analysis. The two basic categories which transport planning has adopted are movement and – by implication – stationary activity (Ortuzar and Willumsen, 1995 or Schnabel and Lohse, 1997). This division is noticeably different from the analysis in time-budget research (see for example Szalai, 1972 or Ås, 1978), which only distinguishes between different types of activity, with travel being one among many. Still, from the perspective of transport planning this privileged position of movement is reasonable and, happily, easy to understand for most respondents.

The movements in themselves need further structure to make them suitable for analysis. These more detailed definitions and implied structures are for professional use. The terms used in the professional context frequently do not match everyday language perfectly. They are therefore not necessarily the concepts or terms to be used directly in a survey. Here, it might be required to use other descriptions and terms for the movement, more familiar to the respondents, to elicit the desired information from them.

The following division of movements into units is internally consistent and was adopted by the MEST and TEST projects (see Table 2-1 for an example and also Table 2-2 for translations of the English terms):

"A *stage* is a movement with one vehicle (as driver/rider or passenger), or on foot.[4] It includes any pure waiting (idle) times immediately before or during that movement.

A *trip* is a continuous sequence of stages between two activities.

A *tour* is a sequence of trips starting and ending at the same location.

A *journey* is a tour starting and ending at the relevant base location of the person.

An *activity* is a continuous interaction with the physical environment, a service or person, within the same socio-spatial environment, which is important to the sample/observation unit. It includes any pure waiting (idle) times before or during the activity." (adapted from Axhausen, 2000).

It is important to note that the crucial aspect of these definitions is not the definition of the elements of movement, but that of activity, as the activity

---

[4] Ignoring animal transport, such as horse riding, for the moment.

determines the number of movements observed (see below). This activity definition does not delineate a pure, single-purpose set of actions, but groups of acts, such as work, shopping, being at home, or visiting friends, which are held together by a shared intent or meaning. "Movement" is equally a basket of actions held together by the overarching intent to travel between two activities in the definition above. Unfortunately, it is easy to construct exceptions, such as the walk in the park or the business meeting in the train. More important in the context of travel, business travel in particular, are streams of actions undertaken while moving. The obvious examples are working (preparing meetings or reports, telephoning colleagues or business partners), meeting friends, eating in train restaurants, shopping on ferries. Given that these intertwined actions can have a major influence on the utility derived from the movement, it might be necessary to capture these subordinate actions in a survey of long-distance travel behaviour. Nevertheless, as they do not constitute the main purpose of the journey as a whole, i.e. the journey would still take place, even if the particular actions were unfeasible – e.g. no restaurant car on the train, prohibition of mobile telephone use on air planes, etc. – transport planning does not use them to define activities and therefore additional trips. This simplification is primarily meant by the privilege given to movement over stationary activities mentioned above. A possible definition for these actions is:

subordinated streams of actions, which are engaged in by the traveller during the movement, but do not constitute the main purpose of the whole journey. From a public transport perspective, between the stage and the trip occur:

customer movements: continuous sequences of (para)transit/public transport stages of a certain type, ignoring any walking stages undertaken to reach the next point of boarding during a transfer.

Different criteria can be used to define the customer movement, the most relevant being; by operator, if the purpose is to allocate revenue between multiple operators within a large (regional) network operating a revenue sharing scheme, as do most continental European systems; by type of vehicle, if one intends to allocate revenue within a firm operating different sub-networks, e.g. between diesel buses, trolley buses, street cars and cable cars; by type of service within a firm or network, e.g. express, normal, night, shared-ride taxi services.

This set of definitions provides a consistent and clear framework to describe the movements of the traveller. The survey designer has to choose which of the levels he/she wishes to employ in the survey at hand. Each level has advantages and disadvantages in terms of ease of understanding by the respondents and usefulness as a data source (see Table 2-1 for the classification of a complex journey).

While the stage is unambiguous, the definition of the trip depends on the definition of the activity to provide its start and end points. Depending on the definition of what constitutes an "activity", it is possible to vary the number of trips, the most frequently-used reference unit in transport modelling. The definition proposed leaves open the way in which the researcher operationalises "important", respectively the respondent. The socio-spatial environment is constituted by the people involved in the interaction and the environment in which it takes place. In the case of the environment, only the type has to remain the same, for example a walk through a park is within one spatial environment. The definition implies that any change in the number of persons involved in the interaction defines a new activity, e.g. somebody leaving early from a joint dinner defines a new activity of the same type; equally each visit to a different store in a shopping mall is a different activity; or a change in the size of the party travelling together would constitute a new trip.

Importance can be defined on one, some, or all of the main dimensions by which activities can be classified:

- **Kind of activity** defines what the person is doing; gardening, talking with someone, operating a machine, walking through a park.
- **Purpose** defines what the person hopes to achieve in an instrumental sense; earning money, relaxing, getting fit, growing food, satisfying the demand for sleep, etc.
- **Meaning** defines what the person hopes to achieve in a moral sense or say about himself/herself; helping someone, fulfilling a promise, taking care of himself/herself, etc.
- **Project** gives the greater context of the activity, the framework under which it is undertaken, e.g. preparing dinner, obtaining a degree, working towards promotion, building a house, etc.
- **Duration**.
- **Effort** accepted to be able to undertake the activity, in particular the detour required to get to the activity location.
- **Expenditure for/income from** the activity participation and the associated additional travel.
- **Urgency** of the activity in terms of the possibility of (further) delay.

This list ignores more descriptive dimensions, such as, for example, the number of people involved, location, kind/type of activity by which the activity could be replaced, how long the activity has been planned, planning effort, possible time horizons for delays, allocation of costs between participants, allocation of costs between participants and non-participants, satisfaction with the activity in terms of goal achievement.

In the context of long-distance travel, the problem of the activity definition is compounded, as one is, in many cases, by not really being interested in an exceedingly fine resolution of the activity description. Here compound activities – or rather, projects – such as visiting a museum, a shopping expedition in the capital city, arriving and staying at a hotel overnight – are a fine enough resolution. Again a trade-off is required between the wishes of the local tourism board, which would be interested in the fine detail, and the willingness and the ability of the respondent to provide this detail in the context of a retrospective survey covering multiple weeks.

While the definition of the trip hinges on the concept of the activity, the definition of the journey requires a reference location or base. In daily travel this will normally be the (main) home of the respondent. Still, some travellers will have multiple reference locations (e.g. weekend home, family home and *pied-a-terre* of the weekly commuter, student dorm and parents' house, multiple homes of children living with their parents and step-parents). In addition, tourists on a round-trip will shift their base location between various accommodations during their holiday. In all cases, it seems reasonable to break any observed tour (from first reference location and back) into smaller units for analysis. These will normally be sub-tours of the main tour, but in some cases they involve the shift from one base location to the next, e.g. the Friday trip/journey from the university town to the parental home. In general, the researcher will not know about the exact status of a reported location and will have to impose an external definition on the movement data obtained. For example, a base location is any location where travellers spend at least one (two consecutive) night(s).

The discussion so far has provided a consistent set of definitions to divide a movement into a set of building blocks. However, these definitions themselves require two further definitions to be operational: one of activity and one of base or reference location. The base location can vary during a holiday, as people move from location to location on a complex journey. Activity is problematic, as the local detail is irrelevant from the long-distance perspective. Whether and how to communicate these concepts is the topic of the next section, which deals with the delimitation of the scope of a survey.

2.3 MEASUREMENT PROBLEMS

The discussion above has hinted at the fact that, in any travel survey, some movements fall outside the scope of the survey, as they are deemed to be without relevance to the objectives of the data collection. This match between stated purpose and requested information is important, as respondents are likely to refuse to answer questions which seem irrelevant or frivolous given the stated purpose of a survey (Gerber, Crowley and Trencher, 1999). Such detail can jeopardise a survey by reducing the response rates. Additionally, in the case of long-distance travel, particular care needs to be taken to avoid such detail to keep the response burden within acceptable limits.

Consider the case shown in Figure 2.2. It is a complex holiday involving a number of places with overnight stays and a number of tours from these temporary bases. It is always assumed that the activities/trips within the destination of a trip are not reported, where the spatial limits of the destination are defined in a suitable and natural way, for example as the boundaries of the municipality[5] or the built-up area. Based on this example a number of different conceivable scopes for a survey can be illustrated:

---

[5] This can create interesting problems, where the legal units are very large, such as English District Councils, or small in relation to the built up area, such as the Boroughs within London or the Municipalities within Brussels.

Table 2-1   Classification of an example journey (activities are groups of actions lasting more than 5 min)

Mode/ Operator	Activity/Event	Activity number	Trip number	Stage number	Customer movement	
					By operator	By mode
	Home	1				
Walk			1	1.1		
Bus/A			1	1.2	1	1
Walk			1	1.3		
	Buy train ticket and provisions	2				
Local train/B	Change train		2	2.1	2	2
Intercity/B			2	2.2	2	3
Walk			2	2.3		
	Check in, work in lounge, board	3				
Flight segment/C	Stop over, wait on board		3	3.1	3	4
Flight segment/C	Change plane		3	3.1	3	4
Flight segment/D			3	3.2	4	4
Walk			3	3.3		
Taxi/E			3	3.4	5	5
Walk			3	3.5		
	Meeting with client	4				
Walk			4	4.1		
Bus/F			4	4.2	6	6
Walk			4	4.3		
	Check in, work in lounge, board	5				
Flight segment/E			5	5.1	7	7
Walk			5	5.2		
Coach/E			5	5.3	7	8
Walk			5	5.4		
Streetcar/A	Change to bus		5	5.5	8	9
Bus/A	Change to next bus		5	5.6	8	10
Bus/A			5	5.7	8	10
Walk			5	5.8		
	Home	6				

In keeping with current practice, walks within a complex or building are not considered as stages, e.g. walks within airports or train stations, although is would be useful to capture them.

Table 2-2   Movement defined in a selection of European languages

English	Dutch	Finnish	French	German	Greek	Italian	Norwegian	Portugese	Serbo-Croat	Swedish
Stage	Rit	Osamatka	Trajet, etape	Etappe	Στάδιο	Tappa	Delreise	Etapa	Etapa	Delresa, reselement
Customer movement			Voyage	Beförderungsfall	κίνηση με Δημόσιες Συγκοινωνίε	Spostamento	Passasjerer		Prevoz, Putovanje	
Trip, linked trip	Ver-plaatsing	Matka	Deplacement, itinénaire,	Weg, Fahrt	Μετα-κίνηση	Spostamento viaggio, spostamento	Enkeltreise	Viagem, deslocacao	Kretanje	
Tour		Matkaketju	Circuit	Tour	Περήγηση	Tour, itinerario	Tur-retur reise		Tura	Tur, returresa
Journey, sojourn, round trip		Matkaketju, Koti-peräinen	Journee	Reise, Ausgang	Ταξίδι	Viaggio	Hovedreise		Putovanje	Huvudresa, resekedja
Activity		Aktiviteetti Toiminto	Activite	Aktivität	Δραστηριότητα	Attività	Aktivitet	Actividade	Aktivnost	
Excursion	Dag trip, excursie	PäivämatkaE kskursio		Tagesreise, Ausflug	Εκδρομή	Escursione	Utflukt	Passeio	Dnevni Izlet	Endagsresa, utflykt
Trip, round trip, travel	Reis, Rondreise, tour	Matka, kiertomat-ka		Reise, Rundreise		Viaggio, percorso circolare,	Rundreise	Excursao	Putovanje	
Visit	Bezoek	Vierailu	Visite	Besuch	Επίσκεψη	Visita	Besøk	Visita	Posjeta	Besök

Concept 1: Report all stages, except for those not crossing a municipal boundary.

Concept 2: Report all stages, except for those which belong to tours not reaching crow-fly destination more than x km from the current base (the current base is a location, where the traveller stays at least two nights).

Concept 3: Report all trips leading to overnight stay locations.

Concept 4: Report all destinations where at least one overnight stay occurred.

Concept 5: Report all destinations where at least one overnight stay occurred and all stages over a certain length.

Concept 6:   Report the destination where the maximum number of overnight stays occurred and where the destination was further away from home than any other with the same number, in case there is a tie.

Concept 7: Report the destination furthest away from home.

Obviously, each is valid, but is also clear that each will produce different results. While each is valid, they are quite different with regards to the ease with which the respondent can understand and implement them. The definition of the scope should be as natural as possible to avoid complex definitions and explanations, which can only confuse and irritate the respondent.

The example definitions have highlighted the elements which need to be discussed and defined:

- Base unit
- Activity
- Minimum distance (see above)
- Minimum duration
- Destination or spatial resolution
- Spatial exclusions
- Temporal exclusions
- Reference location or base

The **base units** discussed above – stage, trip, tour, journey – are all equally valid for the data collection and the description of the respondents movement, but each has its particular advantages and disadvantages, which need to be balanced.

The stage is unambiguous in its definition, but many respondents need special encouragement and attention before they accept the concept. The introduction of a trip purpose "Change of mode or vehicle" is often enough, but this does not cover the various walk stages which are part of every trip. In the context of long-distance travel, the stage can be too detailed unless there are rigorous exclusions which reduce the response load, but these are in turn problematic (see below).

Figure 2.2 Example holiday

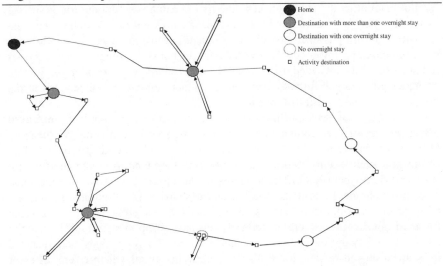

Source: Axhausen (1996), Figure 1

The trip is a unit with which most respondents are familiar (see above). However, the activity definition needs to be comparatively rough if one wants to keep the numbers to be reported within acceptable limits.

The tour is also possible, but in recent reviews (Axhausen, 1995; Youssefzadeh and Axhausen, 1996) no examples of its use are reported. It overlaps, in general, with the journey and where it is most valuable, in capturing sub-tours such as side trips from a holiday location or a work place during lunch, it is too abstract and complex to explain.

The journey is frequently used, as it is again very close to popular understanding, but it can be too all-encompassing a concept for many research questions, as all intermediate stops and purposes are lost. On the other hand, the respondent can provide a quick overview over her travelling at this level, which might be especially important for frequent travellers or regular journeys. In addition, it might be possible to combine the journey with the trip or stage level to achieve the desired resolution.

Given the dependence of the trip definition on the **activity** definition, it is crucial to be clear about what constitutes an activity. In the context of daily mobility, there are well understood summary terms, which naturally group coherent streams of actions, such as work, going to a restaurant, school or shopping. The combination of such terms as pre-coded options with frequently used minimum duration requirements makes it possible to convey to the respondents the desired resolution of the activity stream. At the level of long-distance travel these terms might imply a too-detailed description, especially if one is only interested in destination and, so to speak, the main purpose(s) of a visit. Unfortunately, European languages do not offer suitable terms at this medium level of resolution, the level between "the first evening we went out for dinner for two hours, then we had a drink in the pub and then I went to bed in the hotel" and "I visited the my grandparents for the weekend". Most surveys of long-distance travel employ the lower level terms and try to convey through various signals (number of units provided for on the form, resolution of location suggested, examples given, some formal definitions etc.) that they are only interested in the main purposes of the visit to a location.

All surveys of travel behaviour have either explicit or implicit **minimum distances**, mostly in conjunction with the suggested resolution of location. Surveys of daily mobility ignore movements inside buildings or building complexes, such as universities or factories, and they tend to ignore short walks, rides and drives between different addresses during a set of errands of the same type, say shopping. Long-distance travel surveys have explicit minimum distances, often some round numbers such as 75, 100 or 200. While one could use distance travelled, most surveys prefer crow-fly distance. The first approach has the advantage of tying in with the mental map of the road signs and distance indications on rail tickets, but it also produces distortions where rivers, lakes or mountains create detours. The crow-fly approach is based on the assumption that most travellers have a map-like understanding of their environment. Doubting this themselves, many surveys aim for journeys over 100 km, but ask respondents to describe all journeys over 75 km to cover this grey zone where the mixture of map knowledge and the mental maps of road distance could lead to under-reporting. Best practice is to provide each respondent with a map indicating the appropriate radius around the home location.

Current best practice in travel surveys does not use a **minimum duration** to exclude certain movements. This is in contrast to tourism surveys, which do impose the minimum one-overnight-stay rule.

Travel surveys are interested in the destination of the movements. Respondents must therefore indicate this destination at a suitable **spatial resolution;** street address, name of neighbourhood, name of facility, settlement, village, municipality, city, region or country. While the street address or variants such as name of the place visited (store, restaurant etc.) or nearest street corner are natural for surveys of daily travel, there is no obvious choice for long-distance travel. Most long-distance surveys use municipality, the smallest self-administered unit at the base of the administrative hierarchy. Unfortunately, in many European countries this level is too large and actually often unknown to the respondents; the UK is a good example, where the district councils are irrelevant to most people's understanding of the settlement geography of their area. The neighbourhood or village level would be good for modelling, but it is normally not used, as: a) the available place name databases do not include them; and b) visitors are often unsure about them, especially in large cities. The city or village level is the compromise most long-distance surveys currently adopt, but the rapid progress in place name databases might lead to a switch in the near future (see, for example, the resolution offered by the European route planning tool at www.reiseplanung.de or similar software produced by other providers).

The spatial resolution, at which the respondents are invited to report their movements, implies **spatial exclusions** of certain movements from the record. In long-distance surveys, essentially all movements within the location, i.e. city or village, are factually excluded. Respondents could report them, but experience indicates that they do not. The equivalent in surveys of daily mobility, as mentioned above, are movements within an address, even if they are large complexes, such as factories, universities or shopping centres.

In addition, **temporal exclusions** could be defined in addition to those times which are excluded because the movements occur within the destinations visited. The temporal exclusions could be wider, such as no movement between 22:00 and 6:00 in the daily context, or all movement while you are staying at your destination, resort, second home etc.

The definition of the journey requires, as discussed above, a **base** or **reference location**. This is purely of analytical interest. As its introduction changes the number of journeys to be counted[6], the respondents should not be exposed this concept. Still, in long-distance surveys special care needs to be taken that the respondents report tours originating from the new reference location; the day trip to an attraction from the holiday base, the long shopping trip from the second home, etc. If care is not taken, such journeys would have to be obtained from separate surveys of travel behaviour of visitors, a notoriously difficult undertaking, as both the sampling and the motivation of visitors at their destinations is problematic (See Deussner, Eisenkölb, Hendrich and Lichtenberger, 1996, for an example). Surveys of daily mobility do not have this problem, as they request the reporting of all movements, with the exceptions noted above.

For the analytical purposes mentioned above, a definition which can be imposed on the data when it has been collected is required. Possible definitions are:

- any destination to which the respondent returns without an intervening overnight stay elsewhere; or
- any destination where the respondent stays for more than one consecutive night;
- any destination where the respondent stays for more than x out of y consecutive nights;
- any specific location, i.e. hotel, flat or house, where the respondent stays for more than one consecutive night;

---

6 The tour: home–holiday resort (x+1 days)–home would have to count as two journeys, if one defines the new reference location as any place where the respondent spends more than x days.

In most cases, the second or third possibilities are the ones which can be implemented with the data at hand.

Next to the definition of the scope of the survey, i.e. of the exact survey object, two special problems occur in long-distance surveys: the treatment of frequent travellers and the treatment of repeated, frequent journeys. In daily mobility surveys these problems are ignored, as during the usual one day reporting period trips are not repeated and the survey load of the frequent traveller is acceptable.[7]

The frequent traveller is of particular value to a survey of long-distance travel, as he will provide much data to the overall data yield. This means that one does not want to antagonize such travellers with, for them, excessive requests for details, but, on the other hand, one wants just these respondents to provide such detail. A further consideration is that one does not want to reduce the details for all respondents, so as not to discourage the small share of frequent travellers. As above, a suitable mix of questions at different levels of detail has to be found.

The repeated journey, e.g. the weekly trip between home and second home or the daily long-distance commute by train, is a comparable problem. If one is only interested in the number of such trips, one can satisfy this interest with a question about the frequency of such trips. If one is interested in the details of such trips, in particular departure dates or departure times and trip duration, then one has to insist on detailed individual reports; something which might be too difficult in a retrospective situation, but not in an on-going diary.

The decision of how to treat these two problems will depend on the overall objective of the survey. No optimal solution can be offered.

2.4   CONCLUSIONS

As a summary, Table 2-3 gives two examples of how possible definitions of the scope of travel surveys could be put together. The final choice depends on the aims of the survey at hand. Still, any definition has to maintain an internal consistency which allows the respondent to recognise the interest of the researcher and the researcher to reconstruct the movements of the respondents. In a survey of long-distance travel particular care has to be taken to optimise both response rate and data yield by choosing the reporting period and level of detail in a way which encourages participation and complete reporting of all relevant movements.

The need for a careful definition of the scope of the survey is larger in the long-distance context with its censoring of the domain, but the discussion has shown that surveys of daily mobility would also benefit from the attention. It is, in particular, the definition of the activity, which needs to be considered, as it determines the number of movements reported.

---

[7] The French NPTS did allow the respondents a simplified procedure to report repeated trips, but this is very unusual.

2.5 REFERENCES

Ås, D. (1978) - Studies of time-use: problems and prospects. *Acta Sociologica*, **21** (1) 125-141.

Axhausen, K.W. (1995) - Travel diaries: An annotated catalogue, 2nd edition. *Working Paper*, Institut für Straßenbau und Verkehrsplanung, Leopold-Franzens-Universität, Innsbruck.

Axhausen, K.W. (1996) - Possible contents and formats for long-distance-travel-diaries: Proposals for the first wave of MEST-pilots. *Deliverable*, **D2**, MEST-Project, Fakultät für Bauingenieurwesen und Architektur, Leopold-Franzens-Universität, Innsbruck.

Axhausen, K.W. (2000) - Definition of movement and activity for transport modelling. In D. Hensher and K. Button (eds.) *Handbooks in Transport: Transport Modelling*,Transportation paper, Elsevier, Oxford.

Axhausen, K.W., A. Zimmermann, S. Schönfelder, G. Rindsfüser and T. Haupt (2000) - Observing the rhythms of life: a six-week travel diary. *Arbeitsbericht Verkehrs- und Raumplanung*, **25**, Institut für Verkehrsplanung, Transporttechnik, Strassen- und Eisenbahnbau, ETH Zürich.

Deussner, R., G. Eisenkölb, A. Hendrich and E. Lichtenberger (1996) - Österreich-Matrizen: Urlauberreise- und Urlauberlokalverkehr. *Report to the Austrian Ministry of Science, Transport and Arts, Vienna*, Österreiches Institut für Raumplanung, Vienna.

Eurostat (1995) - Implementation of the EUROSTAT methodology on basic tourism statistics: A practical manual, 2nd draft. *EUROSTAT*, Luxembourg[8].

Eurostat (1998) - Community methodology on tourism statistics. *Internal working paper*, Eurostat, Luxembourg.

Gerber, E.R., M.L. Crowley and S.R. Trencher (1999) - Identity thieves, warrantee cards and government surveys: The ethnography of personal information management. *Paper presented at the International Conference on Survey Non-Response*, Portland, October 1999.

Ortuzar, J. de Dios and L. Willumsen (1994) - Modelling Transport. Wiley and Sons, Chichester.

Richardson, A.J., E.S. Ampt and A.H. Meyburg (1995) - Survey Methods for Transport Planning. Eucalyptus Press, Melbourne.

Schnabel, W. and D. Lohse (1997) - Grundlagen der Strassenverkehrstechnik und der Verkehrsplanung. Verlag für Bauwesen, Berlin.

---

[8] This report was included as item TF/95/9/EN for the "*Joint meeting of the task force on Passenger Transport Statistics and on Tourism Statistics*", 31.1. and 1.2.1995 in Luxembourg

24

Szalai, A. (ed.) (1972) - The Use of Time. Mouton, The Hague.

Youssefzadeh, M. and K.W. Axhausen (1996) - Long distance diaries today: Review and critique. *Deliverable*, **D1**, MEST-Project, Fakultät für Bauingenieur-wesen und Architektur, Leopold-Franzens-Universität, Innsbruck.

Table 2-3   Examples of possible survey object definitions

Element	Type of survey	
	Daily mobility survey	Long-distance travel survey
Target movements	All relevant stages during the reporting period	All relevant trips during the reporting period, which are part of a journey to a destination at least 100 km from the base location.
Base unit	Stage	Trip
Activity definition	Any interaction longer than five minutes, unless a "serve passenger" stop	Main activity, which has motivated the trip to the destination
Reporting period	One day starting at 4:00 am until ending the day at the reference location	Eight weeks, starting Monday 4:00 am of the first week
Minimum distance	Walks under 1 km	None
Minimum duration	None	None
Spatial exclusions	Stages which are part of trips within a closed building or compound, such as factory or office campus; Stages starting or ending outside the study area during the reporting period	Trips which are part of journeys to destinations less then 100 km from the reference location; Trips within destinations
Temporal exclusions	Stages undertaken as work while working, e.g. driving a delivery vehicle	Trips undertaken as work while working, e.g. driving a charter coach bus
Spatial resolution	(Building) address	Municipalities or separately identifiable settlements, e.g. resort complexes, villages, which are part of larger administrative units
Base location	Home address within the study area	Destinations, where the traveller spends at least one night

Source: adapted from Axhausen (2000), Table 2

Country	Name	Year	Frequency	Survey unit	Sample size/year
A	Microcensus Tourism	1969 -	3 years	Individual	1% of residents
A	Survey of Trips Abroad and Expenditures	1988 -	n.a.	Individual	12000
A	Government and Business Travel	1995	-	Individual	1886
B	Holiday Survey	1996	-	Household	2425
B	Quarterly Holiday Survey	1997 -	Quarterly	Household	10000
DK	Tourism Survey	1996 -	Quarterly	Individual	6000
SF	Holiday Survey of residents	1991-95	n.a.	Individual	6200
SF	Revised Holiday Survey	1996 -	Quarterly	Individual	8400
F	Tourism Demand Survey	1989 -	n.a.	Household	8000 10000; >96
D	Tourism Demand Survey	1962-90	n.a.	Individual	0.1% of the population
D	Tourism Demand Survey	1997 -	Quarterly	Household	12000

Chapter 3
Long-distance diaries today: Review and critique

M. Youssefzadeh

28

3. Long-distance diaries today: Review and critique[1]

M. Youssefzadeh

35, Av Dr Paul Benet
F – 82140 St Antonin Noble Val

Abstract

The paper describes the state-of-practice in long-distance survey design and implementation in Europe with some consideration to recent American efforts. It discusses the strength and weaknesses of the various approaches and highlights critical issues.

Keywords

Travel survey, tourism survey, review, Europe, MEST, long-distance travel diary.

---

[1] Preferred citation: Youssefzadeh, M. (2003) Long-distance diaries today: Review and critique, in K. W. Axhausen, J.-L. Madre, J. W. Polak and Ph. L. Toint (eds.) *Capturing Long-Distance Travel*, 27-44, Research Studies Press, Baldock.

3.1   INTRODUCTION

The project "Methods for European Surveys of Travel Behaviour" (MEST) is aimed to develop improved methods for gaining harmonised and comparative data about European long-distance travel behaviour. In a first deliverable (Youssefzadeh and Axhausen, 1996) a review of the existing practice in this field across Europe was conducted to highlight the differences and common points in the data collection methods used in various countries. The review was undertaken in 1996. Due to MEST and other initiatives within the EC and Eurostat (Eurostat, 1995a and Weckström-Eno,1999), an awareness for the need for comparable travel data has been created, which consequently led to considerable work in this area across Europe.

This chapter is an update of the initial review. It includes all surveys mentioned in the MEST Deliverable as well as surveys identified in the follow-up project DATELINE (Schnabel, 2000) and through further investigations of the author. Since the first review, Eurostat has been successful in establishing its standards in Tourism Statistics. The result of these activities has been a number of tourism demand surveys, which have been included in this chapter. Although they are not strictly focused on transport and do not contain detailed information about the movements of the respondents, they were considered valuable to the discussion of European long-distance travel surveys because of their relatively large number on one hand and, on the other hand, because of the work that has been undertaken in Europe to standardise them. The success of this work gives a good example and hope for future long-distance travel surveys.

The second section of this chapter will provide the reader with a brief summary of long-distance travel surveys and related surveys in Europe, focusing on the Western European Countries. In order to provide a comparison, North American surveys have been included. Intercept surveys have not been considered, as they differ considerably from household surveys and should be treated separately. Also, in the second section tourism demand surveys are described and some of their problem areas are compared to those of travel surveys. The third section looks at efforts undertaken by the EU to harmonise data collection of long-distance mobility in Europe. Section four discusses examples of current long-distance travel surveys and comments on and critique of the existing practice are the contents of the fifth section.

A catalogue containing detailed information about the collected surveys is available in Youssefzadeh (forthcoming) on www.ivt.baug.ethz.ch/vp.html.

3.2   SUMMARY OF EXISTING PRACTICE

In almost every European country, information about people's travel is collected using household surveys. Besides the daily urban or regional mobility, long-distance travel behaviour is becoming more interesting for transport operators and planners, environmental groups, the tourism industry and other commercial enterprises. In many countries surveys are conducted which include at least a section on long distance mobility, or even focus entirely on that subject. Considering the growing importance of long-distance travel and its economic, social and environmental implications across national borders, it is still a relatively neglected area in survey research and transport statistics.

Whereas data on daily urban or regional mobility is collected thoroughly in travel diaries, of which the main aim is to capture information on the movement itself, there are far more tourism surveys that look at long-distance travel than there are specific long-distance travel surveys. Inevitably in these surveys, the focus is not on travel from one location to another but mainly on activities and especially on the overnight stays at the destination. Since tourism-demand surveys give useful insight into people's travel behaviour, they need to be considered here, but it should be pointed out that, despite some similarities, they are generally different and should be treated separately.

The following tables provide an overview on the surveys that have been identified.

Table 3-1   Tourism demand surveys

Country	Name	Year	Frequency	Survey unit	Sample size/year
A	Microcensus Tourism	1969 -	3 years	Individual	1% of residents
A	Survey of Trips Abroad and Expenditures	1988 -	n.a.	Individual	12000
A	Government and Business Travel	1995	-	Individual	1886
B	Holiday Survey	1996	-	Household	2425
B	Quarterly Holiday Survey	1997 -	Quarterly	Household	10000
DK	Tourism Survey	1996 -	Quarterly	Individual	6000
SF	Holiday Survey of residents	1991-95	n.a.	Individual	6200
SF	Revised Holiday Survey	1996 -	Quarterly	Individual	8400
F	Tourism Demand Survey	1989 -	n.a.	Household	8000 10000; >96
D	Tourism Demand Survey	1962-90	n.a.	Individual	0.1% of the population
D	Tourism Demand Survey	1997 -	Quarterly	Household	12000
GR	Pilot Survey on Annual Tourism Demand	1995	Yearly	Household	3000
GR	Survey on Leisure and Business Trips	1997 -	Quarterly	Household	8000
Eire	National Household Survey on Tourism	1998 -	Quarterly	Household	12000
I	Holiday Survey	1959-92	3-4 years	Household	24000 – 90000
I	Multipurpose Survey on Daily Life Aspects	1996 -	Yearly	Household	24000
I	Tourism Demand Survey	1997 -	Quarterly	Household	14000
L	Tourism Survey	1996-98	Yearly	Household	1500
NL	Continuous Tourism Survey	1980 -	Continuous	Individual	3000 (net)
N	Holiday Survey	1968 -	4 years	n.a.	n.a.
N	Omnibus Survey (Tourism)	1997 -	Quarterly	Individual	8500

P	Holiday Survey	1988-91	Yearly	n.a.	16000
P	Revised Holiday Survey	1997 -	Quarterly	Individual	6640
E	Holiday Survey	1996	-	Household	3000
E	Holiday Survey "FAMITOUR"	1996 -	Quarterly	Household	8000
S	Tourism and Travel Data	1989 -	Monthly	Individual	24000
UK	United Kingdom Tourism Survey	1989 -	Continuous	Individual	80000
UK	British National Tourism Survey	1960 -	Continuous	n.a.	3000

Table 3-2   Long-distance travel surveys[2]

Country	Name	Year	Frequency	Survey unit	Sample size/year
A	Travel Survey	1995	-	Household	12000 (2500 LD)
B	Travel Behaviour of Belgians	1982 -	2 years	Individual	6000
B	National Survey on Mobility of Households	1999	-	Household	3000
SF	Travel Survey	1992	-	Individual	17500
SF	National Travel Survey	1998/99	-	Individual	18250
F	Transport and Communication Survey	1966,73, 81,93	-	Household	7000-14200
D	Infratest "Mobility"	1990 -	Continuous	Individual	n.a.
D	Long Distance Travel Survey	1979	-	Household	17000 and subsamples
GR	Travel Survey Athens	1995	-	Individual	17000
GR	Survey on Leisure and Business trips	1997 -	Quarterly	Household	8000
Iceland	Travel Survey	1996 -	4 months	Individual	4813
N	National Travel Survey	1985	-	n.a.	4200
N	National Travel Survey	1992	-	n.a.	6000
N	National Travel Survey	1998	-	n.a.	8800
P	Survey on Medium & Long Distance Mobility	1998	-	Household	41845
S	Travel Survey (RVU)	1978,84	-	n.a.	8000
S	Travel Survey (Riks-RVU)	1994-1998	Continuous	n.a.	ca.10000
S	Travel Survey	1999 -	Continuous	n.a.	ca. 8000
UK	Business Traveller Panel	1992,94	-	Individual	400, 600
UK	National Travel Survey	1965,72,7 5,78,85, 1988-	Continuous	Household	5796 (2000)
UK	Long Distance Travel Survey	1975-1978		Individual	30000-50000
CH	Microcensus – Travel Behaviour	1974	5 years	Individual	29000 (7250 LD)
EU	European Travel Monitor	1988 -	Continuous	Individual	400000 (1999)

[2] Including daily mobility surveys with a section on long-distance travel.

CAN	Canadian Travel Survey	1979, 1980-1996	2 years	Household	182000
USA	American Travel Survey	1995	5 years	Household	80000
USA	Travel Survey (NPTS/ATS)	2000	-	n.a.	40000

In the last decade tourism-demand surveys have been booming. Some European countries – notably Greece, Luxembourg, Ireland and Iceland – that had never conducted surveys on domestic and outbound tourism before started to do so, adopting the EU Directives and taking up the set standards from the beginning. Other countries have been revising their existing surveys in order to match the standards of the directives and to raise their quality (see Eurostat, 1999).

Most countries have managed to establish continuous or frequently-repeated surveys on tourism demand which deliver consistent and comparable data. This is not the case for specific long-distance travel surveys, most of which have been either one-off events, or have been repeated only after several years and after considerable changes to the design, therefore not delivering consistent and comparable data.

Whereas Eurostat has been relatively successful in implementing standards for European Tourism Surveys, these are still missing for Long Distance Travel Surveys. A look at the current examples of long-distance travel behaviour research in Europe reveals the non-uniformity in many features. However, the methodological work undertaken in MEST, and in parallel in the Eurostat pilot surveys of long-distance travel (Axhausen, 2000), has led to a EU 5th Framework Project. The project DATELINE is based on the methodology developed and tested in the previous projects and pilot surveys.

As there are more tourism surveys and as they are better harmonised, the information on transport contained here should be interesting to analyse. Moreover, the Swedish experience (section 4.4) shows that it is possible to have both long-distance travel and tourism in the same survey.

One of the major difficulties leading to incomparable results has been the inconsistent definition of the basic unit, i.e. the event that is the main objective of the survey. This can be a trip with a minimum distance or a minimum stay or some other definition. Also for distance, time and purpose different categories are used, which makes a direct comparison of the collected information impossible.

Generally tourism-demand surveys distinguish between holiday and business journeys. Holiday journeys are divided into long holiday journeys, defined by a minimum of 4 overnight stays away from home, and short journeys, with a minimum of one overnight stay. Business journeys generally are considered only if they include one overnight stay (Eurostat, 1999).

The definition 'overnight stay', of course, ignores all day journeys, which account for many long-distance journeys, especially those for business purposes. Some surveys even only consider trips if they include 4 overnight stays. Some surveys exclude specific types of long-distance trips, e.g. Austria excludes medically-prescribed visits to a spa or visits to a rehab. clinic in the Tourism Mikrozensus. This example also demonstrates the focus on aspects other than travel information in tourism-demand surveys.

Specific long-distance travel surveys, on the other hand, define the survey unit mainly by distance, although there are still no standards as to which is the minimum distance for a journey to be considered as a long-distance journey. Often – but not always – 100 km is chosen as the minimum distance from home to furthest destination.

This main difference between the methodology of tourism surveys and long-distance travel surveys mirrors also the different data needs and aims of the data collection. In the field of tourism the factors influencing the choice of destination, means of transport and accommodation and the expenditures are the main objectives and the most difficult items to capture. Due to the relatively rare nature of a 4 night stay away from home, holiday surveys ask details about these journeys up to one year in retrospect, and up to three months for journeys with one overnight stay. The greatest difficulties are encountered when it comes to the expenditures on and for each trip. Memory effects and also the lack of knowledge about the exact amount spent are reasons for this. Business travellers especially often do not know the exact cost of a journey as they do not need to pay for it.

The main objective of long-distance travel surveys is to trace the characteristics of the movement from one location to the other. Accommodation, activities and expenditures are generally only of secondary interest. The main difficulty here is to capture data on the movement on a detailed enough level despite memory effects and lack of knowledge by the respondents. It is therefore questionable whether detailed information about the additional issues covered by tourism surveys could be collected. It is considered to be more sensible to concentrate on the issues of the movement in order to reduce respondent burden.

Most of the collected travel surveys are retrospective, i.e. they collect information on journeys undertaken in a defined period before the survey day. The method of data collection varies between self-completion mail-back, personal face-to-face and telephone interviewing. There is a tendency to use personal and telephone interviews in household surveys, whereas panel surveys make use of self-completion questionnaires, which is easier there than in one-off surveys through better instruction of respondents and the development of routine through repeat surveys.

One option offering a compromise between the cheaper paper method and the personal methods that are more expensive is to use method mix surveys as suggested by MEST. Respondents, in a first step, are contacted by mail and then reminded and motivated to reply with a telephone call. Should the respondent wish to complete the questionnaire on the phone, he/she can do so straight away.

3.3   EFFORTS TOWARDS HARMONISATION

The discussion above proves the need for harmonisation in surveys that collect cross-national data and which deliver information to decision makers in different countries. However, transport and infrastructure have traditionally been seen as a national responsibility, whereas tourism has been considered as a task which affects other countries as well and where the exchange of information is both crucial and natural.

3.3.1   EUROSTAT tourism directive

In 1995 the EU published Council Directive 95/57/EC on Tourism Statistics providing basic guidelines for a harmonised data collection across the EU countries. It was believed at that time that there was a need for legislative measures in order to achieve data conformity in a relatively short period of time.

The Tourism Directive requires the collection, compilation, processing and transmission of harmonised statistical information on tourism supply and demand within the European Union.

Concerning the data collection, the directive establishes the following categories:

- capacity of collective tourism accommodation establishments;
- guest flows in collective accommodation establishments;
- tourism demand.

The data collection is supposed to cover national tourism, including inbound as well as outbound tourism. Tourism is defined as holiday and business journeys, which involve at least one or more consecutive nights spent away from the usual place of residence (Eurostat, 1995b).

The minimum requirement for the collection of travel data within tourism surveys is the main mode of transport used to reach the final destination, the size of the party and the purpose of the journey. However, the participating countries are free to collect more detailed information on transport.

3.3.2   EUROSTAT long-distance surveys

While the Council Directive on Tourism Statistics managed to establish a set of standards for stays in commercial accommodation, the data availability with regards to travel comprising stays with friends and relatives as well as one-day outings is unsatisfactory.

To define the data needs roughly and the means of collecting the required data, in the late 1980s the EC member states supported a COST action (COST 305, 1988). An informal working group co-ordinated by EUROSTAT in 1995 refined the data needs and methodological requirements defined by COST 305. In addition a series of pilot surveys was undertaken in seven member countries (namely Austria, Denmark, France, Italy, Portugal Spain and Sweden) based on the recommendations of the working group.

In parallel, the fourth Framework Programme project MEST was commissioned to develop the methodology for a benchmark survey of long-distance travel behaviour. In contrast to the case of tourism statistics, perhaps following the traditional understanding of transport as a national responsibility, the European Commission refrained from a legislative procedure to establish standards for the collection of long-distance travel data. All efforts were undertaken with the aim of developing a practicable methodology which could form the basis of recommendations to the National Statistical offices of the member countries. Within the fifth Framework programme the EU commissioned a project to develop the methodology recommended further - as a result of MEST -

and to undertake a uniform European long-distance travel survey (DATELINE[3]).

With the exception of DATELINE and ETM (the European Travel Monitor), which is only focused on international journeys, long-distance travel surveys in the European Union member countries remain incompatible.

3.4   EXAMPLES OF THE CURRENT PRACTICE

This chapter describes three approaches to the collection of long-distance travel data in further detail.

3.4.1   French nationwide transportation surveys

Once every decade (1966/67, 1973/74, 1981/82, 1993/94) INSEE, the French National Institute for Statistics, conducts a household mobility survey, covering both daily and long-distance mobility.

The most recent survey (1993/94) consists of three parts, which used different instruments (Madre and Maffre, 1994):

- Face-to-face interview collecting data on trips made on the previous day as well as during the previous weekend;
- 7 day car-diary for daily mobility;
- face-to-face interview (3 months retrospective) and self-completion diary (3 months non-retrospective) for long-distance journeys (more than 80 km from the usual residence).

The major advantages of a combined mobility survey are the relative completeness of the travel information, which allows for cross-checks and a better understanding of mobility patterns of the respondents, and the fact that the information on the household needs to be collected only once. That is why in 2001 the Americans have chosen to merge the NPTS (daily mobility) and the ATS (long distance) in the same National Household Travel Survey. In fact, it is only recently (Madre and Maffre, 1999), that a first attempt at analysis of daily mobility data and long-distance travel behaviour for the same person has been conducted. The downside is clearly the length of the survey (on average 1.5 hours), which means that no more than one person per household can be interviewed.

The general aim of the survey is to understand all aspects that could influence the level of mobility. Therefore all trips have to be described, whatever their purpose, mode of transport, length, period in the year or time of day. Also, the provision of telecommunication is of interest and data about the ownership of telecommunication equipment, the use of telephone during trips and contact opportunities were collected.

In order to collect more information from highly mobile segments of the population, the sample of 20003 respondents was stratified to over-represent households with several cars (except for Paris where the mobility is relatively high

---

[3] See http://www.ncl.ac.uk/dateline/

despite the low car ownership figures).

The results of the data analysis supported the following observations:

- Short journeys made from places other than the usual residence (e.g. destination of a holiday) were not considered in the long-distance instrument, and much under-reported by nature in the interview on daily mobility conducted at home;
- Respondents demonstrate great difficulties in estimating distances. There is a significant under-estimation of distances and times for trips within the same municipality, whereas long-distance trips were overestimated in both time and distance.
- The definition of trip was slightly different in the two parts of the survey, which caused confusion amongst the interviewers and the respondents. As a result, the data were more consistent with regards to distance than the number of trips.

There is no further national survey planned in France for the near future. However, results are available from several regional surveys, which were undertaken recently.

3.4.2   NPTS/ATS 2000

Traditionally, travel data of American residents were collected in two national surveys. Whereas the Nationwide Personal Transportation Survey (NPTS) – conducted by the United States Department of Transportation about every 5 years (1969, 1977, 1983, 1990, 1995, 2001) – collects information about daily trips of people in the US, its counterpart the American Travel Survey (ATS) was conducted irregularly (the more recent ones in 1977 and 1995) by the Bureau of Transportation Statistics.

The ATS 1995 gathered demographic characteristics of all household members and information about journeys to destinations 75 miles and more from their homes taken during 1995. The survey was undertaken in 4 waves. 80,000 sampled households received a notification letter, followed by a survey pack and a telephone call, in which the respondents were encouraged to participate and to note their journeys. Three months later their travel data were collected by telephone. Three more phone calls followed, so that data for a whole year were gathered for each household. Some respondents that were difficult to reach by phone were interviewed personally. The response rate was very high; 65000 households completed all four interviews (Federal Highway Administration, 1998).

For the year 2000 it was planned to combine the two surveys. Several pre-tests were conducted, the main objectives of which were to test the methods for improving response rates and to test the feasibility of using a combined instrument. Three survey designs were tested under two different sampling approaches:

Design	Test
NPTS only RDD	Incentive tests
ATS only RDD	Questionnaire tests
NPTS/ATS Combined RDD	Prospective vs. Retrospective
NPTS/ATS Combined Address-based	None

Due to budget constraints Random Digit Dialling (RDD) was chosen as the main sampling method, which led to response rates of around 30%. In the US, telephone survey response rates are very poor because most people are already inundated with telephone marketing calls, which have created a cultural bias away from being willing to speak on the telephone with strangers for fear of being subjected to sales requests. This is a problem that is not yet very relevant in Europe, but which survey firms will face in the not-too-distant future.

On the other hand, due to the growing market penetration of mobile phones and the difficulties of combining addresses and telephone numbers, RDD seems to be the only possibility to reach certain, and especially highly mobile, segments of the population.

At the moment it is not clear whether the combined NPTS/ATS 2000 will be conducted or not. At the time of writing, the results of the pre-tests have not yet been published.

3.4.3   Mobility

In 1990 Lufthansa German Airlines commissioned Infratest Burke, an international market research company, to undertake a long-distance travel survey in Germany. Infratest realised there was a lack of data on long-distance travel behaviour in Germany, while at the same time there seemed to be an enormous demand from various institutions, be it the travel and tourism industry like railways, airlines and tour operators or the public sector. It was decided to undertake the survey continuously as a multi-client study starting in 1991.

In the first 3 years, due to the lack of telephone coverage, there were different data collection methods used in East and West Germany, CATI in the West and face-to-face in the East. Since 1995, however, telephone interviews were undertaken in the whole country.

The survey covers all journeys over 100km, not excluding any because of their purpose or their destination. Besides gathering information on travel, a standard questionnaire covers background information on the individual. Special questions were added to reflect the needs of the study's clients regarding the awareness and use of travel services, their prices and the satisfaction with the products offered on the travel market (Jochems, 1998).

With up to 30000 interviews per year, covering all times of the year, the "Mobility" survey in Germany delivers a valid base of travel data with updates and reports up to four times a year. It is unique in Europe for a market research institute to set up a national long-distance survey to provide the data needed by industry and the decision-makers in the public sector, because of a lack of initiative from official sources.

3.4.4 Resundersökningen RES 1999

Since 1994 Statistics Sweden has undertaken a continuous National Travel Survey which collects data on daily as well as long-distance journeys. In 1999 the successful Riks-RVU, which was commissioned by several national authorities, including the Railways, the National Tourist Board and the Swedish Institute of Transport and Communication Analysis, was redesigned. The following changes have been made.

Data about daily mobility used to be collected based on journeys. First the respondent was asked about the starting point and the destination of the journey as a whole. Then she or he was asked about all stops made during the journey. This information was collected for each trip. In the new RES the respondent is asked questions trip-by-trip in a strictly chronological order. The CATI-system recognises when a journey is completed, at which point some questions about the whole journey appear on the interviewer's screen. It was hoped that this way of asking would provide more trips and stages that were typically lost in earlier surveys, for example short walks to the bus station.

Some control questions are included in the questionnaire for daily mobility. These are asked when the respondent states a destination for a trip. He/she will then be asked "did you make any other stop on the way to this destination?' If the respondent says yes, another trip is recorded. Another question is whether the respondent undertook any errands at the same time as he/she changed modes. If so, this also results in a separate trip.

The questionnaire for long-distance trips in RES was enlarged. A new funder, the Swedish Tourist Authority, entered the consortium behind the new survey RES. This led to questions about spending (on travel, accommodation and other consumption at the visited location) and about types of accommodation for overnight stays. Because of the new sponsor, some changes were also made to the questionnaire for daily mobility. One of them is the collection of data about the car is used, that is, if it is a car owned by the household and, in case of several cars being available e.g. a rented car or a borrowed car, which one is used for the journey. This to get more information about emission factors and similar questions.

The methodological changes made to the survey have not increased the average number of journeys reported by the respondents. However, there has been a 5 % increase in the number of stages reported, whereas the number of trips has gone up by only one per cent.

Concerning the survey design, the changes seem to have obtained a "smoother" survey for both respondents and interviewers, which ideally should result in a higher data quality. However, users of the survey results are dissatisfied with the quality of the databases (there is a need to improve the geographic coding of addresses and establish effective data quality checks) and the lack of clearly defined processes in terms of data delivery.

Another important issue is the survey sample, which has been reduced to 8000 interviews per year and which, from the viewpoint of the database users, is too small to make significant estimations on a yearly basis.

3.5   CONCLUSIONS, COMMENTS AND CRITIQUE

3.5.1   Non-Uniformity

The most obvious fact about the European long-distance travel surveys of the last years is their non-uniformity. They are inconsistent in sampling and content, many items of which do not match policy needs.

There is also an obvious lack of integration due to the use of different data and sources for sampling in each European country. Only the multi-client studies of the European Travel Monitor show a question consistency and consistency of purpose, even though data collection protocol and sampling methods and sample sizes vary between the different countries.

3.5.2   Data needed and data available

Most of the surveys considered in this report have a similar pattern. There are first some socio-demographic questions including age, sex and location of residence. The second part of the survey consists of questions about travel details, including origin/destination, departure/arrival time and mean of transport used.

Attitudinal questions are extremely rare and reasons for particular choices are never established, e.g. the reasons for mode/mean choice. There is evidence that mode choice is very often influenced by emotional and irrational factors, such as fashion, prestige and habit. But there is a range of factual reasons for mode choice currently not covered, some of which might be interesting to European travel behaviour researchers:

- Actual health status and handicaps.
  Only the National Travel Survey in the UK asks for the health status. The Swedish RVU included a question about handicaps in their surveys up to 1985. After taking the question out of the Riks RVU of 1994 it was included again in the next survey, the RES 2000.
- Luggage (prams, sports equipment, suitcases, etc.)
  The Business Panel conducted in Great Britain is the only one to ask about luggage.
  The Swedish RVU asks about prams to be transported.
- Age and health conditions of accompanying people.
  Two surveys ask about the age of the youngest child in the travel group (Swedish RVU and the French NPTS 1993–94), while there is also information on handicaps and luggage in the French survey, but only for daily mobility.

It could also be interesting for transport planners to understand reasons for not undertaking trips. Often elderly people do not travel themselves but generate trips of relatives and friends to see them. The same is true for families with small children.

From a long-term perspective it is also very important to know how often children have been taken on trips on different modes of transport in order to understand their future mode choice behaviour. Their travel pattern might again be created by habit and a set of values that was influenced by the travel behaviour of their parents.

As mentioned above, most of the surveys are retrospective and ask for a period seldom longer than three months. The researcher is hardly able to see which journeys are frequently undertaken and have similar characteristics (same destination, same mean of transport, same accommodation, same duration, etc.). A simple question about trip frequency would be very helpful in this case, but only the Norwegian National Travel Survey includes one.

Another method that was recently suggested and which helps to reduce the respondent burden of reconstructing information about journeys from their memory is the "Most Recent Trip" (MRT) method. Richardson and Seethaler (1999) suggest that surveys should only capture data on one long-distance journey from each respondent, notably their most recent one. By doing, so every respondent will have one journey to report, which helps reducing non-response in two major sample groups, i.e. the highly mobile and the very infrequent travellers. As every respondent has only one journey to report effects of repetitiveness and also recall effects can be minimised. Whereas memory effects cannot be completely excluded, the way questions are worded and prompting in telephone or personal interviews can achieve better results than is the case with diary-based traditional surveys, since the task is much simpler.

The MRT method has been tested in the NPTS/ATS 2000 as well as the Swiss Microcensus. Results are not yet available.

Mode choice is very often a question of costs. Questions about the costs of transportation are rare and drawing inferences from secondary sources such as car type, season ticket availability can lead only to estimates. Given the car type and the whole trip distance, the costs can be estimated, but then one should know the car occupancy and the person/institution which is paying the costs, e.g. the company, the parents, etc. The availability of a season ticket or other reductions for public transport cannot provide the researcher with the ticket prices all over Europe. Expenditures can consist of a theatre visit or meals in expensive restaurants but no expenses for transportation at all. The experience in tourism surveys across Europe shows that expenditures are a very difficult item to capture. Respondents often either do not remember or do not know the exact amount of their expenditures.

Although it would be interesting to know the allocation of costs between the employer and the traveller for business travel, experience with tourism surveys has shown that respondents often simply do not know the answer as the costs of their travel are not always transparent to them.

3.5.3   The choice of the target population

Long-distance travel covers a vast field of different travel types with extremely diverging impacts on policy decisions. Mode choice, cost considerations and other preferences on business and leisure travel are almost in opposition to each other. Airlines, hotels and public transport providers are increasingly adjusting their services to the different needs of these groups of travellers. Therefore the question of choosing the right target population to cover both types of travel in an appropriate way needs to be addressed by the researcher.

The division of data into business and leisure traveller enables more precise information and therefore a higher data quality.

Another possibility for grouping the target population is the journey duration. While short journeys are usually over short distances, the proportion of short distances will be quite different for long journeys. There will also be a different transport mode choice behaviour.[4]

Dividing the target population into different groups allows for much higher data quality and should be seriously considered in the case of an overall long-distance travel survey, covering many countries.

Most long-distance travel surveys, as well as tourism surveys, focus on the journeys of the population between 15 and 75 years old, i.e. the age span with the highest mobility. Whereas there is great policy interest in the mobility of children and the elderly, these surveys seem not to be interested in collecting information about these population groups.

Also, travelling with children or elderly people or journeys generated by these population groups (e.g. visit to grandmother or visit to see grandchildren) can influence destination and mode choice of the population between 15 and 75 years old and should therefore be considered in a long-distance travel survey.

A gap between different statistical sources and survey data was discovered in the French NPTS 1993/94, which concerned the travel of household members who stay away from their usual place of residence for a longer period of time. These could be students or young people on military service. Their journeys are under-reported compared with available data from the railway companies.

---

[4] There is also a correlation between trip duration and trip distance according to income groups, countries, etc.

3.6 REFERENCES

Ampt, E., L. Buchanan,.I. Chatfield. and A. Rooney (1998) - Reducing the impact of the car – creating the conditions for individual change. *Paper presented at the ETC*, Loughborough.

Axhausen, K.W. (2000) - The Eurostat pilots of long-distance travel diaries: Summary of the final report. *Report to the Österreichisches Statistisches Zentralamt*, Wien and Eurostat, Luxembourg.

COST 305 (1988) - Data system for the study of demand for interregional passenger transport. *Final Paper*, Brussels, Luxembourg.

Eriksson, S. (1999) - Proceedings from the methodological workshop on the implementation of the Council Directive 95/57/EC on Tourism Statistics,*.4/2000/D/no.1*, Luxembourg.

EUROSTAT (1995a) - Definitions and variables of a household survey for mobility, Passenger transport statistics and mobility. *Document T7/95-2/5/EN*, Luxembourg.

EUROSTAT (1995b) - Council Directive 95/57/EC of 23 Nov. 1995 on the collection of statistical information in the field of tourism, Brussels.

EUROSTAT (1999) - Progress report on methodological developments in the EEA Countries of Tourism Statistics following the implementation of the Council Directive 95/57/EC. *Document TOUR/99/32/EN*, Luxembourg.

Federal Highway Administration (1998) - Personal travel: the long and the short of it. *Working Paper published by the Office of Highway Information Management* , Washington D.C.

Jochems, P. (1998) - German long-distance travel: Results of the on-going 'Mobility' survey. *Presentation at the 3rd MEST Workshop*, Pörtschach.

Lyons, G. (1998) - A case study of the development of car dependence in teenagers. *Paper presented at the ETC*, Loughborough.

Madre, J.L. and J. Maffre (1994) - The French national passenger travel survey: the last dinosaur or the first of a new generation. *Paper presented at the International Conference on Transport Behaviour*, Valle Nevada.

Madre, J.L. and J. Maffre (1999) - Is it necessary to collect data on daily mobility and on long distance travel in the same survey? *Transportation Research Circular, E-C026, 343-364, TRB, Washington D.C.*

Richardson, A.J. and R.K. Seethaler (1999) - Estimating Long-Distance Travel Behaviour from the Most Recent Trip. *Transportation Research Circular, E-C026, 237-254, TRB, Washington D.C.*

Schnabel, C. (2000) - DATELINE up-dating review of existing long-distance survey, Socialdata, Munich.

Statistics Sweden (2000) - National Travel Survey, NTS 1999. *Official Statistics of Sweden*, Swedish Institute for Transport and Communications Analysis.

Weckström-Eno, K. (1999) - Long distance passenger travel, *Statistics in focus, Transport*, **Theme 7, Volume 4,** Eurostat, Luxembourg.

Youssefzadeh, M. and K.W. Axhausen (1996) - Long distance diaries today: Review and critique, *Deliverable*, **D1**, MEST-Project, Fakultät für Bauingenieurwesen und Architektur, Leopold-Franzens-Universität, Innsbruck.

Youssefzadeh, M. (forthcoming) - Long Distance Diaries today: A Collection of Recent Surveys. *Arbeitsberichte Verkehrs. und Raumplanung*, 55, Institut für Verkehrsplanung, Transporttechnik, Strassen- und Eisenbahnbau, ETH, Zürich.

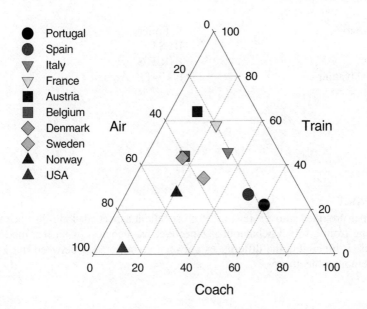

Chapter 4
What is known?

J.-P. Hubert and F. Potier

4.   What is known?[1]

J.-P. Hubert   F. Potier
TRG   DEST
FUNDP   INRETS
B – 5000 Namur   F - 94110 Arcueil

Abstract

This paper provides an overview of the most salient aspects of long-distance traffic in Europe from a travel behaviour perspective; frequencies, distances, modes and purposes. It highlights the differences between countries and between the various socio-demographic groups.

Keywords

Long-distance travel, Europe, surveys, state-of-knowledge.

---

[1] Preferred Citation: Hubert, J.-P. and F. Potier (2003) What is known? in K. W. Axhausen, J.-L. Madre, J. W. Polak and Ph. L. Toint (eds.) *Capturing Long Distance Travel*, 45-70, Research Studies Press, Baldock.

4.1   INTRODUCTION

In Europe, the surveys that produce data about long-distance mobility generally have a national or regional basis. This state of affairs leads to analyses and comparisons of the mobility behaviours at a national level. But unfortunately, transport surveys are quite different, and the spatial reach of long-distance mobility makes it more sensitive to national spatial organisation than local mobility. This makes the comparison between countries difficult, even for a simple indicator like the rate of long-distance journeys per person and month (see Table 4-1).

Several points arise from this table; the link between long-distance mobility and economic development seems strongest for those countries with the lowest average number of long-distance journeys per person. However, Belgium is a rich country with a low journey rate. The small size of the country may explain such a low figure, given that the average distance between Belgium's five largest towns is under 100 km, which is the threshold of the survey. The date of some surveys – especially those of the Portuguese, Italian and Spanish – may also explain some of the differences.

Comparisons between countries are useful and necessary. They are shown here as long as the available data in Europe are sufficiently consistent. But social, geographic or temporal factors specific to each country can influence the selected indicators. That is the reason why this chapter also analyses, in parallel, the effects of such factors on this kind of mobility.

Table 4-1   Average number of long-distance journeys/person and month in different European countries

Country	1998 GDP/capita [x1000 €]	1998 population density [person/km^2]	Year of survey	Minimum distance	Long-distance journeys/ person and month
Norway	29.6	14	1998	100 km	0.54
Denmark	29.4	123	1996-97	100 km	0.60
Sweden	24.0	22	1999	100 km	0.62
Austria	23.3	96	1996	75 km	0.56
France	22.1	108	1993-94	100 km	0.75
Belgium	21.9	334	1998-99	100 km	0.39
Great Britain	21.2	244	1992-98	50 miles	0.70
Italy	18.4	191	1997	100 km	0.48
Spain	13.2	78	1997	100 km	0.27
Portugal	9.8	108	1996	100 km	0.19

Norway and GB data were given as number of trips and were divided by 2 for simplicity in the absence of information about the number of trips/journey. This produces a slight overestimate

The first part of this chapter provides a description of long-distance journeys according to their main descriptive features; distance, transportation mode, length of journey, season when people travel, and purposes of the journey. The data used come from transportation surveys conducted in different European countries. As the documentation is less precise than desirable in many cases, and as the categorisations are often crude, a more detailed analysis is performed on the basis of the French national transport survey of 1993–94, for which the required detail is available.

The second part outlines an analysis of the links between long-distance mobility and the social, demographic and locational characteristics of the travellers. In particular, it is based on work of the European research consortium ARTIST (Agenda for Research on Tourism by Integration of Statistics/Strategies) on international travel and the specific features of the different European countries (see Potier *et al.*, 2000 and Cockerell *et al.*, 2000).

4.2 DEFINITIONS AND SOURCES

Analysis of long-distance mobility from different sources requires homogeneous definitions. But this homogeneity can only be obtained with aggregated categories, which have had to be imposed here on the different data sources.

The main unit of analysis is the (round trip) journey, starting when the traveller leaves home and finishing when he or she gets back. The duration of the journey is the complete time elapsed, including travel time, and it is split here into three categories; same-day travel, short breaks with one to three nights away from home, and long journeys including four or more nights.

Journeys have a main purpose. Classes that are used here are:
- commuting;
- business travel (including journeys of commercial travellers, journeys for meetings or congresses);
- personal business (including trips related to education, health, administrative business, civil or religious ceremonies);
- visit to friends or relatives;
- leisure (including visit to sites of natural or historic interest, cultural shows or sports meetings, stay in a second home, package tour, and holidays).

The first two classes are professional journeys; the last three are private journeys. Purposes that are usually excluded from the scope of long-distance surveys are; moving home, travel of the personnel of transport firms and troop movements. Commuting over long distances is sometimes excluded as well; for instance, in the French national transport survey of 1981–82 or in the American Travel Survey (ATS) of 1995.

Concerning the analysis of distance, the measure unit used is the distance from home to the point furthest away (outward journey). The round-trip distance can also be considered and it is more relevant if the traveller visits many different places. Some travel survey databases are based on single trips. Results on journeys require special processing in these databases and are therefore less frequently published.

A journey is regarded as a long-distance survey if the outward journey is longer than a particular threshold fixed by the survey. The threshold is usually 100 km for the European surveys analysed, except for the British and Austrian cases (respectively 80 km and 75 km). In the USA, the distance threshold for the 1995 ATS was 160 km.

European data that are used in this chapter come from:
- Household surveys supervised by Eurostat in 1996–97 in Austria, Denmark France, Italy, Spain and Portugal. Except for Denmark, the reporting periods are two or three month long and the survey periods were in early spring, or summer in Portugal (Weckström-Eno, 1999);
- National transport surveys undertaken in Belgium in 1998–99 (Toint *et al.* 2001), in France in 1993-94 (Insee, 1998), in Great Britain (DETR, 1999) (the period 1992-98 of this continuous survey was employed), in Norway in 1997–98 (Denstadli, 1999), in Sweden in 1999 (SIKA, 2000). Detailed results and original microdata could be used for the French national survey (referred to as microdata Insee-Inrets, 1993–94). For other countries, results are less detailed.

The respondents had to be:
- more than 5 years in Belgium, France, and Sweden;
- more than 12 years old in Norway;
- more than 15 years old in Great Britain, Portugal and Denmark

The American data source is the 1995 ATS (BTS, 1997).

Some statistics on transport related to tourism are also used because they are relevant for the study of long-distance mobility.

The analyses of international travel by Europeans reported here are based on data from the *European Travel Monitor* survey (ETM), which focuses on trips abroad with at least one night spent in the country visited.

"[The survey is conducted] on a representative sample of the population aged 15 years and over in EU and EFTA countries. In all 250,000 people per year are interviewed in six separate cycles, each of which covers outbound international travel in the preceding two months" same-day trips are excluded. (Potier *et al.*, 2000, page 95).

4.3 WHAT DOES "LONG" DISTANCE MEAN?

Long-distance mobility behaviour is so varied that this mobility cannot be regarded as a well-delimited and specific phenomenon. Could it only be an artefact and the consequence of an analytical definition? No, because thresholds of distance bring qualitative changes in the way that people travel. For most people long-distance journeys are rare events (Table 4-1), even if the numbers of this type of journey are growing faster than any other. Some means of transport are specifically dedicated to long distances, even if most journeys above 100 km are made by car (Figure 4.3). Above all, travelling for long distances frequently results in a temporary change of residence (Table 4-2). But these qualitative changes are never necessary and their occurrence depends on the purposes that have motivated the journeys.

The overall set of long-distance journeys has to be split according to the main descriptive features of the journeys.

4.3.1   The range of distances

If long distances are defined by a lower limiting value, there is no upper limit. What is the distribution of the journeys? The available tables giving the number of journeys by distance class make it possible to draw frequency curves. The percentage of journeys in a certain distance interval is divided by the width of the interval, and this gives an average percentage per unit distance. In Figure 4.1 the matching x-coordinate is the centre of the interval. The curves drawn for different European countries are close to each other and are rapidly decreasing. On the whole, long-distance journeys can be divided in three segments with a share of about one third each: 100 to 150 km, 150 to 250 km and more of 250 km.

This type of figure can be refined to show more detail, as will be done later for the French data (see Figure 4.1). Still, Figure 4.1 shows how the frequency of trips decreases when the length of trips grows. Long-distance trips are mainly made inside a region or between adjoining regions.

Figure 4.1   Distance distribution of trips of more than 100 km

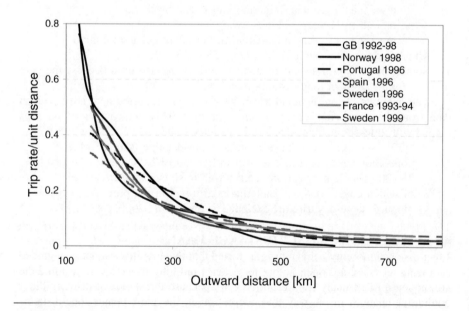

4.3.2   Means of transport

The great majority of long-distance journeys are made by car. The average share of the car for journeys over 100 km is about 70% in Sweden, Norway, Austria (threshold of 75km), Italy and Portugal. In France and Belgium, the share rises to

75%[2]; in Denmark and Spain, the rate is slightly under 65%.

As a comparison, in the United States, car use is even more dominant, with a share of 81% for long-distance journeys over 160 km.

With regard to the usage of the different public transport modes (coach, train and air), the European countries show substantial diversity. Each country has its own profile dictated by its geography, the structure of its transport system and economic conditions (Figure 4.2). In Latin and Alpine European countries, the share of rail and coach is relatively high. In Scandinavian Europe and Belgium, the share of trips by air is higher.

Figure 4.2   Modal split of public transport in different countries

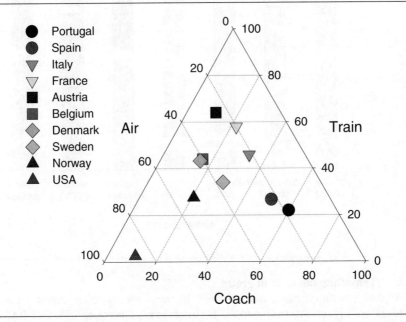

4.3.3   Means of transport and distances

The French data illustrates how the modal split changes when distance increases (Figure 4.3). The car only loses its supremacy when destinations are greater than 750 km, which represents 13% of the total in France. In that distance band, the aeroplane becomes the main public means of transport. The share of train use is also affected by distance, although not as dramatically; it varies between 10% and 20% (maximum in the band 800–1500 km round trip). In France, the share of coach use stays between 3% and 5% in contrast to countries such as Spain or Portugal.

[2] It rises to 84% in Great Britain, but for domestic travel over 80 km (source: DETR 1992–98).

4.4   DIFFERENCES IN THE MOBILITY BEHAVIOUR

The journey distance is only one component of travel. The other characteristics create equally important choices. Such a choice can be private, or made by an employer, or by parents for a child; it can be the choice to travel alone or with other people at a certain period of the year, and for a certain duration.

Figure 4.3   Modal split of journeys by round trip distance in France, 1993–94

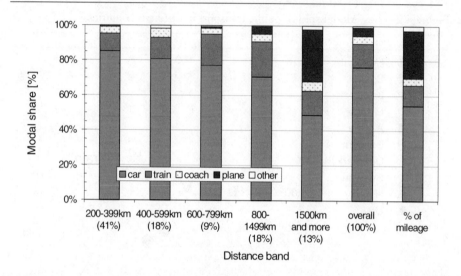

4.4.1   Travelling alone or in group

Unlike daily mobility, many long-distance journeys are made in groups; family, friends or colleagues. According to the Eurostat surveys, between 25% and 40% of journeys are made by single persons in Europe; between 28% and 55% are made by groups of three persons or more (Weckström-Eno, 1999).

In France (Microdata Insee-Inrets, 1993–94), in the case of journeys made by car (75% of journeys), only one long-distance journey in five is made by one person travelling alone, generally a man, because such journey has often a professional purpose[3]. There are two people in the vehicle in 25% of long-distance journeys by car, three in 20% of the journeys, and four or more in the remaining 35%. Such a decrease is not found in the American data, where two long-distance journeys in five are made by one person travelling alone.

---

[3] When the driver is a man, he drives alone in one journey in five; if the driver is a woman: one journey in ten.

4.4.2   Duration of stay, purpose and seasonality: Three dimensions of long-distance travel

Duration of stay
Table 4-2 sums up the distribution of long-distance journeys according to the duration of stay in different European countries. The proportion of journeys with an overnight stay varies from 50% to 70% of the total.

Table 4-2   Distribution of duration of stays

Country	Same day	One to three nights	Four nights and more
France 1993-94	31%	36%	33%
Portugal 1996	37%	39%	24%
Denmark 1996	43%	34%	23%
Belgium 1998-99	47%	32%	21%
Italy 1996	46%	35%	19%
Sweden 1999	48%	27%	25%
USA 1995	24%	50%	26%

Purposes
In our data, journeys with professional purposes (commuting and business trips) represent 20% to 37% of the total.

Commuting over 100 km is at the intersection of long-distance mobility and daily mobility, as the journeys are repeated and stay inside the usual environment of the traveller. They represent an important share of professional journeys because of the strong attraction of large metropolitan areas and the development of motorways and high-speed trains. In France in 1993–94, 6% of all long-distance journeys were for commuting. In Great Britain they represent 13% of domestic trips over 80 km. In Austria, they represent 10% of long-distance journeys (threshold of 75 km), in Denmark, 5% and in Norway, 6%.

In our data, journeys with private purposes represent 63% to 80% of the total. Private purposes are most prominent in long-distance mobility. The three main purposes that compose private purposes account for:
- personal business: 10% to 15%;
- visit to relatives and friends: 20% to 30%;
- leisure: 20% to 45%. The countries where the share of leisure journeys is higher are: Portugal (45%), Italy (39%), France (33%), and Spain (31%).

Seasonality
Individuals' or households' participation in long-distance travel is very sensitive to social and climatic cycles, such as working days and weekend, bank holidays, summertime, wintertime, etc. The number of long-distance journeys per person has

important seasonal variations.

Figure 4.4 and Figure 4.5 show the seasonal variations of the number of private and professional journeys in France, according to their duration. Private journeys of more than four days show the largest variation and are concentrated during the summer. Journeys with one to three overnight stays vary less, though they are quite numerous in spring, as a probable effect of the bank holidays in April and May (Easter, 1 May, 8 May, Ascension Day, Whit Sunday). The comparison of the two figures also shows that private and professional journeys are comparable in number only in the case of same-day journeys.

In addition, we can use data from survey on tourism in Portugal and Italy on journeys with one or more overnight stays (but no specific distance threshold), commuting excluded. There are peaks in the summer season (July, August and September). In Portugal (INE, 2000), more than 35% of Portuguese over 15 years old made at least one journey with an overnight stay in the summer season, which is twice as much as at the other times of the year. In Italy, with similar data, 40% of all journeys with overnight stays (private and professional) are made in the summer season, but only 15% of professional journeys with overnight stays are made in summer (Istat, 1997).

Is the summer peak a southern European or European characteristic? The 1995 ATS survey shows a smaller variation for the USA. However, a peak can be seen for the summer season in some states: e.g., in the state of New York, 34% of journeys are made during the summer, compared to 30% on average. On the contrary, some other states do not have such an increase (e.g. 26% of journeys in summer in Georgia or Kansas).

Figure 4.4   France 1993-94: Seasonal variations of personal journeys (000' journeys)

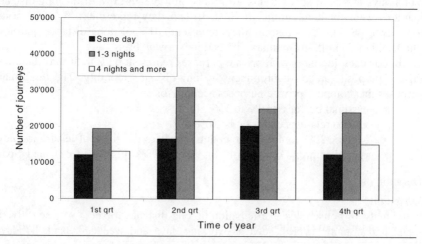

Figure 4.5   France 1993-94: Seasonal variations of professional journeys
                  (000' journeys)

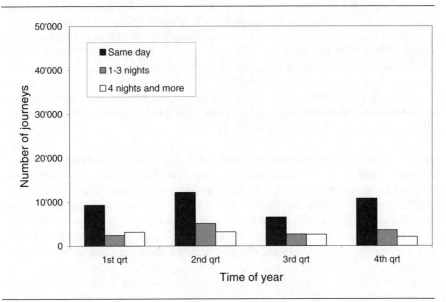

4.4.3   The link between duration of stay, purpose and distance

Aggregate figures result from complex combinations of different behaviours.
Distance distributions are far from being uniform. For instance, in France
professional journeys are on average shorter in duration and in distance. Indeed,
the proportion of private journeys increases both with distance and duration (Table
4-3).

Table 4-3   France 1993-94: Shares of private journeys by distance and by
                 duration of stay

Distance (round-trip distance for journey)	Share [%]
< 400 km	77
400 – 599 km	79
600 – 799 km	81
800 – 1,499 km	84
1,500 km and more	85
Duration of stay	
Same day	61
1 to 3 overnight stays	88
4 and more overnight stays	90

However, in the case of same-day journeys, people travel more kilometres for professional purposes than for private purposes. Typical professional destinations for meetings and conferences, as well as the residential locations of people concerned, make the use of the high speed train or plane frequently possible.

The link between duration and distance is another example of that complexity (Figure 4.6). Not surprisingly, the frequency of same-day journeys decreases with rising distance. The negative influence of distance on frequency is less important for journeys with one to three overnight stays. But, when the journey lasts more than four days, very long distances are no longer an obstacle and the share rises accordingly as travellers seek a complete change of scenery, especially for holidays.

4.4.4   How do purposes combine with other dimensions of journeys?

Distance, mode of transport, duration, season and purpose are combined in the logic of long-distance mobility. After the analysis of long-distance journeys according to their main descriptive dimensions, the main interactions will be identified by looking for the most frequent combinations of purpose and duration in the set of long-distance journeys. Except where indicated, the French 1993–94 NPTS is used as it allows a finer categorisation of purposes than in the previous sections.

Figure 4.6   France 1993-94: Share of private journeys by round trip distance and duration of stay

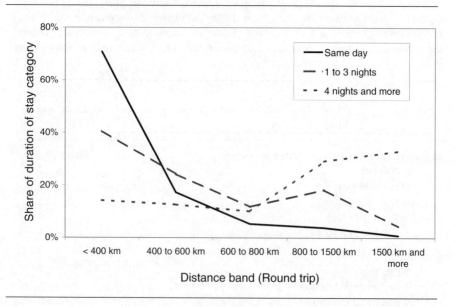

Professional journeys: Commuting
Long-distance commuting mostly generates same-day journeys (three out of four). Average distance is not far above 100 km, which is expected, and in the distance range around 100 km, commuting is the dominant purpose of long-distance travel. In Great Britain, one trip (*i.e.* outward or inward journey) in five in the band 80 to 120 km is a commuting trip (NTS 1992–98).

Commuting trips in France have the distinctive feature of being almost exclusively made by men (86%) from households with above average income. Travellers in the direction of Paris (either as place of residence or as place of work) often use the train (62%).

Professional journeys: Business trips
In France, most business trips last less than four days, 55% of them being same-day journeys. As with commuting, travellers are usually men (80% of business trips). In the 45% of business trips with overnight stays, travellers go to a hotel in about two cases in three.

The car is used for 80% of business trips, which is a little more than average. But train or plane are often used for same-day journeys, especially when people travel for meetings or conferences.

Both commuting and business trips are, of course, essentially weekday trips.

Private journeys: Private business
Private business is a rather heterogeneous category. Like professional business trips, these journeys rarely last more than four days and, in half of the cases, they are same-day journeys. Only one private business trip in three takes place during the weekend.

Private journeys: Visits to relative and friends
Journeys whose purpose is a visit often combine short distances (100 to 150 km), one to three overnight stays and the weekend period. In France, half of the short breaks (one to three overnight stays) are motivated by visits. In Great Britain, a visit to friends or relative is the most common purpose for all trips under 400 km, and they represent about 25% of all the trips over 80 km.

Leisure
This category is very heterogeneous and aggregates very different behaviours. The data of the French national survey made it possible to divide this too-wide category into three: culture or sports related,[4] journeys to a second home, and holiday journeys when the destination is not a second home.

Almost three leisure purpose journeys in five are made during holidays and, in that case, most of them last more than four days.

Leisure journeys with a culture- or sports-related purpose (or mixed, when

---

[4] In the French 1993–94 survey, such journeys can be initiated from home or a temporary residence, especially during holidays.

people go to amusement parks) are, in more than half the cases (54%), same-day journeys. Such same-day journeys generally occur during the weekend, and especially on Sunday; the use of coach is greatest for this type of trip.

The majority of journeys to a second home are made during weekends, outside holiday time: very few journeys are made on the same day only.

Holiday journeys, where to a second home or not, generally last more than four days. But short breaks of one to three overnight stays during holidays to a destination other than a second home are more and more frequent. These short holiday breaks often have remote destination: in one short break in four, the outward distance is over 400 km.

Short holiday breaks are more frequent among people living in the Paris metropolitan area: 35% of travellers on that kind of journeys come from that region.

4.5   SOCIAL AND SPATIAL FACTORS AND LONG-DISTANCE MOBILITY BEHAVIOUR

As with daily mobility, the number of long-distance journeys is distributed very unevenly in the population, especially during seasons other than summer. During the average month, only a minority of Europeans make a long-distance journey: 42% of the population in Norway, 35% in Belgium. In France over a period of three months, 46% of the population still does not travel over 100 km, 26% once, and only 28% more than twice.

At the same time, a very small proportion of the population makes a lot of long-distance journeys, especially commuters; less than 1% of the Norwegian population makes more than 6 journeys per month and totals 11% of all long-distance journeys; 4% of the Belgians make more than 5 during an average month. As with daily mobility, the behaviour depends on age: people in the age band between 25–55 years make more long-distance journeys, but the long-distance mobility of older people has grown substantially recently. Men travel more often than women. In France this is particularly due to professional travel, but in Norway men also make more leisure long-distance journeys than do women.

Long-distance journeys, or tourism in general, are a strong factor of social differentiation. Qualitative studies made from this perspective disclose many social mechanisms. The ambition here is more limited and this section focuses on the quantitative effects of income and residential location on long-distance mobility.

4.5.1   The importance of income

The uneven distribution of long-distance mobility in the population has several causes: some social situations generate frequent long-distance journeys such as living at more than 100 km from the place of work, possessing a second home or studying in another town far from the family home, etc. Some of these situations are correlated with household incomes. On the other hand, a low income acts also as a brake on mobility in general, and for long-distance travel in particular. For instance, among the 40% of the French population who did not go on holidays in

1999, 37% of them said it was for financial reason[5] (Rouquette, 2000).

Cumulated percentages of population, number of journeys and mileage by increasing income show the lower long-distance mobility of people with an income under the median (Figure 4.7). The poorer half of the households make only about the third of long-distance journeys.

In France, people in households with an annual income under FF 75,000 in 1994 (15% of French households[6]), made three long journeys per year versus twelve in households with an income in the top 5% (more than FF 480,000). In the USA, households with more than US$ 50,000 annual income in 1995 (one American household in three) were responsible for 48% of the journeys, while households with less than US$ 25,000 (40% of all American households) account for only 16% of the journeys[7].

Figure 4.7   Cumulative distribution of population, journeys and km by household income

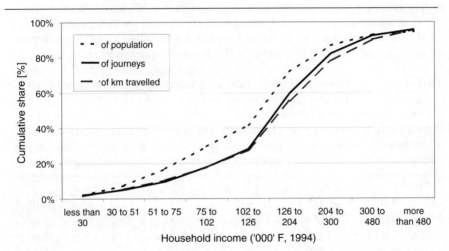

The total is less than 100% as the households with missing income data were included in the calculations.

---

[5] Holidays are defined in the French survey on conditions of living as a leisure trip lasting more than four days, which is probably, though not necessarily, a long-distance journey.

[6] The French NPTS had a question about income, but values and percentages may differ from other sources since there is no official data for income in France as there is in the USA, with census data.

[7] Income limits for each fifth of households were: US$ 14,400; 29,914; 42,002 and 65,124 in 1995 (source: US Census Bureau).

4.5.2 The influence of size of town

Populations in the various European countries have mainly adopted an urban way of life, which was historically usually associated with concentrated housing and activity in manufacturing or services. Since the end the 1970s, urbanisation has been linked to the development of metropolises, where large service industry-based cities, with vast attraction zone, interlace with those of other cities. Metropolisation has produced large conurbations with sprawling suburbs following the famous model of the *Megalopolis* in the North East of the USA. The communication functions of these large cities are essential and require continuous and substantial investment. People living in these large cities or in their metropolitan areas have a better access to transport facilities. Do they have a different long-distance travel behaviour?

If the share of long-distance journeys produced (or attracted) by urban areas grouped in size classes is superior or inferior to the share of the population living in these towns, it can be said that long-distance mobility in a particular class size is above or under the average. The division of the former percentage by the latter gives a indicator centred on the value 1, which can be called a relative production (or attraction) of long-distance journeys (Table 4-4) in a certain group of towns.

Table 4-4   France 1993-94: Relative production and attraction of long-distance journeys by size of town

Population of urban area (1990)	(1) share of population	(2) share of journeys produced	(3) share of journeys attracted	(2)/(1) Relative production	(3)/(1) Relative attraction
Rural area	26%	23%	25%	0.9	0.9
2,000-5,000	6%	4%	6%	0.7	1.0
5,000-10,000	6%	6%	7%	1.1	1.2
10,000-20,000	5%	7%	8%	1.3	1.6
20,000-50,000	7%	7%	9%	1.0	1.4
50,000-100,000	6%	6%	7%	1.0	1.1
100,000-200,000	7%	7%	9%	1.0	1.2
200,000-2,000,000	21%	22%	19%	1.0	0.9
Paris urban area	16%	19%	11%	1.1	0.7

Rural areas are indeed characterised by a low long-distance mobility, but small cities (from 5,000 to 50,000 inhabitants) are clearly above the national average. Medium and large cities are neutral, and the Paris region is over-represented. The small towns are also often places of destination.

The size of towns does not automatically imply more long-distance journeys but it does imply changes in behaviour for the different types of long-distance journeys.

4.5.3 The influence of urbanisation

Grouping towns by their size has the drawback of ignoring the regional context. Many small French towns (fewer than 20,000 inhabitants) which had above-average long-distance mobility numbers might have this particularity because many of them might belong to a large metropolitan area. The next step is to examine regions and to compare their relative production, calculated as before, with a "relative urbanisation" indicator based on the number of people inside a certain administrative region who live in an urban area of more than 100,000 inhabitants. The two indicators were calculated for the French administrative regions and the states of the USA.

Figure 4.8 shows that the size of urban areas does not have the same effect on same day journeys as it does on journeys with overnight stays or holiday departure rate.

Figure 4.8   France 1993–94: Average number of long-distance journeys by type and size of urban area

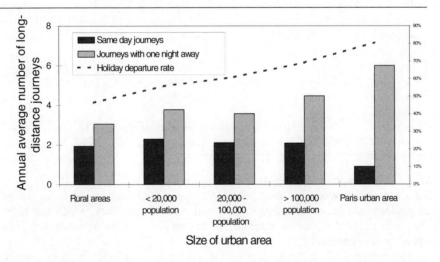

There is a very small negative correlation, which is clearer in the US data, between the number of domestic journeys per inhabitant and the number of people living in a town of more than 100,000 inhabitants (Figure 4.9). In contrast, international journeys are clearly more numerous in more urbanised regions. This is consistent with Norwegian observations: the inhabitants of the ten larger built-up areas make fewer domestic journeys over 100 km, but 25% more international journeys.

It seems from these examples that no general relationship between long-distance mobility and urbanisation should be looked for without analysing separately the different types of long-distance journeys. But cultural patterns and geographical location may have to be taken in account as well.

Figure 4.9   France 1993-94 and USA 1995: Relative long-distance journey
production by degree of urbanisation [8]

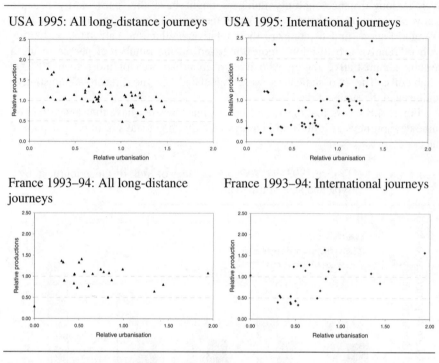

4.5.4   **Geography and long-distance mobility**

The distances between the main cities are specific to each country, as are its
morphology and its surface. Figure 4.10 indicates this diversity, which has to be
taken into account if one is interested in the modal split, as transport networks
depend on this geography.

The analysis of distance distribution above for outward journeys can be
pursued for the French regions in 1993–94, with distance bands of 100 km (see
below).

The frequency curve for France, overall, has some deviations from the
expected continuous decrease. These deviations have moved relative to the

---

[8] Relative urbanisation = share of a region or a state in the population of urban
areas with more than 100,000 people/share in the total population in France:
Agglomérations urbaines of 1990 defined by Insee; in the USA, *Metropolitan
areas* defined by the Bureau of Census, both definitions are based upon
continuously built up areas; 1.0 is the average. Relative production = share of a
region or a state in the production of long-distance journeys/share in the total
population; 1.0 is the average.

observations in 1981–82. The distance band 200 km 300 km was more frequent in 1981–82 and the 500 km 700 km much less so. In these twelve years the number of long-distance journeys increased from 210 million[9] to 319 million (Inrets, 1989, pp. 151 and 155).

Figure 4.10   France   1993-94:   Distance   distribution   for   long-distance journeys by selected regions

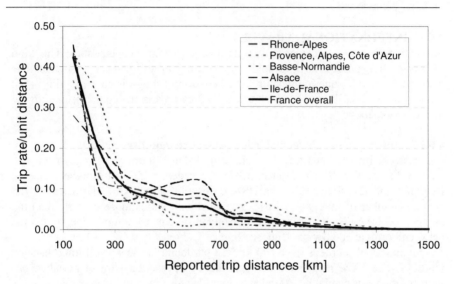

It is noticeable that the richer regions (Ile-de-France, Alsace, and Rhône-Alpes) are above the average curve for distances beyond 400 km and the others are under (except Provence-Alpes-Côte-d'Azur (PACA), that overtakes the average after 800 km). Regional curves have various shapes that can be explained by the location of their major towns inside the French urban network.

Certain regional curves have deviations at distances of 200, 600 and/or 800 km. These distances usually correspond to the average distance between the region and Paris region (Ile-de-France): 200 to 250 km for regions of the Parisian basin (e.g. Basse-Normandie); 550 to 600 km for Rhône-Alpes and Alsace regions; 750 to 900 km for PACA. The attraction and the demographic weight of the Paris region increases the number of trips in the distance range. As regards the Ile-de-France region, its curve shows all these deviations as well.

The Alsace and Rhône-Alpes region curves are significantly concave in the interval 100 to 300 km. Trips of that distance are less frequent than the average. In

---

[9] The French national transport survey of 1981–82 ignored commuting and counted 189 million journeys, but commuting over 100 km was estimated to 21 million journeys (Inrets, 1989, p. 155).

these frontier regions, the largest towns of the urban networks are quite close to one another[10] and large towns of other French regions with a rank higher to the one of the regional capital (Lyon or Strasbourg) are usually more than 400 km away, except Lyon for the south of Alsace and Marseilles for the south of Rhône-Alpes.

These examples show that the signification of distance thresholds is relative to regional or national spatial organisations. It also appears that the evolution of such regional curves can be a useful indicator of structural changes in long-distance mobility behaviours.

4.6   INTERNATIONAL TRAVEL

International travel is a category with its own particular characteristics. This kind of travel often passes the threshold of 100 km journey distance – so that it is justified to include such journeys in the discussion of long-distance mobility – but it does not necessarily do so, which creates a grey area in the comparison with the data reported above.

4.6.1   International travel inside long-distance mobility

The share of international travel within long-distance journeys changes from one country to another: 9% in France, 12% in Sweden[11], 20% in Norway, 47% in Belgium, and less than 5% in the USA (threshold of 160 km). Furthermore, the average number of international trips per inhabitant varies more strongly than the number of long-distance trips per inhabitant (a gap of almost one to twelve between Portugal and Switzerland, see Figure 4.11).

International journeys over 100 km are particular subsets of all long-distance journeys. The ETM data make comparisons of international travel possible, but such comparisons cannot be extended to long-distance mobility in general.

4.6.2   National specifics in the production of international travel

The very large range of international journeys rates requires explanation. Important variations can also be seen in the modal share for international journeys from the producing countries of Western Europe. Overall, car and plane are the two dominant modes (39% each), 15% of international travel is undertaken by coach and 7% by train (Potier, 2000, p. 106[12]). But few countries match the European average. The shares of car and plane are similar (i.e. a difference of less than 10 points) in only five European countries: Austria, Switzerland, Italy, Spain and

---

[10] The distances between Lyon (Rhône) and the second and third largest urban areas of Rhône-Alpes region - Grenoble (Isère) and St-Etienne (Loire) – are, respectively 104 km and 59 km. In Alsace, the distance between Strasbourg (Bas Rhin) and the second urban area, Mulhouse (Haut-Rhin), is 108 km.

[11] In 1999, Swedes made 2 million international journeys of less than 100 km. In comparison, they made 63 million long-distance journeys, 7.6 million of which were abroad (source: SIKA 1999).

[12] It is the main means of transport. When journeys involve ferryboats, they are always allocated to the main terrestrial mode used during the journey.

France (countries are ranked by the value of the difference between the share of car and the one of plane). In the Benelux countries the car is considerably more dominant for international travel. In contrast, the plane is widely dominant in Scandinavian countries, the British Isles and Greece; more than half of international journeys are made by plane in all these countries with the exception of Denmark and Sweden[13] (*ibid.*, p. 110). There is no general relation between the number of international journeys and the preferred mode of transport used, since the car or the plane can be dominant in countries with high or low international journey rates.

Figure 4.11   Europe 1994: Average number of international journeys (/inhabitant and year)

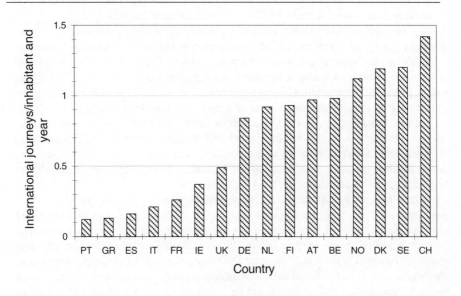

Source: European Travel Monitor (IPK, 1995)

---

[13] The proportion of the population living near the border is well-placed to make a medium long-distance international journey by terrestrial means of transport (car, coach, train). However, not all the borders have the same appeal. European countries differ a lot on this feature. In 2000, less than 5% of the British lived less than 50 km crow-fly distance from a different country, 12% in Spain, 20 to 25% in France, Portugal, Sweden, Norway and Finland, 30 to 35% in Italy and Germany, more than 90% in Austria, Switzerland and Belgium (Hubert and Moriconi, 1999).

Such diversity among European countries has many causes. Some may be found in the geography of the countries. Proximity still appears to be a compelling factor for international journeys, even if this notion integrates not only distance but also political homogeneity and similarity in the standards of living. The international flows of travellers from EU and EFTA countries stay mostly inside Europe (eastern and western) (80%) and, for each country with terrestrial borders, flows are directed towards neighbouring countries in 40 to 60% of the journeys (*ibid.*, pp. 96, 104).

Other causes can be found in the culture and standard of living of the peoples of Europe. Leisure is by far the most prominent purpose of international travel, more than for long-distance mobility in general: 77% of international travel with overnight stays is motivated by leisure, 8% by visits to relatives or friends, and 14% for business. About one leisure journey in five lasts fewer than four days, and short breaks for leisure represent 14% of the overall (*ibid.*, p. 101).

Every country has its own culture of leisure. The leisure required for long-distance travel and the means of transport for that travel have not become affordable to the same extent in the different countries. This contrast is pronounced in the Mediterranean countries, which are a major destination but a relatively minor producer of international journeys. Still, the increase of short breaks in the recent years is a major evolution in this particular long-distance market.

In the Artist project, European countries have been classified into six regional groups according to the characteristics of their outbound flows. The classification is based on factorial analysis and considers such factors as the trip rate, the purposes, the type of destination (seaside, mountain, town), the time period and the travellers' profiles (*ibid.*, pp. 113–14) (See Figure 4.12).

Three regions of Europe have high departure rates around one journey abroad with overnight stays per person and year. In the Rhine region countries (Benelux and Germany), most of the international journeys are motivated by holidays with the family, often to the seaside in the summer. People mainly travel by car; that mode of transport is used in 55% of all international journeys in these countries. In the Alpine countries (Switzerland and Austria), holiday trips are also prominent but journeys are shorter and terrestrial public transport (train in Switzerland, coach in Austria) is more frequently used than in other European countries. In the Scandinavian countries (Sweden, Norway, Finland and Denmark), international journeys are still shorter on average; one third are short breaks either for professional or private purposes. Scandinavian travellers are in the majority men; they often use the plane, and towns are frequent destinations for their trips. More international journeys are made in winter in Scandinavia than in any other countries.

The countries of the British Isles and Iceland constitute a fourth group where departure rates are about 0.5 international journeys per person and per year. The plane is widely used (the modal share is 70%). International travellers are large consumers of organised travel and middle classes are widely represen

Figure 4.12   Europe: Classification of countries by long-distance travel pattern

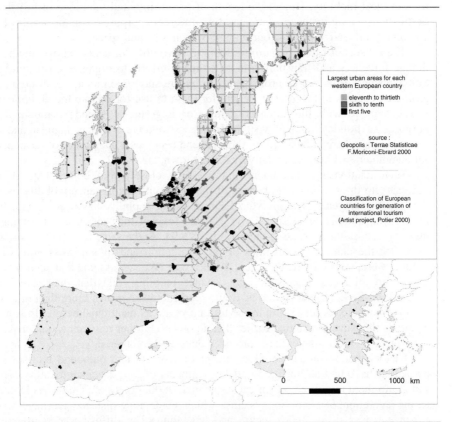

In the last two groups, the departure rates are about 0.2 to 0.3 international journeys per person and per year. Mediterranean countries (Spain, Italy, Portugal and Greece) have the lowest departure rates. For international travel, the share of professional journeys is higher in this group than for other Europeans, and the share of holidays is lower. France is a separate group. The departure rate is low but holidays are a prominent purpose as in the Rhine or Alpine regions, although travellers are older or without children and use planes more than cars.

4.7   CONCLUSION

Either long- or short-distance travel patterns sum up the behaviour of all kinds of people and show great diversity. However, the analysis of long-distance mobility leaves a stronger impression of heterogeneity than that of local mobility. There is no core of regular trips, scheduled by the obligations of daily life, that structures people's local mobility.

Long-distance travel is a relatively rare event. Short private journeys with destinations under 250 km emerge from this as a group, as do long journeys for holiday purposes. But these groups do not play the same role as the home-to-work trips in local mobility. Due to the length of travel time and the range of possible destinations, long-distance journeys for different purposes cannot easily be combined and tend to exclude one another within time and space.

The subsets of travel by purpose seem to have little influence on one another, though travellers and transport companies make efforts to organise them jointly. Some business trips can be prolonged by a leisure stay, free mileage is offered by airline companies to business travellers for them to use for private travel, holiday journeys made with the extended family or a group of friends combine the purposes of holidays and of visit to friends or relatives. It may happen that a second home where citizens go for the weekend becomes a main place of residence for commuters working in a relatively remote town, etc.

Such relationships are interesting to study closely, but before that, it is necessary to draw a complete picture of the trends in long-distance mobility over the last twenty years. The growth of long-distance mobility has been strong. In France, the number of journeys over 100 km (except long-distance commuting) grew by almost 4% per year in the period 1982–94. At the same time (in the period 1980–95) the annual growth rates of the population and of the gross domestic product were, respectively, 0.5% and 2% per year. We can assume that such wave has raised all the segments of long-distance mobility, and that the wave has covered all the European countries. Some segments have grown more than others, such as short breaks for leisure in the last ten years, as mentioned before. In some countries the wave has started earlier than in others. Further research should give a more precise view of the process, provided data can be gathered.

Factors that favoured the development of tourism, and outbound tourism in particular, have had an impact on all the segments of long-distance mobility. We can group them into three sets of causes (Potier, 2000, pp. 97–9). One set is linked to the evolution of transport systems, which made long-distance journeys less expensive, less tiring, more secure and appealing. The diffusion of household motorisation in developed countries is an aspect of this evolution. Long-distance travel has become commonplace. It is seen neither as a luxury nor, on the contrary, as a painful ordeal. This technical and economical evolution has not only favoured long-distance mobility, whatever the purpose of travel may be, but the opportunity to use a modern and efficient mode of transport is an incentive for travelling longer distances.

A second set is linked to the increasing productivity of industry and services and the resulting reduction in working time. The extension of holidays stimulated the demand for leisure. At the same time, the economic system could generate an *industry of leisure*. This mass tourism has created seaside or mountain resorts and, by reaction, another part of the population is attracted by other remote countries or rural regions that were spared by industrialisation and tourism development. As a consequence of the increasing incomes of the population, retired people have better health and income to travel more. The new organisation of production in a global economy multiplies business travel.

A third and more recent cause can be found in the new territorial organisation generated by metropolises that are the economic centres for services and communication and are also cultural and academic centres. The sprawling urban areas and the efficiency of local transport systems increase the chance of daily long-distance journeys. These areas are also important places of commercial or scientific meetings, business meetings, cultural exhibitions, and are therefore frequent destinations of long-distance travel.

The process of European integration is a catalyst for this sets of causes, which are not independent. Their joint evolution provides the stimulus to the growth of that heterogeneous behaviour which is long-distance mobility.

4.8 REFERENCES

BTS (1997) - 1995 American travel survey profile. *US Department of Transportation*, Washington, D.C.

Cockerell, N., N. Barrie, M. Manente, V. Minghetti, E. Celotto, M.C. Furlan, G.R.M. Jansen, M.J.W.A. Vanderschuren, F. Potier, Y. Israeli, S. Blais, G. Röschel, A. Troitiño and R. Vickerman (2000) - Artist Agenda for Research on Tourism by Integration of Statistics/strategies. *Deliverable*, **5**, ARTIST Project, Brussels.

DATELINE Project (2000) - Sampling Methodology. *Deliverable*, **3**, Socialdata, München.

Denstadli, J. M. (1999) - Travel behaviour 1998 - journeys of 100 km or more. *Summary of TOI Report 466/1999*, TOI, Oslo.

DETR (1999) - Transport Statistics Bulletin, National Travel Survey 1996-1998 update. *DETR*, London.

Eurostat (1998) - Community methodology on Tourism statistics. *Eurostat*, Luxembourg.

Hubert, J.-P. and F. Moriconi-Ebrard (1999) - Terrae statisticae. Il database sui comuni d'Europa. *Sistema Terra*, 8 (1-3) 120-125.

INE (2000) - Destaque do INE, Viagens turisticas dos residentes (1999-2000). *INE*, Lisboa.

Inrets (1989) - Un milliard de déplacements par semaine. La mobilité des Français. *La Documentation française*, Paris.

INSEE (1998) - La mobilité à longue distance des ménages en 1994. Enquête transport et communication 1993-1994. *Insee Résultat, collection Démographie-Société*, n°72-73-74,1998, INSEE, Paris.

ISTAT (1997) - I viaggi in Italia e all'estero nel 1997. *ISTAT*, Roma.

Potier, F. (2000) - Trends in Tourism and international flows in Europe, in ECMT (ed.) Transport and leisure. *Report of the 111th Round Table of Transport Economics,* ECMT, Paris.

Potier F., N. Cockerell, G.R.M. Jansen, M.J.W.A. Vanderschuren, M. Manente, V. Minghetti, E. Celotto, M.C. Furlan, O. Heddebaud and G. Röschel (2000)

Analysis of tourism and transport flows and overview of recent trends. *Deliverable,* **1**, ARTIST Project, Brussels.

Rouquette, C. (2000) - Chaque anée, quatre Français sur dix ne partent pas en vacances. *INSEE première, No. 734,* INSEE, Paris.

SES/ESA (1998) - Actes du colloque déplacements à longue distance. Mesures et Analyses. *Département des études économiques du Service Economique et Statistique (SES),* Paris and ESA Consultants, Strasbourg.

SIKA (2000) - RES 1999 Den nationella reseundersöknigen. *Sveriges oficiella statistik,* IKA, Stockholm.

Toint, Ph. L., E. Cornélis, C. Cirillo, Ph. Barette, A. Dessy, T. Jacobs., R. Verfaillie, J.-M. Museux, E. Waeytens, S. Saelens, C. Durand, V. André, K. Van Hoof, E. Heylen and I. Pollet (2001) - Enquête nationale sur la mobilité des ménages: Réalisation et résultats. *Rapport fina,*l. SSTC, Brussels.

Weckström-Eno, K. (1999) - Long distance passenger travel. *Statistics in focus, Transport,* **Theme 7, 4/1999**, Eurostat, Luxembourg.

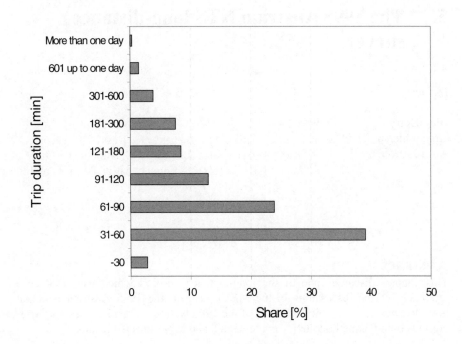

Chapter 5
The 1995 Austrian NTS long-distance survey

M. Herry

72

5.   The 1995 Austrian NTS long-distance survey[1]

M. Herry

Büro Herry
Argentinierstr. 21
A – 1040 Wien

Abstract

This chapter discusses one of the long-distance surveys which was used as a reference for the discussions in the MEST project: the 1995 Austrian National long-distance survey, which was part of the 1995 National Travel Survey (NTS). It presents both the methodologies implemented and some selected results.

Keywords

MEST, long-distance travel, survey design, survey protocol, Austria, National Travel Survey, results.

[1] Preferred citation: Herry, M. (2003) The Austrian 1995 NTS long-distance survey, in K. W. Axhausen, J.-L. Madre, J. W. Polak and Ph. L. Toint (eds.) *Capturing Long-Distance Travel,* 71-84, Research Studies Press, Baldock.

5.1 INTRODUCTION

The task of this chapter is to discuss the experiences gained through the long-distance element of the 1995 Austrian National Travel Survey, which was one of the surveys, and which formed the development of the work in the MEST and TEST projects. It will present both methodological experiences and individual results, expanding those presented in Chapter 4.

The Austrian Federal Transport Infrastructure Masterplan (Österreichischer Bundesverkehrswegeplan; BVWP) (Bundesministerium für Wissenschaft und Verkehr, 1998) was a follow-up to the Austrian Traffic Concept 1991 (Österreichisches Gesamtverkehrskonzept) (Bundesministerium für öffentliche Wirtschaft und Verkehr, 1992). Its main objective was the prioritisation of transport investment across all modes based on detailed national models of transport supply and demand. These were based on a careful analysis and documentation of the existing traffic and transport situation in Austria. Due to the lack of current data at the time, a series of new surveys was commissioned, among which the National Travel Survey (NTS) was the most important. The NTS encompassed both daily mobility and long-distance travel.

5.2 THE NTS SURVEY AND THE VALIDATION STUDY

The main NTS survey, which was carried out by Fessel+GfK and IFES (1996), as accompanied by a validation study carried out by a consortium of the consultancies Herry and Sammer (1996).

5.2.1 Main survey

The main survey was carried out by postal distribution of the survey materials and personal collection of the forms by interviewers. The interviewers checked for the completeness of the forms and were allowed to set a new reporting day/reporting period in cases of incomplete recording during the previous period. The survey had two versions. In the short version the households (2/3 of sample) were asked to record all trips made in one day by their members over 6 years of age. In the long version (1/3 of sample) they were additionally asked to record all trips longer than 50km during the previous 14 days. The household and individual forms were identical in both cases. The daily mobility form was a variant of the well-known KONTIV design (Brög, 2000) and the long-distance form was derived from it (see Figure 5.1).

The respondents were asked for the origin and destination of their trips (street address, name of municipality respectively), departure and arrival time, purpose, modes used, estimated distances (daily mobility only) and number of overnight stays (long-distance mobility only).

The sample was stratified by district/city, which were supplied by the client. Based on the official registry of households every n^{th} member was selected, starting from a randomly-drawn first household. The "n" varied locally depending on assumed rates of quality neutral sample loss due to local differences in the quality and timeliness of the local registries.

74

Figure 5.1   Austrian NTS: Long-distance survey form (main study)

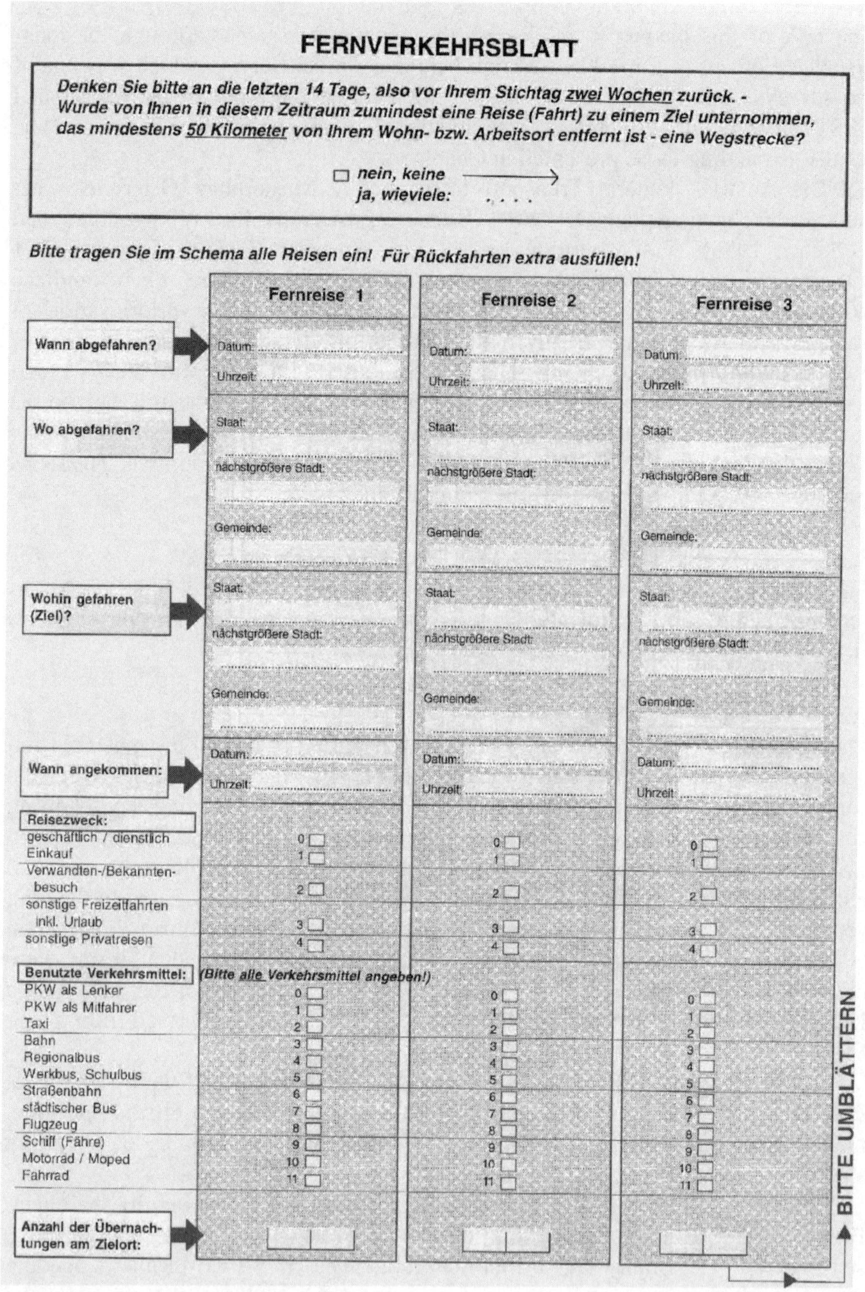

FERNVERKEHRSBLATT

Denken Sie bitte an die letzten 14 Tage, also vor Ihrem Stichtag zwei Wochen zurück. - Wurde von Ihnen in diesem Zeitraum zumindest eine Reise (Fahrt) zu einem Ziel unternommen, das mindestens 50 Kilometer von Ihrem Wohn- bzw. Arbeitsort entfernt ist - eine Wegstrecke?

☐ nein, keine ————————→
ja, wieviele: . . . .

Bitte tragen Sie im Schema alle Reisen ein! Für Rückfahrten extra ausfüllen!

	Fernreise 1	Fernreise 2	Fernreise 3
Wann abgefahren?	Datum:	Datum:	Datum:
	Uhrzeit:	Uhrzeit:	Uhrzeit:
Wo abgefahren?	Staat:	Staat:	Staat:
	nächstgrößere Stadt:	nächstgrößere Stadt:	nächstgrößere Stadt:
	Gemeinde:	Gemeinde:	Gemeinde:
Wohin gefahren (Ziel)?	Staat:	Staat:	Staat:
	nächstgrößere Stadt:	nächstgrößere Stadt:	nächstgrößere Stadt:
	Gemeinde:	Gemeinde:	Gemeinde:
Wann angekommen:	Datum:	Datum:	Datum:
	Uhrzeit:	Uhrzeit:	Uhrzeit:

Reisezweck:

geschäftlich / dienstlich	0 ☐	0 ☐	0 ☐
Einkauf	1 ☐	1 ☐	1 ☐
Verwandten-/Bekannten-besuch	2 ☐	2 ☐	2 ☐
sonstige Freizeitfahrten inkl. Urlaub	3 ☐	3 ☐	3 ☐
sonstige Privatreisen	4 ☐	4 ☐	4 ☐

Benutzte Verkehrsmittel: *(Bitte alle Verkehrsmittel angeben!)*

PKW als Lenker	0 ☐	0 ☐	0 ☐
PKW als Mitfahrer	1 ☐	1 ☐	1 ☐
Taxi	2 ☐	2 ☐	2 ☐
Bahn	3 ☐	3 ☐	3 ☐
Regionalbus	4 ☐	4 ☐	4 ☐
Werkbus, Schulbus	5 ☐	5 ☐	5 ☐
Straßenbahn	6 ☐	6 ☐	6 ☐
städtischer Bus	7 ☐	7 ☐	7 ☐
Flugzeug	8 ☐	8 ☐	8 ☐
Schiff (Fähre)	9 ☐	9 ☐	9 ☐
Motorrad / Moped	10 ☐	10 ☐	10 ☐
Fahrrad	11 ☐	11 ☐	11 ☐

Anzahl der Übernach-tungen am Zielort:

BITTE UMBLÄTTERN →

Source: Herry and Sammer, 1996

Figure 5.2   Austrian NTS: Long-distance survey form (validation study)

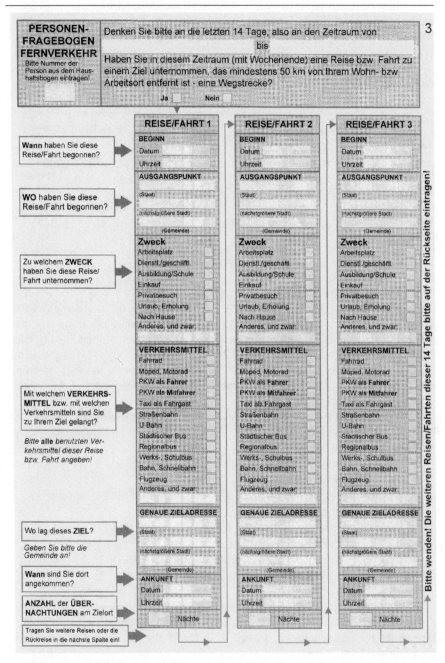

Source: Herry and Sammer, 1996

The survey was carried out in five waves between 9.10.1995 and 18.11.1995. The fieldwork ended in mid-December when all the difficult-to-reach households had been processed. Table 5-1 gives the response behaviour for the main and the validation study. A response rate of 67% was achieved in the main study.

Table 5-1   Austrian NTS: Response behaviour in the main and the validation study

	Main study [Number of households]	Validation study [Number of households]
Sample		1193
Quality neutral losses		177
Net sample	12600	1014
Non – respondents	4160	325
Respondents	8440	689

5.2.2 The validation survey

The validation survey was included in the overall design of the study to provide a control for the main study. While the content was the same, the forms and the protocol were different and more emphasis was put on obtaining high quality data (for the long-distance form, see Figure 5.2).

The sample was constructed from telephone directories as well as from addresses available at Fessel+GfK and IFES. A response rate of 68% was achieved.

The protocol mixed postal and telephonic elements (fieldwork period: 10 November 1995 to 14 December 1995):

- announcement by postcard;
- announcement by telephone;
- 1st mailing of the surveys;
- reminder postcard;
- telephone reminder and change of reporting day/period;
- 2nd mailing of the surveys;
- telephone reminder and change of reporting day/period;
- 3rd mailing of the surveys.

This intense regime was supplemented by telephone interviews of 57% sample of respondents (66% response rate). These interviews were used to probe the respondents for additional trips, as well as to record the mobility of any children under 6 years of age.

Table 5-2 shows the trips which were additionally identified by mode and distance.

Table 5-2   Austrian NTS: Additional trips identified during the quality
             control telephone interviews of the validation study

Number of trips	Distance 0-500 m	500-1000 m	1-2 km	2-5 km	5 km plus
Walking	111	9	21	6	
Bicycle	4	4	4	4	1
Public transport			1	3	5
Car		9	18	16	27

5.3   DATA WEIGHTING AND NON-RESPONSE SURVEY

The data sets were carefully coded and edited. To gross them up, an iterative
sequential weighting procedure was used, which maintained the known marginal
distributions (three iterations required). The main survey used weights for; national
household size distribution; district-specific household size distribution; day of
week distribution; national age by sex distribution; district-specific age by sex
distribution; national distribution of centrality of residence within the districts. The
weighting of the validation survey used one less weight and less specific ones;
national household size distribution; household size distribution by group of
provinces; day of week distribution; national age by sex distribution; age by sex
distribution by group of provinces.

5.3.1 Non-response analysis and survey of initial non-respondents

For the non-response analysis, a subsample of the refusers (of the main survey)
was drawn: 964 people on a telephone-based survey. About every fourth person of
these could not be reached because of "wrong or not existing telephone numbers",
"wrong addresses", etc. Of the remaining 75% we received an answer to the non-
response survey attempt from about 45% of them after extensive contact attempts.
The biggest shares of non-response reason (within the non-response analysis) were:

- "telephone number not available / name could not be found";
- "not willing, hung up";
- "not available on phone".

Table 5-3 shows the reasons of non-response for the survey of initial non-
respondents.

Table 5-3   Austrian NTS: Responses and non-response behaviour of the
             sample for the survey of initial non-respondents

Reason given/behaviour	Share [%]
Not a valid number; person cannot be found	21.7
Person cannot be found at the address reached	3.5
Wrong number	1.6
Person cannot be reached	12.7

"Does not want"; hung up	16.5
No time	6.7
Claims that the forms were already returned	4.3
Unfavourable opinion about the survey ("nonsense")	0.8
Annoyance about the invasion of privacy ("that is nobody's business")	0.6
Fear of data misuse	0.3
Answered	29.0
Partially answered	2.3

Those who did participate were asked about the reasons for not participating in the initial survey. The biggest shares of non-response reasons were:
- "I do not know / cannot remember";
- "Lack of time".

Table 5-4 gives a complete overview of the reasons.

Table 5-4   Austrian NTS: Reasons given for non-response in the main study (survey of initial non-respondents)

Reason given/behaviour	Share [%]
Does not know/cannot remember	31.1
Lack of time	23.5
Other	14.2
No questionnaire received	6.3
Questionnaire was not understandable	4.3
Unfavourable opinion about the survey ("nonsense")	4.0
Fear of data misuse	2.3
Claims that the forms were not picked up	2.3
Did no want to	1.7
No interest	1.7
Annoyance about the invasion of privacy ("that is nobody's business")	1.3
Claims that the forms were already returned	1.3
No reason given	6.0

Table 5-5 presents the average number of trips per person by the number of contacts needed to obtain their response, which shows that the later respondents have a slightly higher trip rate. The respondents in the survey of initial non-respondents indicated a much lower average trip rate (2.4). That means that we did not catch the highly mobile among the non-respondents of the main survey in a appropriate way. The results of the non-response analysis were therefore used only partly for the reweighting of the data.

Table 5-5   Austrian NTS: Average number of trips per person by number of contacts needed to obtain the data (main study)

Number of contacts	Cumulative response rate	Trips per person and day
1	37.5 %	2.97
2	56.0 %	3.02
3	63.9 %	3.01
4	66.5 %	3.02
5	67.7 %	3.03
All		2.99

5.4   AUSTRIAN LONG-DISTANCE MOBILITY

This section focuses on the results for the long-distance element of the survey. Detailed results about the daily mobility of the Austrians can be found in Herry and Sammer (1999).

The share of people undertaking long-distance trips varies considerably between the types of residential location. Unlike for daily mobility, Vienna has the smallest share of mobile people for long-distance mobility. The reason for that is that the share of out-commuters is low in Vienna because of the attractiveness of the capital. The number of trips/mobile person varies again, but this time the large cities, excluding Vienna, have the smallest number, while peripheral locations have the greatest (see Table 5-6).

Among the trip purposes, business (33.4 %) and visiting friends and relatives (25.7 %) dominated. (Return home was recoded to match the outward trip purpose.) There is also a noticeable share of people going to second and vacation homes (Figure 5.3). The car dominated the market, with a total share of 77.7% (driver and passenger), while rail is a distant third (16.5%) (Figure 5.4). The low share of "other" – which is mainly coaches – is due to the fact that the survey period was in the autumn and winter. While the peripheral and provincial locations rely more on rail, when they use public transport the inhabitants of the big cities outside Vienna make also use of "other", which also includes air (Table 5-7).

Two-thirds of all trips were shorter than 90 min., which means on average shorter than 100km (Figure 5.5). It is noticeable that it is the inhabitants of the big cities, other than Vienna in particular, who make long trips, while the Viennese make, on average, the trips of shortest duration (Table 5-8). Equally, public transport is used for longer trips, while the other modes have similar trip duration distributions (Table 5-9).

Table 5-6   Austrian NTS: Share of people undertaking trips over 50km and
average number of long-distance trips/mobile person by type of
home location

Type of home location	Share of persons with long-distance trip (50 km and more) [%]	Trips per person with long-distance trip/14 days
Vienna	21.3	3.4
Big cities (excluding Vienna)	40.1	2.4
Central districts	27.8	3.4
Peripheral districts	30.0	3.9
All	28.6	3.4
Central districts	Defined as urbanised areas outside Vienna and the major cities	
Peripheral districts	Defined as the rest of the country	

5.5   CONCLUSIONS

Within the (previous) Austrian Federal Transport Infrastructure Masterplan
(Österreichischer Bundesverkehrswegeplan; BVWP) the (first) National Travel
Survey (NTS) was commissioned and carried out in 1995 by Fessel+GfK and
IFES, together with a 1995 validation study by Herry and Sammer. These studies
encompassed both daily mobility as well as long-distance travel. This framework
was quite useful because the validation survey was included in the overall design
of the study to provide a control for the main study. While the content was the
same, the forms and the protocol were different and more emphasis was put on
obtaining high quality data.

An essential element of the validation study was the non-response analysis and
survey of initial non-respondents. This analysis showed that the later respondents
have a higher trip rate. The respondents in the survey of initial non-respondents
indicated a lower average trip rate. That means that we did not catch the highly
mobile people among the non-respondents of the main survey in an appropriate
way. This gap was filled out in the non-response survey and analysis.

Figure 5.3   Austrian NTS: Long-distance trip purposes

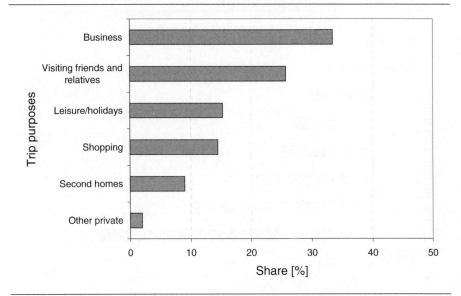

Figure 5.4   Austrian NTS: Long-distance mode shares

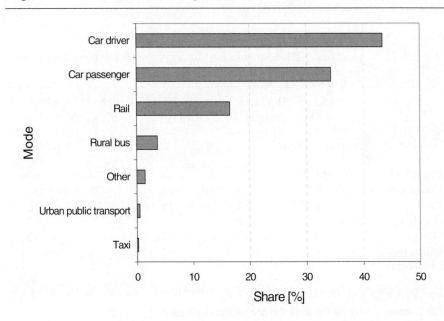

82

Figure 5.5   Austrian NTS: Long-distance trips by trip duration

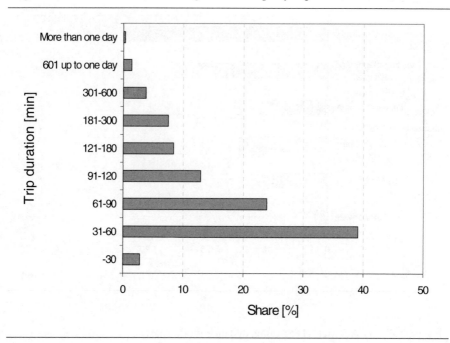

Table 5-7   Austrian NTS: Share of mode for trips over 50km by type of home location

Modes	Vienna	Big cities outside Vienna	Central districts	Peripheral districts	All
	[%]	[%]	[%]	[%]	[%]
Car driver	51	46	44	39	43
Car passenger	46	39	38	26	34
Rail	2	9	15	25	16
Rural bus		1	1	8	4
Other	1	5	1	1	2
Urban public transport			2		0

Central districts	Defined as urbanised areas outside Vienna and the major cities
Peripheral districts	Defined as the rest of the country

Table 5-8   Austrian NTS: Share of trip durations for trips over 50km by type of home location

Duration	Vienna [%]	Big cities outside Vienna [%]	Central districts [%]	Peripheral districts [%]	All [%]
Up to 60 min	52	30	42	41	42
61 to 120 min	39	34	34	39	37
121 to 180 min	7	12	7	9	8
181 to 360 min	1	9	11	6	7
More than 360 min	1	15	6	4	5

Central districts	Defined as urbanised areas outside Vienna and the major cities
Peripheral districts	Defined as the rest of the country

Table 5-9   Austrian NTS: Share of trip durations for trips over 50km by mode

Duration	Car driver [%]	Car passenger [%]	Public transport [%]	All [%]
Up to 60 min	52	46	15	42
61 to 120 min	31	37	48	37
121 to 180 min	7	6	12	8
181 to 360 min	6	6	12	7
More than 360 min	4	5	9	5

5.6   REFERENCES

Brög, W. (2000) - The New KONTIV design: A total survey design for surveys on mobility behaviour. *Paper presented at the ICES II International Conference on Establishment Surveys*, Buffalo, New York.

Bundesministerium für Wissenschaft und Verkehr (1998) - Der Masterplan des österreichischen Bundesverkehrswegeplans. *BMöWV*, Vienna.

Bundesministerium für öffentliche Wirtschaft und Verkehr (1992) - Österreichisches Gesamtverkehrskonzept. *BMöWV*, Vienna.

Fessel+GfK and IFES (1996) – Feldbericht. *Report to the Ministry of Stated Owned Industries and Transportation*, Vienna.

Herry, M. and G. Sammer (1999) - Mobilitätserhebung österreichischer Haushalte, Österreichischer Bundesverkehrswegeplan. *Forschungsarbeiten aus dem Verkehrswesen*, **87**, Vienna.

Herry, M. and G. Sammer (1996) - Österreichischer Bundesverkehrswegeplan: Gewichtung, Hochrechnung und Zusatzerhebung zur KONTIV Österreich. *Report to the BMöWV*, Vienna.

This form is about all journeys that took you more than
65 miles away from your present base between

May 9th and June 5th 1997

A journey starts and ends at the same place.
*We call this place your **present base**. This is normally your home but can
also be anywhere you stayed more than two consecutive days.*

*If you have any questions about how to fill in these forms,
please check the **Example Booklet** we have enclosed.*

TRAVEL FORM

for the selected person   **First name:**

**Please fill in the table below. Give every journey a separate name. That
name will be used again later.**
Started and ended in - the City, town or village, where you started the journey
Destination - the City, town or village and country which was your main destination
for this journey
Date of departure from the origin and *date of return* to the origin of this journey
Size of party - the number of people who travelled with you on this journey.

Journey name	Date of departure	Date of return	Started and ended in	Destination	Size of party
					☐
					☐
					☐
					☐
					☐
					☐
					☐

Chapter 6
MEST survey work

K. W. Axhausen and M. Youssefzadch

6   MEST survey work[1]

K. W. Axhausen

IVT
ETH
CH – 8093 Zürich

M. Youssefzadeh

35, Av Dr. Paul Benet
F – 82140 St Antonin Noble Val

Abstract

The MEST project conducted three waves of pilot studies during the three years of its duration. This chapter traces the development of the approach taken from the first wave based on earlier work in the Eurostat pilots to the draft proposal of a uniform European survey of long-distance travel behaviour. It presents the pilot fieldwork and the associated cognitive laboratory work, which was used to refine the survey approach. While it presents some descriptive statistics, it focuses on the qualitative results of the survey work.

Keywords

MEST, pilot surveys, form design, protocol, scope, development.

---

[1] Preferred citation: K. W. Axhausen and M. Youssefzadeh (2003) MEST survey work, in K. W. Axhausen, J.-L. Madre, J. W. Polak and Ph. L. Toint (eds.) *Capturing Long-Distance Travel*, 85 – 108, Research Studies Press, Baldock.

6.1 INTRODUCTION[2]

One of the main aims of the project MEST (Methods for European Surveys of Travel Behaviour) was the development of a design for a long-distance travel survey suitable for implementation in all member states of the European Union (EU) (MEST Consortium, 1995). The resources provided in the contract allowed for the pilot testing of different designs in four member states chosen to reflect different types of language and attitudes towards survey research: Sweden (S), the United Kingdom (UK), France (F) and Portugal (P). The MEST pilot work overlapped in time with a parallel initiative of the Commission of the European Communities (CEC) chaired by Eurostat and part funded by CEC DG 7 – Transport, which had the aim of testing a particular definition of the scope and content for a long-distance travel survey (Eurostat, 1995a). The results of this work undertaken in Austria, Denmark, France, Italy, Portugal, Spain and Sweden (Axhausen, 1998) will be considered in this chapter and the next. Both the Eurostat-Initiative and MEST reflect the concern about the lack of suitable data for policy making at the European level already expressed a decade earlier (Fabre, Klose and Somer, 1988) and still not resolved at the time the project started (See also Chapter 1).

The definition of the scope of the survey object, discussed in Chapter 2, is only the start of a survey design, which has to address further questions before its implementation is possible (see for example Dillman, 1978 or Richardson, Ampt and Meyburg, 1995):

- **Sample frame and sampling**: Definition of the sample frame and the procedure for drawing the members of the sample from the sampling frame (see Chapter 10 for more detail);
- **Survey protocol**: sequence, type, frequency and content of the interactions with the members of the sample and those responding;
- **Question wording** and sequencing for written and oral interactions with the respondents on survey forms (PAPI – paper and pencil interview), in computer-aided telephone interviewing (CATI), on the web or during computer-aided personal interviewing (CAPI);
- **Form design** for the PAPI elements of the survey protocol;
- **Selection, content and design** for any supporting materials, such as announcement letters, cover letters, reminder cards, explanatory booklets, flyers about the project, etc.

In addition, there are issues which are specific to surveys recording events, such as surveys of travel, tourism, episodes of ill health, victimisation through crime, road accidents, etc, which need to be determined:

---

[2] This chapter is based on work presented in Axhausen and Youssefzadeh, 1999 and MEST Consortium, 1999.

- Duration of the reporting period;
- Temporal orientation of the reporting period (retrospective or non-retrospective diary[3]);
- Base unit of reporting: stage, trip or journey;
- Treatment of frequent travellers;
- Treatment of frequent journeys, trips or stages;

It should be pointed out that these questions need to be answered not only for the main survey, but also for the **validation survey**. A validation survey, normally using a different approach to contact the respondents and to retrieve information, aims to address the problems arising from non-ignorable non-response, both at the sampling-unit level (household or person), and, for episode-oriented surveys, at the episode level also, i.e. the objects, events, episodes which the survey tries to recover, in this case journeys, trips within journeys or stages within trips (see Chapter 9 for more detail). The MEST project did not have the resources to undertake dedicated separate validation surveys and had to restrict itself to some validation work inherent in the protocol of the pilots themselves.

This chapter will present the MEST pilot work, organised into three waves, and discusses the lessons learnt from it, in particular with regard to the structure of the question set, its formulation and size. The issues addressed in each of the waves were selected to address open questions which either arose from the experiences of the MEST and Eurostat work or from the wider experiences of the consortium embers and the experts, who discussed these with the consortium in a series of three workshops organised for that purpose (June 1996, September 1997 and September 1998).

6.2   STRUCTURE AND ISSUES OF THE WAVES OF THE PILOT SURVEYS

The pilots used fractional-factorial experimental designs (Box, Hunter and Hunter, 1978) to maximise the usefulness of the survey work undertaken in each wave. Such a design generates a set of different surveys within each wave, with each survey being a specific combination of the possible attributes (values) of the issues under study. For example, in wave II the project was interested in the variations due to differences in the base unit (stage or trip), layout of the forms (one column/base unit or one page/base unit) and durations of the reporting period (four or eight weeks). In combination with the four countries, a total of 32 ($4 \cdot 2 \cdot 2 \cdot 2$) different surveys would have been possible. Eight of those 32 were selected, which allowed the estimation of linear models of the main effects of each variable (see Table 6-1).

---

[3] The word "prospective" would be natural, but implies in the first instance a survey of intentions, plans and future commitments, but these are not the sought-after contents of a survey, in which the respondents keep a diary of the relevant movements while they are engaged in them.

Table 6-1   Example of the experimental designs: Pilot surveys of wave II

Country	Issues		
	Base unit	Layout of survey form	Duration of reporting period
Portugal	Stage based	Page based	4 weeks
Portugal	Trip based	Column based	8 weeks
UK	Stage based	Column based	8 weeks
UK	Trip based	Page based	4 weeks
France	Trip based	Page based	8 weeks
France	Stage based	Column based	4 weeks
Sweden	Stage based	Column based	4 weeks
Sweden	Trip based	Page based	8 weeks

Table 6-2 gives an overview of the issues addressed in the pilot fieldwork. In Waves I and II experimental designs were used to address a range of issues, while the third wave tested our draft proposal for the survey design in conjunction with a set of four specific issues which were addressed one each in the four countries participating. In the first wave the consortium undertook, in addition to the fieldwork, a set of cognitive laboratory studies to address a number of issues in greater depth, which will be described below. Some initial laboratory testing was also undertaken before wave III to optimise the wording of the surveys.

The experiences available at the time of the design of the first wave, in particular those from the Austrian Eurostat pilot (Axhausen, Köll and Bader, 1996) and from work with surveys of daily mobility (in particular, the experiences gained by Socialdata with their "Neues KONTIV Design"), led to the choice of three issues; temporal orientation, method of data retrieval and respondent workload.

Table 6-2   Overview over the waves: Survey periods, countries and issues addressed

Characteristic	Wave		
	Wave I	Wave II	Wave III
Survey period	Dec. 1996-Jan. 1997	May-June 1997	Jan.-March 1998
Countries	P, S	F, P, S, UK	F, P, S, UK
Surveys	8 (fractional factorial)	8 (fractional factorial)	Draft proposal plus 4 country specific tests
Issues	Temporal orientation Method of data retrieval Respondent workload	Base unit Layout of survey form Duration of reporting period	F: Non-retrospective survey P: Follow-up for stages S: Person sampling unit UK: Route information

Most surveys of long-distance travel (see Chapter 3) have used a retrospective format, i.e. the respondents were asked to report long-distance journeys which they had already undertaken. Still, the consensus for surveys of daily mobility is that it is better to undertake non-retrospective surveys, in which the respondents keep a diary of the movements as they occur, i.e. they receive the diary at the start of the reporting period and return it afterwards. This approach had also been tested in the Austrian pilot studies with promising, but inconclusive results.

In the European context it is clear that no single method of data retrieval can be optimal. The protocol should allow for flexibility in the way in which the respondents can be approached and the data retrieved from them. In current practise, mixed-method surveys, based either on a core self-administered written questionnaire or centred around a CATI survey, dominate. Both postal-based and CATI-based approaches have their specific difficulties: lack of literacy (OECD and Statistics Canada, 1995) and the creation of an initial impression of complexity and high time requirements in the one case, availability of phones for the population, availability of phone numbers for the researcher and availability of the respondent to answer the phone (presence at home, screening through answering machines, etc.) in the other case.

The third issue was the amount of detail which the respondents are willing to report about their movements. The Austrian pilots had indicated that there might be an optimum, which neither overburdens the respondents, nor is too simplistic. This issue was tested again by varying the amount of movement and household detail included in the survey, varying the number of items, as well as the number of pre-coded categories.

The results of the first wave suggested that the stage as a base unit might be too detailed for the long-distance context and that the design of the survey forms needed further attention. The second wave therefore tested both a trip-based and a stage-based approach, two different ways of presenting the base units on the form (2 columns/page or a whole page for one unit). Finally the duration of the reporting period was varied to see how this change in response burden might affect the results.

The project group felt confident enough in the third wave to concentrate on a draft version of its final recommendations, but wanted to use the opportunity to test specific issues; in France a non-retrospective protocol, in Portugal a CATI-add-on retrieving the stages of the trips described, in Sweden a person-detail only design and in the UK an question about the route chosen during the trips.

The evolution of the design can be traced in Table 6-3, which gives the definition of the scope and the elements of the implementation, together with those elements of the protocol which varied between the waves. The survey forms were updated from wave to wave to incorporate those indications, which were clear from each previous wave.

The survey protocol for the mail-back non-retrospective surveys consisted of sending an announcement letter, containing information about the purpose of the survey, followed a couple of days later by the survey package. There were two postcard reminders during the reporting period and up to two reminder letters after the end of the reporting period. The sample participating in the retrospective surveys received an announcement letter followed by the survey package and up to two written reminders afterwards.

In the third wave the reminder postcards were preceded by phone calls aiming to motivate the respondents to participate. If desired, the respondents could use these opportunities to report their travel in a CATI-style context.

In addition, in all waves the postal contact was followed by phone calls to respondents as well as non-respondents. In the third wave the respondents received a thank-you card before this call. Respondents were questioned about their experience with the survey and the dates when the survey was completed. On this occasion, corrections to obvious mistakes and item non-response were made and respondents were also probed about any further journeys that had been omitted. Non-respondents were asked about their reasons for not responding. The interviewers were instructed also to probe for some basic information about the household and the journeys undertaken.

The participants in the non-retrospective telephone interviews received an announcement letter and a memory jogger. They also received two postcards reminding them of the need to note their journeys during the reporting period. At the end of the reporting period, the telephone interviews were undertaken. The retrospective sample received an announcement letter and a memory jogger to note any journeys undertaken in the weeks prior to the telephone interview.

6.3   INSIGHTS FROM THE FIELD WORK

6.3.1   First wave
In the first wave 70% of the Portuguese sample and 54% of the Swedish sample completed a telephone interview with the same contents as the paper instrument (see also next section). The response rate of the self completion mail surveys was about 25% in both countries, not including the respondents contacted in the follow-up telephone interviews. The total response was raised considerably by the interviews with the non-respondents to the paper form, of whom a very high percentage was willing to participate in the telephone interviews. They provided some basic information on their journeys and their socio-demographics. As the follow-up interviews were more successful than previously expected, it was decided that during the following waves more detailed information would be collected from the respondents by this method, if required.

The percentage of respondents who had undertaken at least one long-distance journey was considerably higher in the mail-back survey than in the telephone interviews. Many respondents felt that a travel survey was not relevant to them if they had not made a long-distance journey, even if the instructions on the forms and the announcement letter state the opposite, leading potentially to non-ignorable non-response.

As part of the first wave of MEST pilot surveys, an extensive testing of the instrument as well as the concepts that lie behind travel diaries in general was undertaken in the form of cognitive laboratories (see Sudman and Bradburn, 1983; Sudman, Bradburn and Schwarz, 1996 or Tanur and Fienberg, 1992 for the use of these in the social sciences in general). In these experiments the participants were told that the researcher was not only interested in their answers but also in the methods they used to arrive at them. The respondents were therefore asked to "think aloud" while retrieving the answer from their memory. The interviews were either audio- or videotaped, giving the researcher the opportunity to see which areas of the questionnaire were difficult for the respondents and which areas were answered with ease. The work was performed in either a laboratory style setting or preferably in the respondent's home

This work was carried out in France and the UK and for each respondent consisted of:

- pre-test of one of the survey forms used in the first wave involving think-aloud protocols, respondent observation and discussion;
- three out of five smaller tasks highlighting specific and problematic aspects of travel diary surveys;
- *explaining the concept of the 'stage'* – respondents had to divide hypothetical journeys, described in little stories or drawn on maps into stages according to the explanation given of the concept;

Table 6-3   Design elements of the waves

Element	Wave		
	Wave I	Wave II	Wave III
Scope			
Base unit	Stage, combined with some journey level questions	Stage or trip and journey roster	Trip and journey roster
Activity definition	Main purposes of the trip and change-of-mode	Main purpose at stage or trip level; main purpose of journey	Main purpose at trip level; main purpose of journey
Minimum distance	100 km crow-fly distance to furthest destination of the journey		
Minimum duration	None		
Spatial exclusions	*Movements inside the destinations*		
Temporal exclusions	None		
Spatial resolution	Municipality or built-up area		
Base location	Any locations with more than one overnight stay		
Implementation			
Reporting period	6 weeks	4 or 8 weeks	8 weeks
Temporal orientation	Retrospective and non-retrospective	Retrospective	Retrospective
Frequent travellers	No special treatment		
Frequent journeys	No special treatment		
Protocol (see also text for other elements of the protocol)			
Main form of data retrieval	Self-completion, CATI	Self-completion	Self-completion
Survey pack	Cover letter, household form, movement form, explanatory booklet	Cover letter, household form, movement form, explanatory booklet and explanations on the journey form	Cover letter, household form, movement form, filled-in examples on the relevant forms, map indicating 100 km radius around home location
Incentives	None	None	Offer to send brief report of the results
Survey form	3 columns/page; one column for journey level items	Journey roster on the front and back of the movement instrument 2 columns/page or full page for stages or trips	Journey roster on the front and back of the movement instrument Full page for each trip

- *capturing activities* – paraphrased description of activities had to be assigned to the categories in the questionnaire;
- *car availability* – three types of questions about respondents' car availability were tested: an added page to the person form requiring detailed responses, an added question to the person form and a question about car availability at each stage of a journey added to the travel diary;
- *capturing the route* – respondents were asked to remember recent car journeys, filling in an alternative travel form asking about "bigger towns passed" or "major junctions and important roads" or for public transport journeys, completing a trip diary with an added question about "main points along the route";
- *capturing the mode* – descriptions of modes were to be classified against the mode categories provided in the two versions of the survey form.

During the pre-test of the forms the respondents assessed the following points as very important (see Wofinden and Scott, 1997):

- Consistent layout, making clear whether a number, a written reply or a tick was required;
- Clear and easy guidance through the columns of the travel diary;
- "Not applicable" category for all relevant variables, and the opportunity to give further written descriptions for the "other" category;
- Possibility of multi-response for several questions, e.g. activity coding supported also by the "capturing activities" and "capturing the mode" exercises;
- Larger number of categories to choose from for pre-coded items;
- All pre-coded categories should be obvious and should avoid abbreviations clear only to frequent users of such services, e.g. intercity instead of IC-train or high speed train instead of ICE or TGV.

On the whole, the interviewees did not read the explanation booklet in advance but tended to use it as a reference when they had difficulties in understanding a question.

The "capturing the stage" exercise showed that there were no learning effects, i.e. respondents easily completed the forms for the invented journeys, but had difficulties afterwards in dividing their own journeys into stages.

Repetition had a significant impact, leading to a decrease in the level of detail when a number of stages had to be described. The thinking aloud element also proved that respondents considered short stops en route for any purpose as irrelevant and did not report them. This information about the perception of the importance of information is very useful in assessing the reasons for item non-response.

Public transport users considered the whole question of car availability as irrelevant and tended to skip it. In the UK context it proved to be more effective to ask a question related to the terms of the car insurance, as every driver's name has to be mentioned in the insurance contract.

The exercise about describing one's route proved to be especially successful with car drivers who, almost without exception, had a perfect knowledge of the roads used and had no difficulties in explaining their routes. Whereas for domestic travel, the interviewees remembered the major roads better, in the case of international travel the question about the bigger towns passed was the easier format. The 1989 French border survey, which had asked the foreign respondents to mark their routes on maps, obtained good results even for the routes used.

6.3.2   Second wave

The survey instruments were improved using the results of the cognitive laboratories of the first wave (see Wofinden and Scott, 1997). The results of the first wave of pilots suggested the use of the larger set of questions about the household and so collection of more socio-demographic information about the respondents and their household members. The design of the household questionnaire was improved and some of the questions were re-worded in order to make them clearer.

For the movement instrument, as an alternative to their presentation in columns, a page-based design was developed which gives a better overview of the items and the categories for answer. Readability was improved, especially for the page-based but also the column-based questionnaire. Larger fonts and only two columns per page were used, which also facilitated the guidance through the forms.

The questions about the journeys and the trips/stages were clearly separated to reduce confusion about the different concepts. The journey roster was placed on the front page of the movement form (see Figure 6.1) with space for more journeys on the back page. The question order was changed to be more in line with the way people remembered their journeys in the think-aloud protocols (purpose, origin, destination, accommodation-related questions, size of party, departure and arrival time and finally mode). To increase the involvement of the respondent in the survey and to reduce repetitiveness, the respondents were asked to give each of their journeys a name. This was also done to evaluate how people remembered their journeys and which clues they use to retrieve information about their journeys from memory.

The main issue studied in the second wave of pilots was the quality of the survey instrument. Respondents in general felt more comfortable with the improved design. They still had difficulties dividing their journeys into trips or stages. The main problem was the omission of return trips/stages back to the origin of the journey. Most respondents either simply forgot them or perceived them to be irrelevant, although the instructions on the forms repeatedly asked for the inclusion of return legs of the journey. In these cases and in cases where responses were unclear, wrong or where individual questions had not been answered, the follow up interviews proved to be very helpful, especially as in all four countries, a very high percentage of the respondents who had completed the forms were willing to participate in a telephone interview.

Clearly the page-based layout of the travel diary was preferred by the respondents. The trip design was assessed as being less repetitive and easier to complete. The separation of the items for the journeys from the items for the trips or stages entailed in them was successful. Journeys were omitted only in a minority of cases. Respondents felt that giving a journey a name was a good idea. The analysis of the journey names showed that the vast majority of respondents used either the destination or the purpose as the brief description (name) of their journeys. This result supported the newly implemented question order (Meyburg, 1997), where purpose and destination are the first questions asked instead of the more common order in travel diaries, which starts with origin and departure time, continuing with travel mode and purpose, before a question about the destination is asked.

Overall, item non-response was considerably lower than in the first wave and resulted mainly from the failure to record zero or "not applicable". Missing responses in the household form resulted mainly from questions where the respondents have to indicate the allocation of the costs incurred between different parties (themselves, employer, etc.)

6.3.3   Third wave

Before these surveys were undertaken cognitive laboratory interviews were carried out in Sweden and Portugal. They resulted in some changes in the wording, in the coding categories and in the layout. Comments by participants in the think aloud interviews led to better explanations being developed for the term "trip".

The original landscape design of the household form was changed to a portrait format, allowing enough space to include examples and explanations on the questionnaire itself instead of using an example booklet. Because respondents rarely referred to the example booklet, the examples and explanations for the travel questionnaire were included on the forms as well. This also helped to reduce the amount of material sent. A map with a circle indicating the 100 km distance around the respondent's reference location was included in the survey material, which had been helpful in a series of recent French surveys.

Involvement in the survey topic had proved to be one of the most important reasons for participation in surveys. To raise the respondents' involvement further one additional item was included on the movement form; a question about the personal assessment of the trip (see Figure 6.2, but also Figure 6.1, the journey roster for the named journeys[4]). Additionally, an offer was made to inform the respondents about the results of the survey on request. Following Ampt's recommendations on reducing respondent burden (Ampt, 1997), a more colloquial style of language was implemented, i.e. expressions like "mode", "destination" or

---

[4] The forms used the following throughout: circles for tick mark, boxes for writing numbers and lines for the text for open questions.

"origin" were generally avoided.

The most remarkable result in the third wave was the extremely high response rate of 81% (not including the follow-up interviews with converted non-respondents) in Sweden, where the surveys were carried out by the national statistical office SCB (Statistiska Centralbyran). In other countries, where the surveys were undertaken by market research companies, there were a lower response rates. In the UK and in France, potential respondents used the motivation calls to indicate their refusal to participate in any kind of survey. In Portugal the refusal rate for participation in telephone interviews increased enormously compared to the first wave of pilots, even though both surveys were undertaken by the same company. The most probable reason is the fact that the respondents received the survey material in advance and could more easily judge the likely complexity of the effort involved in cooperating.

The additional tests mentioned above provided additional insights. The test of non-retrospective survey protocol in France revealed in the follow-up telephone interview that most respondents had answered the survey in retrospective fashion, negating any possible benefit from this approach.

Part of the sample in Portugal was successfully interviewed by phone after their written replies had been received about the stages of their reported journeys. This was an attempt to reduce the response burden and still collect information about the stages of the journeys. The advantages of this method were seen in simpler trip based diaries and the opportunity of giving respondents individual explanations and guidance in a personal telephone interview.

The pilot surveys of the first and second wave were based on a mixed household/person approach. The sample was person based and only one person of the household was asked to report their trips, but the socio-demographic characteristics of all household members were requested from the respondent. Difficulties with this approach were concerns about privacy and the respondent's lack of information about the socio-demographic details of all household members. The additional survey undertaken with part of the sample in Sweden was a purely person-based approach, where only information about the chosen member of the sample was collected on a person's form. No significant differences in response behaviour were observable.

For a part of the UK sample, the movement form contained a question about the chosen route for each trip. This design was seen as a possible alternative to a stage base design. Compared to the concept of the stage, which gave respondents severe difficulties, the cognitive laboratory experiments of the first wave had proved that respondents were more comfortable with describing their routes, which in the case of a public transport trip are essentially the stages and in the case of car trips provides valuable detailed information about each route not available elsewhere. Respondents, car drivers and public transport users obviously had no difficulties with the question and even enjoyed describing their trips in this way.

98

Figure 6.1   Second wave movement form: Front page with journey roster

---

This form is about all journeys that took you more than

65 miles away from your present base between

May 9th and June 5th 1997

A **journey** starts and ends at the same place.
We call this place your **present base**. This is normally your home but can
also be anywhere you stayed more than two consecutive days.

If you have any questions about how to fill in these forms,
please check the **Example Booklet** we have enclosed.

TRAVEL FORM

for the selected person   **First name:**

**Please fill in the table below. Give every journey a separate name. That
name will be used again later.**

Started and ended in - the City, town or village, where you started the journey
Destination - the City, town or village and country which was your main destination
for this journey
Date of departure from the origin and **date of return** to the origin of this journey
Size of party - the number of people who travelled with you on this journey.

Journey name	Date of departure	Date of return	Started and ended in	Destination	Size of party
					☐
					☐
					☐
					☐
					☐
					☐
					☐

Source: Axhausen and Youssefzadeh (1999), Appendix K.

Figure 6.2   Third wave movement form: Trip page

Journey name: _____   **Trip No.:** ▢

What was the main purpose of the trip ?

○ Return home
○ Work
○ Education
○ Visiting friends/relatives
○ Leisure/ Holiday

○ Picking up/dropping off someone
○ Picking up/delivering something
○ Shopping
○ Accompanying someone
○ Other _____

Where did you start the trip ?   **Where did you go to?**

How many nights did you stay in this city, town or village before you moved on or returned home?   nights

In what kind of accommodation did you stay overnight ?

○ private *(friends, relatives,...)* ○ commercial *(hotel, hostel, B&B,...)* ○ **Not applicable**

How many people accompanied you on this trip?   people

When did you start the trip?   **When did you arrive at your destination ?**

(date)   (local time)   (date)   (local time)
(Please state if a.m. or p.m.!)   *(Please state if a.m. or p.m.!)*

How did you travel? *(Please tick all that apply!)*

○ Private Car
○ Rental Car
○ Taxi
○ Motorcycle

○ Bus
○ High speed train
○ Other train
○ Plane

○ Underground / Metro
○ Ship
○ Bicycle
○ Other _____

Was there anything which affected your way of travelling?
(Please tick all that apply!)
○ No
○ Yes, more than hand luggage
○ Yes, travelling with young children
○ Yes, physical disabilities
○ Other _____

Was travelling during this trip pleasant?
○ Yes   *(Please tick all that apply!)*
No, because ○ it took too long
○ it was uncomfortable
○ it was too expensive
○ for the following reason:
_____

Who paid for your travel expenses? *(Please tick all that apply!)*
○ Self   ○ Employer
○ Household member   ○ Other _____

Who paid for your overnight stays? *(Please tick all that apply!)*
○ Self   ○ Employer   ○ **Not applicable**
○ Household member   ○ Other _____

Don't forget to complete trip panels for your return home!

Source: Axhausen and Youssefzadeh (1999), Appendix S

6.4   RESPONSE RATES

The response rates to the different surveys vary due to a number of factors, which will be analysed in detail in Chapter 7, jointly with the results of the Eurostat pilots. The raw numbers of Table 6-4 and Table 6-5 have therefore to be considered with care. For a more detailed breakdown by survey type and wave see MEST Consortium (1999). Still, one has to note the importance of the follow-up telephone interview with the non-respondents to the written form. A large share can be converted and are willing to provide the requested information, or at least the core; a description of themselves, their household and a record of their journeys to the standard of the journey roster (see Figure 6.1 above).

6.5   DESCRIPTIVE RESULTS

The socio-demographics of the respondents met the expectations and shall not be reported here, but see MEST Consortium (1999) for the details. The results about the movements of the respondents are of more interest. Given the closer similarity of waves II and III to the final recommendations, only results from those two waves will be presented. Please note the different times of the year, when comparing the results (summer – wave II – versus winter – wave III). The results for wave II are shown separately by duration of the reporting period.

The large variations in the share of persons with zero long-distance journeys due to both the differences in reporting period and time of year are noticeable. Looking at the average number of journeys of the long-distance mobile the differences between the two eight-weeks surveys disappear, while the persons reporting in the four-week survey continue to have higher figures, indicating a need for a proper reweighting due to likely non-ignorable non-response processes for these longer reporting periods. The difference is probably also due to memory effects, which reduce the number of reported journeys over the eight week reporting period. Further breakdowns of these numbers by the socio-demographics of the respondents are available in MEST Consortium (1999), but do not reveal any surprising insights. The average number of trips is consistent with values reported elsewhere (see for example Axhausen, 1999), as is the pattern of concentration of the journeys made on a small share of the travellers (see Figure 6.3).

6.6   RESPONSE BEHAVIOUR

As part of the pilots, the respondents were interviewed about their experiences with the survey instrument. This survey was conducted particularly carefully after the third wave, as the design of this wave was the draft of the recommendations. The results obtained are useful for the further development of the survey design (full results are included in MEST Consortium, 1999).

Table 6-4   Response rates (Percent of sample without quality-neutral losses [%])

Wave	Country			
	France	Portugal	Sweden	UK
Wave I				
CATI only	-	70.5	54.7	-
Postal response	-	27.2	22.3	-
Telephone follow-up	-	55.0	47.2	-
Sum	-	82.2	69.5	-
Wave II				
Postal response	19.8	14.5	21.3	44.8
Telephone follow-up	50.0	62.4	34.6	28.3
Sum	69.8	76.9	56.0	73.1
Wave III				
Postal response	18.1	14.4	59.7	23.6
CATI at respondent's request	3.8	3.3	-	11.0
Telephone follow-up	24.5	27.8	21.0	0.4
Sum	46.4	45.5	80.7	41.9

Table 6-5   Sample size after quality neutral losses

Element	Country			
	France	Portugal	Sweden	UK
Wave I				
CATI only	-	298	179	-
Self-completion	-	298	197	-
Wave II	288	290	300	297
Wave III	758	209	233	236

Most of the respondents across the countries (75%) found the survey interesting, which reflects the general interest people take in travel and mobility. Again, most respondents found the household, person and vehicle form easy or very easy to fill in (91%), but this dropped to 58% for the movement form, which 28% actually found difficult (see Table 6-7). The difficulties were associated with remembering journeys (10%) and specific details (11%) and, most importantly, understanding the concept of the trip (21%).

Table 6-6   Amount of travel by wave

Characteristic	Wave II		Wave III
	4 week reporting period	8 week reporting period	8 week reporting period
Share of persons with no long-distance journey			
France	62	44	53
Portugal	69	21	87
Sweden	73	50	72
UK	38	44	78
Average number of journeys/Person and week			
France	0.17	0.26	0.12
Portugal	0.09	0.14	0.03
Sweden	0.16	0.19	0.07
UK	0.39	0.22	0.19
Average number of journeys/Long-distance mobile person and week			
France	0.29	0.28	0.23
Portugal	0.59	0.30	0.25
Sweden	0.63	0.39	0.37
UK	0.45	0.33	0.26

The easiest part of the questionnaire was the household form. While 83% said that they had no difficulty in replying to the household questions, only 16% had no difficulties with the journey description element of the travel form and only 11% had no difficulties in describing their trips, which is consistent with the overall assessment above. While the majority of respondents found the questionnaires not confusing, a substantial 21% minority were confused by the design of the survey forms. However, there were no clear areas for improvement indicated by the respondents.

For most of the people who responded to the survey, the motivation phone calls were informative (43%) or helpful (37%), whereas 20% felt they were intrusive. Table 6-7 shows that a third of respondents replied after receiving the first motivation phone call. The first phone call can therefore be regarded as very successful. The much lower percentage of replies after the second motivation call and the perception of such calls as intrusive by about a fifth of respondents suggests that only one motivation call could be used and still maintain the goodwill of the respondents.

Figure 6.3   Comparison of the observed against expected share of journeys for long-distance mobile travellers (assuming a uniform distribution)

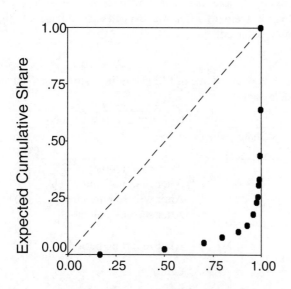

Observed Cumulative Share

The figure is based on the pooled data from Waves II and III

None of the non-retrospective respondents participating in the follow-up interviews had fulfilled the conditions of a non-retrospective survey, which is to complete the forms immediately after the journeys in order to prevent problems arising from the burden of having to recall details of earlier journeys. Also 97 % of the respondents stated that they had not used the memory jogger, intended as an aid to the recall journeys.

Table 6-7   Respondent behaviour: Overall difficulty of forms (Wave III respondents only)

Share [%]	Both questionnaires	Household form	Movement form
Very easy	38.5	20.7	2.3
Easy	44.0	70.7	55.8
Neither easy nor difficult	11.5	6.5	14.0
Difficult	5.6	2.2	27.9
Very difficult	0.4	0.0	0.0

Those 3% who had used the memory jogger, generally did not carry it around as a means to take notes of their travelling activities. As all journeys were reported either after the second motivation phone call, which was close to the end of the survey period, or even after the end of the survey period, data collected in the prospective survey seems very like that from a retrospective survey. Non-retrospective surveys do not seem to offer the expected advantage of higher reliability in the information obtained.

Table 6-8   Respondent behaviour: Time of filling out the instruments (Wave III respondents only)

Retrospective protocol		Non-retrospective protocol	
Time	Share [%]	Time	Share [%]
		After each journey	0.0
		After first motivation call	0.0
		After written reminder	0.0
		After second motivation call	10.5
After reporting period	58.4	After reporting period	89.5
After first motivation call	33.3		
After written reminder	2.7		
After second motivation call	5.5		

Given the complexity of the survey the response burden was relatively low, with a self-assessed average total response time of 25 minutes. Even so, a reported maximum of 4 hours is a concern, which relates also to the main reason given for not responding: lack of time (36%). About a third just did not want to participate; another 8% had no interest and another 7% reported a lost questionnaire. About 7% gave no long-distance travel as a reason for non-response, but less than 1% gave too many long-distance journeys. Various other reasons (18%) made up the rest.

6.7   CONCLUSIONS

The survey work undertaken by the MEST Consortium allowed it to establish an approach to conducting a common survey of long-distance travel which should be feasible across the member states of the European Union. The approach is not optimal in any one country, but this is a necessity for a common benchmark survey. The mixed method protocol involving postal and oral elements is flexible enough to be adjusted to the different preferences of the respondents in the various member states, as the load can be shifted between the written and oral elements while maintaining the uniformity of the survey instruments, definitions and respondent stimuli.

The development of the journey roster and of the route-question within the trip level are substantial advances for travel survey research, as their success indicates that sterile discussions about the proper base unit of response are unproductive in the long-distance context. It is clear from the experiences in MEST that most respondents think about the journey as a whole when they think about longer-distance travel, which for most people is still a rare event (see Table 6-8 above). This is consistent with the observation that many respondents start to use the names of regions or even countries instead of cities when describing the destinations of their long-distance journeys. Still, when guided correctly people are able to provide more detailed break-downs of their travel in a trip-based survey instrument. The "Describe your route" question can provide the necessary detail about the interchanges in the public transport case or the routes in automobile case in this overall context. Telephone follow-up interviews always allow the retrieval of further detail, if required, as these are rarely refused by earlier respondents. These three elements allow the survey designer to distribute the response burden and does allow him/her to limit the burden, if desired, through combinations of the journey roster and a request to describe only a limited subset of those journeys.

The various experiments with non-retrospective protocols could not establish its superiority in spite of the *a priori* expectations based on the experiences with surveys of daily mobility and some long-distance ones (Austrian Eurostat pilots and the US 1995 American Travel Survey). The results of the follow-up interviews made it clear that the respondents treat it the same way as retrospective surveys. Those participating in the end might be a bit more attentive to their travel during the reporting period, but this is balanced by the larger opportunity to drop out during the long duration of a typical long-distance travel survey.

The respondent surveys also made it clear that the form design was good but not yet perfect. Clearly more work needs to be done to improve this, if one wants to maintain a mixed-mode approach (see also next chapter).

6.8   REFERENCES

Ampt, E. (1997) - Respondent burden: Understanding the people we survey. *Paper presented at the International Conference on Transport Survey Quality and Innovation*, Grainau, May 1997.

Axhausen, K.W. (1998) - The Eurostat pilots of long-distance travel diaries: Summary of final reports. *Report to the Österreichische Statistische Zentralamt*, Wien and Eurostat, Luxembourg, Innsbruck.

Axhausen, K.W. (1999) - Surveying long-distance travel: Effects of survey contexts and protocols. In Statistics Sweden (ed.), Official Statistics in a Changing World, Proceedings of the 3rd International Conference on Methodological Issues in Official Statistics, 141-149, Statistics Sweden, Stockholm.

Axhausen, K.W., H. Köll, M. Bader and M. Herry (1997) - Workload, data yield and data quality: experiments with long-distance travel diaries. *Transportation Research Record*, **1593,** 29-40.

Axhausen, K.W. and M. Youssefzadeh (1999) - Towards an European Survey of Long Distance Travel (a new European long distance diary: Second draft of content and structure and a new European long distance diary: Final draft of content and structure. *Report to the CEC, DG VII - Transport, MEST Deliverables*, **D3 and D4**, Fakultät für Bauingenieurwesen und Architektur, Leopold-Franzens-Universität, Innsbruck.

Box, G.E.P., W.G. Hunter and J.S. Hunter (1978) - Statistics for Experimenters. John Wiley and Sons Inc., New York.

Dillman, D.A. (1978) - Mail and Telephone Surveys: The Total Design Method. John Wiley and Sons, New York.

Eurostat (1995a) - Proposal for definitions and variables of a household survey for mobility. *Document T7/95-2/5/EN, Informal Working Group "Passenger Transport Statistics and Mobility"*, Eurostat, Luxembourg.

Fabre, F., A. Klose and G. Somer (Eds.) (1988) - Data system for the study of demand for interregional passenger transport, final report. *COST*, **305**, Commission of the European Communities, Brussels.

Madre, J.L. and J. Maffre (1997) - La mobilite des residants francais: Panorama general et evolution. *Revue Transport and Securite,* **56**.

MEST Consortium (1995) - Methods for European Surveys of Travel Behaviour: Technical Annex, contract with the CEC, DG VII – Transport. *4th Framework Programme*, Brussels.

MEST Consortium (1999) - Methods for European Surveys of Travel Behaviour. final report to the CEC, DG 7 - Transport, *MEST Consortium*, Innsbruck.

Meyburg, A.H.and H.M.A. Metcalf (1997) - Question formulation and instrument design. *Transportation Research Circular*, **E-C008**, II-H/1, TRB, Washington D.C.

OECD and Statistics Canada (1995) - Literacy, Economy and Society: Results of the First International Adult Literacy Survey. *OECD*, Paris.

Richardson, A.J., E.S. Ampt and A.H. Meyburg (1995) - Survey Methods for Transport Planning. Eucalyptus Press, Melbourne.

Sudman, S. and N.M. Bradburn (1983) - Asking Questions. Jossey-Bass, San Francisco.

Sudman, S., N.M Bradburn and N. Schwarz (1996) - Thinking about Answers. Jossey-Bass, San Francisco.

Tanur, J.M. and S.E. Fienberg (1992) - Cognitive aspects in surveys: Yesterday, today and tomorrow. *Journal of Official Statistics,* **8** (1) 5-17.

Wofinden, D. and M. Scott (1997) - Report on the cognitive-laboratory pre-test surveys for the MEST-project. *STRS*, Twickenham.

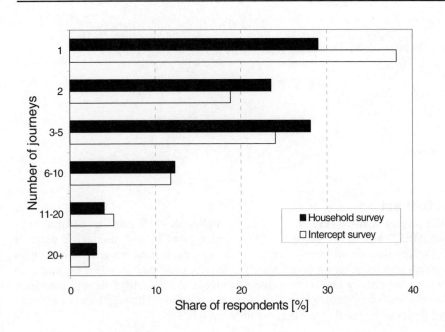

Chapter 7
How reliable are household surveys for the description of air travel?

J.-I. Lian and J.-M. Denstadli

7. How reliable are household surveys for the description of air travel?[1]

J.-I. Lian and J.-M. Denstadli

TOI
N – 0602 Oslo

Abstract

The project reported here was part of the additional work that was undertaken in the MEST and TEST projects. The objective was to test alternative ways of collecting data on air travel. Comparisons were made between general household surveys and intercept air travel surveys. Results show that air travel estimates do not depend heavily on survey method. Intercept and household surveys produce a more or less comparable picture of the air travel market, although some differences are found with regard to trip purpose distributions.

Keywords

Intercept air travel surveys, household surveys, mobility estimates.

---

[1] Preferred citation: J.-I. Lian and J.-M. Denstadli (2003) How reliable are household surveys for the description of air travel? in K. W. Axhausen, J.-L. Madre, J. W. Polak and Ph. L. Toint (eds.) *Capturing Long-Distance Travel*, 109-120, Research Studies Press, Baldock.

7.1 INTRODUCTION

The study reported here was part of the additional work undertaken in the MEST and TEST projects. The objective was to examine to what degree household travel surveys and specially designed intercept air travel surveys yield similar results with regard to air travel patterns. Traditionally, air travel surveys have been conducted as intercept surveys at airports, as is the case for the Norwegian Air Travel Survey. Attempts to identify airline passengers by means of general household surveys have been regarded as almost impossible, because they have represented such a small percentage of the total population. During recent years, however, there has been a substantial growth in air traffic, more people taking the opportunity to fly both for business and private purposes. In the Scandinavian countries, the airlines are referred to as the "winners" in the long haul transportation market, gaining market share at the expense of car traffic. This trend may support alternative ways of collecting data on air travel. For instance, airline passengers should be more easily reached via general household surveys nowadays. Household surveys may represent an effective way of collecting air travel data at the aggregate level, and they offer several advantages to the travel researcher. Generally, they are more easily administered than are intercept surveys; they make possible the collection of information on non-respondents, and, in most cases, the researcher is able to collect more information in household surveys.

A fundamental question that remains is, however, whether these surveys give a valid picture of the airline passengers and the type of trips they make. The effect of survey method on air travel estimates is not well documented in the literature, and we wanted to shed more light on this problem. Therefore, the following questions were raised:

RQ1:   Do household surveys and specially-designed intercept air travel surveys produce diverging estimates of mobility?

RQ2:   Do results derived from household surveys and specially-designed intercept air travel surveys differ with regard to trip and respondent characteristics?

Thus, while the work in the MEST surveys was devoted to the comparison of different survey formats *within* one type of data collection technique (household surveys), this part of the work compared results *between* different data collection techniques.

7.2 DATA

7.2.1 The household survey

The household data were collected in October and November 1997 as part of the Norwegian National Travel Survey (NNTS). This is a nation-wide telephone-based survey conducted every fifth year. A random sample was drawn from the official telephone register produced by Norwegian Telecom. This register is revised every month, and is the most updated register containing personal information available to the public. More than 98% of all Norwegian households have telephone service, making the potential of sampling bias often emphasised in telephone surveys a minor problem.

Twenty-eight people were interviewed each day over a period of one month. The respondents were asked to describe any long-distance trip (over 100 km) undertaken during the month preceding the interview (including any trip made by air). Characteristics of trips and related activities were collected, as well as the number of round-trip flights made within Norway during the previous 12 months, background information on the individual and his/her household, and access to car and public transport. Although the sampling unit is the household, the unit for analysis is the individual. Only one person in each household was interviewed, and only about his/her own travel activities. To obtain a random sample within the households, the interviewer asked to speak to the person in the household who was the last to celebrate his/her birthday. If the prospective respondent was not available at that time, agreement to call back was made with other members of the household whenever possible. If no one answered the phone, up to eight callbacks were made in the following week. Eight hundred and thirty six people completed the interview, which gave a response rate of 58%. 37% (n=308) of the respondents had made at least one round-trip flight within Norway during the previous 12 months. This group is used in the comparison of mobility between the intercept and household survey (RQ1). 12% (n=101) reported one or more flights within Norway during the month prior to the interview. These account for a total of 271 trips, which form the basis for analysing trip purpose and socio-demographic status of airline passengers (RQ2).

7.2.2 The intercept survey

Since 1972 the Institute of Transport Economics (TOI) has conducted nationwide travel surveys among airline passengers. The purpose of these surveys has been to analyse the role and function of air transport and to furnish data for traffic forecasts, airport planning and route planning. Three years ago, TOI initiated the 1997/98 Norwegian Air Travel Survey (NATS). Data were collected at three different points of time; the second week in October 1997, the third week in March 1998 and the first week in August 1998. These dates were chosen based on previous experience, and were intended to represent the three major seasons: autumn, winter/spring and summer respectively. Routes and flights to be surveyed were selected using a system of stratification. The data were weighted by traffic counts within the three periods and the expanded data provided an estimate of all domestic air traffic in Norway in the one-year period from September 1997 through August 1998. To test the research questions raised above, however, only data from October are used. These data are intended to represent the last four months in 1997.

Data were collected using the so-called on-board distribution/on-board collection method (see Richardson, Ampt and Meyburg, 1995). Passengers were handed a four-page questionnaire when boarding the plane, and requested to take a few minutes to answer the questions during the flight. The cabin crew collected the forms upon arrival, and also gave a reminder over the loud speaker during the flight.

	Intercept survey	Household survey
Person	Gender	Gender
	Year of birth	Year of birth
	Occupation	Occupation
	Industry of work	Driver's licence
	Primary area of work	Education
	Position at work	Any disabilities that makes it difficult to travel
	Number of round trip flights within Norway during the last 12 months	Number of round trip flights within Norway during the last 12 months
	Place of residence	Place of residence
	Frequent flyer program membership	Income
Household		Size
		Vehicle ownership
Journey	Departure date and airport	Departure date and place
	Mode of transport to the airport	Mode of transport
	Place of destination	Place of destination
	Time of arrival at the airport	Type of overnight accommodation
	Duration of journey	Duration of journey
	Place of visit	Number of accompanying persons
	Type of ticket and who was paying	Type of ticket and who was paying
	Main purpose	Main purpose
	Whether or not the trip is associated with oil operations	

The questionnaire included information on start/end points of the journey, trip purpose, duration of the journey, the number of round-trip flights made within Norway the previous 12 months, and background variables such as age, gender, occupation and so on. The NATS conducted in October 1997 provided almost 30,000 questionnaires usable for data processing (overall response rate of 45%). Clearly, the two surveys are very unbalanced when it comes to the number of observations. With 101 respondents and 271 trips in the database, the household survey will not produce a complete picture of the air travel market. It will, however, give some valuable indications of whether these surveys are suitable for collecting data on air travel.

7.3   RESULTS

7.3.1   Convergence of mobility between intercept and household surveys (RQ1)

In both surveys, respondents were asked how many round trip flights they had made within Norway during the last 12 months (respondents in the intercept survey were instructed to include the trip they were about to make). *A priori* one would expect household surveys to produce travel estimates that are biased downwards. The most mobile people can be difficult to reach in these surveys simply because they are less often at home (see e.g. Brög and Meyburg, 1982). With intercept surveys, on the other hand, interviewers are bound to meet all kinds of travellers, in both high and low mobility groups, which is likely to help to produce a more valid picture of the market.

Figure 7.1 compares mobility patterns among the household and intercept respondents. Contrary to expectations, the average mobility is slightly higher in the household survey than in the intercept survey. Averages are 4.5 and 4.1 trips per year respectively. The distributions diverge among the low frequency travellers (fewer than six trips) and in particular the single trip makers. 38% of the respondents in the intercept survey are classified as single trip makers, i.e. they report the present trip to be the only one made within the last 12 months, while the corresponding number for respondents in the household survey is 29%. Less divergent distributions are revealed among the high mobility groups (six or more trips). Thus, a first conclusion is that the most mobile air passengers are surveyed as easily at home as at the airports.

7.3.2   Convergence of trip and respondent characteristics between intercept and household surveys (RQ2)

Table 7-1 compares the distribution of trip purpose in the household and intercept survey. In both surveys, business trips dominate, while private trips and combined trips are in a minority. This corresponds to previous air travel surveys conducted in Norway, which have shown a great dominance of business purposes. Hence, both surveys seem to capture this distinctive characteristic of the market. The distributions are, however, diverging, with the proportion of business trips markedly higher in the household survey. The statistical significance of these differences was tested using a chi-square test. The results indicated highly significant differences, with p=0.000 (Pearsons χ^2=16.5, df=2). Hence, to a certain degree the two surveys give a contradictory picture of the air travel market.

Figure 7.1: Trip frequencies

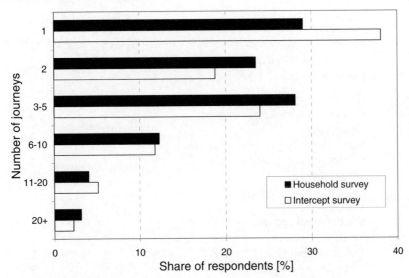

Average trip rate intercept survey: 4.1 trips   (n=29,496)
Average trip rate household survey: 4.5 trips   (n=308)

If we look at the more disaggregate level, differences become even greater (p=0.000, Pearsons χ^2=173.1, df=10). The most striking difference is found within the category "Commute to/from place of work", which is three times higher in the household survey. This may explain the high mobility reported by household respondents. People commuting to/from place of work are generally very mobile. Often these kinds of trips are undertaken on a regular basis, making the overall mobility within the group high. Both in the intercept and the household survey, the commuters report almost twice as high mobility as do respondents travelling for other purposes. Thus, it is obvious that the high share of commuters found in the household survey makes a significant contribution to the results in Table 7-1.

Differences also are revealed among other groups of business travellers. In general, the household survey indicates less traditional business traffic. For instance, 9% of the intercept respondents travel for the purpose of sales/purchasing, while the corresponding number in the household survey is only 3%. A greater proportion of the business trips reported in the household survey are unspecified ("other purposes"). This may indicate that interviewers have done a poor job when classifying trips described by the respondents, which in turn may have affected response patterns in the other categories. Yet, poor classification cannot explain all differences, and the overall impression is that the two surveys produce a divergent picture of the business passengers.

Table 7-1: Trip characteristics (%)

		Intercept survey	Household survey
Purpose[a]	Business	59	71
	Private	35	27
	Combination of business and private purposes	6	2
Purpose specified[b]	Business purposes specified:		
	Commute to/from place of work	11	34
	Conference	19	12
	Sales, purchasing, negotiations, trade fair	9	3
	Service job/consulting work	7	3
	Other purposes	13	19
	Private purposes specified:		
	Visit relatives/friends	21	16
	Holiday/weekend trip	5	2
	Medical treatment	2	1
	Travel to/from place of study	2	1
	Other private purposes	5	7
	Combination of business/private purposes	6	2
Who paid for the ticket[c]	Employer/client	62	68
	Him-herself/another person in the family	29	26
	Sports-/cultural organisation	3	2
	Social Security office	2	2
	Other	4	2
Type of ticket[d]	Full fare	62	53
	Discount	33	42
	Free ticket/bonus	5	5
Sample size		29,496	271

[a]Pearson chi-square: 16.5, p=0.00, df=2   [c]Pearson chi-square: 8.2, p=0.08, df=4
[b]Pearson chi-square: 173.1, p=0.00, df=10   [d]Pearson chi-square: 8.4, p=0.02, df=2

Differences also are found between trips for private purposes, but these trips seem to be less discrepant. Trips to friends and relatives constitute a major part of the total number of trips in both surveys, and both surveys suggest that private trips such as holidays, medical treatment and so on, are rarely undertaken by plane.

The last rows in Table 7-1 compare the distribution of ticket type and who paid for the ticket. With regard to the latter, the employer/client more often seems to pay for the ticket in the household survey. Most likely, this is due to the greater number of business trips found in the household survey. However, differences are only marginally significant (p=0.08, Pearsons χ^2=8.2, df=4), and no clear conclusions can be drawn. Due to the greater number of business trips, we would expect that household respondents more often use full fare tickets (Norwegian domestic flights do not offer business class). This seems not to be the case. 53% of the household respondents report to have travelled on a full fare ticket, while the corresponding number in the intercept survey is 62%. As Table7-2 illustrates, both business and private travellers report more frequent utilisation of discount tickets in the household survey. Table 7-3 compares the distribution of gender, working status and age within the two surveys. The figures are very similar. In fact, no significant differences are found. The table draws a picture of the airline passengers consistent with previous air travel surveys. Men are in the great majority and so are middle-aged people and people in regular work. The results suggest that previous differences are not due to sampling or non-response bias, and, therefore, it is hard to give a reasonable explanation for the contradictory figures in Table 7-3. This question is discussed further in the concluding section.

Table7-2: Trip purpose by ticket type

Survey	Trip purpose	Ticket type			Sample size
		Full fare	Discount	Total	
Household survey	Business	70 %	30 %	100 %	178
	Private	12 %	88 %	100 %	65
Intercept survey	Business	82 %	18 %	100 %	15875
	Private	27 %	73 %	100 %	9595

7.4 DISCUSSION

Results show that air travel estimates depend less on survey method than anticipated. No support was found for the hypothesis concerning survey method and mobility. In fact, the average mobility was higher in the household survey, suggesting that the most mobile airline passengers are surveyed as easily at home as at the airports. Also, the distribution of age, gender and working status within the two samples was remarkably similar, indicating that the results are not a product of sampling or non-response bias. Considering this, it is hard to give a reasonable explanation of the different trip purpose distributions in the intercept and household survey. In particular, the high number of commuting trips found in the household survey, and, consequently, the low number of more traditional business purposes (e.g. sales, marketing and conferences), are remarkable. Although population data are not available, there are reasons to believe that the household survey gives a distorted picture of the business traffic.

Table7-3: Respondent characteristics (%)

		Intercept survey	Household survey
Gender[a]	Male	65	65
	Female	35	35
Working status[b]	Working	84	86
	Not working	16	14
Age[c]	13-29 years	22	20
	30-44 years	38	43
	45-59 years	33	31
	60 +	7	6
Sample size		29,496	271

[a]Pearsons chi-square: 0.00, p=0.98, df=1
[b]Pearsons chi-square: 1.02, p=0.31, df=1
[c]Pearsons chi-square: 2.96, p=0.40, df=3

The dominating number of trips to/from work is not consistent with previous air travel surveys, and, quite certainly, these trips are over-represented in the household survey. Memory effects may have had an impact on the results. In the intercept survey respondents were only asked to report on the trip they were about to make, while household respondents were requested to describe all trips made within the previous month. The retrospective approach makes memory effects a potential problem, and several studies have shown that omission of trips due to memory effects can lead to considerable bias in data (e.g. Denstadli and Lian, 1997; Armoogum and Madre, 1996). Commuting trips may be more easily remembered due to their regularity, while sporadic trips are more often forgotten. This is supported by Wermuth (1985), who found that regular trips were better reported than irregular ones.When interpreting these results we must have in mind the low number of observations in the household survey. As mentioned previously, the survey was conducted as part of the Norwegian National Travel Survey. Among the respondents only 12% reported that they had made one or more trips by air within the reporting period, indicating that airline passengers are not reached as easily at home as expected. The relatively low number of observations makes results susceptible to "outliers", i.e. respondents with extremely high mobility. A closer investigation of the results reveals that a few people dominate the commuting trips – three respondents count for one-third of the total number of trips to/from work in the household survey. If these respondents are excluded from the analysis, the share of commuting trips drops to 25%. However, they did not have an unreasonably high mobility, and, therefore, they were included in the sample. Nevertheless, it illustrates the potential impact of small sample size. Most likely, the distributions of trip purpose would have been less divergent if the number of observations in the household survey had been greater.

The overall impression is that household and intercept surveys produce a more or less comparable picture of the air travel market. The correspondence between the surveys does, however, assume that each type is conducted according to recognised sampling and surveying principles. It is also important to bear in mind that the area of application is different. If one aims to establish OD-matrices, intercept surveys are the only true alternative. At the route level, household surveys are still insufficient, due to the small number of observations. Household surveys do, however, represent an alternative way of collecting air travel data at the aggregate level if one ensures a sufficient sample size.

7.5   REFERENCES

Armoogum, J. & J.L. Madre (1996) - Accuracy of Data and Memory Effects in Home Based Surveys on Travel Behaviour. *MEST working paper.*

Brög, W. and A.H. Meyburg (1982) - Consideration of Nonresponse Effects in Large-Scale Mobility Surveys. *Transportation Research Record 807*, 39-46.

Denstadli, J.M. and J.I. Lian (1997) - Memory Effects in Long Distance Travel Surveys. *TEST Working paper.*TOI, Oslo.

Richardson, A.J., E.S. Ampt and A.H. Meyburg (1995) - Survey Methods for Transport Planning. Eucalyptus Press, Melbourne.

Wermuth, M. (1985) - Errors arising from incorrect and incomplete information in surveys of non-home activity patterns. *In E.S. Ampt, A.J. Richardson and W. Brög (Eds.), New Survey Methods in Transport,* VNU Science Press. Utrecht, Holland, 333-347.

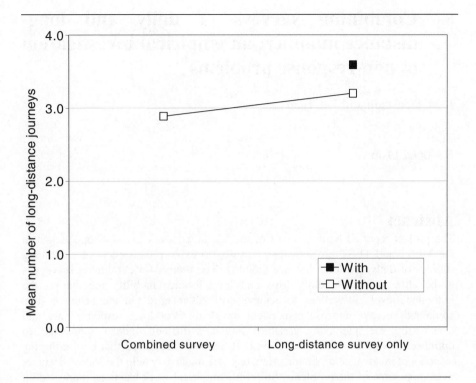

Chapter 8
Combining surveys of daily and long-distance mobility: an empirical investigation of non-response problems

J.-M. Denstadli and J.-I. Lian

8. Combining surveys of daily and long-distance mobility: an empirical investigation of non-response problems[1]

J.-M. Denstadli and J.-I. Lian

TOI
N – 0602 Oslo

Abstract

The project reported here was part of the additional work that was undertaken in the MEST and TEST projects. The aim was to explore the effects of combining surveys of daily and long-distance mobility. The motive for combining surveys is to be able to analyse daily trips and long-distance mobility together at the individual level, as well as to achieve cost advantages. On the negative side, combined surveys increase respondent workload. Workload, response rates and data quality are interacting variables, and it is difficult, indeed impossible, to optimise all variables at the same time. It has been suggested that contacting the respondent in advance of the interview (e.g. via mail) may help the survey designer overcome some of the problems. Still, little empirical work has been published on the effects of combining surveys versus conducting separate surveys of daily and long-distance mobility, and the potential impact of pre-contact. In this paper, results are reported from an experiment designed to test effects of respondent workload (i.e. combined surveys versus separate surveys of long-distance mobility) and pre-contact. Results indicate that unit non-response and item non-response (i.e. the number of trips reported) change systematically with changes in the experimental variables: Separate surveys and advance-notice letters generate increased response rates and increased number of trips reported.

Keywords

Advance notice, combined travel surveys, non-response, long-distance travel survey, daily mobility.

---

[1] Preferred citation: Denstadli, J.-M. and J.-I. Lian (2003) Combining surveys of daily and long-distance mobility: An empirical investigation of non-response problems, in K. W. Axhausen, J.-L. Madre, J. W. Polak and Ph. L. Toint (eds.) *Capturing Long-Distance Travel*, 121 - 132, Research Studies Press, Baldock.

8.1 INTRODUCTION

The study reported here was part of the additional work undertaken in the MEST and TEST projects. The purpose was to explore possible reasons for variations in unit non-response and item non-response (i.e. under-reporting of mobility) other than those examined within the MEST surveys. These were impacts of (i) *workload,* in the sense of combining surveys of daily and long-distance mobility versus running separate long-distance travel surveys, as was the case for the MEST surveys, and (ii) *pre-contact,* i.e. sending respondents a letter/warning prior to the interview.

Combining surveys of daily and long-distance mobility is a common practice when conducting analysis of travel behaviour. There are strong arguments for doing this. For instance, it enables the researcher to analyse daily and long-distance mobility together at the individual level, and it reduces total survey costs. But the combined survey has disadvantages. Travel surveys form the basis for transport planning and estimation of origin-destination matrices. To estimate these matrices, each journey reported by the respondent must be described by a minimum number of items, including origin/destination, length of journey, mode of transport, purpose, departure time and date and so on. Hence the questionnaire must cover a certain set of items on both daily trips and long-distance journeys. Consequently, the combined interview will be time-consuming and demanding on the respondent, and will increase respondent burden. In turn, high workload increases the probability of respondent fatigue and diminished motivation, and can be expected to influence both the willingness to participate and the quality of reporting.

Some of these problems may, however, be overcome by contacting the respondent in advance of the interview (e.g. via mail). Still, little empirical work has been published on the response effects of combining surveys of daily and long-distance mobility versus conducting separate surveys and the potential impact of pre-contact. Therefore, the following questions were raised in the study:

RQ1: How does respondent workload, in the sense of combining surveys versus running a separate long-distance survey, affect unit and item non-response in household travel surveys?

RQ2: How do prior letters affect unit and item non-response in household travel surveys?

8.2 METHODOLOGY

8.2.1 Sampling

Three samples were drawn from the official telephone register produced by Norwegian Telecom. This register is revised every month and is the most frequently updated register containing personal information available to the public. More than 98 percent of all Norwegian households have telephone service, making the potential of sampling bias often emphasised in telephone surveys a minor problem.

Although the sampling unit is the household, the unit for analysis is the individual. Only one person in each household was interviewed, and only about his/her own travel activities. To obtain a random sample within the households, the interviewer asked to speak to the person in the household who was the last to celebrate his/her birthday, a common practice. If the prospective respondent was not available at the moment, an agreement to call back was made with other members of the household, whenever possible. If no one answered the phone, up to eight call backs were made in the following week.

8.2.2 Experimental design

In order to test the questions raised above, three different designs were outlined. Each design had a questionnaire containing questions on travel details such as origin location, destination location, mode, purpose and so on. For long-distance travel, the common definition using a 100 km minimum was employed for a reporting period of one month. In addition, information was collected on household characteristics (size, location, income and demographics of all members of the household), personal characteristics (e.g. age, gender, income, and education) and the number and type of available vehicles. The experimental variables which were varied between the designs were respondent workload and pre-contact.

Workload is considered a product of survey type, i.e. whether or not the respondent was asked to report both daily and long-distance mobility, or long-distance trips only. In the introduction, the respondents were informed that it would take approximately 20 and 10 minutes respectively to complete the interview.

Pre-contact describes whether or not the respondent received a letter prior to the interview. The letter was sent about a week before he/she was contacted and provided a general background of the survey, a request to interview the person in the household who was the last to celebrate his/her birthday and the type of questions that would be asked. In addition, the letter included a memory jogger.

The questionnaires were randomly assigned to the three samples. The data were collected in October and November 1997 as part of the Norwegian National Travel Survey, with an equal number of interviews made each day of the surveying period. In order to minimise possible interviewer bias, questionnaires for the experimental groups were systematically assigned to interviewers so that each person conducted an approximately equal number of calls within each sample. Table 8-1 gives a description of the samples.

Apart from the experimental variables, the designs are identical. Thus, comparing non-response rates in sample 1 and 2 reveals the effects of respondent workload, and comparing sample group 2 and 3 indicates effects of contacting the respondent prior to the interview. Consequently, sample 2 can be used as the reference group when testing for effects of both workload and pre-contact. An examination of socio-demographic characteristics showed small differences between the samples. Neither of them was found to be statistically significant.

Table 8-1   Description of samples

	Sample 1	Sample 2	Sample 3
Workload	High Combined survey	Low Long-distance trips only	Low Long-distance trips only
Introduction	Respondents were informed about the topic of the study, the purpose, and that it would take app. *20 minutes* to complete the interview.	Same as in sample 1, but interviewing time was estimated to be *10 minutes.*	Same as in sample 2.
Pre-contact	No	No	Yes
Number of respondents	424	410	426

8.3   RESULTS

8.3.1   Impacts of workload and pre-contact on unit non-response

Table 8-2 gives a description of the response behaviour in the three experimental groups. The first row describes the number of households in the sampling frame. "Non-contact" is the number and percentage of households that could not be reached within eight attempts. "Refusal" refers to those who were reached but who refused to participate. The refusal percentage is calculated by dividing this number by the total number of people reached (row C). "Terminated" is the number and percentage of respondents who first agreed to participate, but later terminated the interview. Finally, "response" refers to the number and percentage of respondents who completed the interview, divided by the number of persons we actually accessed ("refusal"+"terminated"+ "response").

All groups achieved a response rate well above 50 percent. This is in the upper range compared to commercial telephone surveys conducted in Norway. Hence, making an overall comparison, unit non-response is relatively low within all groups, which indicates that travel surveys are perceived as legitimate surveys. However, differences between groups do exist. The effect of workload is found by comparing sample 1 and 2. As can be seen from the table, the response rate is increased by 9 percentage points when the perceived workload is halved (row F). Thus, there is no doubt that the 10 minutes extra interviewing time in the combined survey has a negative effect on respondents' willingness to participate. Also, when comparing sample 2 and 3 to explore the effects of pre-contact, differences are revealed. The response rate increases by another 9 percentage points when respondents are contacted prior to the interview.

Table 8-2   Response behaviour

Step		Sample 1 Combined survey without warning		Sample 2 Long-distance survey without warning		Sample 3 Long-distance survey with warning	
		[%]	Sample	[%]	Sample	[%]	Sample
A	Sampling frame	100	910	100	759	100	696
B	Non-contact	B/A	15	140	16	119	16	110
C	Total number reached	C/A	85	770	84	640	84	586
D	Refusal	D/C	44	337	35	226	27	158
E	Terminated	E/C	1	9	1	4	0	2
F	Response	F/C	55	424	64	410	73	426

Running a logistic regression to test the significance of these differences, both effects are found to be significant at the 5 percent level (Wald statistics 10.99 and 10.10; p=0.002 and 0.001 respectively). The results lead to the conclusion that both reducing the perceived workload and contacting the respondent prior to the interview seem to pay off when it comes to unit non-response.

As can be seen from Table 8-2, few respondents terminated the interview (row E). By their nature, telephone interviews can be terminated quite easily: respondents may hang up without any notice. This, however, was not a problem in these experiments. This suggests that once people have agreed to participate, the length of the interview does not appear to be a problem. Finally, the proportion of unreachable households (non-contact) is independent of experimental group, as would be expected (row B).

Looking at reasons non-respondents gave for refusing, there are indications that pre-contact makes people more interested in the subject under investigation. Table 8-3 summarises reasons given for not participating. In sample 2 (no pre-contact), 25 percent of non-respondents explain the refusal as due to lack of interest in the subject. The corresponding percentage in sample 3 (prior letter) is 14 percent, indicating that a prior letter increases personal interest and motivation. In sample 3, non-respondents are dominated by the hard-core refusers, i.e. those who never participate in telephone surveys, no matter what the subject is. This also seems to interact with survey length, suggesting that some respondents rationalise their refusal with this reason rather than the true reason of "too long". What can also be seen from Table 8-3 is that the proportion of proxy refusals, i.e. refusals given on behalf of the selected respondent by the person who answered the telephone, is smaller in sample 3. Although differences are not statistically significant, it indicates that households receiving a prior letter may feel more obliged to participate.

8.3.2 Impacts of workload and pre-contact on item non-response

The second part of the non-response problem deals with the completeness of information, and in particular how to reduce the problem of under-reporting of mobility. Two aspects of under-reporting are identified and analysed: (i) the proportion of respondents reporting to have made at least one long-distance trip within the last month; and (ii) average trip rate among the travellers.

Table 8-3   Reasons for refusing

	Sample 1 Combined survey without warning		Sample 2 Long-distance survey without warning		Sample 3 Long-distance survey with warning	
	[%]	Sample	[%]	Sample	[%]	Sample
Proxy refusals	36	11	16	7	6	4
Respondent is ill	12	4	3	1	7	4
No time	30	9	23	10	14	9
Don't participate in telephone interviews	96	28	46	21	54	34
Interview too long	10	3	-	-	-	-
No interest in the subject	69	21	56	25	22	14
Do not feel competent	8	2	14	6	9	6
Other reasons	30	9	27	12	13	8
No reason given	46	13	41	18	33	21
Total	337	100	226	100	158	100

Proportion of respondents reporting to have made long-distance trips

Table 8-4 summarises the proportion of respondents who reported having made long-distance trips (over 100 km) within the previous month. As can be seen from the table, no real differences are found. In all groups, approximately 50 percent of the respondents report having made at least one trip. The chi-square test shows no significant differences. Thus, neither reduced workload nor a prior warning appear to affect the number of people reporting long-distance travel.

In order to reduce under-reporting, aided recall questions were built in to follow up zero trip respondents. The probing was done by listing common trip purposes, and then asking respondents if they had made one or more of the trips mentioned. In addition, respondents were asked how many air trips they had made during the previous year, and, if one or more, how many of these were made within the previous month. Table 8-5 shows the results of these attempts to stimulate recall[2].

---

2 Probing questions were included only in the long-distance surveys.

Table 8-4   Proportion of respondents reporting to have made long-distance trips ("pre-probe")

Experiment	Sample size	Share [%]
Sample 1 Combined survey without warning	201	50
Sample 2 Long-distance survey without warning	204	50
Sample 3 Long-distance survey with warning	198	48

Pearsons chi-square: 0.197, p=.906, df=2

Table 8-5   Effects of aided recall questions

Number of respondents reporting to have made long-distance trips	Sample size	Share [%]
Initial numbers	402	49
After probing	424	52

Twenty-two people (five percent of the initial non-travellers) responded positively to the probing questions, increasing the number of respondents who reported having made long-distance trips from 49 to 52 percent. Hence, probing questions can be an effective way to stimulate respondents' minds, and, to a certain degree, reduce the problem of memory lapses.

Trip rate
The second aspect of under-reporting deals with the reported mobility. Table 8-6 summarises the average reported trip rate within the three experimental groups. As can be seen from the table, the smallest number of trips occurred in the combined survey. Compared to sample 2, the reference group, the trip rate is approximately 11 percent lower among respondents receiving the combined survey, suggesting that high workload increases the probability of under-reporting. On the other hand, the prior letter sent to respondents in sample 3 seems to reduce under-reporting. Compared to the reference group, the average trip rate is increased by approximately 12 percent.

Using the negative binomial regression model for count data, an extension of the Poisson model, the "true" effects of the experimental variables can be analysed. In Table 8-7 we have modelled trip rate as a function of the two experimental variables (combined survey and prior letter) and respondent characteristics (working status, education, gender and driving licence).

Table 8-6   Average trip rate (trips over 100km) within experimental groups (non-travellers excluded from analysis)

Experiment	Mean	Std. deviation	Sample size
Sample 1 Combined survey without warning	2.89	1.98	201
Sample 2 Long-distance survey without warning	3.20	2.33	204
Sample 3 Long-distance survey with warning	3.59	2.25	198

Table 8-7   Analysis of long-distance mobility (# trips) using the negative binomial model (non-travellers excluded from analysis)

Variable	Parameter	T-statistics	
Constant	0.6859	4.315	**
Combined survey	-0.0722	-1.137	
Prior letter	0.1487	2.555	**
Working	0.1059	1.277	
University education	0.1708	3.216	**
Male	0.1753	3.175	**
Driving licence	0.2042	1.217	
Overdispersion parameter α	0.0823	3.375	**
N		599	
Log-likelihood		-1194.2	

**$p<.05$

Corresponding with the results in Table 8-6, the parameter estimates in Table 8-7 suggest that the combined survey leads to under-reporting of long-distance mobility compared to separate long-distance surveys. The effect, however, is not statistically significant. Therefore, no clear conclusions can be drawn concerning the relationship between high workload and reported mobility. On the other hand, the effect of prior letters is significant, indicating that contacting the respondent in advance of the telephone call increases the number of trips reported. The socio-demographic variables reveal the expected pattern: men are more mobile than women, and education level positively affects the amount of long-distance travel. The significant overdispersion parameter indicates that the negative binomial regression is preferred in comparison with the Poisson model.

130

Figure 8.1   Trip rates for travellers by survey design

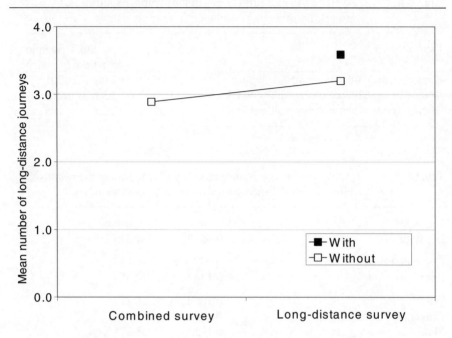

8.4   DISCUSSION

From the results presented above, it is evident that combined travel surveys are vulnerable to non-response errors. Both unit non-response and under-reporting of mobility is higher in the combined survey than in the separate long-distance survey. Although the response rates reported here are in the upper range compared to commercial telephone surveys conducted in Norway – indicating that travel surveys are perceived as more legitimate surveys – almost 50 percent of the prospective respondents in the combined survey refused to participate. The sensitivity towards interview length clearly affects willingness to participate in surveys. In addition, the high workload produced by a combined interview seems to reduce the completeness in reporting of mobility, although the overall results were not significant. However, the data indicate that respondents get tired, and, deliberately or not, omit some of the trips they have made.

These findings weigh against combining surveys of daily and long-distance mobility. Still, the tactical implications may not be the same for all researchers. If one aims to analyse daily trips and long-distance mobility together at the individual level, few alternatives to combined surveys exist. One must, however, be aware of the potential bias created by decreased response rates and under-reporting of mobility.

The lower response rates can to some extent be corrected by contacting the respondents in advance of the interview. A prior letter seems to pay off, when it comes both to response rates and to more accurate reporting of mobility. It is also evident that the letter does not need to be lengthy. In the present study, the letter only gave a short introduction to the study, describing the sponsors, the purpose of the study and the kind of questions that the respondent would be asked, in addition to a list where respondents could record their previous and intended travel activities. Thus, the important matter is that a prior letter is sent and not the amount of information it contains.

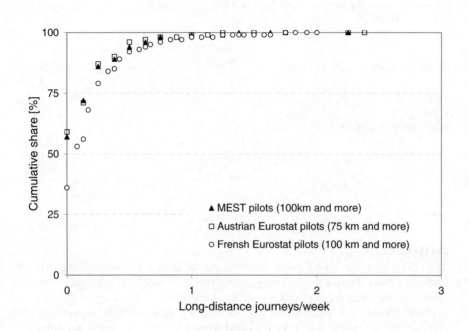

Chapter 9
Analysis of the MEST and related survey work

K. W. Axhausen

9. Analysis of MEST and related survey work[1]

K. W. Axhausen

IVT
ETH
CH – 8093 Zürich

Abstract

The analysis of the MEST pilots and two related data sets (Austrian and French Eurostat pilots) focuses on the linear regression analysis of the aggregate response rates and the disaggregate analysis of the data yield. In both cases the relative insensitivity of the respondents to the survey form design is verified. In comparison, the protocol and the temporal orientation have a significant influence on both dimensions.

Keywords

Response behaviour, long-distance travel, MEST pilots, Eurostat pilots, aggregate models, disaggregate models.

---

[1]Preferred Citation: K. W. Axhausen (2003) Analysis of MEST and related survey work, in K. W. Axhausen, J.-L. Madre, J. W. Polak and Ph. L. Toint (eds.) *Capturing Long-Distance Travel*, 133 - 150, Research Studies Press, Baldock.

9.1 INTRODUCTION

The data collected for MEST (see Chapter 6) and for the Eurostat pilot surveys (Axhausen, 1998) provide a rich source for the analysis of the performance of different types of mixed-method protocols, which formed the core of these efforts. Two aspects of the performance were most relevant in the context of MEST and will be reported here: the response behaviour of the sample and the data yield as a function of the characteristics of the protocol, scope of the survey and form design. The optimisation of those two goals - response and data yield - which in itself requires a trade-off between number of movements reported and the amount of detail reported about each, is, in the final analysis, the task of the survey designer.

The chapter will discuss two sets of models, each addressing one of these questions; first, a set of aggregate models relating the characteristics of each survey to the response rate obtained (see also Axhausen and Youssefzadeh, 1999; or Axhausen, 1998); second, a set of disaggregate models relating the data yield in terms of reported number of journeys to the characteristics of the survey and the survey forms (see also Axhausen and Youssefzadeh, 1999; or Axhausen, 1999a, b, c). The final section of the chapter raises issues for future research. For a discussion of the scope of the surveys and of their implementation see Chapters 2 and 6.

9.2 RESPONSE BEHAVIOUR: AGGREGATE MODELS

The aggregate modelling attempts to relate the response rates (see below) to the overall description of the surveys and the protocols employed. All three waves are included. It will not look at the data yield at the aggregate level (number of journeys and trips/stages reported), as one could not correctly account for the socio-demographic differences within the samples. The appropriate disaggregate analyses will be reported below. In principle, it is possible to conduct the analysis of response behaviour at the disaggregate (household or person) level, if appropriate prior information is available about each unit in the sample. The work by Armoogum and Madre (1997) has shown the usefulness of this approach. The more limited test of comparing those who responded in writing to those who responded only on the phone, will not be pursued here, as the effects of excluding the double non-responders (not in writing and not on the phone) cannot be properly assessed (see Axhausen *et al.*, 1996; Polak and Ampt, 1996; or Kitamura and Bovy, 1987 for such tests).

The dependent variable, response rate, will be analysed in three forms:

- **postal response** (where relevant): Share of sampled persons replying in writing;
- **telephone response**: Share of sample answering on the phone who had not answered in writing (full interview in the case of CATI surveys; non-response interviews in the case of postal surveys covering person and household detail and a roster of the journeys undertaken);
- **total response**: Sum of the above.

This is necessary, as it is known from earlier studies, that the characteristics of the postal survey influence both partial response rates and that a trade-off has to be made between these two to obtain an optimal response rate.

In the interpretation of the results below one should keep in mind that it was impossible to get the protocols defined perfectly consistently in the tenders of the pilots implemented. There were various misunderstandings on the part of the survey firms, which generated deviations from the ideal. In addition, the constructions of the sample frames varied widely between countries and waves, and could not be standardised within the budget available. The list below describes the relevant points:

Wave I:
- Portugal: The sample was screened through an initial recruitment call.
- Sweden, Portugal: Did not execute the full non-response interviews. For the purpose of this analysis they were still counted towards the telephone response rate.
- Sweden: The CATI interviews had to be repeated with a less complex experimental design due to software problems in the original survey period (one of the two alternative designs).

Wave II:
- UK: The sample was drawn from a pool of responders, who had stated during an earlier survey that they were willing to participate in further transport related surveys.

Wave III:
- Sweden: The survey firm changed to the new low bidder, the National Statistical Institute.

The results of the linear regressions for the three dependent variables are presented below for two different datasets:

- **all surveys***:* a variable set focusing on the administration method, the country and the wave of the pilots (Table 9.1);
- **surveys excluding the CATI-only surveys of the first wave** *:*describing the surveys with variables related to the protocol and to the survey form (Table 9-2).

9.2.1 All surveys

The analysis across all surveys with a relatively small variable set consistently gave the best fit, as measured by the adjusted R^2. The estimated equations are jointly highly significant as measured by the F-values. Weighting the dependent variables with the size of the sample did not change the conclusions drawn from the results. They are therefore not reported.

Table 9-1   Aggregate analysis of the response rates: All surveys
              (unweighted linear regression)

Variable	Kind of response rate					
	Postal returns		Telephone		Sum	
	Para-meter	Signi-ficance	Para-meter	Signi ficance	Para-meter	Signi ficance
Constant	-8.6		79.8	**	71.2	**
Self-administered form part of protocol	25.2	**	-12.0	**	13.2	**
France	5.0		-8.6	**	-3.6	
Sweden	6.7		-22.1	**	-15.4	**
UK	16.6	**	-23.1	**	-6.5	
Swedish third wave contractor (SCB)	36.3	**	6.6		42.9	**
Recruitment from a panel of prior respondents	8.8		-6.7		2.2	
Telephone screening of sample	9.6	*	-11.3	**	-1.7	
Summer holidays during survey period	-4.5		0.4		-4.8	
MEST 2nd wave	0.4		-7.9	*	-7.5	
MEST 3rd wave	-2.1		-32.7	**	-34.8	**
F	21.2		36.9	**	17.4	**
Adjusted R^2	0.89		0.94		0.87	
N	26		26		26	

*	$\alpha = 0.10$
**	$\alpha = 0.05$

Source: adapted from Axhausen and Youssefzadeh (1999), Table 35

In the analysis of the postal returns, the dummy variable 'Self-administered form' acts as an additional constant. The willingness to participate in writing is equally low in Sweden, France and Portugal; only in the UK there is a significantly higher willingness to respond in writing, even having adjusted for the fact that, in the second wave, the UK sample was drawn from a panel of prior respondents to a different prior travel survey. The new contractor in the third wave in Sweden had a substantial positive impact. The MEST pilots profited here from the trust in the Statistical Central Bureau (SCB), which acted as our contractor in this wave.

The sample screening in the first wave in Portugal had also a significant positive effect.

The changes between the first and the second and the first and the third wave in both design and protocol had no recognisable impact on the written response, in spite of the size of the change. Roughly a quarter of the sample was willing to participate in each country, all other things being equal. It seems as if there is a core of willing respondents who participate out of interest, a sense of civic duty or curiosity.

The telephone returns, either CATI-only returns or returns to the complex non-response interview, are higher overall (43% on average across all surveys and countries). A written element sent prior to the telephone contact had a significant negative impact on the willingness to respond on the phone, which was further reduced by the more complex design of the second MEST wave and even more so by the protocol of the third wave (see below for further discussion).

In addition, there are noticeable country effects. While, *ceteris paribus*, the Portuguese are quite willing to respond on the phone, this willingness is significantly lower in France and even lower in Sweden and the UK. In spite of the positive effect on the postal return, the effects on the telephone returns obtained by SCB were not large.

The overall response, averaged over all surveys, was satisfactory, at 66%. The negative effect of the third wave protocol, resulting from the reduction in the telephone responsiveness, is a disappointment, but the further analysis might shed light on the reasons for this effect.

9.2.2 All surveys excluding the CATI-only first wave surveys

An initially tested, but problematic, complexity variable was replaced for this analysis with a dummy variable identifying forms, following the design adopted for the second and third wave of MEST.

The analysis of the postal returns confirms the results so far: strong country, contractor and sampling effects and no significant effects of the forms and the survey design as such. The temporal orientation effect is nearly but not quite significant at alpha = 0.14 (see also Axhausen et al., 1996 which identified this effect as significant).

The telephone returns are dominated by country and contractor effects. The effect of the MEST design is larger than in the postal return model, but it is far from being statistically significant. The only scope and survey form design variable, which is significant, if only at the 10% level, is the dummy indicating an eight-week reporting period. It reduces overall response by about 10%, but this result has to be seen against the background of an overall model, which is only weakly significant with an F-value of 3.1.

The results for the overall response reflect the results for the parts: country, contractor and sampling effects being significant.

Table 9-2   Aggregate analysis of the response rates: All surveys excluding
                   CATI-only first wave surveys (unweighted linear regression)

Variable	Kind of response rate					
	Postal returns		Telephone		Sum	
	Para-meter	Signi-ficance	Para-meter	Signi-ficance	Para-meter	Signi-ficance
Constant	17.6	**	74.8	**	92.4	**
France	6.5		-18.2	**	-11.6	
Sweden	7.7		-28.6	**	-20.9	**
UK	15.3	**	-35.7	*	-20.4	**
Swedish third wave contractor (SCB)	33.9	**	0.6		34.5	**
Recruitment from a panel of prior respondents	10.3	*	10.2		20.5	**
Telephone screening of sample	16.4	*	-13.3		3.1	
Summer holidays during survey period	-4.3		11.7		7.4	
Page versus column-based form	3.3		-8.4		-5.0	
Concurrent diary versus retrospective survey	-6.0		2.2		-3.8	
Trip-based versus stage-based description	1.3		-0.5		0.8	
MEST 2nd and 3rd wave style form	-2.5		-10.8		-13.2	
Reporting period: 4 weeks versus 6 weeks	0.0		0.0		0.0	
Reporting period: 8 weeks versus 6 weeks	-3.8		-7.5		-11.3	*
F	11.9	**	5.2	**	3.1	*
Adjusted R^2	0.86		0.69		0.53	
N	23		23		23	

* $\alpha = 0.10$
** $\alpha = 0.05$

Source: adapted from Axhausen and Youssefzadeh (1999), Table 37

9.2.3   Summary of the aggregate results

The results presented above have to be treated with care, given their aggregate base
and the specific nature of the sample of surveys analysed. Still, certain main points
are clear:

- *Country effects:* The effects of the countries are strong and generally significant. Respondents in Portugal, Sweden and France are less willing to reply in writing, while the French, Swedish and English are less willing to reply on the phone. The first result could be the effect of an orally-oriented culture in Portugal, which does not prioritise the written word. The unwillingness to reply on the phone in the northern European countries could be the result of an increasing amount of telephone interviewing and sales, which reduces the general willingness to participate. Portugal might therefore catch up, as time goes by.

- *Sampling effects:* The effect of pre-selection, either through the use of a panel of prior respondents or screening, is visible only for the written reply, as one would expect. Its use can only be recommended if it does not bias the sample drawn. Further research is required here.

- *Contractor effects:* The country effects above confound country and contractor effects for France, Portugal and the UK. The interpretation above is based on the assumption that the firms employed are representative for private sector survey firms in these countries. There is no reason not believe this.

- The case of Sweden is instructive, as we can contrast a private sector firm with the official Statistical Office acting as a consultant. Given the scale and skill differentials between a small private firm and the national statistical office, it is difficult to judge what has contributed to the substantially larger response obtained by SCB. More empirical work is required to establish the advantage of using an official body as the fieldwork firm in comparison to a private survey firm of similar size. At this point it is not yet possible to extrapolate the results from Sweden to other countries.

- *Design effects:* With the exception of the negative effect of concurrent diary (non-retrospective) protocol on postal response, no consistent design effects could be identified at this level. The designer seems therefore relatively free in his or her choices.

- The design effects are more visible and stronger in the telephone response. The respondents who did not participate in the written element of the survey were less willing to participate in the telephone element of a task, which they must have perceived as being difficult. The negative, but not significant, effect of the Wave 2 and 3 form design variables indicates this.

- This conclusion is supported by the negative and significant effect of the Wave 2 and Wave 3 dummy variables in the analysis of the telephone response across all surveys. This result is disappointing, but may be not surprising. The design changes reflected the responses of the participants in the cognitive laboratories, which are likely to belong to the group of respondents willing to participate in the written element – no effect there of the design changes. Still, the design seems to have been perceived as complex by a significant share of the respondents and lowered their willingness to participate, at least in the telephone element of the protocol.

- *Wave III*: The disappointment of Wave 3 is based on the unsatisfactory participation in the telephone element. The response to the written element was no worse than before.

- The contrast between the results obtained by the private firms in Portugal, France and the UK and the results obtained by Statistics Sweden raises the issue of to what extent the protocol of the third wave or the performance of the firms is at fault. Given the general competence of the firms employed, it is unlikely that the main fault can lie with the firms. In addition, there were special circumstances in each case: in France the survey was conducted by a firm also heavily involved in electoral opinion polling and it was felt by the firm that their name reduced the willingness of the sampled to participate; in the UK the survey was conducted in an economically polarised area with both the poorer and the richer population over-represented, both of whom are known to be less willing to participate than are middle-class respondents; in Portugal the negative effect of the written material, perceived by many as complex, was felt strongly; in Sweden SCB might have been particularly enthusiastic in this, their first involvement in MEST, whereas the other firms might have been professional, but not as keen in their second or third wave of the project.

- Still, even accounting for this, the telephone response was not satisfactory. The survey firms felt that giving the potential respondent the opportunity to refuse by calling them to offer help was not advantageous. The firms were asked to prepare for the task and to use suitable interviewers, but it might be possible that the preparation period and the training were not sufficient. The results obtained by the CBS in the Netherlands and Socialdata in Germany with this style of protocol for surveys of daily mobility indicates that there probably is scope for improvement through better training and selection of the interviewers, but in the case of CBS, an official agency bias might be at work as well.

9.3   DATA YIELD: DISAGGREGATE MODELS

The analysis of the response behaviour has to be balanced by an analysis of the data yield, i.e. the number of movements of a given detail reported by the respondents, as the overall quality of a survey has to be assessed using both dimensions. The maximisation of the total number of reported journeys through sampling and oversampling highly mobile persons will be discussed in Chapter 10. Three sources of data are available to shed light on the interactions between survey protocol, definition of the scope of the survey and the design of the survey form: the MEST surveys (see Chapter 6), the Austrian Eurostat pilots (Axhausen *et al.*, 1996) and the French Eurostat pilots (IPSOS, 1997; Axhausen, 1998 and 1999b). All three used experimental designs to explore the effects of different dimensions on response behaviour and data yield.

The framework for the analysis of the data yield is the negative binomial regression approach, a generalisation of the Poisson regression for count data (Greene, 1995 and 1997). The probability that we observe a particular number of movements, here journeys, is under the Poisson assumptions:

$$P(Y = y_i) = \frac{e^{\lambda_i} \lambda_i^{x_i}}{y_i!} \quad \text{with} \quad \ln \lambda_i = \beta_i x_i$$

The rigid Poisson assumption that the mean and the variance of the distribution are equal is relaxed in the negative binomial case by allowing for overdispersion in the variance:

$$Var[y_i] = E[y_i](1 + \alpha E[y_i])$$

which results in the following probability distribution:

$$P(Y = y_i) = \frac{\Gamma(\theta + y_i) u_i^2 (1 - u)^{y_i}}{\Gamma(\theta) y_i!}$$

with $u_i = \dfrac{\theta}{\theta + \lambda_i}$, $\theta = \dfrac{1}{\alpha}$, β_i the vector of parameters to be estimated for the variables x_i.

9.3.1 Austrian Eurostat pilots

The Austrian pilot was a response to both the Eurostat pilots as well as to the disappointing results of the long-distance element of the then recent national travel survey (Herry and Sammer, 1999). Within the framework of a mixed method protocol preferred by the national government, the experiments focused therefore on three elements:

- duration of the reporting period (four weeks, eight weeks);
- temporal orientation (retrospective, non-retrospective (concurrent diary)) ;
- level of detail of the household, person and movement description (minimum required by Eurostat (1995), larger set coded in more detail).

Otherwise, the Eurostat minimum requirements were used, in particular the level of aggregation (stage) and the minimum distance (100 km, implemented as 75km to avoid errors at the boundary). All possible eight combinations were tested.
The protocols involved the following contacts:

Non-retrospective surveys	*Retrospective surveys*
Announcement letter	*Announcement letter*
Survey distribution	Survey distribution
Two letters during the reporting period reminding the respondents	
Reminder letter	Reminder letter
Redistribution as a retrospective survey	Redistribution survey
(Non)-response telephone interview	(Non)-response telephoneinterview

In the case of a written response the telephone interviews were used to interview the respondents about their experiences with the survey (including their likes and dislikes), to clarify any obvious errors, to probe for not-yet-reported journeys and to ask about the household income in four classes.[2] In the case of no written response, the telephone interviews were used to obtain a roster of the journeys undertaken in the reporting period, but no stage details, to ask for the reasons for the non-response and to establish some household characteristics, including household income.

Given the nature of the study, a representative sample of 1500 residents of Innsbruck with telephone numbers was obtained from an address dealer, as official sampling frames could not be obtained. From this list we removed those without a phone number or a different address in the most recent official telephone directory CD and used 200 for a pre-test, leaving a sample of 1080, which was divided equally between the eight experimental surveys. See Table 9-3 for the response rates. A full non-response interview was counted as a response, as it provided the core information about the level of mobility and the minimum household details. The survey period covered March to June 1996, with the last telephone interviews taking place in July.

9.3.2 French Eurostat pilots

The most recent French NPTS (Armoogum and Madre, 1998) had been conducted as a sequence of face-to-face interviews, including diaries between the visits. It included, among other elements, a substantial long-distance survey. The French ministry used the opportunity of the Eurostat initiative to test some questions of interest to it. It decided to concentrate on three elements:

---

[2] The item non-response for income was corrected using a class mean imputation using number of cars and number of persons over 15 years in the household to define the classes.

- duration of the reporting period (three months retrospectively or three one-month periods – first retrospective/the following two non-retrospective);
- type of data retrieval (CATI or postal self-completion);
- type of sampling frame (fresh random sample or sample from a panel of people who had indicated their willingness to participate in future surveys).

Again, the Eurostat (1995) content requirements and definitions were used. The protocol started with official announcement letters, followed by the survey material. No reminders were performed. The newly designed and untested postal form provided a matrix for the recording of the stages (A3 folded) and was distributed only to those self-completing. The CATI sub-sample received a one-page memory jogger. Both sub-samples received a covering letter, a map showing the home location of the respondent and a 100km circle around it and a brief flyer explaining the study.

A sample of 1000 respondents was achieved, distributed between the eight experimental conditions. The response rates are calculated based on the number of persons contacted initially. See Table 9-3 for the response rates. The survey was conducted in the Rhone-Alpes region around Lyon during the first quarter of 1997.

Table 9-3   Austrian and French Eurostat pilots: Response rates (not corrected for sample loss)

Country	Survey			Postal Response [%]	Telephone Response [%]	Total Response [%]
Austria	Non-retro spective	4 weeks	Minimum	22.2	24.4	46.7
			Large	28.9	18.5	47.4
		8 weeks	Minimum	23.7	20.7	44.4
			Large	25.9	14.1	40.0
	Retro spective	4 weeks	Minimum	35.6	15.6	51.1
			Large	33.3	23.7	57.0
		8 weeks	Minimum	36.3	10.4	46.7
France	Random sample	CATI	Monthly	-	48.7	48.7
			Quarter	-	49.2	49.2
		Postal	Monthly	24.4	-	24.4
			Quarter	34.7	-	34.7
	Panel based	CATI	Monthly	-	43.5	43.5
			Quarter	-	47.2	47.2
		Postal	Monthly	45.4	-	45.4
			Quarter	42.7	-	42.7

Source: Axhausen (1998), Table 5

A first inspection of the table reveals strong design effects on the response behaviour of the samples. In the Austrian case the temporal orientation has a strong effect (about 10% average difference between retrospective and non-retrospective surveys), which is in the opposite direction to the current experience with surveys of daily mobility. In the case of France, a strong interaction between the method of administration and the duration of the reporting period is visible. The total response rates are at the lower limit of the acceptable for surveys of this type, but not critical, given the relatively small number of contacts with the respondents and the experimental nature of the survey materials.

In Austria the response rate for the follow-up interviews with those who had replied in writing was nearly 100%.

9.3.3 Analysis

For each of the three data sources negative binomial models of the number of journeys reported were estimated, trying to keep these models as comparable as possible, but not reducing the set of variables included to the lowest common denominator. In all three cases, the negative binomial model provided a better fit than the simple Poisson model, but more complex formulations, such as the zero-inflated negative binomial model, did not consistently improve the fit further and will therefore not be reported here (see Axhausen, 1999a, b and c for earlier estimates). The interaction terms of the experimental design variables were significant only for French data and are included here in the model presented. See Figure 9.1 for uniform Q-Q plots of the three datasets comparing the observed with expected distribution.

The most striking point of Table 9-4 is the lack of significance of the survey form design variables. It seems as if the form design has no impact on the number of movements reported as long as a minimum standard is met. This is consistent with the assumption of a core of postal respondents, who are basically willing to engage with forms.

In contrast, the impact of the protocol variables is striking. In the Austrian case, the retrieval by phone during the follow-up telephone survey is not significant, but this overlaps with the need to redistribute the survey form after a long period of non-response, which indeed does reduce the number of reported trips. The interactions of the protocol variables in the French case are interesting. All three variables reduce the number of journeys reported, but these reductions are balanced for particular combinations of them: a self-administered form reduces the number of journeys reported, but this effect is balanced by combining it with fresh random sample or monthly reporting. Equally, the negative main effect for recruitment from a pool of prior respondents is balanced if they are approached monthly, by phone.

The differences between the surveys visible in the effect of the reporting period [weeks] are difficult to interpret, as survey design, country, sponsor, field work firm, season and survey form effects interact. The relatively low value for the French Eurostat pilot is nevertheless noticeable and might be due to the long reporting period of 12 weeks for the CATI respondents and, additionally, the untested survey form for the postal respondents.

The socio-demographic variables, in spite of the different sets available, all tell the same story; that the wealthier (Austria: household income/month; France: socio-economic class), better connected (MEST: number of telecom links at home), the better educated (MEST, Austria; university education or students) and the economically active (MEST; full-time work; Austria: males; France: head of family and full-time work) are more likely to undertake long-distance travel.

The impact of car ownership is not consistently significant, but the relative effects are the same throughout; people in households without a car make significantly fewer long-distance journeys (MEST, France) than households with one car, while those with two or more make significantly more (Austria, France). The chosen coding is a compromise as a log (number of vehicles)-term is not feasible, given the households without cars.

The overall quality of estimates is reasonably good. The overdispersion parameter of the negative binomial model is always highly significant and associated with large gains in the Log-Likelihood function.

Figure 9.1   Uniform Q-Q plots of the frequency of long-distance travel distribution

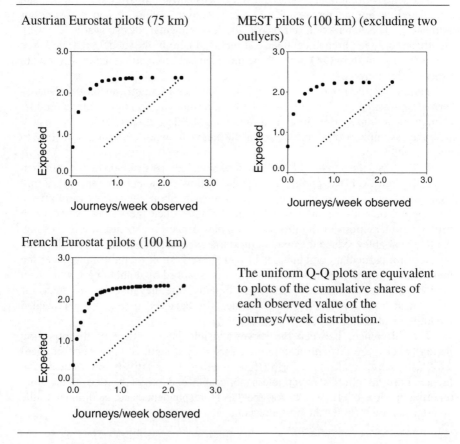

Austrian Eurostat pilots (75 km)

MEST pilots (100 km) (excluding two outlyers)

French Eurostat pilots (100 km)

The uniform Q-Q plots are equivalent to plots of the cumulative shares of each observed value of the journeys/week distribution.

Table 9-4   Results of the negative binomial regression analyses: Number of person journeys

MEST Wave II and III (100km +)			Austrian Eurostat pilots (75km+)			French Eurostat pilots (100km +)		
Variable	Para-meter	Sig.	Variable	Para-meter	Sig.	Variable	Para-meter	Sig.
			Constant	-1.1938	**	Constant	-1.0235	**
Constant	-3.9177	**						
Duration of reporting period	0.1898	**	Duration of reporting period	0.1628	**	Duration of reporting period	0.0958	**
			Redistribution	-0.4479	**			
			Phone retrieval	-0.0544				
Retrospective	0.1646		Retrospective	-0.1894	**	Postal contact	-0.0259	**
						Prior respondent	-0.1112	**
Page/Unit	0.2086							
Trip based	0.1213					Monthly report	-0.0565	**
Detail for all household members	0.0249		Amount of detail	0.0742		Recruitment * Contact	0.0848	**
MEST 2nd wave	1.4493	**				Recruitment * Monthly	0.1404	**
						Monthly * Contact	0.1188	**
UK	1.2628	**						
France	1.1899	**						
Portugal	-0.2377							
			Male	0.5617	**	Head of family	0.2585	**
						Below 20 years	-1.1093	**
University education	0.3832	**	University education	0.6582	**			
Student	0.6214	**				Student	0.6081	**
Fulltime work	0.5678	**				Fulltime work	0.3705	**
						Parttime work	-0.2630	**
Number of telecom links at home	0.1532	**				Semi-rural location	-0.4826	**
Second home	0.3737	**						
			Below 20000 ATS/month	-0.4205	**	Socio-economic class (++)	0.3683	**
			Between 20000-40000 ATS/month	-0.2721	**	Socio-economic class (+)	0.3045	**
No car in Household	-0.5979	**	No car in household	-0.0428		No car in household	-0.7925	**
Two or more cars in household	0.0272		Two or more cars in household	0.2437	**	Two or more cars in household	0.2793	**
Alpha	1.1257	**	Alpha	0.7703	**	Alpha	1.1319	**

N	688	1632	62655
L(0)	-1202.2	-2218.8	-161087
L(Poisson)	-1018.1	-1936.6	-141661
L(Negative binomial)	-878.8	-1829.5	-112377
ρ^2	0.269	0.175	0.302

**: $\alpha = 0.05$
France: Weighted data set

9.4   CONCLUSIONS AND OUTLOOK

The analyses reported in this chapter are based on a rich, but by no means conclusively large, data set of surveys. Still, a number of conclusions are possible, which can be used to formulate recommendations for the developing practise in long-distance travel surveys.

It is obvious that the survey designer has to accept trade-offs; retrospective surveys improve participation, but seem to reduce the number of journeys reported (clear in the Austrian pilots and less so in the French Eurostat pilots). The surveys have shown that self-administered surveys can still be used in a wide range of countries, but they have also shown that they have to be supplemented by a telephone element to reach a wider number of the respondents than the core postal respondents. This core seems to be relatively insensitive to the survey form design, but the non-core members are influenced by it in their willingness to reply later on the phone, which implies a further trade-off to be considered.

Sampling from pools of known respondents and advance telephone screening improves response, but it raises potentially more issues than it resolves. Both approaches can bias the sample and require rather comprehensive screening interviews about the socio-demographics of the sample and their travel behaviour, which defeats the purpose of the screening or the sampling from the pool of known respondents. Still, if possible, one should draw from a sampling frame which includes information about the household and its members, such as a census or population register.

The results from the French Eurostat pilot seem to indicate, that a reporting period of 12 weeks might be too long. The other results indicate, on the other hand, that eight weeks might be acceptable in conjunction with the 100km minimum distance to the furthest destination of the journey.

The lack of clear-cut results on the survey form design variables makes the formulation of recommendations difficult. The qualitative results reported in the last chapter indicate that a more generous layout and the separation of the journey roster from the journey detail is a viable approach. Still, one has to remember that no real alternative form design was tested within the MEST survey work.

The work reported here has not exhausted the research question about the optimal balance between response rates, data yield and level of detail of the reported data. In particular, the interaction between written and oral response needs to be explored in more detail. The possibilities of web-based surveys need to be explored, particularly for highly mobile respondents, but with special care with regard to sampling biases.

Statistically, there is more work needed on the statistical similarity of data from different sources: Is it really possible just to merge data from survey forms and telephone interviews? The first results from the Austrian survey indicate no differences, but one sample is not enough.

9.5 REFERENCES

Armoogum, J. and J-L. Madre (1998) - Weighting or imputations ? The example of non-responses for daily trips in the French NPTS. *Journal of Transportation and Statistics*, **1** (3), 53-64.

Armoogum, J. and J.L. Madre (2000) - Item non-response, sampling and weighting. *in P.M. Jones and P. Stopher (eds.) Transport Surveys: Raising the Standards*, Transportation Research Cicular, **E-C008**, II-D-1-II-D-19, TRB, Washington D.C.

Axhausen, K.W. (1998) - The Eurostat pilots of long-distance travel diaries: Summary of final reports. *Report to the Österreichische Statistische Zentralamt*, Wien and Eurostat, Luxembourg, Innsbruck.

Axhausen, K.W. (1999a) - Surveying long-distance travel: effects of survey contexts and protocols, in Statistics Sweden (ed.). *Official Statistics in a Changing World, Proceedings of the 3rd International Conference on Methodological Issues in Official Statistics,* 141-149, Statistics Sweden, Stockholm.

Axhausen, K.W. (1999b) - Non-response and data yield: Experiences from Austria and France. *Paper presented at ICNS 1999, Portland, October 1999, Arbeitsberichte Verkehrs- und Raumplanung,* **8,** Institut für Verkehrsplanung, Transporttechnik, Strassen- und Eisenbahnbau, ETH, Zürich.

Axhausen, K.W. (2001) - Methodological Research for a European Survey of Long-Distance Travel. *Transportation Research Circular*, **E-C026**, 322-342, TRB, Washington, D.C.

Axhausen, K.W., H. Köll, M. Bader and M. Herry (1997) - Workload, data yield and data quality: experiments with long-distance travel diaries. *Transportation Research Record*, **1593,** 29-40.

Axhausen, K.W. and M. Youssefzadeh (1999) - Towards an European Survey of Long Distance Travel incorporating A new European long distance diary: Second draft of content and structure and A new European long distance diary: Final draft of content and structure, report to the CEC, DG VII – Transport. *MEST Deliverables*, **D3 and D4**, Fakultät für Bauingenieurwesen und Architektur, Leopold-Franzens-Universität, Innsbruck.

Eurostat (1995) - Proposal for definitions and variables of a household survey for mobility. *In Minutes of the Task Force on Passenger Transport and Tourism Statistics*, Luxembourg, 31. 1.-1. 2. 1995.

Greene, W.H. (1997) - Econometric Analysis. Prentice Hall, Upper Saddle River.

Greene, W.H. (1995) - Limdep Version 7.0. Econometric Software, Bellport.

Herry, M. and G. Sammer (1999) - Österreichischer Bundesverkehrswegeplan: Verkehrsbefragung, part A3-H/2. *Report to the Austrian Ministry of Science and Transport*, Wien and Graz.

IPSOS Region (1997) - Survey on long-distance mobility. *Report to the French Ministry of Transport*, IPSOS Region, Lyon.

Kitamura, R. and P.H.L. Bovy (1987) - Analysis of attrition biases and trip reporting errors for panel data. *Transportation Research*, **21A** (4/5) 287-302.

Polak, J.W. and E.S. Ampt (1996) - An analysis of response wave and non-response effects in travel diary surveys. *Paper presented at 4th International Conference on Survey Methods in Transport*, Steeple Aston, September 1996.

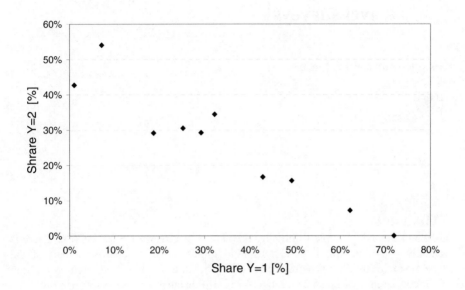

Chapter 10
Weighting and correcting long-distance travel surveys

J Armoogum and J-L Madre

10 Weighting and correcting long-distance travel surveys[1]

J Armoogum and J-L Madre

INRETS
F – Arcueil

Abstract

It is not always possible to obtain complete data directly from a survey. There is usually something missing: a household might refuse to answer; a part of the questionnaire might not be returned; some trips are omitted; or an item is missing or inconsistent (for instance, an over-long trip distance or a too-short trip duration, suggesting an unreasonable speed). In this chapter we will discuss methodologies to cope with this non-response by weighting procedures. After a presentation of the most important concepts useful in this field, we will consider these corrections from a theoretical and practical point of view, illustrated with examples drawn from a methodological survey (VATS) and from the French National Personal Transportation Survey (NPTS). This chapter then presents original methodologies developed for the MEST project.

Keywords

Non-response, unconfounded non-reponse, confounded non-response, weighting, imputation, calibration on margin, Calmar, under-reporting.

---

[1] Preferred citation: Armoogum, J. and J-L Madre (2003) Weighting and correcting long-distance travel, in K. W. Axhausen, J.-L. Madre, J. W. Polak and Ph. L. Toint (eds.) *Capturing Long-Distance Travel*, 151 - 170, Research Studies Press, Baldock.

10.1 INTRODUCTION

Long-distance travel is very unevenly distributed in the population. Thus, in order to collect information on this topic, it seems adequate to over-sample highly mobile groups. For the calculation of mobility rates or of total amounts of distance travelled (see Section 2), it is useful to collect information on both travellers and non-travellers. But if we only need information on some characteristics of the trips, for instance in order to calculate Origin-Destination matrix flows (see Section 3), it seems pointless to survey non-travellers. In this case, a clear objective has to be defined: How important is a good uniform relative accuracy on each flow, which is almost impossible to achieve with a reasonable sample size when these flows are of different magnitude or do we need only to estimate the main flows with a high accuracy? Thus, a sample scheme strategy is generally a compromise between different purposes, which depend on the information available for drawing the sample, which might, for example, allow for the stratification of the sample.

10.2 CONCEPT AND DEFINTIONS

All surveys are susceptible to a variety of different types of error that affect different parts of the survey process, which have different implications for data quality and are amenable to different forms of prevention or compensation (Groves, 1989; Richardson, Ampt and Meyburg, 1995).

10.2.1.1 Types of non-response

Non-response errors are those generally associated with the failure of sample units to participate fully in the survey. It is usual to distinguish between two different forms of non-response.

- **Unit non-response** refers to the failure of a unit in the sample frame to participate in the survey. In the context of travel diary surveys, unit non-response can arise for a number of different reasons including refusal, non-contact, infirmity or temporary absence (see, e.g., Bróg and Meyburg, 1980, Kim et al., 1993; Richardson and Ampt, 1994; Stopher and Stecher, 1993 ; Thakuriah, Sen, Sööt and Christopher, 1993).
- **Item non-response** refers to the failure to obtain complete information from a participating unit. In the context of travel diary surveys, the most significant form of item non-response is probably the under-reporting of trip-making due to respondents' failure to recall and/or record all the relevant journeys correctly (see, e.g., Ampt and Richardson, 1994; Bróg and Meyburg, 1981; Bróg, Erl, Meyburg and Wermuth, 1982, Hassounah, Cheah and Steuart, 1993). Item non-response can be regarded as a particular form of the more general problem of measurement error in survey research (Groves, 1989).

As it appears in the definition, the difference between unit and item non-response is that we have less information about unit non-response than about item non-response. Indeed, for a selected unit the only information that we can extract without error is geographical and even if the sample is picked from a prior official census return, the figures there are not necessarily up-to-date. But we know much more about the units which do not reply to some questions (from the responses given to the other questions).

10.2.1.2   The best way to deal with non-response is to avoid it

Even if non-response is inevitable, we should take measures to avoid it. Zmud and Arce (1997) deal with this problem comprehensively in the case of travel surveys. In a mobility survey, for example, is it necessary to ask for trip distance that people do not always know, or estimate poorly? Or is it possible to calculate it from origin and destination on which there are almost no missing data (Flavigny and Madre, 1994)? Missing trips are often due to memory effects or to an over-long reporting period. Some of these memory effects can be avoided through the use of memory joggers. Either way, most people remember their daily mobility only for the day before the interview, and their long-distance trips for about one month (Armoogum and Madre, 1996).

10.2.1.3   Re-weighting or imputing data?

There is a wide range of different techniques available for addressing the problems of non-response in the post-processing of a survey. These can be classified into two main methods:

- **weighting procedures**, which consist of an expansion of the respondent's weight;
- **imputation procedures**, which replace a non-response by the response of some respondent.

Generally, unit non-response is corrected by weighting procedures and item non-response by imputation procedures. However, we can also correct total non-response by imputation procedures (for example, in a households survey, by duplicating the response of a respondent household for a non-respondent household), and under-reporting (which is considered to be item non-response) by weighting procedures (Armoogum and Madre, 1997).

Let us suppose that we are measuring two variables of interest, Y1 and Y2. If the unit k does not respond to both Y1 and Y2, it is common to give the unit k the weight 0, and to increase the weight of the respondents. If the unit k responds to Y1 and not to Y2, it is usual to replace the missing value by one (or many) plausible value(s). This process is commonly called imputation. We will consider this process when re-weighting is a reasonable solution, and when it is better to implement imputation procedures.

Let us now suppose that we are measuring three variables of interest, Y1, Y2 and Y3. If the set of missing data for Y1 and Y2 is not the same as for Y1 and Y3, we will have to run two different re-weighting procedures, and their result will probably not be identical for the total of Y1. Thus, re-weighting has only to be implemented when a unit is totally missing (for instance in the case of missing trips) or when almost all the important variables describing a unit are missing. For instance, in the French NPTS, all car diaries for which interviewers suspected missing trips (about 5%), or in which there was at least one trip with not enough information to implement the imputation procedure (less than 1% of diaries), were skipped. Thus, a data file was obtained which contained more than 94% of the diaries collected, with a single weight set and with no missing data left for the main variables; trip, distance, and no trip omitted (checked by the odometer).

10.2.1.4 The quasi-randomisation approach

This approach considers that the default of response adds a supplementary phase in the sample schemes. Each person selected in the sample has a probability of responding to the survey (conditionally to being in the sample selected). The problem is that this probability is unknown. The difficulty is that the survey designer does not know *a priori* the distribution of the response probability (i.e. the response mechanism), and s/he must make assumptions about it. Once the response mechanism is estimated, the estimation of the total of a target variable of the survey is derived from these probabilities for a design-based estimation (or randomisation inference).

Definition of design-based inference; suppose that s is a sample selected from the population U, and π_k the probability of the element k (of U) to be in the sample s. The total of the target variable y is: $Y = \sum_{k \in U} y_k$ and the design-based

inference is estimated by : $\hat{Y} = \sum_{k \in s} \dfrac{y_k}{\pi_k}$.

10.2.1.5 Unconfounded or confounded non-Response

A useful characterisation of the non-response mechanism is in terms of the concept of being "unconfounded".

Let s be a sample drawn from the population U, y a target variable and x: J auxiliary variables. The respondent sample r is picked from the sample s according to an unknown mechanism that follows a conditional probabilistic law q(r/s). The general form of a response mechanism is:

$$q(\, . \, |s) = q(\, . \, |s, y_s, x_s)$$

$$\text{where} : y_s = \{ y_k : k \in s \} \text{ and } x_s = \{ x_k : k \in s \}$$

Deville and Särndal (1994) define a "unconfounded" response mechanism when:

$$q(\, . \, |s) = q(\, . \, |s, x_s)$$

This last definition resembles the definition of ignoability introduced by Rubin (1976). In the context of an "unconfounded" non-response, the response mechanism depends only on the auxiliary variables and not on the target variable, and therefore the response probability can quite easily be estimated.

10.3   WEIGHTING PROCEDURES TO CORRECT NON-RESPONSE

10.3.1.1   Correction of unconfounded unit non-response with a weighting procedure

In countries where the sample is drawn from prior official census returns, it is usual to re-weight the sample with a two-stage weighting method. In the first stage we correct the non-response by a post-stratification on the variables that explain the response mechanism (a preliminary stage consists in analysing auxiliary variables that explain the response mechanism, which can be done, for example, with a logit model which shows the influence of each variable, everything being equal in other respects). By crossing these variables, we obtain classes, which form the framework for post-stratification. This is implemented by dividing the initial weight (reciprocal of the household's selection probability) by the individual's selection probability and by the response rate of the individual class.

$$\text{weight} = \frac{\text{initial weight}}{\text{Individual's selection probability}} * \frac{1}{\text{response rate}}$$

The second stage involves a calibration on margins to rectify the remaining sampling error. The most well-known function of calibration is the raking ratio, but in Calmar (Sautory, 1995), a software package developed by the French National Institute of Statistics and Economics Studies, three other functions are available (linear, truncated linear and logit).

Calibration on margins

Consider a finite population $U=\{1,2,...,k,...,N\}$ of N individuals, from which a probability sample s is drawn. The probability of selection of an individual k, in s is π_k (the weight of an individual k is $d_k=1/\pi_k$). In our survey we measure the variable of interest Y (the objective is to estimate the total $Y = \sum_{k \in U} y_k$) with which we also associate J auxiliary variables $X_1,...,X_j,...,X_J$, for which we know the population totals: $X_j = \sum_{k \in U} X_{jk}$.

Note $x'_k = (x_{1k},...,x_{Jk})$ and $X' = (X_1,...,X_J)$, an estimation of the total is :

$$\hat{Y} = \sum_{k \in s} \frac{y_k}{\pi_k} = \sum_{k \in s} d_k * y_k$$

If we want to take the auxiliary variables into consideration, we estimate the total Y with another function such as $\hat{Y} = \sum_{k \in s} w_k * y_k$, where weights w_k

are as close as possible, in an average sense for a given metric, to d_k, while respecting the calibrations equation: $\forall j = 1...J \quad \sum_{k \in s} w_k x_{jk} = X_j$.

To solve this kind of system, we choose a metric function $G(x)$, with $x = \dfrac{w_k}{d_k}$ as the argument, to measure the distance between the w_k and the d_k; $G(x)$ must fulfil certain conditions: it must be positive, convex and $G(1)=G''(1)=0$.

Once the $G(x)$ function has been chosen, the problem is to find the weights w_k ($k \in s$) which are the solution of the following system:

$$\underset{w_k\, k \in s}{\text{Min}} \ \sum d_k \ G(\frac{w_k}{d_k}) \ \text{under the constraint} \ \sum_{k \in s} w_k x_k = X$$

Let L, be the Lagrange vector of this system,

$$L = \sum_{k \in s} d_k \ G(\frac{w_k}{d_k}) - \lambda\left(\sum_{k \in s} w_k x_k - X\right)$$

The first-order condition leads to: $w_k = d_k F\!\left(x'_k \lambda\right)$ where F is the reciprocal of the first derivative of G.

The vector λ is calculated by solving a non-linear system of J equations to J unknowns, determined by the equations of calibration.

$$\sum_{k \in s} d_k F(x'_k \lambda) x_k = X$$

Calmar numerically solves this system by the Newton iterative method. Convergence is reached when the difference between the division of weights $\dfrac{w_k}{d_k}$ obtained for two successive iterations is small enough:

$$\text{Max}\left|\frac{w_k^{(i+1)}}{d_k} - \frac{w_k^{(i)}}{d_k}\right| < \varepsilon, \text{ with } \varepsilon > 0.$$

Calmar permits a choice between four different functions for $G(x)$:

a) linear function

$$G(x) = \frac{1}{2}(x-1)^2 , x \in R \text{ and } F(u) = 1+u$$

b) raking ratio function

$$G(x) = x\log(x) - x + 1, x > 0 \text{ and } F(u) = \exp(u)$$

c) logit function

$$G(x) = \left((x-L)\log\left(\frac{x-L}{1-L}\right) + (U-L)\log\left(\frac{U-x}{U-1}\right) \right)\frac{1}{A}, \text{if } L < x < U(+\infty \text{if not})$$

$$\text{with } A = \frac{U-L}{(1-L)(1-U)}$$

$$F(u) = \frac{L(U-1) + U(1-L)\exp(Au)}{U-1+(1-L)\exp(Au)} \in \,]L, U[$$

d) truncated linear function

$$G(x) = \frac{1}{2}(x-1)^2 , \text{if } L \leq x \leq U(+\infty \text{if not})$$

$$F(u) = 1 + u \in \,]L, U[$$

The technique of calibration reduces biases and increases precision in the estimates (Deville, Särndal and Sautory, 1993). If we use the distribution of the population according to the main socio-demographic variables (which also explain mobility) we should have good estimates of transport behaviour (Armoogum and Madre, 1996).

Two stage or single stage procedure?
As has been shown with the Australian VATS data presented above, within small homogeneous population groups, travel behaviour of non-respondents does not differ significantly from the behaviour of respondents (Ampt and Polak, 1996). Thus, the post-stratification according to the crossed categories with homogeneous response rates is essential. The information used for the calibration is different from the sample base, because of households which have moved or dwellings built since the last census. In a case where we implement only a post-stratification, we correct non-response but do nothing for the sampling error. Therefore, another way of adjusting the data is to calibrate the respondent sample over the margins of the population, a method implemented in Austria (Sammer, 1996). However, we have to ensure that the response mechanism is explained by the variables chosen for the

calibration (Deville, 1997)

The analysis of the non-response mechanism presented here can only be implemented when the sample is drawn from the census, or when much effort is dedicated to a non-respondent survey (see VATS example below). Nevertheless, calibration on margins can be run, when the structure of the total population (if possible by zone) is known. Indeed, the size of conurbation is generally the best explanatory factor of total non-response, but a geographic post-stratification is not sufficient to get a good fit of the sample and an expansion consistent with other data sources. For instance, calibration on age groups could be useful for demographic modelling (following cohorts) (Armoogum, Bussière and Madre, 1994 and 1995).

10.3.1.2 Correction of unit confounded non-response with a weighting procedure

Suppose that we have a mail-back questionnaire where the sample is asked to describe their long-distance journeys, and some percentage does not participate. In such situations we do not know why some of the questionnaires were not returned – was the individual too busy to fill out the form (for example: too much travel), or perhaps the individual did not travel at all and so assumed the questionnaire would be of no importance. It is usual to classify this type of non-response as a confounded non-response since the probability of responding depends on the response itself.

We are interested in the qualitative variable Y with I levels (for example, Y could be a dichotomous variable, such as whether or not the person had made a journey). The sample is divided into H groups h=1, ..., H, and $H \geq I$, for example the groups could be the regions or zones of residence.

Let us postulate a response model such that only i influences the response generating a response with a P_i probability and a non-response with a $\overline{P} = 1-P_i$ probability. We intend to estimate P_i.

Thus: Y a qualitative variable with I levels

$y_k = 1,...,i,....,I.$

$R_k = 1$ if the individual k responds, otherwise 0.

therefore we can classify the observations into H groups and thus:

$$n_h = \sum_{i=1}^{I} n_{h,i} + n_{h,?} \ within \ each \ h \ group \begin{cases} y_k = 1 \ for \ n_{h,1} \ units \\ ... \\ y_k = i \ for \ n_{h,i} \ units \\ ... \\ y_k = I \ for \ n_{h,I} \ units \\ y_k = ? \ for \ n_{h,?} \ units \end{cases}$$

Let us pose the following model:

Probability($R_k = 1 \mid y_k = i$) = P_i

Probability($y_k = i \mid k \in (h)$) = m_{hi}

Conditional to the sample s that gives the size of the known n_h, the exact number $n^*_{n,i}$ ($i = 1$ to I and $i = ?$) is one of the model's parameters. But we will prefer to

take $m_{h,i} = \dfrac{n^*_{h,i}}{n_h}$ as parameters. Note that we have the relation $\sum\limits_{i=1}^{I} m_{h,i} = 1$ in each

H groups. Since the n_{hi} follow an L multinomial distribution (n_h ; $m_{hi}P_i$;

$\sum\limits_{i=1}^{I} m_{h,i}\overline{P_i}$) and we can write the likelihood logarithm as:

$$\log(L) = \sum_{h=1}^{H}\left(\sum_{i=1}^{I} n_{h,i} \log\left(m_{h,i}P_i \right) + n_{h,?} \log\left(\sum_{i=1}^{I} m_{h,i}\overline{P_i} \right) \right)$$

With H Lagrange multiplier L_h associated with the H constraints ($\sum\limits_{i=1}^{I} m_{h,i} = 1$),

the maximum likelihood equations are as follows:

for h = 1 to H; i = 1 to I;

(1) $\qquad \dfrac{\partial \log(L)}{\partial m_{h,i}} = 0 \Leftrightarrow \dfrac{n_{h,i}}{m_{h,i}} + n_{h,?} \dfrac{\overline{P_i}}{\sum\limits_{i=1}^{I} m_{h,i}\overline{P_i}} + \lambda_h = 0$

for i = 1 to I;

(2) $\qquad \dfrac{\partial \log(L)}{\partial P_i} = 0 \Leftrightarrow \dfrac{\sum\limits_{h=1}^{H} n_{h,i}}{P_i} - \sum\limits_{h=1}^{H} n_{h,?} \dfrac{m_{h,i}}{\sum\limits_{i=1}^{I} m_{h,i}\overline{P_i}} = 0$

We can write the first equations at fixed h:

$$n_{h,i} + n_{h,?} \dfrac{m_{h,i}P_i}{\sum\limits_{i=1}^{I} m_{h,i}\overline{P_i}} + \lambda_h m_{h,i} = 0$$

then if we add for i = 1 to I, we find that $\lambda_h = -n_h$ The equations become:

For h = 1 to H; i = 1 to I ;

$$(3) \qquad m_{h,i} = \frac{n_{h,i}}{n_h - \dfrac{n_{h,?}\overline{P}_i}{\displaystyle\sum_{i=1}^{I} m_{h,i}\overline{P}_i}}$$

For i= 1 to I;

$$(4) \qquad P_i = \frac{\displaystyle\sum_{h=1}^{H} n_{h,i}}{\displaystyle\sum_{h=1}^{H} \dfrac{n_{h,?}m_{h,i}}{\displaystyle\sum_{i=1}^{I} m_{h,i}\overline{P}_i}}$$

An algorithm to estimate probabilities
In the first stage of this algorithm, we consider that response is missing only by random, so we initiate the processes by: $m_{h,i} = \dfrac{n_{h,i}}{n_h - n_{h?}}$ then we calculate the

$$P_i = \frac{\displaystyle\sum_{h=1}^{H} n_{h,i}}{\displaystyle\sum_{h=1}^{H} n_h m_{h,i}} \text{ , and estimate } Q_h = \frac{n_{h,?}}{\displaystyle\sum_{i=1}^{I} (m_{h,i}\,\overline{P}_i)}$$

the other stages of the process consist of estimating the $m_{h,i} = \dfrac{n_{h,i}}{n_h - Q_h \overline{P}_i}$, make

the m_{hi} keep the relation for all h : $\displaystyle\sum_{i=1}^{I} m_{h,i} = 1$ then calculate the $P_i = \dfrac{\displaystyle\sum_{h=1}^{H} n_{h,i}}{\displaystyle\sum_{h=1}^{H} Q_h\, m_{h,i}}$,

then we estimate the quantity $Q_h = \dfrac{n_{h,?}}{\displaystyle\sum_{i=1}^{I} (m_{h,i}\,\overline{P}_i)}$ and finally make:

$Q_h = \dfrac{Q_h}{\displaystyle\sum_{h=1}^{H} Q_h} * \displaystyle\sum_{h=1}^{H} n_h$. The algorithm stops when the differences between two

successive P_i are less than ε.

We can approach the solution by two other methods. If we suppose that $\frac{n_{h,?}}{\sum_{i=1}^{I} m_{h,i}\overline{P}_i} = n_h$, it follows that (3) $\Rightarrow$ (4) and above all : $m_{h,i} = \frac{n_{h,i}}{n_h P_i}$.

Let V_i be: $V_i = \frac{n_{h,i}}{n_h}$ so for h= 1 to H;

$$(5) \qquad m_{h,i} = \frac{V_i}{P_i} \; .$$

From the equations (5) we propose two other methods to estimate the P_i.

Econometric method
If we transform the equations (5) in :

$$\sum_{i=1}^{I} \frac{1}{P_i} V_i = 1 + \varepsilon_h \; \text{(because} \; \sum_{i=1}^{I} m_{h,i} = 1)$$

where the ε_h follow a normal distribution with a small variance and 0 as mean. In the equations of (5) only the P_i and the ε_h are unknown, so in doing a regression we can directly estimate the P_i .

Data analysis method
First of all we have to do a principal component analysis, with all the V_i (i=1, ...,I), V_i defined as above. Then, we calculate the components of the hyperplan whose dimension is equal to I-1, passing through the central point of gravity of all points. The P_i are given by the intersection of this hyperplan with the variables V_i.

Result of a simulation
Let us see the results of a simulation of the three methods. Suppose that Y is a qualitative variable with 2 levels (y_k =1 or y_k =2). Let P_1 (=0,710) be the probability that unit k responds knowing y_k = 1, and P_2 (=0,499) be the probability that unit k responds knowing y_k = 2.

The sample is divided into 10 subsamples. After simulating the first sample we select the non-respondent with P_1 and P_2 (Table 10-1).

Figure 10.1 shows the scatterplot of Y=1 against Y=2, which could be used to fit a linear regression. The estimates of P_1 and P_2 with the three methods give similar results and are very close to each other.

The bootstrap technique allows us to calculate the confidence interval at 95% for both estimators. We have drawn 1000 samples of 1000 units with replacement from the sample with non-response, then we calculate 1000 estimators of de p_1 and de p_2 with the three different methods. The upper range (respectively lower range) is for each technique the 25th highest value (respectively lowest). Here, the 3 procedures also give similar results (Table 10-2).

The last French NPTS is a good example of confounded non-response, for which we have implemented the weighting procedure described above. In each selected household an individual was asked to report his or her long-distance journeys in a mail-back questionnaire, but only 60% of the forms were returned. It was found that a person who travels is more interested in participating in the survey (Armoogum, 1997).

Table 10-1   Simulation of the two samples

Group	Sample without non-response		Sample with non-response			Size of the group
	$Y = 1$	$Y = 2$	$Y = ?$	$Y = 1$	$Y = 2$	N_h
1	2	94	54	1	41	96
2	7	91	38	7	53	98
3	25	71	50	18	28	96
4	34	61	42	24	29	95
5	49	57	44	31	31	106
6	40	50	30	29	31	90
7	53	31	34	36	14	84
8	92	36	45	63	20	128
9	95	16	34	69	8	111
10	92	4	27	69	0	96
Sum	489	511	398	347	255	1000

Table 10-2   Estimation of the P_1 and P_2 probabilities and their confidence intervals at 95%

		Algorithm	Econometric	P. C. A.
P_1	Estimator of $\hat{P}_1$	0.719	0.711	0.710
0.710	Lower range	0.652	0.653	0.648
	Upper range	0.783	0.779	0.783
P_2	Estimator of $\hat{P}_2$	0.493	0.510	0.499
0.499	Lower range	0.442	0.455	0.443
	Upper range	0.554	0.571	0.559

10.3.1.3 Correction of under-reporting with a weighting method

When we want to accurately measure a rare event in a retrospective survey – a long-distance journey, for example – an easy method is to increase the duration of the reporting period. But, in doing so, we may face memory effects. For example, in the last French NPTS respondents were asked to list all the journeys they had made during the previous three months. In order to avoid non-response, high mobility people (who had made more than 6 journeys during the last month) had to describe in detail only those journeys they had made during the previous month.

Figure 10.1   Position of the groups

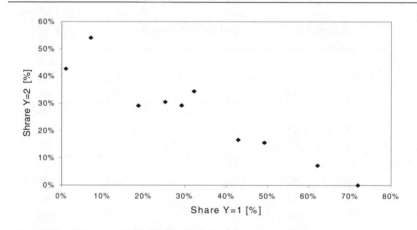

Since seasonal effects have been avoided by conducting the survey throughout the year, the distribution of journeys has to be uniform during the 13 weeks (3 months) of the reporting period. Figure 10.2 shows that this is true for those high mobility respondents. But for those with a lower mobility, three phenomena interfere:

- there are few journeys during the week before the interview because of the need to be at home (the long-distance interview takes place during the second visit by the interviewer); for the same reason, few journeys reported in the self-administered questionnaire end during the first week;
- trips omitted due to memory effects become more apparent as we refer to earlier weeks,
- for the first week there is an 'edge effect'; people unsure of the exact date of a journey tend to place it at the beginning of the reporting period.

Between the interviewer's two visits, the interviewee had to fill a memory jogger to help the recall of journeys. The experience of our colleagues from Norway tends to show that this has been useful, since we have collected 29%

journeys during the first month, 34% during the second month and 37% during the third, while for the Norwegian survey those figures are 15%, 35% and 50% (MEST, 1996a).

In order to correct memory effects for low mobility people, we have to avoid the problem of them needing to be at home. Consequently, in building the memory effects model only individuals who did not change their appointment with the interviewer were taken into account.

Figure 10.2   Distribution of journeys during the reporting period for high and low mobility persons

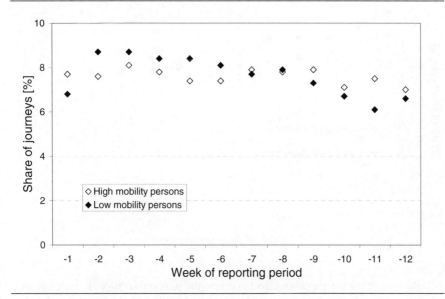

As can be seen in Figure 10.2, the distribution of trips for this group decreases from the first week. We classify the trips into three homogeneous categories, shown in Figure 10.3: Private trips of less than 500 km; private trips of more than 500 km; and business trips. People appear to forget their business trips more often than their short private trips and the latter more than their long private trips. In each category we estimate the number of trips as a function of the number of weeks between these trips and the interview. Empirically, an exponential function gives a stable result, and consequently this function was chosen to adjust the data (Armoogum and Madre, 1997).

Besides this test of different functions to adjust memory effects, we might also investigate whether the three dimensions (frequency, purpose and length) of the journeys considered are best for estimating memory effects models. Denstadli and Lian have shown in an analysis of under-reporting errors in the Norwegian National Travel Survey that trips made by train are better reported than those made by car, and that private trips are better reported than business ones.

Is it interesting to take into account either only personal characteristics or the means of transport (for instance, are car trips better reported when they are made as driver than as passenger?). As when identifying unit non-response mechanisms, logit modelling (explaining the proportion of journeys ending during the last month) should be used to identify those which are well reported and those subject to memory effects.

Figure 10.3   Distribution of journeys of low mobility persons by purpose

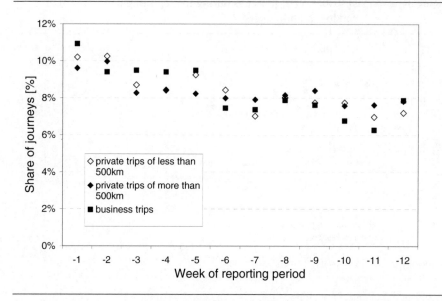

Re-weighting for memory effects offsets the bias on average, but we are not sure that it gives a correct distribution, since it adds the omitted trips of people who have described some and not to those who have declared none. In fact, in the French NPTS, if we compare the distribution of weekend trips made by individuals interviewed on the following Monday with those obtained from later interviews, the proportion of zero trips explains less than 10% of the difference for average mobility (up to one third for trips under 2 km). Thus, this re-weighting method, which compensates on average for the under-reporting of short weekend trips, does not seem to introduce too much bias into the distributions. An alternative solution to re-weighting would be imputations, but we lack information to implement it for those individuals who have described no trip at all.

10.4   CONCLUSIONS

Although many applications of the methods presented here have been implemented in real surveys, this chapter could seem rather theoretical. The best methods are not always those which are the most complex to implement; if we take the example of the post-stratification. But in the case of confounded non-response, as there is a correlation between travel behaviour and response behaviour, more complex techniques have to be implemented, since the impression given by raw data can be substantially distorted.

However, the list of methods presented here is not exhaustive. This chapter has concentrated on statistical approaches, while promising methods based on artificial intelligence have been studied by FUNDP (parsers) and by INRETS (neural networks) for the companion project TEST. A general issue for both approaches is to determine, without being too normative, what data are considered consistent and what data have to be corrected.

10.5   REFERENCES

Ampt, E.S. and A.J. Richardson (1994) - The validity of self-completion surveys for collecting travel behaviour data. *Proceedings 22nd European Transport Forum*, PTRC, London.

Armoogum, J., Y. Bussière, Y. and J.L. Madre (1995) - Demographic dynamics of mobility in urban areas: The Paris and Grenoble case. *World Conference on Transport Research Society*, 1995.

Armoogum, J. and J.L. Madre (1996) - Non-response correction in the 1993-94 NPTS: The example of daily trips. *Proceedings 4th International Conference on Survey Methods in Transport*, Steeple Aston, September 1996.

Armoogum, J., J.L. Madre, J.W. Polak, X.L. Han and M. Herry (1996) - Sampling and weighting schemes for travel diaries: review of issues and possibilities. *MEST Deliverable*, **D6**, INRETS, Arcueil

Armoogum, J. (1996) - La pondération de l'enquête Transports et communications 1993-94; note de l'Insee N°1068/F410, December 1996.

Armoogum, J. and J.L. Madre (1997) - Accuracy of data and memory effects in home based surveys on travel behaviour. *Paper presented at the 76th Annual Meeting of the Transport Research Board*, Washington, D.C., January 1997.

Armoogum, J. and J.L. Madre (1997) - De l'opimisation du plan de sondage au redressement d'une enquête: l'exemple des voyages à longue distance dans l'enquête Transports et Communications, Rennes, June 1997.

Armoogum, J. (1997) - Correction of a non-response due to the potential response: Case of the French N.P.T.S., *8th IATBR conference*, Austin, September 1997.

Armoogum, J. and J.L. Madre (1997) - Interview et présence au domicile. *Symposium of Statistic Canada*, Ottawa, November 1997.

Brög, W. and A. Meyburg (1980) - The non-response problem in travel surveys - an empirical investigation. *Transportation Research Record*, **775**, 34-38.

Brög, W. and A. Meyburg (1981) - Considerations of non-response effects on large scale mobility surveys. *Transportation Research Record*, **807**, 39-46.

Brög, W., E. Erl, A. Meyburg and W. Wermuth (1982) - Problems of non-reported trips in surveys of nonhome activity patterns. *Transportation Research Record,* **891**, 1-5.

Bushnell, D. (1994) - The National Travel Survey; Report on the 1991 Census-Linked Study of Survey Non-response. *Office of National Statistics,* London.

de Heer, W. and G. Moritz (1997) - Respondent sampling weighting and non-response. *Paper presented to the International Conference on Transport Survey Quality and Innovation,* Grainau, Germany, May 1997.

de Leeuw, E.D. (1992) - Data Quality in Mail, Telephone and Face to Face Interviews. *PhD thesis,* Universiteit Amsterdam.

Deville, J.-C. (1998) - La correction de la non-réponse par calage ou par échantillonage équillibré. *Paper presented at the 25th annual meeting of the Statistical Society of Canada,* Sherbrook, Canada, May 1998.

Deville, J.-C. and C.E. Särndal (1992) - Calibration estimators and generalised raking techniques in survey sampling. *Journal of the American Statistical Association,* **87** (418) 376-382.

Deville, J.-C. and C.E. Särndal (1994) - Variance estimation for the regression imputed Horvitz-Thompson estimator. *Journal of Official Statistics,* **10** (4) 381-394.

Deville, J.-C., C.E. Särndal and O. Sautory (1993) - Generalised raking procedures in survey sampling. *Journal of the American Statistical Association,* **88** (423) 1013-1020.

Flavigny, P.-O. and J.-L. Madre (1994) - How to get geographical data in the household survey. *Paper presented at the 7th Conference of the International Association for Travel Behaviour Research,* Valle Nevada, July 1994.

Groves, R. (1989) - Survey Errors and Survey Costs. John Wiley and Sons Inc., New York.

Hassounah, M., L.S. Cheah and G. Steuart (1993) - Underreporting of trips in telephone interview surveys. *Transportation Research Record,* **1412**, 90-94.

Kalton, G. (1983) - Compensating for Missing Survey Data. *Institute for Social Research,* University of Michigan, Ann Arbor.

Kim, H., J. Li, S. Roodman, A. Sen, S. Sööt, and E. Christopher (1993) - Factoring household travel surveys. *Transportation Research Record,* **1412**, 17-22.

Lessler, J.T. and W.D. Karlsbeek (1992) - Nonsampling Errors in Surveys. John Wiley and Sons Inc., New York.

Little, R.J.A. and D.B. Rubin (1987) - Statistical Analysis with Missing Data. John Wiley and Sons Inc., New York.

Madre, J-L. and J. Maffre (1994) - The French National Travel Personal Survey: The last of the dinosaurs or the first of a new generation? *Paper presented at the 7th Conference of the International Association for Travel Behaviour Research*, Valle Nevada, July 1994

Polak, J.W. and E.S. Ampt (1996) - An analysis of wave response and non-response effects in travel diary surveys. *Proceedings 4th International Conference on Survey Methods in Transport*, Steeple Aston, September 1996.

Richardson, A.J. and E.S. Ampt (1993) - The Victoria Integrated Travel, Activities and Land-Use Toolkit. *VITAL Working Paper,* **VWP93/1**, Transport Research Centre, University of Melbourne.

Richardson, A.J. and E.S. Ampt (1994) - Non-response effects in mail-back travel surveys. *Paper presented at the 7th Conference of the International Association for Travel Behaviour Research*, Valle Nevada.

Richardson, A.J., E.S. Ampt and A. Meyburg (1995) - Survey Methods for Transport Planning. Eucalyptus Press, Melbourne.

Rubin, D.B. (1987) - Multiple Inputation for Non-response in Surveys. John Wiley and Sons Inc., New York.

Rubin, D.B. (1983) Conceptual issues in the presence of nonresponse. *In W.G. Madow, I Olkin and D.B. Rubin (eds.) Incomplete Data in Sample Surveys, Vol II : Theory and Bibliographies,* 125-142. Academic Press, New York.

Rubin, D.B. (1976) - Inference and missing data. *Biometrika,* **63**, 581-592.

Särndal, C-E. and B. Swensson (1987) - A general view of estimation for two phases of selection with applications to two-phase sampling and nonresponse. *International Statistical Review,* **55** (3), 279-294.

Särndal, C-E., B. Swensson, B. and J. Wretman. (1992) - Model Assisted Survey Sampling. Springer, Heidelberg.

Sautory, O. (1993) - Redressement d'un échantillon par calage sur marges, INSEE Document de travail N° F9310. *INSEE*, Paris.

Sautory, O. (1995) - La statistique descriptive avec le système SAS, INSEE - Guides N°1-2. *INSEE*, Paris.

Simpson, S. and D. Dorling (1994) - Those missing millions: implications for social statistics of non-response in the 1991 Census. *Journal of Social Policy,* **23** (4) 543-67.

Stopher, P. and C. Stecher (1993) - Blow up: Expanding a complex random sample travel survey. *Transportation Research Record,* **1412**, 10-16.

Thakuriah, P., A. Sen, S. Sööt and E. Christopher (1993) - Non-response bias and trip generation models. *Transportation Research Record,* **1412**, 64-70.

Wermuth, M. (1985) - Non-sampling errors due to non-response in written household travel surveys. *In E.S. Ampt, A.J. Richardson and W. Brög (eds.) New Survey Methods in Transport*, 349-365, VNU Science, Utrecht.

Zmud, J. and C. Arce (1997) - Item non-response in travel surveys: causes and solutions. *Transportation Research Circular*, **E-C008**, II-D/20, TRB, Washington D.C.

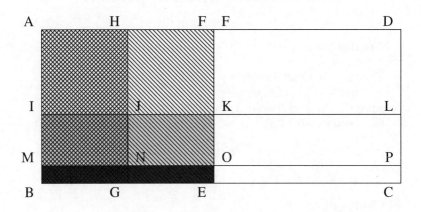

Chapter 11
Imputation with non-ignorable missing values:
a stochastic approach

X. L. Han and J. W. Polak

11 Imputation with non-ignorable missing values: a stochastic approach[1]

X. L. Han and J. W. Polak

Centre for Transport Studies
Department of Civil Engineering
Imperial College of Science Technology and Medicine
UK - London, SW7 2BU

Abstract

This paper presents a new approach to the imputation of missing data, in the presence of non-ignorable non-response. The approach is a Bayesian generalisation of existing expectation maximisation (EM) approaches. The paper outlines the proposed approach and describes an application using data from a travel diary survey and linked follow-up survey. The empirical results are encouraging, indicating that provided some information is available on the nature of the non-response mechanism, the proposed approach is able to significantly reduce the bias in the estimation of relevant population parameters.

Keywords

Imputation, non-ignorable non-response, Bayesian stochastic expectation maximisation (EM), imputation, VATS.

1 Preferred citation: Han, X. L. and J. W. Polak (2003) Imputation with non-ignorable missing values: A stochastic approach, in K. W. Axhausen, J.-L. Madre, J. W. Polak and Ph. L. Toint (eds.) *Capturing Long-Distance Travel*, 171 - 186, Research Studies Press, Baldock.

11.1 INTRODUCTION

Imputation – filling-in missing data with plausible values – is a very common practical technique for handling non-response in surveys. Various procedures of imputation for missing data have been suggested by researchers and practitioners (see, for example, Madow *et al.*, 1983; Little and Rubin, 1987; Schafter, 1997). In this study we will introduce a general imputation approach and apply it to a travel diary survey data.

The travel diary data used in this study was collected as part of the VATS project initiated at the Transport Research Centre, University of Melbourne in the early 1990s and subsequently continued at the Royal Melbourne Institute of Technology. The aim of this project was to assemble a collection of data and analysis tools to underpin the analysis and planning of transport within the Melbourne region. A fuller description of the background and objectives to the VATS project is given in Richardson and Ampt (1993).

The VATS data were collected in a one-day travel diary exercise carried out in the spring of 1994. In total, 6000 households were approached, of which 4637 finally participated in some way in the survey. Each person in a participating household was asked to complete a stage-based travel diary in which they were required to record all their trips and out-of-home activities on the survey day. Following the initial mailing in which the survey forms and instructions were first distributed, up to four reminders were subsequently sent to participants, with the third reminder containing a replacement set of survey forms and instructions. At each reminder, a new travel day was allocated to the potential participant.

In the current context, the key feature of the survey procedure is the inclusion of an auxiliary validation study that provided information on the mobility and demographics of a subset of the main sample frame, including both responders and non-responders to the postal survey.

During the construction of the sample frame, a subset of approximately 10% of the selected households was allocated to a validation study subset. Households in the validation subset were treated identically to those in the main study throughout the main postal survey. However, after the end of the main survey, households in the validation study subset were visited by an experienced interviewer and were strongly pressed to participate in a personal face-to-face interview. In the case of households that had responded to the initial postal survey, the original self-completed form was used as a memory jogger, whereas for households that had not responded to the postal survey a new interview was undertaken.

In the analysis that is presented in this paper we concentrate on the validation sub-sample, which comprised a total of 461 household interviews, 330 of which were undertaken with households that initially responded to the postal questionnaire and 131 of which were undertaken with households that had refused or failed to return the postal questionnaire.

Figure 11.1 is a sketch map showing the sampling structure. To make it a little simpler, we assume that in the validation sub-sample there are no unit and item non-responses. Area ABCD is the total population of interest. Area ABEF is the sample frame of households. Under a good sampling design, ABEF should be representative of ABCD. Area AMOF represents the respondents to the postal survey, among which area AIKF represents the respondents who returned complete questionnaires (no item missing) and area IKOM represents those containing item missing, and area MBEO represents the non-respondents to this survey. If the respondents and the non-respondents are different in the sense of the relevant analysis variables, then area AMOF is not representative of the total population ABCD. Area ABGH is the validation sub-sample in the VATS data. A randomly chosen sub-sample will provide a representation of both ABEF and ABCD (in the sense that they belong to a same population). Area AMNH represents the respondents who also participated in the sub-sample validation interview, among which area AIJH returned complete questionnaire and area IMNJ did not. Area MBGN represents the non-respondents to the postal questionnaire who participated in the sub-sample validation interview.

Figure 11.1   Sampling structure

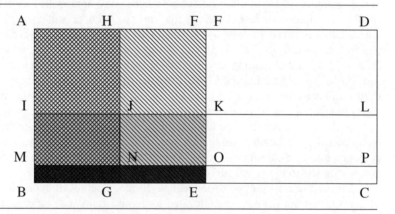

The important fact is that data from area IJNM may provide the information about the item missing mechanism, whereas data from area MNGB may give us the information about the unit missing mechanism.

Suppose $Y = \{Y_{ij}\}$ is the matrix of complete data in the sample (area ABEF), where $i = 1, 2,..., n$ is the unit indicator and $j = 1, 2,..., k$ is the item indicator, Y_i denotes the i-th row of Y.

Denote Y_{obs} as the observed part of Y and Y_{mis} the missing part of Y so that $Y=(Y_{obs}, Y_{mis})$.

Define $R = \{R_i\}$, $i =1,2,..., n$, as the respondent indicator vector with

$$
\begin{cases}
R_i = 0 & i\text{-}th\ unit\ is\ respondent \\
R_i = 1 & i\text{-}th\ unit\ is\ non\text{-}respondent
\end{cases}
$$

and $r = \{r_{ij}\}$ as the item response indicator matrix with

$$\left\{ \begin{array}{ll} r_{ij} = 0 & ij\text{ - th item is not missing} \\ r_{ij} = 1 & ij\text{ - th item is missing.} \end{array} \right.$$

Obviously when $R_i = 1$ all $r_{ij} = 1$ for $j = 1, 2,..., k$.

We will consider an imputation approach, which is based on statistical models, to fill in missing items in area JKON and missing units in area NOEG.

Assume that Y_i are independently, identically distributed draws from some multivariate distribution $f(Y_i ; \theta)$, where θ are unknown parameters associated with f, and (R_i, r_{ij}) belong to some distribution g

$$Prob(Y, R, r; \theta, \beta) = \prod_i f(Y_i, \theta) g(R_i, r_{ij}; \beta \mid Y_i). \quad (1.1)$$

$(R_i, r_{ij} ; \beta \mid Y_i)$, where β are unknown parameters associated with g and β and θ are distinct.

When the missing mechanisms are ignorable, i.e.

$$Prob(R, r; \beta \mid Y) = Prob(R, r; \beta \mid Y_{obs})$$

(ignorability was first defined by Rubin, 1976; see Little and Rubin, 1987 for an extensive presentation and discussion of the concept), the expectaion maximisation (EM) algorithm (Dempster, Laird and Rubin, 1977), which is a widely applicable approach for computing maximum likelihood estimates (MLE) for parametric models when the data are not fully observed, is one of the natural options for imputation because under this condition the maximum likelihood estimates of θ will not involve the missing mechanism g. We must notice that in some problems the E-step in the EM algorithm actually does correspond to filling in the missing data in the sense that it replaces Y_{mis} with its average or expected value $E(Y_{mis} \mid Y_{obs}, \theta)$ under the assumption $\theta = \theta^{(t)}$. In other problems, however, it does not. In particular, when the complete-data probability model f falls in a regular exponential family, E-step actually fills in the missing portions of the complete-data sufficient statistics, rather than Y_{mis}. However, once the EM algorithm has reached its convergence point, we may always take $E(Y_{mis} \mid Y_{obs}, \theta)$ at the final value of θ as the imputation of Y_{mis}, or produce a sample from $Prob(Y_{mis} \mid Y_{obs}, \theta)$ for the multiple imputation (see Rubin, 1987 for the detailed discussion of multiple imputation).

The procedure below is to apply an EM algorithm to impute missing values in VATS data:

- Step 1: Get θ^*, the maximum likelihood estimate of θ, by EM algorithm on data in area AFOM+MNGB;
- Step 2: Impute missing items in area JKON by $E(Y_{mis} \mid Y_{obs}, \theta^*)$ under model f;
- Step 3: Impute missing units in area NOEG by drawing a sample from distribution $f(Y_i ; \theta^*)$.

But strong evidence suggests that neither item nor unit missing tend to be ignorable in travel diary surveys (Polak and Ampt, 1996). And, more importantly, we may obtain the information about the missing mechanism through the analysis of validation data (area IJNM and NMGB) in VATS data and then use it to reduce the biases caused by ignoring the missing mechanism.

While the missing data mechanism is non-ignorable, usually the imputation will involve much more complex distributions because of the conditional distribution of missing data which should be considered is $Prob(Y_{mis} | Y_{obs}, R, r, \theta, \beta)$ rather than $Prob(Y_{mis} | Y_{obs}, \theta)$. The EM algorithm would not be straightforward in most cases.

A derivative of the EM algorithm called *stochastic EM* (Celeux and Diebolt, 1985; Diebolt and Ip, 1996) might be a good alternative to tackle this difficulty. Stochastic EM involves iterating two steps. At S-step in stochastic EM, which is the replacement of E-step in EM algorithm, a single draw is made from $Prob(Y_{mis} | Y_{obs}, \theta^{(t)})$, then at M-step the pseudo-complete sample is used to get the maximum likelihood estimation of $\theta^{(t+1)}$ exactly same as M-step in EM algorithm. Rather than converging to the maximum likelihood of $l(\theta|Y_{obs})$, the M-step in stochastic EM will produce a Markov chain $\{\theta^{(t)}\}$ which converges to a stationary distribution under mild conditions. Once $\{\theta^{(t)}\}$ has converged to the stationary distribution, the estimate of θ may be obtained by sample mean

$$\theta^{\#} = \frac{1}{m} \sum_{t=T}^{T+m} \theta^{(t)}.$$

This estimate does not agree with MLE in general. In the exponential family case $\theta^{\#}$ differs from MLE by $O(1/m)$ (Ip, 1994).

Of course, while the missing data mechanism is non-ignorable we need take a draw from the distribution $Prob(Y_{mis} | Y_{obs}, R, r, \theta, \beta)$ at S-step in stochastic EM and it is not a simple task in many situations. However, consider the fact that

$$Prob(Y_i | R_i, r_{ij}) \propto f(Y_i; \theta) g(R_i, r_{ij}; \beta | Y_i) \quad (1.2)$$

and the relationship expressed by (1.1) we may adopt an MCMC (Markov chain Monte Carlo) technique called *Metropolis-Hastings algorithm* (Metropolis *et al.*, 1953; Hastings, 1970) to produce it indirectly if we may obtain estimation of θ and β somehow.

The following stochastic EM procedure may be used to impute missing values in VATS data:

Step 1: Use validation data (area AHGB) to obtain β^{*}, the estimate of β under model g;

Step 2: Run stochastic EM on data in area AFOM until $\{\theta^{(t)}\}$ converges to the stationary distribution; at M-step adopt model f and at S-step draw the sample by the Metropolis-Hastings algorithm under the probability expressed by (1.2) under the current values $\theta^{(t)}$ and β^{*};

Step 3: Estimate θ by $\theta^{\#}$ and take any set of values produced in the S-step as the single item imputations, or take a few sets of values produced in S-step as the multiple item imputations;

Step 4: Impute the missing units in area NOEG by drawing a sample from distribution

$$Prob(Y_i \mid R_i = 1) \propto f(Y_i; \theta^{\#}) g(R_i = 1; \beta^* \mid Y_i)$$

again through the Metropolis-Hastings algorithm; indirectly.

Toward item imputations, the Bayesian stochastic EM imputation procedure described above tends to have larger variance on the imputed values for single imputation because they are a simple random draw from a plausible multivariate distribution. When the multiple imputation is not of interest we may wish to impute somewhat best-fitted values to those missing items. To reach this target here, we introduce an inhomogeneous Markov chain optimisation method, *simulated annealing*, to find a set of single item imputation values which may maximise the probability function under the current estimated values of parameters, i.e. try to get Y_{mis} which maximise

$$Prob(Y_{misi} \mid Y_{oubi}, R_i = 0) \propto f(Y_i; \theta^{\#}) g(R_i = 0; \beta^* \mid Y_i) \quad (1.3)$$

for all i with not all $r_{ij} = 0$, where $Y_{mis, 1}$ and $Y_{obs,i}$ are the missing part and observed part of unit I, respectively.

Originating from Statistic physics as part of the Markov chain Monte Carlo (Metropolis *et al.*, 1953, Geman and Geman, 1984), simulated annealing is seen as a general technique for approximately solving large combinatorial-optimisation problems when no additional information about the structure of the function to be optimised is used (Kirkpatrick, Gelatt and Vecchi, 1983).

Our version of the simulated annealing algorithm here is very simple: after the estimate of θ is obtained through the Bayesian stochastic EM, say at time $t=t_0$, we use the Metropolis-Hastings algorithm further to produce a series of imputed missing values, denoted as Z^t. Rather than producing them from the distribution expressed by (1.2), denoted as π, we produce Z^t with

$$Prob(Z^t) = c\pi(Z)^{\frac{1}{k_t}}$$

where c is the normalisation constant which depends on the values of k_t and $1 \geq k_t > 0$ is a function of time t.

Notice the fact that

$$if \ \pi(Z_i) > \pi(Z_j) \quad then \ \pi(Z_i)^{\frac{1}{k_t}} > \pi(Z_j)^{\frac{1}{k_t}} \quad \forall \ k_t > 0$$

and the fact that

$$if \ \pi(Z_i) > \pi(Z_j) \quad then \ (\pi(Z_i)/\pi(Z_j))^{\frac{1}{k_t}} = \infty \quad when \ k_t -> 0$$

start from $k_{t0} = 1$ and let $k_t \to 0$ sufficiently slow when $t \to \infty$, we may expect that the simulated annealing algorithm will converge to the maximum probability point (for theory on simulated annealing refer to Laarhoven and Aarts, 1987).

The remainder of the paper is structured as follows. Section 2 presents the unit imputation method on VATS data. Section 3 describes item imputation method on VATS data. Section 4 is a brief concluding remark.

11.2   UNIT IMPUTATION

For simplicity, we assume that each unit contains only 4 items, namely: the size of household, which is an integer from 1 to 8; the number of cars in the household, which is an integer from 0 to 5; the income of the household, which ranges from 1.5 thousand to 170 thousand; and the main interest of this survey, the number of trips made in the household, which is an integer from 0 to 57.

In order to make a comparison we will only use the validation data, which contains 461 household records, to do the imputation, i.e. based on the data of 330 respondents to impute the 131 units of non-respondents. Of course, it will make no sense to compare the imputed values with the true values of each household in unit imputation, so the comparison will be made on the distribution sense, i.e. comparing the distribution of imputation with the true empirical distribution obtained in the validation.

We assume that the data model $f(Y; \theta)$ belongs to a multivariate normal distribution, i.e.

$$f(Y_i) = \frac{1}{(2\pi)^2 |V|^{1/2}} \exp[\frac{1}{2}(Y_i - \mu)'V^{-1}(Y_i - \mu)] \quad \text{for all } i \quad (2.1)$$

where $i = 1, 2, ..., 461$ is the unit index,

$$E(Y_i) = \mu \quad Var(Y_i) = V$$

and thus $\theta = (\mu, V)$. Although the normal model may not fit the data exactly in this case, it can be an effective tool for imputing ordinal data in general (see, for instance, Schafter, 1997).

We further assume that the unit missing mechanism follows a logistic model, i.e.

$$f(R_i | Y_i) = (\frac{e^{Y_i \beta}}{1 + e^{Y_i \beta}})^{R_i} (1 - \frac{e^{Y_i \beta}}{1 + e^{Y_i \beta}})^{1-R_i} \quad \text{for all } i. \quad (2.2)$$

By logistic regression under model (2.2) on the validation data we found that only two variables are significantly relevant to the unit missing – the size of household and the number of cars in the household – and the estimation of β is

$\beta^* =$ -1.035 [intercept],

0.245 [coefficient for size of household],

-0.381 [coefficient for number of cars]

By linear regression under model (2.1) on the validation data of respondents (330 units), we obtained $\theta^* = (\mu^*, V^*)$, the initial estimation of θ, as:

$\mu^* =$ 2.63 [household size],

1.56 [cars],

40.75 [income],

9.79 [trips]

$V^* =$ 1.716 0.612 14.91 6.509

0.612 0.854 14.22 972.2

14.91 14.22 972.2 85.05

6.509 2.769 85.05 82.84

Because we will not consider the item imputation on these 330 units, the initial estimation of θ is also the final one.

Next we will produce a sample of 131 units by the Metropolis-Hastings algorithm (general approach of the Metropolis-Hastings algorithm see Hastings, 1970; Han, 1993; or Gamerman, 1997). Each of the units will (nearly) identically and independently belong to distribution

$$f(Y_i; \theta^* \mid R_i = 1; \beta^*) \propto f(Y_i; \theta^*) f(R_i = 1; \beta^* \mid Y_i)$$

$$= \frac{1}{(2\pi)^2 |V^*|^{1/2}} \exp\left[\frac{1}{2}(Y_i - \mu^*)' V^{-1}(Y_i - \mu^*)\right]\left(\frac{e^{Y_i \beta^*}}{1 + e^{Y_i \beta^*}}\right) \quad (2.3)$$

Now we will compare the distribution of whole validation data, the distribution of respondents in the validation data and the distribution of respondents plus imputed units for non-respondents.

We use mean and standard deviation of all variables to present the corresponding distributions.

Table 11-1 and Table 11-2 are the result. Row 1 shows the means and variances of whole data including respondents and non-respondents; row 2 shows the means and variances of respondents, which will be the estimations of whole data if there are no imputations; row 3 shows the means and variances of average of the 10 imputations.

As a result of the fact that the means and variances of respondents are not too far away from those of the whole data set – which implies that, although the non-response is not ignorable, the influence of non-response is not very strong in this case – the improvement of estimation from our imputation process is not great. However, the imputation process may provide important information about the uncertainty caused by non-response, i.e. it shows the variances (or standard deviations) of those estimations of means and standard deviations of variables.

11.3 ITEM IMPUTATION

Due to some problems of technique with the VATS data we did not receive the original records (in the questionnaire) of the validation data. As a result the necessary information to analyse the mechanism of item missing is unavailable. We will therefore use a simulation method on the validation data to demonstrate the procedure of imputation for the item missing mechanism suggested by us.

We will use the validation data of respondents (330 units) as the base on which we will construct an item missing mechanism, as below. We assume that the first 220 units are under validation so that we are able to get the required information about the parameters of item missing mechanism. Thus we only need to do item imputation on the last 110 units if there are any missing items there.

Table 11-1   Mean of the variables

	Size of family	Number of cars	Income	Number of trips
Validation data	2.698	1.511	38.98	10.02
Respondents	2.633	1.566	40.75	9.79
Unit imputation	2.704	1.543	41.09	10.07
	(sd=0.066)	(sd=0.038)	(sd=2.00)	(sd=0.52)

Table 11-2   Standard deviations of the variables

	Size of family	Number of cars	Income	Number of trips
Validation data	1.324	0.945	30.15	8.733
Respondents	1.310	0.924	31.18	9.102
Unit imputation	1.303	0.935	30.34	8.820
	(sd=0.036)	(sd=0.013)	(sd=1.11)	(sd=0.281)

We further assume:
- there are no missing items on the size of household;
- the missing items on the number of cars are purely at random with

$$Prob(r_{i,2} = 1 \mid Y_i, R_i = 0) = \frac{e^{\eta_1}}{1 + e^{\eta_1}} \quad (3.1)$$

where η_1 is an unknown parameter (we set $\eta_1 = -1$ in the simulation process);

The item missing on household income is dependent on the number of cars and household income (non-ignorable item missing) with

$$Prob(r_{i,3} = 1 \mid Y_i, R_i = 0) = \frac{e^{\eta_2 + \eta_3 Y_{i,2} + \eta_4 Y_{i,3}}}{1 + e^{\eta_2 + \eta_3 Y_{i,2} + \eta_4 Y_{i,3}}} \quad (3.2)$$

where η_2, η_3, η_4 are parameters in the model (we set $\eta_2 = -3$, $\eta_3 = 0.6$, $\eta_4 = 0.025$ in the simulation process), $Y_{i,2}$ and $Y_{i,3}$ are the number of cars and household income in unit j respectively.

The item missing on number of trips is dependent on household income (ignorable item missing) with

$$Prob(\ r_{i,4} = 1 \mid Y_i, R_i = 0) = \frac{e^{\eta_5 + \eta_6 Y_{i,3}}}{1 + e^{\eta_5 + \eta_6 Y_{i,3}}} \quad (3.3)$$

where η_5 and η_6 are the parameters in the model (we set $\eta_5 = -2$, $\eta_6 = 0.025$ in the simulation process).

Simulation
Based on the values of $\{Y_{i,j}\}$ ($I = 1, 2, ..., 330$; $j = 1, 2, 3, 4$) we produce a random matrix $\{r_{i,j}\}$ from distribution (3.1), (3.2) and (3.3) [Notice that $Prob(r_{i,1}=0) = 1$]. All those $Y_{i,j}$ with $r_{i,j} = 1$ are the assumed missing items.

We will produce five such matrices $\{r_{i,j}\}$ to reflect the uncertainty and variations of missing items, and correspondingly we will repeat the imputation procedure five times on these five different $\{r_{i,j}\}$.

Imputation
We will use four methods to impute the missing items for comparison.

- **Mean value imputation**: we simply use the mean value of the same variable observed (i.e. which in validation data and in the responded data) as the imputation value.
- **EM algorithm**: we ignore the item missing mechanism (or equivalently we assume that all items missing are ignorable) and use the standard EM algorithm to do the imputation under model (2.1).
- Bayesian stochastic EM algorithm:
- Step 1: Using the assumed validation data Y_i and $\{r_{ij}\}$ $I=1, 2, ..., 220$ to estimate η through logistic regression under model (3.1), (3.2) and (3.3); using the whole validation data to estimate β under model (2.2);
  Step 2: By maximum likelihood under model (2.1) on the validation data of respondents (220 units), we obtain the initial estimation of $\theta = (\mu, V)$ as

$$\mu^* = \begin{array}{ll} 2.69 & \text{[household size]} \\ 1.62 & \text{[cars]} \\ 41.24 & \text{[income]} \\ 9.65 & \text{[trips]} \end{array}$$

$V^*=$	1.672	0.609	14.50	6.222
	0.609	0.867	13.11	2.400
	14.50	13.11	995.2	75.89
	6.222	2.400	75.89	84.82

Step 3 (item imputation): Based on the relationship

$$\text{Prob}(Y_i \mid R_i = 0, r_{ij}) \propto f(Y_i; \theta) g(R_i = 0, r_{ij}; \eta \mid Y_i)$$

$$(\frac{e^{\eta_2 + \eta_3 Y_{i,2} + \eta_4 Y_{i,3}}}{1 + e^{\eta_2 + \eta_3 Y_{i,2} + \eta_4 Y_{i,3}}})^{r_{i,3}} (\frac{1}{1 + e^{\eta_2 + \eta_3 Y_{i,2} + \eta_4 Y_{i,3}}})^{1 - r_{i,3}} (\frac{e^{\eta_5 + \eta_6 Y_{i,3}}}{1 + e^{\eta_5 + \eta_6 Y_{i,3}}})^{r_{i,4}} (\frac{1}{1 + e^{\eta_5 + \eta_6 Y_{i,3}}})^{1 - r_{i,4}} \quad (3.4)$$

$$= \frac{1}{(2\pi)^2 |V|^{1/2}} \exp[\frac{1}{2}(Y_i - \mu)' V^{-1}(Y_i - \mu)](\frac{1}{1 + e^{Y_i \beta}})(\frac{e^{\eta_1}}{1 + e^{\eta_1}})^{r_{i,2}} (\frac{1}{1 + e^{\eta_1}})^{1 - r_{i,2}}$$

we will use the Metropolis-Hastings algorithm to do the item imputation by systematically visiting the missing items;

Step 4: Re-estimate parameter $\theta = (\mu, V)$ by the maximum likelihood on the pseudo-complete data set (330 units) under model (2.1);

Step 5: Repeat Step 3 and Step 4 fifty times;

Step 6: Using the last 30 iterations in Step 5 to get the final estimation of θ and obtaining the imputed missing items by taking the final state of the Metropolis-Hastings algorithm.

- Bayesian stochastic EM with simulated annealing algorithm:
  Step 1 - Step 6 same as Bayesian stochastic EM;

  Step 7: Under the estimated values $\theta = \theta^{\#}$, $\beta = \beta^*$, $\eta = \eta^*$ we use the Metropolis-Hastings algorithm to do further item imputation by systematically visiting the missing items according to distribution π_k

$$\pi_k \propto [f(Y_i; \theta^{\#}) g(R_i = 0, r_{ij}; \beta, \eta \mid Y_i)]^{\frac{1}{k_t}} \quad (3.5)$$

Here we just take 100 further runs, i.e. $t = 1, 2, 3, \ldots 100$, and set $k_t = 1/t$ although $O(1/\log(t))$ is the sufficient slow speed to reach the maximisation from an arbitrary set of configurations (Geman and Geman 1984, Gidas 1985, Laarhovenand Aarts, 1987).

Define: $bias = E(\hat{y} - y)$ $bias\ coefficient = bias/E(y)$

and $MSE = E(\hat{y} - y)^2$ $MSE\ coefficient = \sqrt{MSE}/E(y)$

Let us use the *bias* and *MSE* to compare the results of four imputation methods with 5 different sets of $\{r_{i,j}\}$ produced by simulation. Table 11-3 shows the bias of three variables by four methods with five runs, Table 11-4 shows the MSE of three variables by four methods with five runs.

The following points should be noted:

When the item missing mechanism is ignorable, the number of cars and the number of trips, under the condition that the other variables are observed in the same unit, EM imputation works well as we might have expected, i.e. it tends to have smaller biases and smaller MSE. However, the Bayesian stochastic EM imputation method, with simulated annealing, works as well as does EM.

In the case that the item missing mechanism is non-ignorable, the income of household, the Bayesian stochastic EM imputation methods, both with and without simulated annealing, perform better than the EM imputation approach because they take the item missing mechanism into consideration.

Table 11-3   Bias and bias coefficient of the imputations

	Mean Imputation		EM Imputation		Bayesian Stochastic EM		Simulated Annealing	
	bias-coef.	bias [%]	bias-coef.	bias [%]	bias-coef.	bias [%]	bias-coef.	bias [%]
Number of cars	0.575	36.8	0.028	1.8	0.060	3.8	0.212	13.5
	-0.800	-51.2	0.197	12.6	0.320	20.4	0.360	22.9
	-0.540	-34.6	0.146	9.3	0.324	20.6	0.270	17.2
	-0.120	7.6	-0.327	20.9	-0.080	-5.1	-0.160	-10.2
	-0.588	-37.6	0.160	10.2	0.235	16.0	0.352	22.4
Average	-0.294	-18.8	0.040	2.6	0.171	10.9	0.201	12.8
Income	25.11	61.5	-11.85	-29.0	0.118	0.2	-1.281	-3.1
	29.68	72.5	-16.71	-40.9	8.125	19.2	-5.363	-13.1
	32.60	79.9	-17.00	-41.6	-9.300	-22.8	-6.136	-15.0
	27.80	68.1	-17.46	-42.8	10.09	24.7	-5.411	-13.2
	33.41	81.8	-17.13	-41.9	-11.07	27.1	-5.159	-12.6
Average	29.72	72.9	-16.03	-39.3	-0.407	0.9	-4.670	-11.4
Number of trips	2.857	29.1	-1.181	-12.0	3.428	35.0	-0.942	-9.6
	2.700	27.5	-1.064	-10.8	-2.433	-24.8	-1.100	-11.2
	-1.000	-10.2	1.425	14.5	1.040	10.6	1.200	12.2
	2.323	23.7	-1.692	-17.2	-1.484	15.1	-1.454	-14.8
	3.500	35.7	-2.060	-21.0	-1.764	-18.0	-1.617	-16.5
Average	2.075	21.2	-0.914	-9.3	0.242	-2.4	-0.782	-7.9

Although the Bayesian stochastic EM imputation, with simulated annealing, tends to have a systematic bias compared with the Bayesian stochastic EM without simulated annealing process in dealing with non-ignorable missing items, the income of household its overall performance (MSE) is much better than the latter due to the huge reduction in variances.

The model-free imputation method, mean imputation, is the worst for all variables in this case, partly due to the fact that the simulation of missing items itself is model-based.

Table 11-4   MSE and MSE coefficient of the imputations

	Mean Imputation		EM Imputation		Bayesian Stochastic EM		Simulated Annealing	
	MSE	M-coef.	MSE	M-coef.	MSE	M-coef.	MSE	M-coef.
Number of cars	1.424		0.611		1.272		0.575	
	1.200		0.350		0.880		0.440	
	0.864		0.396		0.756		0.486	
	0.600		0.462		0.880		0.400	
	1.117		0.614		1.058		0.647	
Average	1.041	65.1%	0.486	44.5%	0.969	62.8%	0.509	45.5%
Income	1942		1308		1516		1189	
	2070		1348		1146		1155	
	2561		1578		1337		1413	
	2264		1594		1894		1280	
	2233		1362		1012		1169	
Average	2214	115.4%	1438	93.0%	1381	91.1%	1241	86.4%
Number of trips	61.6		50.5		95.2		48.4	
	93.0		66.9		69.3		66.1	
	82.2		54.4		55.3		55.6	
	74.4		56.8		77.6		59.1	
	80.2		55.0		67.5		52.4	
Average	78.2	90.3%	56.7	76.9%	72.9	87.2%	56.3	76.6%

11.4   CONCLUDING REMARKS

We have proposed a stochastic approach of imputation for both missing item and unit. The Bayesian stochastic EM imputation, with simulated annealing process, is particularly useful to reduce the biases in dealing with non-ignorable item missing data. In Section 3 we demonstrate that it performs very well in case of non-ignorable items missing, as well as in the case of ignorable items missing.

Of course, its implementation requires some information on the item missing mechanism when the item missing is non-ignorable. Quite often this information may be obtained from the same or relevant surveys such as the validation survey in VATS data and on other occasions they may be available from some other resource. Nowadays more and more survey practitioners and researchers realise the importance of non-response mechanism and consider the implications for the survey protocol and design at the earliest possible point during the survey development.

Another advantage of the stochastic approach of imputation is its flexibility and robustness. The spin-wise imputation through the Metropolis-Hastings algorithm is quite simple to program under various statistical model assumptions. For instance, the removal of the condition on independence between units, which we have imposed on VATS data, will cause no difficulty at all in performing the algorithm: in fact, only minor adjustment in the statistical model is required. As we have shown on VATS data the statistical model assumptions are also quite loose.

Basically we only need to specify some reasonable model on the data structure, i.e. the relationship on variables of interest, and usually the logistic model is quite proper for the missing mechanism. In short, it is fairly straightforward for practitioners and researchers to write a computer program to perform the imputation task using the Bayesian stochastic approach for a specific survey data set. Software for general use should also not be too difficult to produce.

11.5   REFERENCES

Celeux, G. and J. Diebolt (1985) - The SEM algorithm: a probabilistic teacher algorithm derived from the EM algorithm for the mixture problem. *Comp. Statist. Quart.,* **2,** 73-82.

Dempster, A.P., N.M. Laird and D.B. Rubin (1977) - Maximum likelihood estimation from incomplete data via the EM algorithm (with discussion). *Journal of the Royal Statistical Society Series B,* **39,** 1-38.

Diebolt, J and E.H.S. Ip (1996) - Stochastic EM: Method and application. *In W.R. Gilks, S.Richardson and D.J. Spiegelhalter (eds.) Markov Chain Monte Carlo in Practice,* 259-273, Chapman and Hall, London.

Gamerman, D. (1997) - Markov Chain Monte Carlo: Stochastic Simulation for Bayesian Inference. Chapman and Hall, London.

Geman, S. and D. Geman (1984) - Stochastic relaxation, Gibbs distributions, and the Bayesian restoration of images. *IEEE Proc. Pattern Analysis and Machine Intelligence,* **6**, 721-741.

Gidas, B. (1985) - Nonstationary Markov Chains and convergence of the Annealing Algorithm. *J.Statis. Phys.,* **39**, 73-131.

Han, X.-L. (1993) - Markov Chain Monte Carlo and Sampling Efficiency. *PhD thesis*, University of Bristol, Bristol.

Hastings, W.K. (1970) - Monte Carlo sampling methods using Markov chains and their applications. *Biometrika*, **57**, 97-109.

Ip, E.H.S. (1994) - A stochastic EM estimator in the presence of missing data-theory and applications. *Technical report, Department of Statistics,* Stanford University, Palo Alto.

Laarhoven, P.J.M. van and E.H.L. Aarts (1987) - Simulated Annealing: Theory and Applications. R. Reidel Publishing Company, Dordrecht.

Little, R.J.A. and D.B. Rubin (1987) - Statistical Analysis with Missing Data. John Wiley and Sons Inc., New York.

Madow, W.G., I. Olkin and D.B. Rubin (eds.) (1983) - Incomplete Data in Sample Surveys, Theory and Bibliographies **2**. Academic Press, New York.

Metropolis, N., A.W. Rosenbluth, M.N. Rosenbluth, A.H. Teller and E. Teller (1953) - Equations of state calculations by fast computing machines. *The Journal of Chemical Physics,* **21**, 1087-1092.

Polak, J.W. and E.S. Ampt (1996) - An analysis of wave response and nonresponse effects in travel diary surveys. *Proceedings 4th International Conference on Survey Methods in Transport*, Steeple Aston, September 1996.

Richardson, A.J. and E.S. Ampt (1993) - The Victoria Integrated Travel, Activities and Land-Use Toolkit. *VITAL Working Paper,* **VWP93/1**, Transport Research Centre, University of Melbourne.

Rubin, D.B. (1976) - Inference and missing data. *Biometrika ,* **63**, 581-592.

Rubin, D.B. (1987) - Multiple Imputation for Non-response in Surveys. John Wiley and Sons Inc., New York.

Schafter, J.L. (1997) - Analysis of Incomplete Multivariate Data. Chapman and Hall, London.

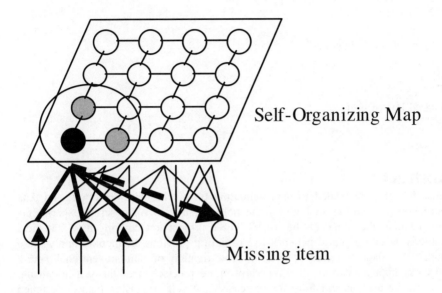

Self-Organizing Map

Missing item

Chapter 12
New correction methods: Neural nets and self-organised maps

S. Midenet and F. Fessant

12   New correction methods: Neural nets and self-organising maps[1]

S. Midenet and F. Fessant

DEST
INRETS
F – 94110 Arcueil

Abstract

This chapter is dedicated to data validation (erroneous data detection) and data correction (imputation methods) in the field of surveys. We describe experiments conducted in the scope of the MEST-TEST project for studying new statistical methods based on neural networks. Considering previous attempts to apply these models for data correction tasks, the investigation of non-conventional neural networks appears worthwhile. We show more precisely that the self-organising map can be used successfully for these tasks. A self-organising map is designed and calibrated according to available observations, described through a set of correlated variables handled together. The map can then be used both to detect erroneous data and to impute values to partial observations. These two processes can be associated in an integrated system, first to discard atypical observations that are declared as being erroneous, and secondly to perform imputation on the remaining observations. We experiment with this principle on the vehicle description file from the MEST pilot surveys database. We show that the performances of our imputation model are very promising compared to other classical methods, and that the use of a self-organising map for data correction provides an integrated and performing system for data validation, data correction and data analysis.

Keywords

Erroneous data detection, imputation methods, surveys, neural networks, self-organising map (SOM).

---

[1] Preferred citation: Midenet S. and F. Fessant (2003) New correction methods: Neural nets and self-organised maps, in K. W. Axhausen, J.-L. Madre, J. W. Polak and Ph. L. Toint (eds.) *Capturing Long-Distance Travel*, 187 – 204, Research Studies Press, Baldock.

12.1   THE NEED FOR CORRECTION METHODS IN SURVEYS

Non-responses and erroneous data remain impossible to avoid in surveys. Their treatment is known to be critical, and time and money consuming. Data treatments consist in detecting erroneous and missing data, and giving them a correct value thanks to an imputation procedure. The imputation procedure depends whether it deals with total non-response – none of the variables of interest is measured for an observation – or with item non-response – only partial information is obtained from a participating respondent. Our investigations concern item non-responses and imputation techniques that apply when only few variables are missing simultaneously. Indeed, total or near total non-responses usually require different types of methods to be handled, based on re-weighting rather than imputation (Little and Rubin, 1987; Armoogum and Madre, 1996).

The purpose of imputation techniques is to assign a value to missing items, with the underlying hypothesis that available items provide enough information to allow the reconstruction of the missing ones. The most commonly-used imputation methods are:

- **deduction** methods: a missing value is deduced through logical rules from the other items of the same observation;
- **substitution** methods: a missing value is replaced by the corresponding value of a similar observation ; this similar respondent can be chosen in the current survey (hot-deck methods) or in other sources (cold-deck methods);
- **prediction** methods: the whole data set is used to build a model for predicting one item value given correlated items. Among classical prediction imputation methods, we can mention class mean imputation and regression-based approaches.

The detection of erroneous data is often a hand-driven or hand-made procedure. Beside straightforward methods for getting rid of coarsely erroneous items – like range validity checking or logical rules verification – it remains very difficult to design an automatic procedure for discarding erroneous data.

In the scope of the MEST-TEST project, we wanted to handle this unavoidable problem of data correction by investigating different and complementary aspects of this issue; we studied several techniques for imputation and error detection, some of them classical and some more innovative, in order to contribute to improve both theoretical methods and computing techniques. The FUNDP research group (Namur, B) concentrated their effort on improving the automation of incoherence detection and imputation method choices thanks to intelligent correction procedures using suitable artificial intelligent computing technologies (see Chapter 13); the Imperial College research group (London, UK) experimented with the expectation minimisation algorithm and its potential as an imputation paradigm (see Chapter 9). At INRETS we have investigated other new statistical methods, the neural network models.

This chapter begins with a state-of-the-art review concerning this application field of neural networks. We then discuss our motivations for investigating the self-organising map architecture and describe the basic principles we propose for using this model for data correction tasks. Then we report our experiments and results on the vehicle description files coming from the MEST Pilot Surveys.

12.2 NEURAL NETWORKS AS PREDICTION METHODS FOR IMPUTATION

12.2.1 Neural networks models for data correction

Neural network (NN) models have been intensively studied for the last fifteen years. They are usually presented as a particular kind of non-parametrical statistical models. Their most interesting characteristics are non-linear modelling capacity, robustness to noisy data and ability to deal with high dimensional data (Hertz *et al.*, 1991; Rumelhart *et al.*, 1986). The multi-layered perceptron (MLP) is one of the most popular NN models and has been widely used for practical applications during the last decade; its performances as a non-linear regression model have been frequently proven. The radial basis function (RBF) model is another kind of multi-layered feed-forward model that has also become popular (Bishop, 1995). Neural network models can provide an alternative to classical prediction imputation methods. Several authors have already investigated this use of NN models but very few attempts to apply them to real surveys or census data have been published.

12.2.2 Item imputation with multi-layered feed-forward neural networks

Most of the publications on this topic concern the multi-layered feed-forward network and, more precisely, the MLP model. The imputation scheme usually exploited consists in training one multi-layered feed forward network to predict one or more variables given the other correlated variables; variables to be predicted stand as output nodes in the neural network, whereas correlated variables stand as input nodes (see Figure 12.1). The learning phase – or calibration – uses all the complete observations. After learning, missing values can be imputed with the network's output. Several authors have successfully applied this imputation principle in various domains, for instance Lopez-Vazquez (1997), Murtagh *et al.* (1998), Sharpe and Solly (1995).

In the field of real size surveys or census data analysis, Nordbotten (1996) uses an MLP to impute values on the Norwegian 1990 population census data. He exploits information from register data source as input to a single MLP that gives the whole set of survey variables. The author validates the resulting model with the estimation of population proportions: he shows how the NN model can contribute to improve statistical estimates based on imputed values for an entire population, compared with traditional estimates.

Semmence (1997) tests feed-forward multi-layered neural network models for missing data imputation on the British family resource survey. He first reports preliminary studies where he compares RBF and MLP architectures with alternative classical imputation methods. He uses as many neural networks as there are variables to impute; only complete observations are used during learning.

Figure 12.1   Imputation scheme with a multi-layered feed-forward neural
               network

Input layer   Hidden layer   Output layer
Correlated Variables   *variable to be imputed*

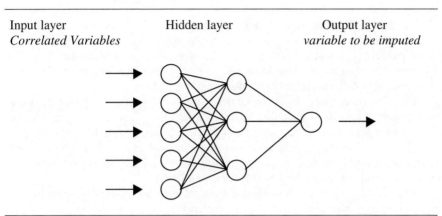

The conclusion from this first stage is promising: neural networks consistently outperform the other methods investigated, the RBF network giving the best results. The author then reports the design of an operational system based on RBF network imputation model and tested on several annual Family Resource Surveys. It appears that the results of the operational system are disappointing. After reading the publications one can assume that the main problem lies in the necessity to make use of enough data for every network to be trained, while keeping only complete data. The system creates only a small number of networks because of the lack of training data, and the learning process does not occur properly.

Cruddas *et al.* (1997) evaluate a feed-forward multi-layered neural network model as a possible alternative to hot-deck methods for imputation in the UK decennial census. The reported experiments concern the 1991 census and six variables to be imputed. Six different feed-forward neural networks are trained, one for each variable; only the complete observations are used, some values being artificially discarded for model evaluation. Cruddas *et al.* report their comparison between the NN system and the hot-deck system generally used for the decennial census treatment. A preliminary test shows that the neural network solution leads to consistent shape for imputed variables distributions, but the operational system based on neural networks underperforms compared to the hot-deck system. Very few details on the NN system are given but one can suspect unsatisfying learning conditions; the lack of complete observations, among other circumstances, may explain such disappointing results.

In any case it appears clearly that this simple imputation scheme can reasonably be considered only if there are few different simultaneous missing items combinations, or if the missing items are concentrated on the same few variables. Standard supervised multi-layered feed-forward networks need a large amount of data – complete data – to be calibrated. These conditions are hardly ever satisfied in real size missing data applications, like survey correction. That is the main reason why experiments with NN systems appear promising on small size test sets but disappointing in a real size application context.

12.2.3 Towards other neural network-based solutions for data correction tasks

Consequently, it is worth looking for some more sophisticated neural networks solutions that enable us to take incomplete observations into account, and to deal simultaneously with several different dimensions to impute.

The first interesting solution consists in investigating particular network architectures and/or data encoding schemes where the missing data is taken into account in a specific way. Some authors propose to code explicitly the lack of a value – known / unknown – for each variable (Vamplew *et al.*, 1996; Muller *et al.*, 1998); or to use thermometric coding (Mitra and Pal, 1995) where the lack of a value can be naturally represented (Muller *et al.*, 1998).

The use of a recurrent multi-layered neural network constitutes a promising alternative, as it enables the use of data with missing items occurring on the input variables, and even allows us to give them values during the same process of predicting the output value (Gingras and Bengio, 1996). Feedback connections are added between hidden units and input units. The basic idea of the model is to use the hidden units to predict an output, and at the same time to capture the relations between the input variables that contribute to the prediction. The network is trained to minimise an output function thanks to a specific adaptation of the back-propagation algorithm called *back-propagation through time*. The imputation process and the output prediction process are performed and learned simultaneously. Considering that this solution for handling simultaneously several missing dimensions in a data set appears both very attractive and more mature than the coding scheme based solutions, we decided to experiment such a model in the scope of the TEST project (Fessant and Midenet, 1999). Our conclusions were not very encouraging. The recurrent model is quite difficult to master and calibrate. Moreover, such a model seems well suited for *using* incomplete items in the explanatory variables, but not for *imputing* values to them.

We turned to a third solution based on another kind of neural network model, to take incomplete observations into account and to handle several dimensions in the imputation process simultaneously. The self-organising map – or SOM – is a well known and quite widely used neural network model that belongs to the unsupervised neural network category concerned with classification processes. We show in the following sections how such a paradigm enables us to represent the joint distribution of a whole set of variables, and to use this representation for data correction (both error detection and imputation).

12.3 THE SELF-ORGANISING MAP

A self-organising map is a neural network model made out of a set of prototypes (or nodes) organised on a map which is a 2-dimensional grid, as depicted in Figure 12.2. Each prototype j has fixed coordinates in the map and adaptive coordinates W_j called *weights* in the input space. The input space designates the definition space of the observations.

Two distance measures are defined, one in the original input space and one on the map. Let us call:

N :   number of input units (dimension of the input space);

i :   subscript used for input dimensions;

d_N :   distance in the input space (we use Euclidian distance);

X :   observation (N-dimensional vector);

K :   number of nodes in the map;

j :   subscript used for the nodes (also called prototypes);

d :   distance in the map between nodes (we use Euclidian distance and integer coordinates in the map);

Y_j :   activity level of node j (scalar);

W_j :   input weight vector of node j (N-dimensional vector);

The self-organising process consists in slightly moving the prototypes in the data definition space – i.e. adjusting W – according to the data distribution. The distinguishing characteristic of the model lies in the fact that the W adjustment is performed while taking into account the neighbouring relations between prototypes in the map. The weight vectors $\{W_j, 1 \leq j \leq K\}$ are gradually adjusted according to observations as follows.

At time t:

1. presentation of a randomly selected observation X (t);
2. selection of the best matching node j* called the *image-node*, such that: $d_N (X(t), W_{j*}(t)) = \min_j d_N (X(t), W_j(t))$;
3. computation of the activity pattern in the map by determining image-node's neighbourhood:
$Y_j(t) = h_{j*}(j,t) = h(d(j,j^*), t)$
with h_{j*} being a decreasing function of the distance in the map between node j and image-node j*, and whose extent in the map also decreases with time;
4. learning for all nodes in the map:

$$W_j (t+1) = W_j(t) + \Delta W_j(t)$$
$$W_j(t) = \varepsilon(t) . Y_j(t) . (X(t) - W_j(t)) = \varepsilon(t) . h_{j*}(j,t) . (X(t) - W_j(t))$$

with $\varepsilon(t)$ decreasing with time for stabilisation purposes.

Such a learning law $(\Delta W = \alpha(X-W))$ makes the weight vector move in the input space and get closer to the observation. The term $h_{j*}(j,t)$ gives a learning ability to the image-node and its direct neighbours. The neighbourhood function $h_{j*}(j,t)$ and the learning rate $\varepsilon(t)$ are defined as follows (Ritter *et al.*, 1989):

$$h_j (k,t) = \exp \left(\frac{-d^2(j,k)}{2\sigma^2(t)} \right)$$

with t_{max} being the number of learning steps, σ_i, σ_f, ε_i and ε_f the learning parameters

$$\varepsilon(t) = \varepsilon_i \cdot (\frac{\varepsilon_f}{\varepsilon_i})^{\frac{t}{t_{max}}}$$

$$\sigma(t) = \sigma_i \cdot (\frac{\sigma_f}{\sigma_i})^{\frac{t}{t_{max}}}$$

The self-organising map is traditionally used for classification purpose. The exploitation phase consists in associating an observation with the closest prototype, called the image-node. The mapping between observations and prototypes is then said to preserve topological relations insofar as observations that are close in the original input space will be associated with prototypes that are close on the map. For a complete description of the self-organising model, please refer to Kohonen (1995).

Figure 12.2   The self-organising map model

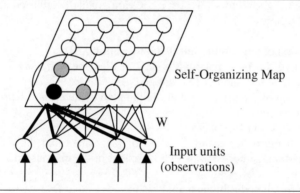

Self-Organizing Map

W

Input units
(observations)

12.4   DATA IMPUTATION AND VALIDATION WITH ONE SELF-ORGANISING MAP

12.4.1   Designing a self-organised map

Once the described entity on which to perform the data correction tasks has been identified, the point is to isolate a set of correlated variables that contribute to defining and specifying this entity. The idea is to take all these variables into account for the model design; the data correction processes will consider all of them together. The standard self-organising map process is then applied, as described in the previous section. The selected correlated variables define the input space; the map is gradually developed based on observations from the data set.

It is important to point out that all the available observations can intervene in the map's development, even the incomplete ones. The principle is quite straightforward. When an observation with missing items is presented, the missing variables are simply ignored when distances between observation and nodes – d_N (X, W_j) – are computed, using only the available dimensions. Such a principle is applied both for selecting the image-node – step 2 – and for updating weights – step 4.

The capacity of the SOM to deal with missing data during the learning and exploitation phases has already been pointed out. Samad and Harp (1992) have tested it on different artificial problems. They showed that for the applications studied, the model degradation is not linearly correlated with the rate of missing data: up to some degree of incompleteness, missing data do not damage the clustering performance of the SOM. The authors also noticed that performances are always better when incomplete examples are used during the weight update, compared to training on the complete examples only; the difference is slight for low dimensional problems but significant for high dimensional ones.

Ibbou (1998) confirms these conclusions with his own empirical results, obtained on both artificial classification tasks and on application with socio-economic data. He shows that the map distortion measure he proposes increases smoothly with the proportion of missing items used during calibration, until a threshold proportion – 50 % in his application – where the degradation becomes substantial. This threshold can be even higher when the original classes are easily separable. Ibbou also checks that for a given proportion, concentration of missing items on few variables is much more penalising than equal distribution.

12.4.2 SOM use for imputation of missing data

The principle of the SOM-based imputation model is illustrated in Figure 12.3. When an incomplete observation is being presented to the SOM, then the missing variables are ignored during the selection of the image-node. The incomplete observation is associated with an image-node and neighbour's values in the missing dimensions are used for imputation. The imputation process can be described as follows :

1. presentation of an incomplete observation on the input layer;
2. selection of the image-node by minimising the distance between observation and prototypes *in the available dimensions only*; the other dimensions corresponding to missing values are simply ignored during the image-node determination;
3. selection of the activation group composed of image-node's neighbours in the map;
4. determination of the value given to the missing item based on the weights of the activation group's nodes in the missing dimension.

This particular way of exploiting a SOM has been already studied and applied to another category of regression-type problems. The LASSO model (stands for Learning Associations by Self-Organisation (Midenet and Grumbach, 1994)), consists in associating output vectors to input vectors through a map, after self-organising it on the basis of both input and desired output vectors given altogether. The LASSO model had been tested on pattern recognition tasks (Midenet and Grumbach, 1994; Idan and Chevallier, 1991). The use of LASSO for recognition of phonemes or hand-written digits leads to good recognition rates and provides interesting abilities concerning knowledge representation.

More recently, Ibbou (1998) analysed the SOM-based imputation process. We have already mentioned his experiment concerning the SOM model robustness regarding incomplete observations during learning. He noticed that the same robustness could be observed for the imputation process relative to the missing data rate, even if the imputation process is obviously sensitive to the wrong classification of observations due to missing values. The author recommends the use of such an imputation method on homogeneous classes, and for sufficiently correlated variables.

Figure 12.3   The self-organising map model for imputation

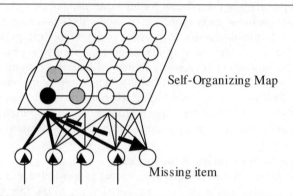

12.4.3   SOM use for erroneous data detection

The self-organising map can be seen as a vector quantification method. Knowing that the quantification error can provide a way to measure the typicality of an observation, the self-organising map proves useful for the detection of erroneous data. The basic idea is to use distances between image-nodes and observations as an indicator of the erroneous character of an observation. The map is used to detect erroneous data in the following way:

A.   Presentation of each observation from the learning set. This step allows the computation for each node of the SOM of the mean value of its distance to observations associated to it ; let us call it *dist_mean(j)* for node j;

B.   followed by:

   1)   presentation of a new observation X from the test set;

   2)   selection of image-node j* by minimising distance between the observation and the prototypes in all the dimensions;

   3)   determination of the measure of representativeness CR(X) for the observation X. This measure compares the distance between X and its image-node j*, with the mean distance *dist_mean (j*)*:

$$CR\,(X) = exp \; \frac{-d_N(X,W_{j^*})}{2dist\_mean(j^*)}$$

4)   if CR(X) < *threshold* then X is suspected of being erroneous.

A low CR measure indicates an observation unusually far from its representative node. That can lead us to suspect that there is an erroneous value in the observation and to check it further. Grabowski (1998) also proposes this kind of measure to detect erroneous observations in databases, although he does not give any experimental results.

12.5   APPLICATION ON MEST PILOT SURVEY

The three waves of the MEST-TEST pilot survey gave project participants the opportunity to experiment with data correction methods on common data sets. FUNDP and INRETS research teams agreed to work on the vehicle description file, with common calibration and test files, in order to compare all the studied imputation methods among which the SOM-based model.

12.5.1   MEST vehicle description

The MEST-TEST pilot survey includes a section devoted to the description of a household's vehicles. It gives information such as owner, main user, type of vehicle, participation in a car sharing scheme, year of purchase, mileage, etc. We decided to focus on variables describing vehicle usage in terms of annual mileage: this entity is described with a set of correlated variables that can be described together and that are not a matter for deduction-type imputation methods.

We selected the following variables:

- presence of a catalytic converter (or cat) with 2 categories {yes,no};
- year of purchase (or yop);
- total mileage given by odometer reading (or current);
- mileage during last 12 months estimated by respondent (or vmt).

The vehicle description file, with observations gathered from the three pilot surveys, initially holds 1050 observations. The rate of missing data is relatively high: 7 % for cat, 6 % for yop, 10 % for current and 11 % for vmt ; only 860 observations out of 1050 are complete.

12.5.2   Data sets' constitution for calibration and test

Our concern was to test the SOM-based imputation model and to compare it with classical imputation methods. It was not possible to keep real non-responses for which we could not calculate the imputation error. We decided to use one part of the complete observations set for testing the imputation model on artificially-generated missing items. One third of the complete observations were selected randomly for the creation of the testing set.

Although incomplete observations can be taken into account during a map's development, as previously mentioned in Section 4.1.2, we did not use incomplete observations for the model calibration. The learning set was chosen to contain the two-thirds remaining complete observations. The comparison of the SOM results with other more classical methods is made more equitable when the same set of observations are strictly used for calibration.

12.5.3 The map design

The four selected variables defining the input space observations from the learning set are used to gradually calibrate the self-organising map.

The **number of learning steps** t_{max} has been kept fixed and chosen so that each observation can be presented 100 times on average. We know from previous experience with the SOM model that this is sufficient and that the self-organising process is not overly sensitive to this parameter.

However, the **size of the map** and the **coding** of the observations are known to be critical for the calibration phase. They both have a strong influence on the selective treatment among variables that is performed by the map.[2] We studied each of these two parameters in order to point out their influence on map self-organisation and on imputation results. For tuning these parameters, we experimented with a range of values for each of them and looked at the average of 10 imputation results given by 10 maps with different initial weights. We proceeded as follows.

Concerning the size of the map or K number of nodes, we used a square map in order to avoid border effects due to the shape of the map. We experimentally determined the size of the map by testing a whole range of values between 2 x 2 and 7 x 7. The best size was found to be 4 x 4. A smaller size does not allow the capture of the data distribution in a satisfactory way, whereas a larger size leads to a description that reveals itself as specific to the learning set (overfitting).

Concerning the coding of the variables, we used previous experience with the model and adopted the following coding scheme (Midenet and Grumbach, 1994). The numerical variables are normalised; each one is represented by one input unit. The categorical variable (*cat*) is represented with two input units corresponding to the two categories (yes, no). The unit associated with the represented category is set to one, whereas the other unit is zero. We end up with five input nodes defining the input space. The significance given to each variable during calibration is tuned thanks to parameters called *coding values*; they are used for weighting the input dimensions during distance computation. These values M have to be fixed experimentally. We ended up with the following: $M_{cat} = 0.5$, $M_{yop} = 10$, and M equal to 1 for *current* and *vmt*. The influence of the coding values on imputation results and on the map organisation is further discussed in Fessant and Midenet (1999).

12.6 THE DESIGNED SOM

Figure 12.4 presents the weight maps for the SOM we selected for producing the

---

[2] The intrinsic dimensionality of the map (which is 2-dimensional in our case) has been intentionally kept fixed despite its influence on the self-organising process. Indeed this process can be implemented with a 3-dimensional 'map' (or more) which obviously leads to a more detailed and complete description of the data distribution by the prototypes. On the other hand a 2-dimensional map enables the analyst to benefit from the visual data analysis abilities provided by the SOM model, as illustrated in Section 6.

results reported in this chapter. For each input unit the weights **W** of its connections with the map nodes are represented as in the map. There are as many weight maps as input dimensions: two weight maps for the *cat* variable – one for each category – and one weight map for each numerical variable. A weight value is represented by a square with the following colour code: a *dark* square means a low weight whereas *light* square means a high value.

The weight maps reveal some relationships between the variables. Areas representing categorical variables are easily distinguishable as they correspond to light squares on the weight maps. For example, we can observe that the presence of a catalytic converter (*cat*) is linked to the year of purchase (*yop*); the probability of having a converter is higher for recent cars: the representing areas overlap. It seems more difficult to relate total mileage (*current*) and mileage during the previous 12 months (*vmt*) to catalytic converter presence (*cat*) and to year of purchase (*yop*). High *current* values are associated with old age and high *vmt* values; mean *current* values may be associated with various *vmt* and *yop*. Recent years for *yop* are associated with low *current* values and high *vmt* values.

It is important to notice that this qualitative analysis performed by the SOM is stable: given the coding scheme and experimental conditions, several maps calibrated from different initial weights lead to the same qualitative organisation: we will see in the following section that these maps also lead to the same quantitative imputation results with a narrow distribution of the error rates.

Figure 12.4   Selected 4 by 4 self-organising map: the weight maps

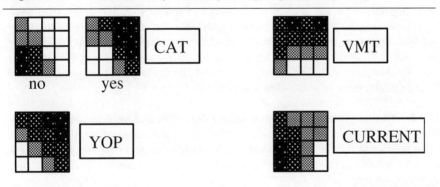

12.7   DATA VALIDATION AND CORRECTION WITH THE DESIGNED SOM

12.7.1   Imputation results

Imputation results for the testing set are presented in Table 12-1 in terms of mean squared error for the numerical variables and in terms of error percentage for *cat*; we also report the standard deviation for imputation errors over ten other SOMs calibrated under the same experimental conditions but with different initial weights. These results concern the SOM-based imputation model with the activation group reduced to the image-node; please refer to Fessant and Midenet (1999) for an analysis of the activation group influence. The results are compared to those obtained on the same databases and variables by the FUNDP research team. The FUNDP's imputation system is described in detail in Lothaire (1999). It allows the use of several standard imputation methods that are respectively for the variables studied:

- Hot-deck with "year of production" (yop) as auxiliary variable for "catalytic converter" (cat) imputation;
- regression, function of current for *yop* imputation;
- regression, function of *yop* for current imputation;
- regression, function of *yop* for each current value for *vmt* imputation.

Table 12-1 presents FUNDP's best result for each variable. Let us stress the fact that SOM results are obtained through one single model for the whole set of variables simultaneously. The SOM-based method leads to better results for 3 out of 4 variables: *vmt* is the only one that is better imputed with a classical imputation method.

The main errors on the *cat* variable come from middle-aged vehicles (*yop* from 1992 to 1994) which almost equally have or do not have a converter. Errors are less numerous for old or new vehicles: the correlation between *yop* and *cat* is clear in these cases. It should be interesting to use additional information like year of *production* (which may be earlier than year of *purchase*) and motor size, because in many countries catalytic converters have been made compulsory at different times depending on the year of production and motor size. We could then have been more precise in the imputation of the *cat* variable. Concerning the *yop* variable, errors mainly come from old vehicles; atypical *yop* values like the seventies or the sixties are difficult to impute. *Vmt* and *current* values seem difficult to impute; we show in the next section that our model is severely damaged because of erroneous values in the observations.

12.7.2   Global system for erroneous data detection and imputation
We noticed a lot of suspicious values in the raw vehicle description file: a *current* value inferior to the *vmt* value, or either *current* value or *vmt* value equal to 0; such an observation can obviously be suspected to contain erroneous data (or missing data with a wrong code).

Table 12-1   Comparison of the imputation results for the whole test set (error percentage, mean squared error – MSE)

Variable	Measure of error	SOM		Standard methods	
		Mean	St. dev	Mean	Method
Catalytic converter	% error	22.0	1.60	39.0	Hot-deck
Year of production	% error	4.5	0.09	4.8	Regression
Current mileage	MSE	46300	580	49050	Regression
Annual mileage	MSE	11150	170	8080	Regression

For the previous experiment these kinds of observations were not discarded from the testing set.

However, they should not be considered for the standard imputation process before being checked and corrected; besides, they lead to high error measures that must not be attributed to the imputation method. We propose to use the erroneous data detection ability of the self-organising map in order to isolate and discard atypical observations that need further data checking; then the imputation process can be performed on the remaining non-suspicious observations.

Using the selected SOM, we discarded from the artificial test set the 10% of data with the lowest CR measure (see Section 12.4.3). These observations were declared not treatable with our imputation model: they stand too far from the main part of the distribution to be treated properly and deserve further checking. The 90% of observations with the highest CR measure have been separately tested: they constitute the clean testing set. Imputation error rates obtained on this reduced testing set are given in Table 12-2.

Applying the model on non-atypical observations significantly improves our numerical results for *current* and *vmt* variables: the SOM model leads to very good results for all variables. These encouraging results show that our erroneous data detection method can be used advantageously to discard atypical observations (almost surely erroneous), to declare them as non-treatable and reach very good results on the remaining observations.

Table 12-2   Imputation results on non-atypical observations with the elected SOM (error percentage, mean squared error – MSE)

Variable	Measure of error	Value
Catalytic converter	% error	23.0
Year of production	% error	4.5
Current mileage	MSE	43350
Annual mileage	MSE	6910

12.7.3   Additional results

The good behaviour of the self-organising map-based model in data correction tasks has been confirmed by other results obtained with another database. The *trip description* file of the 1993–94 French National Personal Transport Survey gave us the opportunity to work on a large real-size data set, and to benefit from both the *raw file* of trip descriptions right after coding and *the cleaned file* established by the SES-MELTT Department from the French Ministry of Transport. These two files enable us to compare our method with the actual correction process. We worked on the following correlated variables: trip duration, crow-flight distance, transport mode (five categories) and trip purpose (three categories).

We compared the SOM model to other classical imputation methods like the hot-deck method or multilayered perceptron, which necessitate the calibration of one specific model per variable to impute. The global results obtained with the SOM are satisfying compared to those of the other tested imputation methods, insofar as a single map has been used instead of variable-specific models. The MLP model outperforms the others on numerical variables thanks to its ability for function approximation, whereas the SOM model is a prototype-based method. We noticed that categorical variables are difficult to impute whatever model is used.

We have extensively investigated the effect of the categorical data coding values on the imputation results and on map organisation. The coding values used for the categorical variables enable us to control their influence during the self-organising process as they affect the weights in the distance computation during image node selection. It appears that the optimal coding values of categorical variables do not lie in the same area for each variable we want to impute. A compromise solution was found, the objective being the imputation of all the variables with one single SOM model: medium coding values for each categorical variable gives satisfactory results for all the variables.

Concerning the erroneous data detection process, we applied the same principle as previously described in Section 12.4.3. This method enables us to detect almost half of the hand-corrected observations (erroneous observations), while detecting less than 10% of non-corrected ones (likely to be non-erroneous). Our experiments and results are extensively described in Fessant and Midenet (1998 and 1999).

12.8 CONCLUSIONS

Our experiments on the MEST-TEST pilot surveys vehicle file confirm that a single self-organised map can be designed and calibrated for the treatment of **a whole set of variables**. Such a property is valuable insofar as it allows consistency while imputing missing items wherever they stand in the observation, and the avoidance of a sequential imputation process with different imputation models for different items. If the number of variables becomes too large a single map may not be sufficient, unless its size and/or intrinsic dimension increases too. However, we have shown in our example that a compromise map may be found in order to treat all the variables of interest together. The size of the map and the coding values for the observations constitute crucial parameters for a compromise map to be found; they can be tuned through a cross-validation type process.

These results also confirm that the **same map used for imputation can be used to detect suspicious observations**. Even if such a tool does not allow the detection of all kind of erroneous data but only of atypical observations that will have to be checked afterward, it enables us to deal simultaneously and with the same model with missing item imputation and erroneous data detection.

Being a prototype-based method, the self-organising map requires significantly less learning observations for calibration than other methods, especially the multi-layered feed-forward neural network based model. This property again may be very important in practice.

The self-organising map is not a black-box type model. On the contrary, the calibration process can be easily interpreted, as illustrated with the weight maps analysis in our vehicle description example. Besides, the SOM model has mainly and traditionally been used for non-linear data analysis and visualisation tasks.

Further experiments for investigating the self-organising map for data correction tasks still have to be carried out. The exploitation of incomplete observations deserves further investigation: it would be very useful to clarify under what conditions the use of incomplete observations during calibration could improve imputation results; that would add a significant argument in favour of SOM's use in the data correction tasks.

12.9   REFERENCES

Armoogum, J. and J.L. Madre (1996) - Non-response correction in the 1993-94 NPTS, the example of daily trips. *Proc. 4th International Conference on Survey Methods in Transport*, 342-361, Steeple Aston, September 1996.

Bishop, C. (1995) - Neural Network for Pattern Recognition. Clarendon Press, Oxford.

Cruddas, M., J. Thomas and R. Chambers (1997) - Investigating neural networks as a Possible Means of Imputation for the 2001 UK Census. *Proc. Symposium of Statistics Canada: New directions in Surveys and Census*, 153-158, Quebec, November 1997.

Fessant, F. and S. Midenet (1998) - Imputation of partial non-responses in surveys with a self-organising map based model. *Paper presented in ACSEG'98 Fifth International Meeting on Connectionist Approaches in Economics and Management Sciences*, Louvain-la-Jeune, November 1998.

Fessant, F. and S. Midenet (1999) - A knowledge-based parser: neural network based approaches; development of a neural network based imputation system for travel diary data. *TEST Deliverable* **D5-B**, INRETS, Arcueil.

Gingras, F. and Y. Bengio (1996) - Recurrent neural networks for missing or asynchronous data. *In Proc. NIPS 8 Advances in Neural Information Processing Systems*, 395-401, MIT Press, Cambridge, USA.

Grabowski, M. (1998) - Application of self organizing maps to outlier identification and estimation of missing data. *Proc. IFCS'98 Sixth Conference of the International Federation of Classification Societies*, 279-286, Rome, July 1998.

Hertz, J., A. Krogh and R.G. Palmer (1991) - Introduction to the Theory of Neural Computation. Addison-Wesley, Redwood City.

Ibbou, S. (1998) - Classification, analyse des correspondances et méthodes neuronales. *Thèse de l'Université Paris 1 Panthéon Sorbonne*, Paris.

Idan, Y. and R. Chevallier (1991) - Handwritten digits recognition by a supervised Kohonen-like learning algorithm. *Proceedings of IJCNN '91 International Joint Conference on Neural Networks*, 2576-2581, IEEE, Piscataway.

Kohonen, T. (1995) - Self-Organizing Maps. Springer, Heidelberg.

Little, R., and D. Rubin (1987) - Statistical Analysis with Missing Data. John Wiley and Sons Inc., New York.

Lopez-Vazquez, C. (1997) - Application of ANN to the prediction of missing daily precipitation records and comparison against linear methodologies. *Proc. EANN'97 International Conference on Engineering Applications of Neural Networks*, 337-340, Stockholm, June 1997.

Lothaire, O. (1999) - A knowledge-based parser: implementation of a tool-box. *TEST Deliverable* **D5-A**, FUNDP, Namur.

Midenet, S. and A. Grumbach (1994) - Learning Associations by Self-Organization: the LASSO model. *NeuroComputing*, **6**, 343-361.

Mitra, S. and K. Pal (1995) - Fuzzy multilayer perceptron, Inferencing and generalization. *IEEE Trans. on Neural networks*, **6**, 51-63.

Muller, S., P. Garda and J.D. Muller (1998) - Un codage neuro flou pour le traitement de données incomplètes par réseaux connexionnistes. *Proc. IPMU'98 Seventh Conference on Information Processing and Management of Uncertainty in Knowledge-based Systems*, 973-980, EDK Editions Médicales et Scientifiques, Paris.

Murtagh, F., G. Zheng, J. Campbell, A. Aussem, M. Ouberdous, E. Demirov, W. Eifler and M. Crepon (1998) - Data imputation and nowcasting in the environmental sciences using clustering and connectionist modeling. *Proc. CompStat 98 International Conference on Computational Statistics*, 401-406, August 1998, Bristol.

Nordbotten, S. (1996) - Neural network imputation applied to the Norwegian 1990 population census data. *Journal of Official Statistics*, **12-4**, 385-401.

Ritter, H., T. Martinetz and K. Schulten (1989) - Topology conserving maps for learning visuo-motor coordination. *Neural Networks*, **2**, 159-168.

Rumelhart, D., G. Hinton and R. Williams (1986) - Learning internal representations by error propagation. *Parallel Distributed Processing: Explorations in the Microstructure of Cognition, Volume 1: Foundations*, in Rumelhart D. and McClelland J.(eds.), 318-362, MIT Press, Cambridge, USA.

Samad, T. and S. Harp (1992) - Self organization with partial data. *Network*, **3**, 205-212.

Semmence, J. (1997) - Family resources surveys: a practical example of imputation. *Proc. Symposium of Statistics Canada: New directions in Surveys and Census*, 149-152, Quebec, November 1997.

Sharpe, P. and R. Solly (1995) - Dealing with missing values in neural network based diagnostic systems. *Neural Computing and Applications*, **3**, 73-77.

Vamplew, P., D. Clark and A. Adams (1996) - Techniques for dealing with missing values in feedforward networks. *Proc. of Australian Conference on Neural Networks*, 251-254, Camberra.

The probability of two different individuals i and j of the population U to be in the sample s is usually called the double inclusion probability and noted p_{ij}. For example, if s is a simple random sample without replacement then,

$$p_{ij} = \frac{n}{N} \frac{n-1}{N-1}.$$

The total T, of long-distance trips made by the population U is:

$$T = \sum_{i \in U} y_i$$

An unbiased estimator of the total is:

$$\hat{T} = \sum_{i \in s} \frac{y_i}{p_i}$$

Then the variance of the total is:

$$V(\hat{T}) = \frac{1}{2} \sum_{\substack{i=1 \\ j \neq i}}^{N} \sum_{j=1}^{N} (p_i p_j - p_{ij}) \left(\frac{y_i}{p_i} - \frac{y_j}{p_j} \right)^2$$

Chapter 13
Sample selection

J. Armoogum and J.-L. Madre

13   Sample selection[1]

J. Armoogum and J.-L. Madre

INRETS
F – Arcueil

Abstract

Optimising the sample is very important, especially for long-distance travel diaries, because, although not every person or household undertakes long-distance journeys, those who do generally travel a lot. It seems obvious, then to over-represent this type of people in the sample when we want to undertake a survey on long-distance mobility. The issue varies depending on whether we want to estimate the global number of trips or to calibrate an origin-destination (O-D) matrix.

Keywords

Sample schemes, stratified random sampling, proportional allocation, optimum allocation, two-phase sampling, origin, destination flows.

---

[1] Preferred citation: Armoogum J. and J.-L. Madre (2003) Sample selection, in K. W. Axhausen, J.-L. Madre, J. W. Polak and Ph. L. Toint (eds.) *Capturing Long-Distance Travel*, 205 - 222, Research Studies Press, Baldock.

13.1   INTRODUCTION

Long-distance travel behaviour is very unevenly distributed in the population. Thus, in order to collect information on this topic, it seems adequate to over-sample highly mobile groups. For the calculation of mobility rates or of total amounts of distance travelled (Section 2), it is useful to collect information on both travellers and non-travellers. But if we need information only on some characteristics of trips – for instance, in order to calculate O-D matrix flows (Section 3) – it seems almost irrelevant to survey non-travellers. And in this case, a clear objective has to be defined: Is a good uniform relative accuracy needed for each flow, which is almost impossible with a reasonable sample size, when these flows are of different magnitude or do we need only the identification of the main flows with a maximal accuracy? Thus, a sample scheme strategy is generally a compromise between different purposes, which depends on the information available to draw the sample – whether or not to allow stratification, for instance.

13.2   SAMPLE SCHEMES FOR GLOBAL AMOUNTS OF LONG-DISTANCE TRIPS

Notation: let

- U be the Population and the size of U is N.
- s be a sample collected from U of size n, and
- y the interest variable (for example, y could be the number of long-distance trips made by an individual during the period under review).

The probability of the individual i of the population U to be in the sample s is usually called the inclusion probability and noted p_i. For example, if s is a simple random sample, then $p_i = n/N$.

The probability of two different individuals i and j of the population U to be in the sample s is usually called the double inclusion probability and noted p_{ij}. For example, if s is a simple random sample without replacement then,

$$p_{ij} = \frac{n}{N} \frac{n-1}{N-1}.$$

The total T, of long-distance trips made by the population U is:

$$T = \sum_{i \in U} y_i$$

An unbiased estimator of the total is:

$$\hat{T} = \sum_{i \in s} \frac{y_i}{p_i}$$

Then the variance of the total is:

$$V(\hat{T}) = \frac{1}{2} \sum_{i=1}^{N} \sum_{\substack{j=1 \\ j \neq i}}^{N} (p_i p_j - p_{ij}) \left(\frac{y_i}{p_i} - \frac{y_j}{p_j} \right)^2$$

An estimation unbiased of $V(\hat{T})$ is:

$$\hat{V}(\hat{T}) = \frac{1}{2} \sum_{i \in s} \sum_{\substack{j \in s \\ j \neq i}} \frac{(p_i p_j - p_{ij})}{p_{ij}} \left(\frac{y_i}{p_i} - \frac{y_j}{p_j} \right)^2$$

13.2.1 Simple random sample without replacement

When s is a simple random sample drawn without replacement from U, and the size of s is n, the inclusion probability of i ($\forall\ i \in U$) is $p_i = \dfrac{n}{N}$, and the double inclusion probability of i and j ($\forall\ i \in U$, $\forall\ j \in U$ and i≠j) is $p_{ij} = \dfrac{n}{N} \dfrac{n-1}{N-1}$.

T is estimated by:

$$\hat{T} = \frac{N}{n} * \sum_{i \in s} y_i$$

The variance of $\hat{T}$ is:

$$V(\hat{T}) = N^2 (1 - \frac{n}{N}) \frac{S^2}{n}$$

where:

- S^2 is the corrected variance, $S^2 = \dfrac{1}{N-1} \sum_{i \in s} (y_i - \bar{y})^2$

- $\bar{y} = \dfrac{1}{N} \sum_{i \in s} y_i$

The goal of optimising the sample schemes is to reduce the variance of $\hat{T}$ under the constraint of the survey budget. When auxiliary information is available on the population, it is essential to use them to increase the precision of the estimates. Stratification is an example of the use of auxiliary information.

13.2.2 Stratified random sampling

When the population U can be divided into H sub-population of $N_1, N_2, ..., N_H$

units, these sub-populations are non-overlapping and together they comprise the whole of the population, so that :

$$N = N_1 + N_2 + ... + N_H$$

The sub-populations are called strata. We will suppose that we know the size N_h (h=1,2,...,H) of the H sub-populations. When the strata have been determined, a sample s_h is drawn independently from each different strata. The sample size of s_h h (h=1, 2,...,H) is denoted by n_h. Stratified random sampling consists in drawing H random samples (i.e. one in each stratum).

An unbiased estimation of the total T_{st} is $\hat{T}_{st}$ (st = stratified):

$$\hat{T}_{st} = \sum_{h=1}^{H} \hat{T}_h = \sum_{h=1}^{H} \frac{N_h}{n_h} * \sum_{i \in s_h} y_i$$

If a simple random sample is taken in each stratum, the estimated variance is:

$$V(\hat{T}_{st}) = \sum_{h=1}^{H} N_h(N_h - n_h) \frac{S_h^2}{n_h}$$

where:

- S_h^2 is the corrected variance, $S_h^2 = \dfrac{1}{N-1} \sum_{i \in s_h} (y_i - \bar{y}_h)^2$

- $\bar{y}_h = \dfrac{1}{N_h} \sum_{i \in s_h} y_i$

Proportional allocation

Let: f be the sampling rate ($f = \dfrac{n}{N}$). If the same sampling rate is taken in each stratum this is called proportional allocation, and therefore $n_h = n\dfrac{N_h}{N}$.

An estimation of the total is $\hat{T}_{prop}$ (prop = proportional):

$$\hat{T}_{prop} = \sum_{h=1}^{H} \hat{T}_h = \frac{N}{n} * \sum_{h=1}^{H} \sum_{i \in s_h} y_i$$

The estimated variance if a simple random sample is taken in each stratum is:

$$V(\hat{T}_{prop}) = \frac{N-n}{n} \sum_{h=1}^{H} N_h S_h^2$$

Using a sample with proportional allocation is generally better than a simple random sample, and it really improves the precision whenever the variable used for the stratification is 'close to' the interest variable, because in this case the within-stratum variance is minimum.

Optimum allocation
Suppose that c_0 is an overhead cost for the survey and c_h the cost for one interview in the strata h (h= 1, 2,..., H). Therefore the overall budget is then C:

$$C = c_0 + \sum_{h=1}^{H} n_h \, c_h$$

Within any stratum the cost is proportional to the size of sample, but the cost per unit c_h may vary from stratum to stratum.

In stratified sampling the values of the sample sizes n_h (h=1, 2,...,H) in the respective strata are chosen by the sampler. Optimum allocation is when the nh (h=1, 2,...,H) are chosen to minimise the variance of the total $V(\hat{T}_{st})$ under the constraint of the budget. This optimum is also known as the Neyman allocation (Neyman, 1934).

In stratified random sampling with a cost function like that described above, the variance of the estimated total T_{st} is a minimum for the Neyman allocation and:

$$n_h = \frac{N_h S_h}{\sqrt{c_h}} \frac{(C - c_0)}{\sum_{h=1}^{H} N_h S_h \sqrt{c_h}}$$

This leads to the following rules of conduct. In a given stratum, take a larger sample if:

- the stratum is larger;
- the stratum is more heterogeneous internally;
- sampling is cheaper in the stratum.

Note that if the cost and also the s_h are invariant in each stratum, the optimum allocation is the proportional allocation.

Because of the use of auxiliary information, stratification produces a gain in precision. This gain is substantial when it is possible to divide a heterogeneous population into internally homogeneous sub-populations.

13.2.3 Example of gain with stratification (proportional and optimum allocation)

Suppose that we know for each individual of the whole population the number of cars in their household, then we can divide this population into 3 strata: the individuals who have no car in their household; the individuals who have one car in their household; and the individuals who have at least two cars in their household. Information about the population is reported in Table 13-1.

Table 13-1   Size and mobility in each stratum

Strata	Number of individuals	Number of trips	Standard deviation (trips)
0 car	300	29	0.30
1 car	500	1748	1.00
2 cars	200	1457	3.78
Total	1000	3234	3.11

If we take 50 individuals in the population according to 3 sample schemes (simple random sample, stratified random sample with proportional allocation and stratified random sample with optimum allocation), the expected mean and variance are illustrated in Table 13-2.

Table 13-2   Expected mean and variance

Sample scheme (n=50)	Mean of number of trips	Variance of the total $V(\hat{T})$
Simple random sample	3234	42 883
Stratified random sample (proportional allocation)	3234	25 355
Stratified random sample (optimum allocation)	3234	13 712

In this example, the variance of the total for the stratified sample with the proportional allocation [$V(\hat{T}) = 25355$] is 40% less than the variance of the total for the simple random sample [$V(\hat{T}) = 42883$]. But the variance of the total for the stratified sample with the Neyman allocation [$V(\hat{T}) = 13712$] is 70% less than the variance of the total for the simple random sample.

13.2.4   The example of the French NPTS
The French National Personal Transportation Survey 1993–94 is the fourth survey conducted by INSEE (the National Institute of Statistics and Economics Studies) since the mid sixties on this topic. It retains the definitions and the essential principles used previously to maintain the statistical continuity so as to enable the measurement of evolution. The purpose of this survey was to describe the trips made by households who are living in France, as well as their use of public and private transport means.
A sample of 20,002 dwellings was drawn from the census of 1990 and from the list of new residences built since that date: 20,053 address cards were made due to divided dwelling (dwellings which have been divided into two or more separate residences since the last census). The survey objective was to collect as much information as possible about the trips; thus, we made an over-representation of the mobile households having several cars (except in Paris, where we did not change the draw probabilities because a large share of Parisians do not favour motorisation). Although there has been a question about car ownership in every

census since 1968, this was the first time that this information had been used to stratify a transport survey sample. The sample was spread over 8 waves from May 1993 to April 1994 in order to neutralise the seasonal effects, which are significant for private trips.

One person was selected from the eligible individuals in the household to answer about his or her long-distance mobility (over 5 years old, who are present at the moment of the survey and able to respond). The probability of being chosen was 2/3 for the most mobile person (in terms of long distance) and the other members of the household shared equally the 1/3 remaining probability of being selected.

Therefore the over-representation households having several cars combining with the over-representation of mobile persons produces a gain in terms of number of described journeys of +23%, compared with a sample scheme without any over-representation. The global amount of long-distance trips ($\approx$650 millions) is known in a confidence limit of $\pm$ 4.8% at 95% degree of confidence (with about 75,000 records in the long-distance survey file).

13.3   SAMPLE SCHEMES FOR O-D FLOWS

A long-distance travel survey is not used only to estimate the global amount of trips but also to calibrate O-D matrices. The question is then: does the optimisation of the sample schemes for the global amount give accurate estimation for each O-D flow, or does the optimisation of the sample schemes for each O-D flow give an accurate estimation of the global amount? Obviously the response is 'no' in both cases.

13.3.1   Representativeness of all regions

The question of optimisation of each O-D flow is complicated. For example, if we want to improve the accuracy of the flow where the origin is i and the destination is j, we have to select people who often make this kind of trip. Whenever we select people, we never know *a priori* if he or she will travel between i and j, but if we select individuals living in the regions i or j we will increase the probability of their making these kind of trips and thus the accuracy of this O-D flow, because the O-D flow where the origin is i and the destination is j is mainly undertaken by people living either in the region i or in the region j.

Therefore, if we want to calibrate an accurate O-D matrix we have to improve the accuracy of the total number of trips in each region. With the optimum allocation that gives the number of individuals to be selected in each region, if the cost of an interview is the same in all regions, we have:

$$n_h = n * \frac{N_h S_h}{\sum\limits_{h=1}^{H} N_h S_h}$$

As we can see in the above equation, with optimum allocation we have to sample 'more' if the size of the region is important or if the corrected variance (S_h^2) is important, which is the case in very large regions. In fact, optimum allocation is generally used for global optimisation. Conversely, if we want the same precision in each region in term of the coefficient of variation (CV) that implies:

For h=1,2,...,H and K>0:

$$CV(\hat{T}_h) = K$$

For h=1,2,...,H:

$$CV^2(\hat{T}_h) = \frac{V(\hat{T}_h)}{\hat{T}_h^2} = N_h^2 \left(\frac{1}{n_h} - \frac{1}{N_h} \right) \frac{S_h^2}{\hat{T}_h^2}$$

Therefore, when $N_h \gg n_h$ (which is usually the case) the variance of the total of our interest variable in the region h is:

$$V(\hat{T}_h) \approx N_h^2 \left(\frac{1}{n_h} \right) S_h^2$$

The variance of the total in a region depends on the region's size to square (N_h^2). If the corrected variance is similar for all regions and if the size of the regions is very different from one to another, the totals are accurate for 'small' regions (n_h small) and inaccurate for 'large' regions (n_h large).
The variance of the total is:

$$V(\hat{T}) = \sum_{h=1}^{H} V(\hat{T}_h) \approx \sum_{h=1}^{H} \left(\frac{1}{n_h} \right) S_h^2 * N_h^2$$

Consequently, if the variance for large regions is important, the variance of the overall total over the population will also be important, hence the total of our interest variable will not be accurate.

13.3.2   Two intermediate solutions
Optimising the sample schemes for the global amount among the population and optimising the sample schemes for the global amount in each region leads to different allocation of the sample size for the H regions. An intermediate solution has been proposed by Bankier (1986): the idea is to find the minimum of:

$$\sum_{h=1}^{H}[(X_h)^{\alpha}.CV(\hat{T}_h)]^2$$

Where:

- $CV(\hat{T}_h)$ is the coefficient of variation in the sub-population h (h=1, 2,…,H);
- X_h is an auxiliary variable correlated to T_h (X_h could be for example a rough estimation of T_h);
- $0 \leq \alpha \leq 1$ and α chosen by the survey designer.

The minimum is achieved when:

$$n_h = n \frac{(X_h)^{\alpha} \frac{S_h}{T_h} N_h}{\sum\limits_{h=1}^{H} (X_h)^{\alpha} \frac{S_h}{T_h} N_h}$$

Note if we take $X_h = T_h$ and:

- $\alpha=1$, the result is then the Neyman's allocation (with identical cost in all regions),
- $\alpha=0$, then the coefficient of variation of the total is quasi invariant in a first approximation.

Consequently, when $0<\alpha<1$, we have an intermediary situation in between an accurate overall total number of long-distance trips over the population and the same relative accuracy for the H regions. But, if we want to use this solution we need to have:

- an auxiliary variable X_h, correlated with T_h;
- the corrected variance in each stratum S_h^2; and
- the size of each regions N_h.

The problem is that we do not always have this information. Another solution is, therefore, proportional allocation.

The Neyman allocation is very interesting when there is significant variability between the S_h (h=1,2,…,H), otherwise proportional allocation gives similar global results to the optimum one. The advantage is that for regional statistics, proportional allocation is much better than optimum allocation, because the variance of a total number of trips in the region h is:

$$V(\hat{T}_h) = N_h \left(\frac{N-n}{n} \right) S_h^2$$

$V(T_h)$ is proportional to the region's size. The coefficient of variation of the total number of trips in the region h is:

$$CV(\hat{T}_h) = \sqrt{N_h \left(\frac{N-n}{n} \right)} \ \frac{S_h}{N_h \hat{\bar{y}}_h}$$

Where: $\hat{\bar{y}}_h$ is the estimation of the mean number of trips made by one person in the strata h, $\hat{\bar{y}}_h = \dfrac{1}{n_h} \sum_{i \in s_h} y_i$.

Then:

$$CV(\hat{T}_h) = \frac{\sqrt{\left(\dfrac{N-n}{n} \right)}}{\sqrt{N_h}} \ \frac{S_h}{\hat{\bar{y}}_h}$$

$CV(\hat{T}_h)$ is in reverse proportion to the square root of the region's h size. In fact we have a better coefficient of variation in very large regions than in small regions, but we have also valuable variance of the total in small regions and in important regions. So this is a good choice from which to estimate global and regional results.

13.3.3 Optimisation of each region's sample scheme
After choosing the number of households that should be in the survey in each region, we have to optimise each of the region's samples by interviewing the most mobile households to improve the accuracy of the total number of trips. Most European countries do not use the census as a sample base, thus if we want to select the most mobile households the solution is a two-phase sampling.

Two-phase sampling
Long-distance trips are rare events: for instance, in France a person makes about one journey every couple of months. Therefore, if we could divide the population according to their long-distance mobility – for example, those who travel and those who do not – it seems uneconomical to interview the different groups in the same way. A common practice is to select a large sample in the population, ask each person about their mobility habits and then take a smaller sample from the large one. This technique is called two-phase or double sampling, since the unit is not

measured completely but is sampled. For example, we could take a large sample from the population, ask them the number of cars they own or the number of long-distance trips they have made since the previous year and then draw a larger sample from those with a higher mobility. In our case, another important discussion is whether to interview all members of a household (which was done in the 1981–82 French NPTS), or to select one person in the household with a higher probability of being the most mobile person (the method used in 1993–94).

As the variance of the total $\hat{T}$ is (cf § 2.):

$$V(\hat{T}) = \frac{1}{2} \sum_{i=1}^{N} \sum_{\substack{j=1 \\ j \neq i}}^{N} (p_i p_j - p_{ij}) \left(\frac{y_i}{p_i} - \frac{y_j}{p_j} \right)^2$$

We can have the variance of the total equal to zero if we always have the relation $\forall (i, j) \in U x U ; i \neq j$:

$$\left(\frac{y_i}{p_i} - \frac{y_j}{p_j} \right) = 0$$

This last formula means that for all unit i of the population U, p_i is proportional to y_i.

The problem is that our interest variable y is unknown, so we must find out an auxiliary variable X proportional to y and $X_i > 0$. Another problem is that if we have two interest variables y and z, and z is not proportional with y, then our estimation of the total of z will not be accurate.

We have to find out auxiliary variables which are proportional to long-distance mobility. There are many variables that we can look at; for example:

- Number of cars in the household;
- Number of long-distance trips made during the previous year;
- Total salary of the household;
- Profession of the household head;
- Urban / rural zone of residence;
- Age of the household head.

Results from the French NPTS

According to the last NPTS 1993–94 (Table 13-3), we should sample more people when:

- they are living in a multi-car household;
- the total salary is above 19,000 Euros;
- the size of the household is between 2 to 5 persons;

- the social category of the household's head is Craftsman/Tradesman or Senior executive or Intermediary or Employee.

The example of the French Eurostat pilot

The French long-distance Eurostat pilot survey relies on a two-stage over-sampling. The first stage consists of the over-representation of the municipalities with household with a high social category and the second stage is to select the person in the household who has to describe her/his journeys.

Sample allocation for the first stage

For the first stage of this sample scheme, the precision for the average of number of trips per household is approximately the same for the stratified optimum allocation and for the stratified proportional allocation, but these two allocations are better than the Eurostat-Ipsos allocation, and the gain of precision is about 29% (see Table 13-4 and Table 13-5).

Sample allocation for the second stage: Selection of one person from the household

The methodology of the 'Kish' person is to select at random only one individual from the selected household. This can be done by a 'sample simple random' with an equal probability (each individual of the household has the same probability of being selected) or with an unequal probability (some individual(s) of the household may have more chances of being selected). At the first contact, Ipsos asked each eligible individual (those over 5 years old) the number of trips they had made during the previous 12 months. Ren and Armoogum (1998) tested two methodologies for the second stage:

1. a selection with equal probability;
2. a selection with unequal probability (a person is selected proportionally to her/his mobility).

Simulation of the two procedures of selection leads to a preference for the second procedure because we have about 22% of more journeys described and the variance is reduced by a quarter.

13.3.4   One person/complete household to be interviewed

Suppose that all members of a household behave exactly the same: it seems to be uneconomical to interview all of them. Interviewing just one is enough (even if it is cheaper to interview another member of this household than another person in another household).

Table 13-3   Long-distance mobility according to the characteristics of the traveller

Units: number of trips during 3 months	Population (in 1000)	Sample size - French NPTS 1993-94	Average number of journeys $\hat{\bar{y}}_h$	Total number of journeys $\hat{T}_h$ (in 1000)	Standard deviation of the number of journeys s_h
Number of cars of the household					
0 car	8995	2 635	0.80	5 172	1.87
1 car	25 897	6 519	1.79	28 953	4.09
2 or more cars	18 169	4 914	2.46	25 935	4.75
Total salary of the household (in 1000 EURO)					
11.3 < S	9 460	2 978	0.96	6 149	2.49
11.3 ≤ S < 19.0	13 121	3 452	1.38	11 381	3.36
19.0 ≤ S < 30.8	16 003	3 872	2.00	19 275	4.73
30.8 ≤ S < 45.5	7 897	2 021	2.80	13 397	5.18
S ≥ 45.5	6 579	1 745	2.78	9 859	4.06
Size of the household					
1 person	6 367	2 953	1.46	6 339	2.70
2 persons	14 273	4 402	1.69	16 158	3.15
3 persons	10 453	2 736	1.99	12 430	5.03
4 persons	12 204	2 507	2.28	15 410	5.11
5 persons	6 474	1 076	2.23	7 597	5.27
6 persons or more	3 289	394	1.40	2 126	2.57
Social-category of the household's head					
Farmer	1 428	398	1.27	1 061	4.02
Craftsman/Tradesman	3 448	883	2.01	4 130	2.89
Senior executive	6 353	1 660	3.71	12 949	5.40
Intermediary	8 075	2 113	2.83	12 931	5.19
Employees	5 204	1 442	1.69	6 159	4.08
Blue collar workers	13 424	2 871	1.35	10 779	4.37
Retired/Students	12 002	3 834	1.02	9 204	2.04
Unemployed	3 127	867	1.41	2 849	3.07
Population	53 060	14 068	1.13	60 061	4.07

Sources: INSEE-INRETS French NPTS 1993-94

Table 13-4   Mobility in each stratum for the French Eurostat pilot survey

Strata Category of municipality	Household in the population (%)	Average of number of trips per household (12 months)	Standard deviation (trips)
Higher social category ++	29	24.5	22.9
Social category +	27	20.2	25.6
Social category -	22	15.2	22.3
Lower social category --	22	17.1	29.3
Total	100	19.6	24.6

Sources: Eurostat-Ipsos, 1997 and Ren and Armoogum, 1998.

Table 13-5   Different sample allocations for the French Eurostat pilot survey

Strata Category of municipality	Sample allocation (Eurostat- Ipsos)	Proportional Allocation	Optimum allocation
Higher social category ++	470	277	254
Social category +	284	258	266
Social category -	99	210	189
Lower social category --	102	210	246
Sample size	955	955	955
Variance for the mean of number of trips	0.93	0.66	0.65

Sources: Eurostat-Ipsos, 1997 and Ren and Armoogum, 1998.

Interviewing one person in a household constitutes a two-phase sampling. The double inclusion probability p_{ij} is equal to 0 (because if i and j belong to the same household and i is different from j, if i is interviewed j is not), and therefore an estimation of the variance of the total number of trips made by a household is:

$$V(\hat{T}) = \frac{1}{2} \sum_{i=1}^{N} \sum_{\substack{j=1 \\ j \neq i}}^{N} p_i p_j \left(\frac{y_i}{p_i} - \frac{y_j}{p_j} \right)^2$$

Where:

- T is the total number of trips made by each person in the household;
- y_i is the number of trips made by the individual I; and
- N the size of the household.

Thus, if each person in a household travels the same amount as the others, then the best inclusion probability is to take $p_i = 1/N$ (because in this case we have $\left(\dfrac{y_i}{p_i} - \dfrac{y_j}{p_j} \right) = 0$).

When some members of the household travel a lot and the others much less, we have to take p_i proportional to y_i then the estimation of the total number of trips made by this household should be accurate.

13.3.5   O-D matrix from NUTS1 or NUTS2 level ?

If we take the example of France, where there are 22 NUTS2 zones and 8 NUTS1 zones, and if we consider that a trip from region A to region B is equivalent to a trip from B to A, this means for a French NUTS2 O-D matrix 253 potential flows and only 36x36 potential flows for a NUTS1 matrix. Obviously the NUTS1 O-D matrix is more precise, but also less accurate in terms of geography. Another result is that the flows of the NUTS2 matrix are more sensitive in terms of cluster effect (the same persons making the same kind of trips).

In the last French NPTS for a NUTS2 O-D matrix, we started from the flow 'Centre – Ile-De-France' with 24.4 million of trips known at the level of ± 22% (at 95% confidence level) to many flows ('Corse-Limousin' for instance) where we have no record. After 100 highest flows, we can state only that they represent less than 0.5 million of trips per year. The intra-zone flows are about 21% of the total number of trips; most of them are inside the largest regions. 34% of the total number of trips concern flows with the Paris region. There are also significant flows between large adjacent regions.

For a NUTS1 O-D matrix we start from the ZEAT1 (Paris) – ZEAT2 (around Paris) with 89.7 million trips known at the level of ± 14% (at 95% confidence level) to ZEAT3 (East) – ZEAT7 (South-West) with 1.1 million trips known at the level of ± 44% (at 95% confidence level). The intra-zone flows are about 35% of the total number of trips, and we have another 35% for the flows with the Paris ZEAT.

13.4   CONCLUSIONS

Optimising the sample is very important in long-distance travel diary surveys, especially when we want to build Origin-Destination matrices. It is then necessary to over-represent the most mobile households or persons in the sample. As the information needed for a direct over-sampling is seldom available (for instance, the cooperation of the National Institutes of Statistics is necessary to use the census), we propose to capture this information with a two-phase sampling. We require a stratification at the regional level to have all regions duly represented in the sample. When the data are collected, we must use the theory of 'small area estimation' to improve the accuracy of each Origin-Destination flow (for instance, by introducing a calibration of traffic counts in the calculation).

We have shown that, compared to uniform sampling, the optimisation of sample schemes can increase considerably the volume of information collected and the accuracy of estimates. However, clear objectives have to be defined on the variables (total distance travelled, the main O-D flows, etc.) for which the accuracy has to be maximised. But even when it is the case, the achievable precision with a reasonable sample size seems modest compared to traffic counts, which are available only for air and rail, and tell much less than surveys on travel behaviour.

13.5 REFERENCES

Ampt, E.S. and A.J. Richardson (1994) - The validity of self-completion surveys for collecting travel behaviour data. *Proceedings 22nd European Transport Forum*, PTRC, London.

Armoogum, J. and J.L. Madre (1996) - Non-response correction in the 1993-94 NPTS, the example of daily trips *Proceedings 4th International Conference on Survey Methods in Transport*, Steeple Aston, September 1996.

Armoogum, J., X.-L. Han, J.-L. Madre, and J.W. Polak (1997) - Improved methods for weighting and orrecting of travel diaries. *MEST Deliverable*, **D8**, CEC, Brussels.

Armoogum, J. and J.-L. Madre (1997) - De l'opimisation du plan de sondage au redressement d'une enquête: l'exemple des voyages à longue distance dans l'enquête. *Transports et Communications*, Rennes, June 1997.

Armoogum, J. (1997) - Correction of a non-response due to the potential response: Case of the French N.P.T.S. *8th IATBR Conference*, Austin, September 1997.

Armoogum, J. and J.-L. Madre (1997) - Interview et présence au domicile. *Symposium of Statistic Canada*, Ottawa, November 1997.

Bankier, M.D. (1986) - Estimator based of several stratified samples with applications to multiple frame surveys. *Journal of the American Statistical Association*, **81**, 1074-1079.

de Heer, W. and G. Moritz (1997) - Respondent sampling weighting and non-response. *Transportation Research Circular*, **E-C008**, II-C/1, TRB, Washington D.C.

de Leeuw, E.D. (1992) - Data Quality in Mail, Telephone and Face to Face Interviews. PhD thesis, Universiteit Amsterdam, Amsterdam.

Ettema, D., H. Timmermanns and L. van Veghel (1996) - Effects of Data Collection Methods in Travel and Activity Research. *European Institute of Retailing and Service Studies*, Technical University of Eindhoven.

Groves, R. (1989) - Survey Errors and Survey Costs. John Wiley Inc., New York.

Kim, H., J. Li, S. Roodman, A. Sen, S. Sööt and E. Christopher (1993) -Factoring household travel surveys. *Transportation Research Record*, **1412**, 17-22.

Madre, J-L. and J. Maffre (1994) - The French National Travel Personal Survey: The last of the dinosaurs or the first of a new generation? *Paper presented* at the *7th Conference of the International Association for Travel Behaviour Research*, Santiago, Chile, July.

Polak, J.W. and E.S. Ampt (1996) - An analysis of wave response and non-response effects in travel diary surveys. *Proceedings 4th International Conference on Survey Methods in Transport*, Steeple Aston, September 1996.

Richardson, A.J. and E.S. Ampt (1993) - The Victoria Integrated Travel, Activities and Land-Use Toolkit. *VITAL Working Paper,* **VWP93/1**, Transport Research Centre, University of Melbourne.

Richardson, A.J. and E.S. Ampt (1994) - Non-response effects in mail-back travel surveys. *Paper presented at the 7th Conference of the International Association for Travel Behaviour Research*, Santiago, Chile, July.

Richardson, A.J., E.S. Ampt and A. Meyburg (1995) - Survey Methods for Transport Planning. Eucalyptus Press, Melbourne.

Chapter 14
PDA-based CASI: Implementation and experiences

I. Haubold

14 PDA-based CASI: Implementation and experiences[1]

I. Haubold

Institut für Eisenbahnwesen
Leopold-Franzens-Universität
A – 6020 Innsbruck

Abstract

Work package two (WP2) of the project Technologies for European Surveys of Travel Behaviour (TEST) comprised an assessment of how new mobile pocket computing technologies were applicable to the improvement of current practice in long-distance travel behaviour surveys.

The work started with an investigation of new mobile computer technologies with regard to their potential to enhance the data capture, data quality and cost-effectiveness of travel survey work. Every major mobile computer obtainable at the time was analysed with regards to the issues involved in selecting the initial target machine for the implementation of a CASI (computer-aided self interview) application: an electronic travel diary application (TDA). Two examples of pen computer-based travel diary applications (TDA) were designed, developed, implemented and tested: the first on a handheld PC (HPC) and then on a palm-sized PC (PPC). These implementations are described in detail. First experiences with the travel diary applications were gained through field trials in Austria, Sweden, France and Portugal. The respondents carried a handheld or palm computer during the whole survey period, allowing them to record their travel "on-line". Respondents had the opportunity to edit their answers at any time and anywhere, e.g. before, during or after a journey, at home or in the office, on the train or bus. The results of the Austrian field tests, which involved a small panel of respondents using both implementations, will be presented. The comparison of both computer-assisted data collection implementations evaluates their acceptability and effectiveness.

Keywords

Long-distance travel diary, self-administered computer interview, handheld computer, palmtop computer.

---

[1] Preferred citation: Haubold, I. (2003) PDA-based CASI: Implementation and experiences, in K. W. Axhausen, J.-L. Madre, J. W. Polak and Ph. L. Toint (eds.) *Capturing Long-Distance Travel*, 223-242, Research Studies Press, Baldock.

14.1 INTRODUCTION

The efficient collection of travel data is crucial for travel behaviour analysis, as the results produced are only as good as the data collected. New developments in mobile computer technologies, specifically the launch of a variety of cheap, hand-held (HPC) and palm-sized organisers (PPC), the so-called PC companions or personal digital assistants (PDAs) introduced the opportunity to conduct complex travel diary surveys in near-time, i.e. close to the occurrence of the event to be reported. These pocket-sized computers allow the completion of complex travel diary surveys, which should improve the data collection experience for the respondent and the data quality for the analyst. The TEST project took advantage of these new technologies by implementing two Computer Assisted Self-administered Interviews (CASI) on two different machines.

A travel diary application (TDA) was designed, implemented and tested on two different types of mobile computer, a handheld PC (HPC) and a palm-sized PC (PPC), differing in the first instance in size and weight, but also in their computing facilities. In February 1997 this task began with the evaluation and selection of appropriate software and hardware-tools for the development of the data collection software. After in-house tests of the first TDA version running on a desktop PC, the program was redesigned in a more user-friendly way for the field trial, running on the HPC selected. Several TDA versions in various European languages were created for use in small pilot surveys in Austria, France, Sweden and Portugal.

The arrival of a second device class in the spring 1999, the so-called palm-sized PC, led to the development of a second electronic travel diary, utilising the results of the previous field trials. Both TDA systems, HPC and PPC, were used in a six-week pilot survey in Innsbruck, Austria. Respondents carried the mobile computer during the whole survey period, allowing them to record their travel "on-line". The respondents had the opportunity to edit their answers at any time and everywhere, e.g. before, during or after a journey, at home or in the office, on the train or bus. The results of the field trails are reported, compared and evaluated.

A summary concludes this chapter and includes an evaluation of the acceptability and effectiveness of both electronic data collection systems and suggestions for future TDA improvements.

14.2 TRAVEL DIARY APPLICATION – TECHNOLOGY OPTIONS

14.2.1 Hardware and development environment

The development of a mobile computer-based travel diary depends on the available hardware. Three main directions in this market were identified and evaluated, in terms of device design and functionality, operating system and development environment. The target devices finally chosen, the HPC Philips Velo 1 and the PPC Compaq Aero 2120, both belonged to the PC companion group running Windows CE:

- *The communicator product group*: The device includes an organiser with personal information management (PIM) and GSM. In April 1997 the Nokia 9000 was the only device available on the market.

- *The personal digital assistant group*: The PDA-group included a variety of devices with personal information management functions, but different in design, architecture, performance, operating system and software, such as the Apple Newton, Sharp Zaurus, U.S. Robotics Pilot or Psion Series. There were large differences between these systems with regard to their features.
- *The PC companions group*: All handheld PCs and palm-sized PCs, such as the Philips Velo or Compaq Aero, running the operating system Windows CE.

The advantage of the first group was the high frequency of use of the phone and organiser. That could have resulted in more travel data recording by the respondent, because the respondent would be reminded of the travel data application with every opening of the device. The disadvantages were the device-specific operating system, lack of screen readability and the lack of an integrated development environment (IDE) spanning between the target device and a PC. In addition, the GEOS operating system available for these devices was not compatible with the common PC operating system and so the data exchange would have been complicated.

The second group, e.g. the Psion range, had three different development environments. Debugging requires cables and a target machine and no on-screen simulator exist. With its OVAL language, Psion provided a language which was the 'spitting image' of Visual Basic. Such an interpreted language suffers performance deficiencies. Various other products were available, but none of them had an installed base of at least one million units, which reduced the developer support.

Why was a PC companion running Windows CE the best available technology option for the development of an electronic travel diary at the time? Windows CE was a new operating system that had a similar look and feel to Windows 95 or Windows NT. The widespread use of the operating system family, Windows 9x, reduced the learning effort for respondents through the familiarity with the Windows interface. This multimedia operating system used graphical user interfaces (GUI) which were intuitive to learn and easy to use. It offered a true multitasking and multithreaded operating system. It could run two or more applications at the same time and it operated on handheld and palm-sized computers.

14.2.2 Technology impact

Windows CE is an operating system (OS) designed by Microsoft for portable computing applications able to interchange data via synchronisation between a desktop PC and a PC companion. At the time of writing, this included handheld PCs with keyboards and palm-sized PCs with pen-based data entry. The extant version of Windows CE also lent itself to the development of "embedded systems" – any specialised device that needed to be controlled by a computer. The operating system provided easy access to applications and included scaled-down versions of Excel, Word, Internet Explorer, E-Mail, Fax and Schedule. These applications were a potential incentive to use the device frequently and to report on more journeys.

Cost-effective solutions for future computer-based surveys require the common use of the questionnaires programs on different device platforms. The Windows CE platform delivers an open architecture that permits flexibility in the device used and allows rapid redesign of the travel diary programme. The desktop PC-based integrated development environment ensured that the substantial existing Windows programmer experience is available to develop customised applications because creating and debugging of Win CE code is identical to desktop code.

In order to achieve a leadership position, Microsoft built strategic partnerships with more than twenty Original Equipment Manufacturers (OEM), which has created competition and ensured worldwide use of PC companions. OEMs had to include specific hardware features (e.g. back-lightning, modem, infrared serial communications (IRDA), coloured screen, voice recording) to a standard outlined and required by Microsoft. Most leading consumer electronics manufacturer launched their PC companions, which lead to increased price competition, performance and speedier technical improvements.

The benefits of an electronic data collection instrument using a PC companion running Windows CE comes from its ability to take advantage of the familiar Windows interface, flexibility in the device used, existing programmer skills, data exchange – ODBC standard and mobile pocket sized devices.

14.3 DESIGN OF THE SURVEY INSTRUMENT

The output of a CASI survey depends on the ease of use for the respondents and survey administrators. Selection of the appropriate device type and suitable application design influence the electronic data collection in quantity and quality. The next subsections present the experiences gained by the TEST project in Austria. The HPC-based travel diary program was created in English, German, French, Portuguese and Swedish, using the questionnaires of the company project MEST (Youssefzadeh and Axhausen, 1996). A difference to the MEST design was the reduction of the minimum travel distance to 25 km. For the palm-sized PC a German travel diary program was built using Visual CE 4.0.

14.3.1 Target devices

The evolution of mobile computing created two device types, the handheld PC and the palm-sized PC. These devices operated on Windows CE and utilise a standard architecture.

Handheld PC – Philips Velo 1

At the start of the TEST project in April 1997, just seven different models of handheld PCs had been launched in America, although not all of them were obtainable in Europe. The available products were compared directly in functionality and design (e.g. user-friendliness, power management, available memory, weight and size, price, included equipment, etc.). After this comparison it was decided to choose the Philips Velo1 (see Figure 14.1) for the development of the prototype Travel Diary Application, because it was the fastest, most expandable and most richly-configured HPC of those on the market. The hardware design of all handheld PCs was similar as a result of the Microsoft standards for the manufacturers. The differentiating points were performance and the inclusion of various further software items and accessories (e.g. CPU, RAM, docking cable or docking station).

Palm-sized PC – Compaq Aero 2120
The palm-sized PCs were launched in September 1998 in Europe. The PPC device was really pocketable compared to the HPC, because it was smaller and weighed less than a handheld PC and therefore might be more appropriate for electronically data collection on the move. Europe's first available Windows CE based PPC, the Philips Nino 300, with an LCD display of four grey shades, was used for the early stages of the application development. The first PPCs with a colour display and German Windows CE were obtainable by May 1999 in Europe. The Compaq Aero 2120 was chosen as the target device for the Austrian field test. As the only device in this price category, the Aero had a high reflective TFT display able to represent 256 colour with more than ten hours battery-life time. This resulted in better readability of the PPC screen than the HPC grey scale screen, especially for elderly respondents or those with glasses (See Figure 14.2).

14.3.2 Application development and implementation
The project implemented two different version of the TDA-CASI tool. The first TDA was developed in Visual C++ running within the Windows CE emulator on a desktop PC. The development of the travel diary application started without a companion device, because in April 1997 not one companion PC was obtainable in Europe. The PC system configuration required Windows NT, NT Service pack, Visual Studio, C++ and the add-in Beta Win CE toolkit to be able to use the development support of the HPC screen emulator. Using the TDA desktop beta version, an in-house test was carried out and the constructive critique of respondents was reflected in the redesign for the first version of the TDA, thus improving the program before the field trial.

The project served as a beta tester for Microsoft and was rewarded with 3 free Philips Velo 1 devices in December 1997. Additional delays and increased workloads were caused by a variety of development problems due to beta testing. The arrival of these HPCs offered new opportunities to realise the TDA within the project time schedule.

The HPC-TDA version used in the field trials was build using Visual CE 2.12 running on a PC running Windows NT, which had to be connected to a handheld PC. Visual CE applications are complex database applications, which provide interfaces for data collection and display the data to the user chosen design. The TDA applications can share data held in the HPC databases with any desktop application that is ODBC (Open Data Base Connectivity) enabled (e.g. Excel, Access, etc.).

Figure 14.1   HPC target device: Philips Velo 1

Figure 14.2   PPC target devices: Philips Nino 300 and Compaq Aero 2120

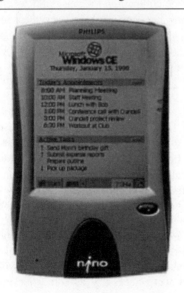
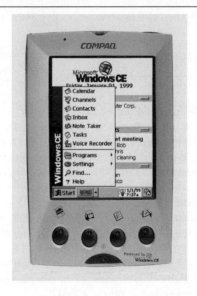

Handheld PC based TDA

The handheld PC-based travel diary application (TPA) guided and supported the respondents during a pilot survey in Innsbruck. The final version consisted of four independently running tools. When respondents open the device clamshell, the TDA icons were displayed in the centre of the screen to direct their attention to the survey. The TDA databases collected data via visual display forms that respondents manage. They typed, listed and changed the data as they wished. It was designed for input by both keyboard and stylus. When the user pressed the stylus to the screen, the input focus moved to the object under the stylus. The respondent could go back a level to correct a mistake at any point during the data entry process. The following figures show a selection of the most frequently encountered screens of the journey questionnaire (See Figure 14.3 and Figure 14.4).

Figure 14.3   HPC TDA: Journey form – Top half

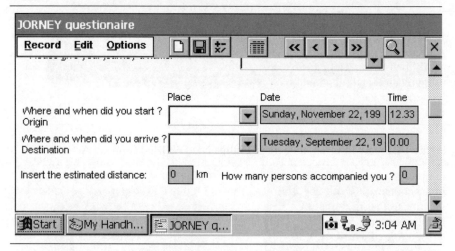

Palm-sized PC-based TDA

Using the experiences gained with the first implementation on a Windows CE platform, the HPC-based TDA, a second, now-PPC-based travel diary application was designed, developed, implemented and field-tested during 1999. The development of the PPC-based travel diary application started using a beta version of Visual CE 4.0 provided by Syware, including instruments to create programs for coloured graphic user interfaces (GUI). Two independently running programs were created. *Haushalt.exe* covered the background questionnaires regarding to household, person, vehicle details and *Reisetagebuch.exe* for travel data collection. The ODBC database of the HPC TDA was reused for the PPC TDA to ensure comparability as far as possible (see also Tables 14-1 to 14-3 for the variables included). Slight changes in the variable set were necessary as some questions were dropped or others added.

Figure 14.4   HPC TDA: Journey form – Bottom half

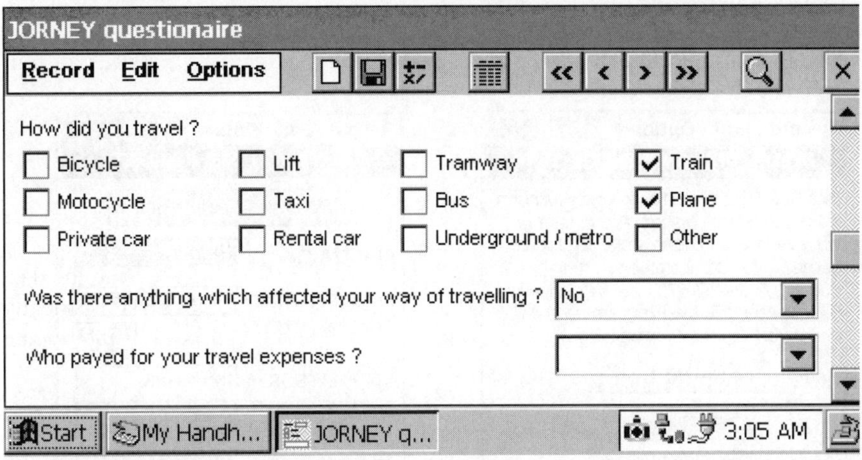

14.4   DEBRIEFING THE RESPONDENTS

After testing the TDA programs on both devices the respondents were interviewed about their understanding of the questions, their views about the screen designs, user guidance and functionality of the data collection tools.

14.4.1   Handheld PC

The questions about journey, trip and stage confused some respondents and so the redesigned version of the TDA focused consistently on the trip level. Most respondents preferred to enter their travel data after rather than before the journey in order to avoid having to make amendments arising from changes to their plans in the course of the journey. Respondents with limited experiences of computer use mentioned that the time used for data entry decreased rapidly when they became familiar with the electronic questionnaires. The effect was noticeable after entering and editing the first two to three records. Respondents without any computer experience needed substantially more time for the first electronic questionnaire to become familiar with the device and the data entry. Elderly respondents in particular had problems reading the grey scale screen.

14.4.2   Palm-sized PC

Both device types – the handheld PC and the palm-sized PC – were used by 15 respondents. Fourteen of those respondents preferred the PPC device because of the stylish design and the sharp colour display. Although the PPC was smaller and lighter, which made it easier to carry than the HPC, some respondents still refused to carry the device during travel. Most preferred to enter their journeys after travelling to avoid possibly corrections. One respondent mentioned his worry about damage or losing the PPC. In particular, respondents with no computer experience had some difficulties entering their travel data.

232

Figure 14.5   PPC TDA: Important screenshots

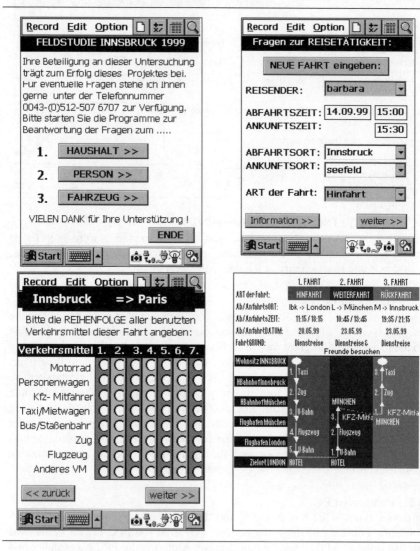

Table 14-1   Variables included: Household

Variable name	Description	Available from		Captured auto- matically
		HPC	PPC	
Hstart	Start time for data entry of household questionnaire		x	x
Plz	Postal code of residence	x	x	
Land	Country	x	x	
Name	Dummy variable	x		x
Kfz	Number of vehicles belonging to the household	x		
Wohnart	Type of accommodation	x	x	
Wohntyp	Tenant or owner	x	x	
Tel	Number of telephones belonging to the household	x	x	
Handy	Number of mobile phones belonging to the household	x	x	
www	Access to the Internet	x	x	
Fax	Fax access at home	x	x	
Hend	End time for data entry of household questionnaire		x	x
HNR	Survey administrative household number		x	x

14.5   FIELD TEST DESIGN AND DATA CAPTURED

Two field tests were conducted in Innsbruck, Austria. Both pilot surveys were carried out in three two-week reporting periods by respondents carrying a PC companion-based survey instrument to enter their travel data on the move. The availability of the device during the whole reporting period gave other household members access to the TDA, which might have increased the response rate. The mobile computer-based Travel Diary provided the respondents with three ways to enter data – past journeys, current on-going journeys and planned future journeys. Table 14-5 lists the main survey design characteristics. The main difference was the absence of an incentive payment in 1999, but fortunately most respondents could be motivated to participate again.

Table 14-2   Variables included: Person

Variable name	Description	Available from		Captured automatically
		HPC	PPC	
Pstart	Start time for data entry of person questionnaire		x	x
HNR	Survey administrative household number		x	x
Name	First name	x	x	
Geburtsjahr	Year of birth	x	x	
Geschlecht	Gender	x	x	
Nationalität	Nationality	x	x	
Familienstand	Marital status	x	x	
Behinderung	Disability	x	x	
Studying	Studying towards (?)	x		
ZwsPlz	Postal code of second residence	x	x	
ZwsLand	Nation of second residence	x	x	
ZwsGrund	Reason for second residence	x	x	
ZesBes	Visiting second residence	x	x	
Beruf	Work status	x	x	
Std	Weekly working hours	x	x	
VC,FP,KMB, VB,AUA,LH	Travel discount card	x	x	
FKO,A,B,C,D, E,F,G	Frequent flyer card	x	x	
Bildung	Obtained degree	x	x	
Tätigkeit	Job title	x	x	
Pend	End time for data entry of person questionnaire		x	x

Table 14-3   Variables included: Vehicle

Variable name	Description	Available from		Captured auto-matically
		HPC	PPC	
Fstart	Start time for data entry of vehicle questionnaire		x	x
Kfzart	Type of vehicle	x	x	
Kfzmarke	Brand/make	x	x	
Baujahr	Year of production	x	x	
KfzBesitzer	Owner of the vehicle	x	x	
KfzHauptnut	Main user of the vehicle	x	x	
KfzNutzer1	Name of vehicle-user 1		x	
KfzNutzer2	Name of vehicle-user 2		x	
Fixkost	Payers fixed costs	x	x	
Verbrauchs-kost	Payers variable costs	x	x	
JahresKm	km per year	x	x	
Treibstoff	Fuel/Petrol	x	x	
Katalysator	Catalytic converter	x	x	
Leasing	Leased car	x	x	
Fend	End time for data entry of vehicle questionnaire		x	x
HNR	Survey administrative household number		x	x

The aim of the development and testing of the mobile computer-based travel diary was to trial a new way of data entry rather than data production. The records of the four major data categories – household, individual, vehicle and travel – were stored as database records on the mobile devices. The PPC version of the TDA provided the easier way to transfer captured survey data via a docking station and data synchronisation to a Microsoft-Access™ database on the desktop PC.

14.6   SURVEY RESULTS

The small sample does not allow an extensive analysis of the reported trips and journeys. The reported average of 3.2 journeys/reporting period is reasonable, although dependent on one (1998) or two (1999) people who reported their daily long-distance commutes (see

Figure 14.6). A t-test concluded that there was no significant difference between the two years, nor between males and females and between employed and not-employed persons.

Table 14-4   Variables included: Travel

Variable name	Description	Available from		Captured auto-matically
		HPC	PPC	
Rstart	Start time for data entry of travel		x	x
Reisender	First name of travel person	x	x	
Journey	Main purpose of journey	x		
Abreise	Date and time of departure	x	x	
Ankunft	Date and time of arrival	x	x	
Abfahrtsort	Origin of stage/trip	x	x	
Ankunftsort	Destination of stage/trip	x	x	
Distance	Estimated travel distance	x		
Fahrttyp	Journey there/journey return/journey continued		x	
Reisegrund (Fahrtzweck)	Reason for this trip/stage; 7 dummy variables for work, education, business, shopping, leisure, visiting, dropping off & picking up	x	x	
AnzMitreisende	Size of travelling party	x	x	
VM1 to VM7	Transport modes used (up to 7)	x	x	
GrundVM	Reason for choosing a certain transport mode	x	x	
VM	Main transport mode	x	x	
Reisekosten	Who paid travel costs	x	x	
AnzÜN	Number of overnight stays	x	x	
ArtÜN	Type of accommodation	x	x	
KostenÜN	Who paid overnight stays	x	x	
Fahrt-Nr	Survey administrative trip number		x	x
Rend	End time for data entry of travel questionnaire		x	x
HNR	Survey administrative household number		x	x

Table 14-5   Description of the Austrian field trials

Element	HPC field test	PPC field test
Type of survey	Stage and trip based long-distance data with minimum distance of 25 km	Trip based long-distance data with minimum distance of 25 km
Recruitment of Respondents	Telephone recruitment, interview due by Fessel Institute, Vienna; 19 respondents selected by gender, mobility and computer knowledge	14 respondents out of the first field test; 4 new respondents recruited locally
Incentives	1000 ATS per respondent	No incentive
Introductory Interview	Introductory interview took about 20 to 40 minutes; handing over of respondents materials, demonstration of device handling, introduction of travel diary program and data definitions	Introductory interview took 20 to 30 minutes; handing over of respondents material, demonstration of device handling, introduction of TDA program and data definition
Respondent Materials	HPC, battery backup, power cable and fact sheet	PPC and power cable
Respondents Burden	A minimum of 51 questions including 37 questions on household, persons and vehicles and 14 questions for one stage or trip	A minimum of 39 questions including 23 questions on household, persons and vehicles and 16 questions for one trip
Debriefing interview	Face-to-face about respondents understanding of questions, screen designs, user guidance and functionality of the TDA program, return of respondents' materials	Face-to-face about respondents understanding of and screen design; user guidance and functionality of the TDA program user; return of respondents' materials
Survey periods	15.6 – 28.6.98 29.6 – 12.7.98 13.6 – 27.7.98	23.8. – 5.9.99 6.9. – 19.9.99 20.3. – 3.10.99
Information letter	About the progress of the HPC field test	About the progress of the PPC field test

The respondents reported 291 trips, forming parts of journeys reaching destinations at least 25km away from home. The distance and travel time distributions of the trips follow the same pattern of a mixture of day trips plus a share of really long-distance trips (See Figure 14. and Figure 14.8).

The car dominated as the main mode, with a share of 86% of all reported trips. The non-car alternatives, in the main the various forms of public transport, increased their shares for the longer distance and travel time trips and journeys. They also had a higher share for the shorter trips distances.

14.7   ASSESSMENT AND RECOMMENDATIONS

The experiences gained with the two hand-held devices demonstrated the feasibility of using this approach to collecting travel diary data. The quality of the data was good and the respondents reported satisfaction with these experiences, while preferring the colour device of the second experiment. This impression is reinforced by the results of the larger scale Portuguese field trials in the winter of 1998/99, where the HPC device received good grades from the respondents.

Figure 14.6   Distribution of the number of journeys (HPC and PPC pilot tests)

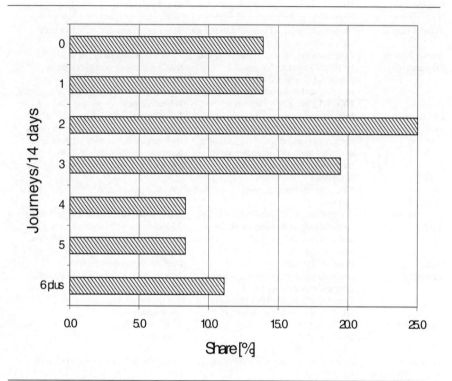

The tests showed that it is possible to obtain representative samples of respondents, even if the survey tool is computer-based. While the novelty of the devices will have helped in these trials, there is no reason to believe that this willingness to participate will disappear. Clearly, participants with little computing experience need extra support, but this is not an insurmountable hurdle.

The reluctance of the respondents to enter their data during their journeys was disappointing. It could be due to fears about damaging or losing the devices, which the respondents had only on loan. This obstacle will disappear in the future as more people own and carry these types of device for their own purposes. WAP-enabled mobile phones would be a prime example. Alternatively, this reluctance can be due to an unwillingness to interrupt the day for data entry, an activity which will never become so frequent as to become quasi-automatic and easy. If this is the main reason, then a combination of passive tracking with a GPS-equipped device (mobile, PDA) plus some active data entry at the end of the day (on the WAP mobile or via a web-site) might be more promising in the future. The prompted data entry during the day could then be directed to those queries, which relate to that moment exactly: mood and satisfaction, planned activities, perceived choice sets, etc.

Figure 14.7   Distribution of trip distances (HPC and PPC pilot tests)

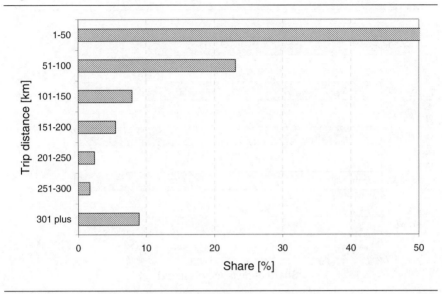

Figure 14.8   Distribution of trip travel times (HPC and PPC pilot tests)

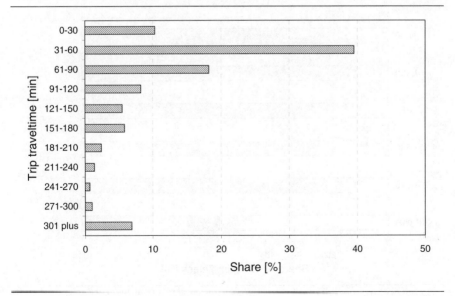

Figure 14.9   Share of modes by trip distances (HPC and PPC pilot tests)

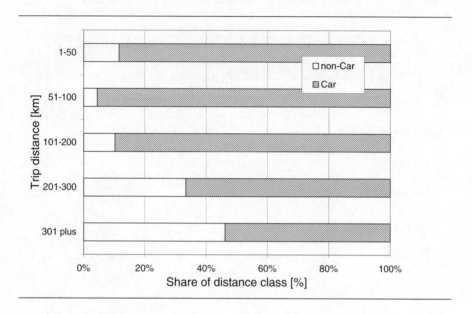

Figure 14.10   Share of modes by trip traveltimes (HPC and PPC pilot tests)

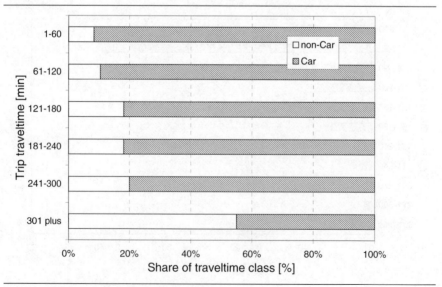

241

14.8 REFERENCES

Ampt, E. (1997) - Respondent burden: Understanding the people we survey. *Resource paper prepared for an International Conference on Transport Survey Quality and Innovation, Raising the Standard*, Grainau, May 1997.

Axhausen K.W. (1996) - Possible contents and formats for long-distance travel diaries: Internal review and critique. *Report to the CEC, DG VII, Transport Research Programme of the 4ᵗʰ Framework Programme, MEST Deliverable,* **D1**, Fakultät für Bauingenieurwesen und Architektur, Leopold-Franzens-Universität, Innsbruck.

Haubold, I., K.W. Axhausen, P. Jackson and J.W. Polak (1997) - Technology Assessment, report to the CEC, DG VII. *Transport Research Programme of the 4ᵗʰ Framework Programme, TEST Deliverable,* **D1**, Fakultät für Bauingenieurwesen und Architektur, Leopold-Franzens-Universität, Innsbruck.

Kalfs, N. and W.E. Saris (1996) - New data collection methods in travel surveys. *Paper presented at the Fourth International Conference on Survey Methods in Transport*, Steeple Aston, September 1996.

MEST (1996) - Methods of European Surveys of Behaviour: Technical Annex. *Transport Research Programme of the 4ᵗʰ Framework Programme*, Fakultät für Bauingenieurwesen und Architektur, Leopold-Franzens-Universität, Innsbruck.

Riede, T. (1993) - Zur Einsetzbarkeit von Laptops in Haushaltsbefragungenin der Bundesrepublik Deutschland, Schlußbericht SAEG-Studie. *Ausgewählte Arbeitsunterlagen zur Bundesstatistik,* **20**, Statistisches Bundesamt, Wiesbaden.

Stecher, C.C., S. Bricka and L. Goldenberg (1996) - Travel behaviour survey data collection instruments. *Paper presented at the Fourth International Conference on Survey Methods in Transport*, Steeple Aston, September 1996.

TEST (1996) - Technologies for European surveys of Travel Behaviour: Technical Annex. *Transport Research Programme of the 4ᵗʰ Framework Programme*, Fakultät für Bauingenieurwesen und Architektur, Leopold-Franzens-Universität, Innsbruck.

TEST (1997) - Technologies for European Surveys of Travel Behaviour: Detailed work package descriptions, report to the CEC, DG VII. *Transport Research Programme of the 4ᵗʰ Framework Programme*, Fakultät für Bauingenieurwesen und Architektur, Leopold-Franzens-Universität, Innsbruck.

Youssefzadeh, M. and K.W. Axhausen (1996) - Long-distance diaries today: Initial review and critique, report to the CEC, DGVII. *Transport Research Programme of the 4ᵗʰ Framework Programme, MEST Deliverable,* **D2**, Fakultät für Bauingenieurwesen und Architektur, Leopold-Franzens-Universität, Innsbruck.

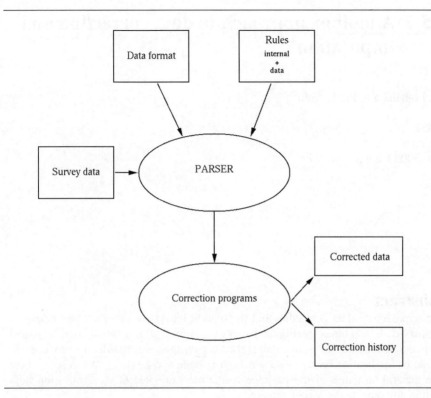

Chapter 15
A toolbox approach to data correction and imputation

O. Lothaire and Ph. L. Toint

15 A toolbox approach to data correction and imputation[1]

O. Lothaire and Ph. L. Toint

TRG
FUNDP
B – 5000 Namur

Abstract

An approach to data correction and imputation based on a toolbox philosophy is discussed. It combines intelligent parsing strategies with a set of more classical imputation methods in a modular software package. Safeguards are proposed to make its application on real data sets both reliable and flexible. We describe here the general structure of the package and some examples of its application both within and outside the MEST project.

Keywords

Travel survey, imputation, item non-response, toolbox approach.

---

[1] Preferred citation: Lothaire, O. and Ph. L. Toint (2003) A toolbox approach to data correction and imputation, in K. W. Axhausen, J.-L. Madre, J. W. Polak and Ph. L. Toint (eds.) *Capturing Long-Distance Travel*, 243 - 254, Research Studies Press, Baldock.

15.1 INTRODUCTION

Travel surveys always contain incomplete and wrong data, and different types of incomplete data may occur. The more severe is *unit non-response,* which refers to the failure of a unit in the sample frame to participate in the survey. This kind of problem is usually taken care of by means of reweighting strategies. A second type of missing data is *item non-response,* which refers to failure of a respondent to respond to one or more item(s) (questions) in the survey. This type of problem is often handled using imputation procedures. Most surveys, including travel surveys, are, of course, designed to reduce unit non-response or item non-response. Some classical strategies to reduce both types of non-response include the use of incentives, follow-ups and non-response interviews. Memory joggers may also be used to help the respondent to remember past trips and to reduce the difficulties arising from memory effects (Madre and Zmud, 1997; Denstadli and Lian, 1998). Furthermore, some new technological tools, such as web-based or CATI surveys, include error checking routines which can reduce the amount of incoherent responses. But even if non-response and erroneous response rates can be reduced by appropriate surveys design or approaches based on new technology (web-based surveys or handheld PC-based surveys, see Chapter 14), the problem of erroneous data and item non-response cannot be avoided completely. For the foreseeable future, a data processing step remains necessary. This observation is the basic motivation that drove the work described in this chapter.

The purpose of what follows is to discuss a software package whose purpose is to detect and correct errors that occur in travel survey-related files, as well as item non-response. Our primary goal, at the start of this development, was flexibility and reliability. We also wanted an approach that did not require substantial additional work from the user when applying the new tool to a different data set. For these reasons, we have chosen to develop our package as a very flexible toolbox with a relatively straightforward user interface. Being also interested in maximal transferability (in terms of cost and environment stability), we also chose to make the greatest possible use of public domain software. The combination of these objectives led us to choose an approach based on a parsing strategy rather than on classical programming tools. In such a design, an ensemble of methods is gathered and applied according to a set of rules or to user-defined specifications to a set of variables occurring in ASCII files with no constraint on variables' definition, order or number. These parameters are also specified by means of easily constructed specification files, which are read at the beginning of the process, before the imputations take place. This makes the software applicable to different kinds of travel surveys, avoiding their being limited to the MEST data formats (however, as they were readily available, these were used to validate the algorithms).

This chapter is structured as follows: in the second section, we review some known imputation methods from a theoretical point of view, and compare their main characteristics. The third section discusses the design and architecture of our software package, while some typical results are shown in Section 4. Some conclusions are finally drawn in Section 5.

15.2   IMPUTATION METHODS FOR ITEM NON-RESPONSE

We start by presenting a brief survey of some imputation methods which form the most commonly used methodological basis for handling item non-response. We refer the reader to Armoogum *et al.*, (1998), Madre and Zmud (1997), Dagnelie (1992), Lehtonen and Pahkinen (1996), and Little and Rubin (1987) for more detail.

Different elements are requested as input for the parser. These elements are:

- **mean imputation**: all missing or wrong values for an item are replaced by the respondents' mean for that item; this method can be dangerous in practice, unless the amount of non-response is negligible. When non-response is significant, the means for the imputed items are artificially enforced, and variances as well as standard errors are underestimated.

- **Stratified means imputation**: this method consists in partitioning the unit response set into imputation classes, which are defined according to the values of properly chosen auxiliary variables. The mean of the variable of interest is calculated for each defined class and missing or wrong values are then replaced by the mean value of their class.

- Stratified means imputation goes a long way in avoiding the problems that occur with mean imputation if the reference variables are chosen so that the differences between classes are significant.

- **Hot-deck:** in hot-deck imputation, missing responses are replaced by values selected from respondents in the current survey. The files are sorted for variables correlated to the variable to impute, thereby defining strata in the data set. The previous observation showing the same characteristics as the observation with missing response (e.g. belonging to the same stratum) is then selected to replace the missing or erroneous one.

- Hot-deck is a very widespread procedure. It avoids the problems which can be generated by stratified means method as the variables distributions are not distorted by artificial concentrations on the mean value of each stratum. The main assumption used in hot-deck procedures is that non-response probabilities, even if they can vary from one stratum to the next, are equal within each stratum.

- **Cold-deck** procedures are similar to hot-deck procedures but use data sources other than the current survey.

- **Regression imputation**: the data set is used to fit a regression for the variable for which one or more imputations are needed using other available variables. As can be expected, the correlation between the dependent and independent variables must be significant to ensure reliable results.

- **Random imputations:** a number of procedures based on random numbers have been proposed, including overall random imputation (imputation values are attributed randomly, without limits on random values fixed by probability distributions), and random imputation with limits on random values fixed by probability distributions, for global distributions or distributions within classes (defined by auxiliary variables values as for the stratified means method). We have retained overall mean imputation. The method is applicable if the rate of missing values is not too high. When classifications or distributions are to be considered, other methods should be preferred.

Besides the above-mentioned mathematical imputation algorithms, a set of logical error correction routines was also implemented in our package in order to handle some specific variables for which values must be consistent with each other, e.g. number of household members in the household file must be consistent with the number of household members in the people file.

Another promising approach relies on the *Expectation Minimisation (EM) algorithm* investigated in MEST (see Armoogum *et al.*, 1998, or Chapter 11). This term refers to a broad class of iterative methods of model-based imputation. The basic idea is to compute a mutually consistent set of model parameters and imputed values by means of an appropriate iterative scheme. Unfortunately, time constraints did not allow us to include this more complex approach in our package.

15.3 PACKAGE ARCHITECTURE

As briefly explained in the introduction, the package aims to be applicable to different surveys. This implies that it must be able to work when different data structures are given as input. This, in turn, requires considerable flexibility regarding the order in which data is presented in the data files, but also regarding the detailed format of these files. In effect, this order and these formats may be rather arbitrary.

We were thus led to develop our software around the concept of a parser, which is a specialised tool that analyses the structure of the data (based on keywords and « tokens ») and only subsequently affects the data read in the files to their appropriate logical data structure. Such software tools are quite widely known, and we chose to use one of their most famous (and freely available) incarnations: the combination of the LEX and YACC packages. We refer the reader to Mason and Brown (1990), for further information. All the information needed by the system is then specified by suitable specification files. This set of files does not only define the input data files and the output files, but also specifies the list of variables contained in each data file and the associated methods that are to be applied on their values. These specifications files have a very simple and readable structure and are very easy to modify without requiring modifications to the programs themselves. Each specification file is itself analysed by a parser which converts the specifications into a formal program, without user intervention.

With the set of above-mentioned imputation methods implemented as independent functions and the data parser, it is thus theoretically possible for the user to associate any imputation method to any variable, but, if one wishes to maximise the quality of the results obtained by the procedure, this association cannot be made blindly. The difficulty is that one needs to control the lists of variables to avoid inconsistency and to check if the chosen related imputation methods are consistent with each variable's nature. These constraints may be summarised as follows:

- some variables, such as binary variables, have a restricted finite set of acceptable values. We must know these sets of values, which can vary from one survey to another for the same variable (for example, modes of transport or journey purposes can be designed to regroup some subcategories);
- some variables have a restricted continuous range of acceptable values, which must be known;
- most imputation methods need auxiliary variables that must be correlated with variables to be imputed. These correlations must be checked for relevance.

Moreover, we have to take into account the fact that the user can define his or her own variables, which means that any checking technique based on a catalogue of usual variables and associated methods would typically be incomplete.

In order to ensure quality of the results, the software first checks the correlation factors between variables for methods requiring auxiliary variables. It also takes the rate of missing values into account, as some methods are inadvisable if this rate is too high (stratified means, regression). However, these verifications can never be completely foolproof, because we cannot be sure that the user has made an appropriate choice of imputation technique. For instance, let us imagine that one chooses the mean imputation method for a discrete variable. The mean value of the variable may then be a real number. If we round it to the nearest integer value, we may lose significant information as each value may have a distinct meaning (consider for example variables such as *mode of transport*, *journey purpose*, *marital status*,...). Thus, and despite the embedded verification techniques implemented in our package, user knowledge and competence remains the best guarantee of good results.

The architecture of our package is described in Figure 15.1. This figure shows the different elements that are requested as input for the parser. These elements are:

- the survey data;
- the data format, in the form of a set of files that define the variables' labels, and, for each variable, the imputation methods and their associated auxiliary variables;
- a set of rules to validate the chosen imputation methods, including, for instance, routines that check the correlation factors and the rates of missing values as explained above.

The specification files (data format and validation rules) are first read and their content interpreted, verified (as discussed above) and correction/imputation tools are produced that comply with the user specifications. The survey data is then fed into the program which effectively applies the correction/imputation tools produced by the previous step of the process. The corrected data is finally written in corrected data files, while the correction history files contain a detailed history of the imputation process.

Provision of a correction history is an important element, as very often corrections and imputations are performed in a very *ad hoc* manner and typically left undocumented. Beside the list of items that have been imputed, the correction history files also contain a set of statistical parameters (means and standard deviations) that reflect the (un)successful nature the imputation. The variations of these parameters between uncorrected and corrected data show how the imputation process affects the original distributions. A small variation indicates that the imputation process is successful, under the assumption that the non-response mechanisms are ignorable (Armoogum *et al.*, 1998). A more detailed description of these outputs can be found in Lothaire (1999).

Figure 15.1   General architecture of the toolbox

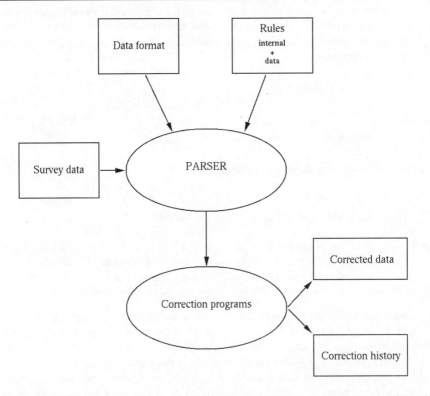

15.4   SOME RESULTS

We now present some results that indicate the effect of applying our package to real surveys. We start by considering its application to the MEST data sets, and focus on the vehicle description files taken from the three pilot waves (wave 1: Portugal; wave 2: Portugal, Great Britain, France, Sweden; and wave 3: Portugal,

Great Britain, France, Sweden), for a total of 1050 observations. We refer the reader to Chapter 5 for a more detailed description of the MEST surveys. The variables describing the vehicles in these data files are:

- presence of a catalytic converter (or *cat*);
- year of purchase (or *y_o_p*);
- total mileage (or *current);*
- mileage during last 12 months (or *vmt*).

The rate of missing data for these variables is relatively important (6.6% for *cat*, 6% for *y_o_p*, 10.2% for *current* and 11% for *vmt*), which is why they were chosen as natural candidates for the application of imputation techniques.

For the purpose of a controlled experimentation, we extracted from all files the 860 complete observations and randomly introduced artificial missing variables in a third of them. Different imputation methods were then investigated, depending on the nature of each variable. For each variable, the related methods and typical results are presented in Table 15-1. This table reports the mean squared error (for *y_o_p*, *current* and *vmt*) and the error percentage (for *cat*) as measures of the quality of the imputation.

Table 15-1   Example results

Variable	Method	Result
Cat	Hot-deck with y_o_p as auxiliary variable	39%
y_o_p	regression, function of current	4.8
Current	regression, function of y_o_p	49044
	Hot-deck with y_o_p as auxiliary variable	52201
Vmt	division of current by y_o_p	12263
	regression, function of current for each y_o_p value	9355
	regression, function of y_o_p for each current value	8083

The main errors for the *cat* variable occur for middle-aged vehicles (*y_o_p* ranging from 1992 to 1994) which have or do not have a converter with a great diversity.This type of error is less frequent for old or new vehicles as the correlation between *y_o_p* and the value of *cat* in these cases is clearer.

The main errors on the variable *y_o_p* are associated with old vehicles: atypical *y_o_p* values for vehicles from the sixties or the seventies are difficult to impute. The imputation results for the *vmt* variable gives interesting results if regressions within classes are performed (*vmt* is then seen as a function of *current* for each *y_o_p* value, or as a function of *y_o_p* for each *current* value). On the other hand, the somewhat naive method of dividing *current* by *y_o_p* to obtain *vmt* does not provide adequate results, mostly because *vmt* is not constant over time, but decreases slightly for old or middle-aged vehicles.

We also had the opportunity to test our package with data from the Austrian

National Travel Survey, which is a substantially larger data set. We have considered the journey description file from this survey and performed hot-deck imputation procedures for the *trip duration* variable. Two procedures have been tested:

- hot-deck with *transport mode* (or mode) as auxiliary variable;
- hot-deck with *transport mode* and *journey purpose* (or *purpose*) as auxiliary variables.

The rate of missing values for this variable is very low (0.5 %), but many records contain negative or obviously erroneous values, caused by incorrect values of reported departure and arrival times. In a first correction step, we have excluded the values outside a 3σ range from the mean value (where σ is the standard deviation of the distribution) and the negative values, thereby increasing the global proportion of missing and erroneous values to 14 %. We then applied the imputation procedures on the corrected data.

Table 15-2 presents the mean and standard deviations for *trip duration* for the original file, the corrected file (excluding erroneous values) and the imputed files.

Table 15-2   Effects of initial correction and hot-deck imputation for trip duration in the Austrian National Travel Survey

	Original data	Excluding erroneous values	Hot-deck by mode	Hot-deck by mode and purpose
Mean	266.8	163.5	165.5	168.5
Std. deviation	6503.7	444.4	455.5	450

Erroneous items in the data file produce large distortions in the variable's distribution. The two hot-deck procedures give very similar imputation results: mean and standard deviation are kept very close to their (corrected) values. This indicates that these procedures seem to be suitable for the imputation of trip duration, a very common variable in travel surveys. These results also indicate that it is safely applicable to large-scale surveys where all the auxiliary variable values are present in a sufficient number of observations. Finally, and most importantly for our purpose, the very fact that we could apply our package to this survey without any modification outside the specification files indicates that our initial design purpose has been reasonably achieved.

15.5 CONCLUSIONS

Three main conclusions can be drawn from the work presented here. The first is that a flexible package based on a toolbox philosophy and implementing reasonable (but, inevitably, imperfect) safeguards can effectively be designed, built and applied to different surveys with varying structure. The second is that the above can be achieved by exploiting public domain software, thereby enhancing transferability, especially from the points of view of price and computing environment stability. The last conclusion is that suitably safeguarded automatic imputation methods can substantially improve the quality of the data with minimal time or resource investment from the user.

15.6 REFERENCES

Armoogum, J., X. Han, J.-L. Madre and J. Polak (1998) - Improved Methods for Weighting and Correcting of Travel Diaries. *Report to the CEC, DG VII, MEST Deliverable,* **D8,** Fakultät für Bauingenieurwessen und Architektur, Leopold-Franzens-Universität, Innsbruck.

Armoogun, J., M. Herry, J.Polak and J.-L. Madre (1996) - Sampling and Weighting Schemes for Travel Diaries: Review of issues and Possibilities. *Report to the CEC, DG VII, MEST Deliverable,* **D6,** Fakultät für Bauingenieurwessen und Architektur, Leopold-Franzens-Universität, Innsbruck.

Axhausen, K.W. (1997) - The Eurostat pilots of long-distance travel diaries: summary of intermediate reports. *Report to the Österreichisches Statistischs Zentralamt,* Wien and EUROSTAT, Luxembourg, Institut für Straßenbau und Verkehrsplannung, Leopold-Franzens-Universitat, Innsbruck.

Axhausen, K.W. and M. Youssefzadeh (1997) - Tender documents: Second MEST pilots, report to the CEC, DG VII, *MEST Internal Working Paper,* **IWP03 and IWP04,** Fakultät für Bauingenieurwessen und Architektur, Leopold-Franzens-Universität, Innsbruck.

Babbie, E. (1990) - Survey Research Methods. Wadsworth Publishing Company, Belmont.

Cornelis, E. (1997) - PACSIM users' manual. *FUNDP - Transportation Research Group,* Namur.

Dagnelie, P. (1992) - Statistique théorique et appliquée. Les presses agronomiques de Gembloux, A.S.B.L, Gembloux.

Denstadli, J.-M. and J.-I. Lian (1998) - Memory effects in long distance travel surveys. *TEST Working Paper,* TOI, Oslo.

Haccou, P. and E. Meelis (1994) - Statistical Analysis of Behavioural Data - An Approach Based on Time-Structured Models. Oxford University Press, Oxford.

INRETS (1996) - Correction de l'enquête transports et mobilite 1993-1994. *Working papers,* **1/42 - 40/42,** INRETS, Arcueil.

Jensen, K and N. Wirth, (1997) - PASCAL, manuel de l'utilisateur et rapport de définition. Eyrolles, Paris.

Lehtonen, R. and E.J. Pahkinen (1996) - Practical Methods for Design and analysis of Complex Surveys (Revised Edition). John Wiley & Sons, Chichester.

Little, R.J.A. and D.B. Rubin (1987) - Statistical Analysis with Missing Data. John Wiley & Sons, Chichester.

Lothaire, O. (1999) - A Knowledge-based Parser: Implementation of a Tool-box, report to the CEC, DGVII. *TEST Deliverable,* **D5A,** Groupe de Recherche sur les Transports, Facultés Universitaires Notre-Dame de la Paix, Namur.

Madre J.-L. and J. Zmud (1997) - Transport surveys, raising the standards: workshop 3: item (sampling, weighting, non-response). *Transportation Research Circular,* **E-C008,** II-D, TRB, Washington D.C.

Mason, T. and D. Brown (1990) - Lex and Yacc. O'Reilly, Sebastopol.

Richardson, A.J., E.S. Ampt and A.H. Meyburg (1995) - Survey Methods for Transport Planning. Eucalyptus Press, Melbourne.

Skinner, C.J., D. Holt and T.M.F. Smith (1996) - Analysis of Complex Surveys. John Wiley & Sons, Chichester.

Youssefzadeh M. and K.W. Axhausen (1996) - Tender documents: First MEST pilots, report to the CEC, DG VII. *MEST Internal Working Paper,* **IWP01 and IWP02,** Fakultät für Bauingenieurwessen und Architektur, Leopold-Franzens-Universität, Innsbruck.

Youssefzadeh M. and K.W. Axhausen (1998) - Tender documents: Third MEST pilots, report to the CEC, DG VII. *MEST Internal Working Paper,* **IWP05 and IWP06,** Fakultät für Bauingenieurwessen und Architektur, Leopold-Franzens-Universität, Innsbruck.

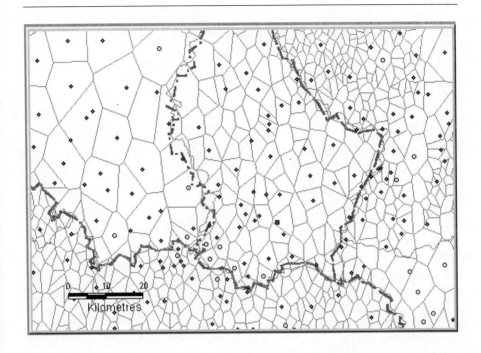

Chapter 16
GIS-based enrichment

J.-P. Hubert

16   GIS-based enrichment[1]

J.-P. Hubert[2]

TRG
FUNDP
B – 5000 Namur

Abstract

Geographical information allows us to reach essential objectives of a survey on personal mobility: making regional O-D matrices; accurate measurement of distance; setting personal behaviours in the geographical context. It is also useful for validation of raw data, during database construction.

Collecting geographical information depends on the different possible survey methods that can be used for long-distance surveys. New technologies enable the collection of such information in GIS format directly. But most survey methods still collect place names that have to be translated into geographical coordinates to enrich the mobility datasets. Such an operation, known as geocoding, relies on complementary information that is to sought in geographical databases, which prove to be a valuable capital of information for transportation studies.

Keywords

GIS, geocoding, database, geographical coordinates, place name.

---

[1] Preferred citation: J.-P. Hubert (2003) GIS-based enrichment, in K. W. Axhausen, J.-L. Madre, J. W. Polak and Ph. L. Toint (eds.) *Capturing Long-Distance Travel*, 255 - 276, Research Studies Press, Baldock.

[2] Now member of GRT, FUNDP, B-5000 Namur.

16.1 INTRODUCTION

Travel diary surveys provide information about the number and spatial distribution of the movements of a population. In addition, modal and temporal characteristics are provided. The analysis of the choices is one of the main uses of travel diary data, another is, in many cases, the derivation of origin-destination (O-D) matrices from the data. Travel surveys also give useful information on transport geography and accessibility of regions. It is usually not possible to exploit transportation data at the smallest geographic level because samples are too small. However, the exact localisation of the stages: origin, destination and route, is crucial. O-D matrices require them obviously even if, in the case of long-distance travel survey, the geographic level of such matrix is only regional: estimates of distances by the respondents are not as good as estimates derived from exact locations of stopping places. The choice models depend on the provision of the description at a local level of the non-chosen alternatives, which can only be obtained by positioning survey data within the complete network. Thus, choice models also require exact locations and this information must be available and exploitable in the data set. However traditional transportation survey datasets do not often contain spatial data. This chapter aims to present how geographical information can be integrated into a travel diary survey and its data set.

After an overview of the benefits brought by the exact knowledge of the locations of stages and stopping places, we will discuss the degree of precision that can be aimed at with respect to the objectives and methodologies of transportation surveys. We will also present the different means of acquisition of geographical information and the database organisation that this kind of data implies.

16.2 USE OF GEOGRAPHICAL INFORMATION

16.2.1 Computing distances and consolidating travel data

An ideal travel diary survey should capture an exact description of all the places, roads, railways, etc., where respondents actually travelled. More modestly, the knowledge of the exact location of stopping places makes it possible to determine a probable route and compute an estimate of the travel distance. Such a method does not give the actual travel distance, but it is a far better estimate that the one which can be obtained from respondents. When the locations of activities are known and transportation networks are available, a minimum path algorithm can compute a probable estimate of the real distance, of the average speed, and split it up into different portions according to the mode or type of road used (Figure 16.1).

Small black crosses are the nodes of a road network extracted from Bartholomew's *Euromaps* main and secondary road, and motorway layers, all integrated in one particular GIS layer. Large spots and dotted polylines indicate a route between Lisbon and Covilha, as positioned in Bartholomew's *Euromaps* database. They can be stored in a specific layer as an add-on to the original set of data.

258

Figure 16.1　　　Route generated with the help of a minimum path algorithm

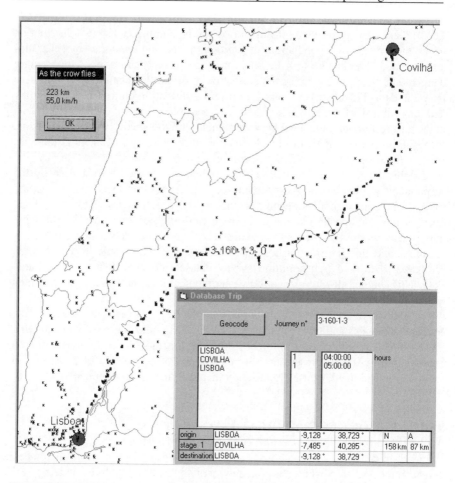

The crow-fly distance between these two towns is 223 km, which leads to an approximate average speed of 55 km/h (duration is four hours). With the parameters chosen, the route is 245 km long and split between 158 km of secondary road and 87 km of motorway.

It is worth noticing that if this distance can be computed during the interview, this may detect some mistakes in place names (e.g. if a trip Geneve-Nyon in Switzerland is confounded with a trip from Genova in Italy to Lyon in France, the average speed will immediately appear excessively high). Collecting place names is prone to errors. Generally, misspelled names do not correspond to actual places, but, since many names are similar, a wrong name may derive from several right names, and it is not always easy to find out which one was actually visited.

Computing distance and average speed is one of the simple ways of verification and validation of geographical information that does not require supplemental questions.

16.2.2 Understanding the influence of local factors on mobility choices

People determine their choices according to the possibilities that they encounter locally, provided they are informed about their existence. That is the reason why some local factors, rather than regional, can explain much of the organisation of transportation. It is therefore important that modelling transportation should be able to integrate these local factors. Place characteristics give the opportunity to build two kinds of set of places: discontinuous sets defined by typologies (according to the population, economic activity, touristic attraction, etc.), and continuous sets (or clusters), such as metropolitan areas or regions. Then, some trip variables (trip purpose or mode for instance) can be crossed with types of places, or tabulated by regions.

Geographical databases are organised according to different levels of territorial statistics. The municipal level is generally the basic level and is referred to as Nuts5 in European statistics[3]. It is therefore particularly important to locate municipalities, or "Nuts 5 units", where changes occur, in order to cross transportation data with territorial variables. Some variables, such as: density, local income, active population, etc. are "internal variables" of the municipalities since they describe the social and economical contents of these geographical areas. The situation within a spatial structure (e.g.: central core, inner/outer suburb, peripheral belt, etc.), the connections with other Nuts 5 areas (e.g.: number of commuters between two municipalities, etc.) are "external" or "situational variables" of the geographical areas. The French national personal transportation survey (NPTS) has shown, for instance, a noticeable grading of duration and distance of daily trips according to a situational variable based on a centre/periphery model of spatial organisation (Madre and Maffre, 1997).

Finally, it is important to produce analyses that are relevant to the Nuts 5 level, and not only to the regional level, since local authorities are often responsible for various aspects of the transport organisation and need information on these topics.

Statistical criteria of representativeness often force the analyst to aggregate results at a regional level. But this aggregation hides the fact that these results are obtained, most probably, from a very small number of dense zones, either for the origin or the destination of the stages. According to the analysis of the two latest French NPTSs, indeed, it can be assumed that the probability of a place being quoted in a travel diary survey is very closely related to the distribution of

---

[3] *"Nomenclature Unifiée des Territoires et Statistiques"*. The fifth level is commonly the municipal one, except for UK and Portugal. The level zero is the one of the national states.

population: 22.6% of the French municipalities counted more than 1000 inhabitants in 1990, and capture 83.5% of the population; 82% of the places appearing as destinations in the 1993-94 French NPTS (both for long distance and daily mobility) belong to that size category. In the 1981-82 survey (for daily mobility only), 21% of the municipalities had more than 1000 inhabitants (according to the 1982 census); they captured 82.7% of the national population and represented about 81.5% of the names recorded in the survey.

Cumulative distribution of names in the surveys, as well as distribution of population, as a function of the size of the municipalities, follow almost exactly the same curve (Figure 16.2). If the municipality size is scaled by the logarithm of the population, the function follows a logistic curve. From 500 to 200,000 inhabitants, the logistic curve is very close to a line, as a regression analysis made for this interval shows (Table 16-1). Results are very similar for daily mobility, either in the 90s or in the 80s (Hubert, Flavigny and Madre, 1999). This result is related to a statistical law credited to the American statistician Zipf, and identified in 1903 by the German geographer Aushofer (Le Bras, 1996).

Table 16-1   Correlation between French municipal populations in 1990 and frequency of their place-names as stage destination in the French National Transportation Survey of 1993-94

Statistical population and place names	Cumulative probability = (%)
Long distance national trips of 93-94 F. NPTS (38 140 destinations in 5 434 places)	$32.51 \times \log10 (\text{population}90) - 82.23$ [0.026] [0.093] $r2=0.997$
1990 municipal population (56.53 millions inhabitants in 36 570 places)	$33.36 \times \log10 (\text{population}90) - 82.98$ [0.015] [0.048] $r2=0.997$

This study, based on French cases, leads to the point that the frequency of the place names mentioned follows the distribution of population in geographical places. Therefore, the list of the 'N' first geographical places in the population should allow the geocoding of a percentage of destinations equivalent to the fraction of the total population that live in these 'N' places. This rule implies that the problem of geocoding has two parts. There are, on the one hand, highly visited places that can be immediately geocoded, and, on the other hand, small places that seldom appear and may be very difficult to locate.

Figure 16.2   Superimposition of cumulative frequency of place-names and
                   of cumulative percentage of population according to the place
                   populations

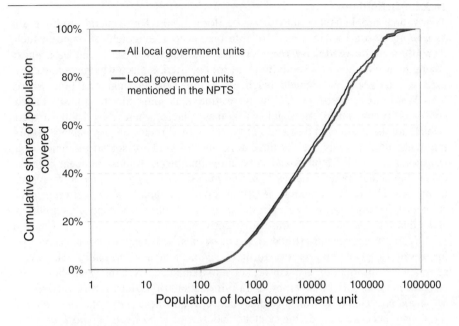

16.3   GEOCODING OBJECTIVES AND DEFINITION

16.3.1   Geocoding data for a long-distance travel survey

The main issue of geocoding is not to find the exact locations of stages and
activities but to produce a relevant geographical position. In the case of long-
distance travel diary surveys, this position should be precise enough, as seen, to
cross social and economical statistics with travel behaviours and also to
reconstitute a virtual but probable stage. In the European context, this goal can be
achieved by finding the names of the municipalities (or Nuts 5 unit) where the
respondent stopped and then measuring the distances between their centres, giving
a sensible approximation. Territorial level "Nuts 5" is therefore a privileged
reference for the events recorded in the survey.

In the case of surveys inside one urban area, it is necessary to work on
another scale and to use smaller divisions; sometimes postal address is the
desirable spatial reference. The minimum path algorithm can be substituted by
more precise methods, such as asking people to draw their travels on a city map or
to carry in their car a GPS (Global Positioning System) receiver backed with a

recorder (e.g. a palmtop computer, see Thill, 2000). This last method obviously raises new problems because of the autonomy and 'inquisitiveness' of electronic devices, which presently seem insoluble for a long-distance travel survey.

16.3.2 Definitions

Terms and problematics must now be formalised. The general problem of *geocoding* is to associate a piece of information to a geographical object, which then becomes its *spatial reference*. That spatial reference can be either a place where an event (such as an activity in a trip) occurred, a place which contains any kind of statistical individuals (such as a town or an agglomeration where households are settled) or it can be a line that joins all the places linked continuously by a trip. Respondents' homes, places where they have stopped (which are the origin and destination of a stage), and routes of respondents' stages that make up a journey are the three fundamental kinds of spatial reference in a transportation survey. Homes and stops are point objects, routes are linear objects. Collecting actual routes requires a *tracing tool* and a *mapping device* to represent them. An alternative solution is to generate probable routes between data collection and analysis. In that case, the spatial references of a stage are simplified and reduced to a sequence of consecutive activities.

Spatial references are stored in a geographical information system (GIS)) as the result of geocoding in the form of *mathematical coordinates*. However, geographical information is always relative to a reference system. Then, their level of precision can only be given by extra information, of various forms, referred to as *metadata*. Geographical metadata concern all these sets of *conventional references* necessary to define a clear and scientific *measure of position* at a certain level of accuracy.

When positions are measured very precisely, as in the case of bridges, tunnel construction, or navigation, geographical metadata are mainly contained in the *geodetic datum*, because the method of measurement is purely geometrical. When the method of localisation is based on interviews and investigations about places visited during some journeys, the term metadata is more metaphoric and points out the reference geographic databases and their characteristics which limit the possible precision of location and are related to questions such as: "How many points are there in each region or country?", "What is the nature of the point known by its coordinates - is it the place of a town hall, a gravity centre in terms of population, the geometric centre - or centroid -, or a post office?", "What is the accuracy of the coordinates (many geographical coordinates are only available in degrees and minutes of terrestrial arc, which implies an accuracy of only one nautical mile)?"

16.4 GEOGRAPHICAL INFORMATION AND SURVEY METHODOLOGIES

16.4.1 Various ways of collecting geographical information

Since the spatial referencing of data increases their quality, geocoded data should be integrated very early in the survey process. But such an objective has to cope with heavy technical requirements on software and database content. It is a very general issue in survey design to find a balance between the resolution of information, their statistical significance and their cost. In the case of geographical information, a balance has to be found between the accuracy of geocoding and the spatial and temporal coverage of the survey. Geocoding requires numerical geographical databases of places and transportation networks. Thus, the criteria to compare are on the one hand, the size of the place-name database, which should be as large as possible to contain in advance all the various possible answers, the cost of acquiring and updating such databases, and the speed of a query of such a very large database. On the other hand, the criteria should be the number of similar names or homonyms which can artificially produce ambiguities and errors, the low interest of an accurate localisation in a low density area, rarely chosen destinations of respondents' journeys, and the relatively small number of places actually visited in a survey in most regions.

The various survey methods give different kinds of geographical indications which are the input of a geocoding process. Indeed, the different survey techniques rely more or less on the respondent's memory of the names of places. In order to indicate how to go somewhere, one uses both names and indications of movement and distances; for instance: '15km after Metz [Moselle, F], on the road to Thionville' [Moselle, F]. Methods used in travel diary surveys do not collect relative indications but only conventionally-referenced place-names. They mostly rely on the respondent's memory of names and not on the memory of movements, unless maps or navigation instruments are used to represent the stages, which are movements within space; and when a survey is based on personal interviews, interviewers do bring maps for this purpose, either paper or digital on a laptop computer (which can be also used to record the stages and geocode them instantly). Lists of names can also help to find a name that has been forgotten. More and more paper maps have indexes of places printed on their back, and large lists of places are easy to query on a computer during a telephone interview. If tracing devices could be used, appeals to the respondent's memory would no longer be required (Flavigny and Madre, 1994). Let us examine then, various ways of collecting geographical indications, and the different methods to geocode them and to integrate geographical information into the set of data.

16.4.2 Methods using mapping devices (from paper to internet)

It is possible to give, as an annex to the survey form, one or more maps to the respondents for drawing their stages during the survey period. This procedure assumes that they will be able to draw their journey on a paper map, which is not easy for everybody. To be exploited, marked maps have to be processed by a scanner or digitizer linked to a computer. A dedicated application is needed to drive the digitizer or load scanned images, to transfer routes drawn on paper into the GIS by clicking on the map or on the screen, to check positions if the operator has clicked a little aside, etc. Scanned images have advantages compared to digitised data because they can be stored and they do not move when processed. Scanners are cheap, but digitizers are more helpful for prolonged use.

Assuming that the paper map is designed and printed with great care, the last problem is to translate centimetres on paper sheets or pixels on screen into geographical coordinates accurately, so that clicking on a point on the map can geocode an activity. Map design must include special indications, such as targets in the corners, to set formulas of translation between the paper and geographical coordinates systems. However, this solution reaches limits when the reference territory is very wide, such as the 15 countries of the EU. The scale of a map of all European Union on an A3 sheet (29.7 x 42 cm) cannot exceed 1:5 000 000, which is hardly consistent with visibility of Nuts 3 areas, especially in densely populated regions with small Nuts 3 territories (Ile-de-France, most western-German *Länder*).

All these problems with the design of the paper map and the transfer to a computer disappear when the respondent can use a software application integrating a digital atlas, and specific functions to draw the stages and store them. But it is very difficult to put such instruments into practice outside costly surveys made with personal interviews assisted by a laptop computer. In the near future, surveys will probably be made through the Internet, but it seems that, at the moment, the use of the Internet strongly biases the sample of respondents. Even though they also belong to the future of long-distance travel surveys, electronic positioning instruments have rapidly become widespread and are worth mentioning. Common GPS receivers can record some points but, as yet, not enough to follow somebody during a complete journey of several days. The receiver has to be linked to a computer that records the stream of geographical coordinates. Post-processing the data is necessary, first to identify stopping places out of this stream, and, if high precision is required, to correct the errors due to the occultation of a satellite, in order to find, for instance, roads actually taken by vehicles. The main problems raised by this method for long-distance mobility studies, which require very long survey periods, are the autonomy of such a device and its bulk, given the present state of technology. This method is nevertheless successfully used for daily mobility studies (Zito *et al.*, 1994, Batelle, 1997)[4].

16.4.3 Without a mapping mediator and with more uncertainty

The most common and cheapest way to obtain locations is to ask the respondents to report verbally or write down the places where they stayed. This geographical information is obtained in its lexical form with all the possible mistakes, as mentioned before, especially when a respondent has been abroad. The sole place-name is often not sufficient geographical information to prevent geocoding errors

---

[4] Triangulation from radio emitters identified by RDS signals seems to represent a much lighter method in terms of hardware equipment, energy consumption, etc. Its accuracy would not be comparable to GPS but seems consistent with long-distance survey requirements (Flavigny and Bouvier, 2000).

due to homonyms, all the more frequent as the space covered by the survey is large. Therefore, if there is no interaction between interviewers and respondents, the questions about the place-name should be accompanied at least by others about the region, country or closest town to it.

In an interactive procedure, such as a telephone or personal interview, answers concerning geographical items can be controlled by interviewers who have maps and/or lists of places at their disposal. It is worth noticing that most computer-assisted telephonic interviews are presently conducted in a non-graphic software environment that precludes using a GIS during the interview. Therefore, only lists of place names can be used and these lists should include specific complementary fields for the interviewer to cross-check names with indications given by the respondent (name of the region, but also the size of the locality, the river that flows through the place, etc.).

If geographical information is stored in the form of one or several place-names, geocoding procedures must contain a second step to associate these names to their positions in mathematical space. Geographical coordinate assignment is based on character string comparison between place-names from transportation survey datasets and tables of georeferences, or *geographical indexes*. Such comparisons lead to three kinds of results, depending on the number of place-names in the reference index that match with a name from the survey dataset. Let these matching georeferences be called *geographical candidates* of a place (see Figure 16.3).

If there is no geographical candidate, the process may search in two directions: other geographical indexes or looser rules for matching. A *searching strategy* must have been previously defined, including the use of a parser application to correct misspelled names (a very first step in this strategy being the elimination of diacritic marks; see next section). If there are several geographical candidates – and even if there is only one, since the criterion is not certain – rules are needed to validate the most plausible candidate and/or eliminate impossible cases. Such a *validation strategy* is primarily based on consistency with other information from the journey, especially the duration of the stage. If no candidate appears at the first attempt, a second step in the searching strategy is initiated, with looser matching rules and/or larger geographical indexes. Both possibilities normally lead to a larger number of candidates[5]. The diagram below schematically

---

[5] This is due to geography and history. A geographical reason is that when a city is large, it is known throughout a large area and cannot have the same name as other cities around, while villages have to be known only inside rather small areas. Therefore distant villages can have the same name without confusing many people, whereas towns have sometimes to modify their names because of possible confusions with other towns. A recent example is, in France, Châlons-sur-Marne, 48,500 inhabitants, capital city of the region Champagne-Ardennes (Nuts 1) and of a *département* (Nuts 3 Marne) which changed its name in 1998 for Châlons en-Champagne because of confusions with Chalon-sur-Saône (*sous-préfecture* of Saône-et-Loire), 54,600 inhabitants. An historical reason is that the older human

describes this geocoding process.

16.4.4 Implementing geocoding

A searching strategy slackens matching rules by steps: fewer common letters are required at each level, until a minimum number is reached. For compound names (e.g. La Línea de la Concepción, Andalucia Esp), partial matches are valuable but for articles. If the last step is reached without success, and no complementary place-names database can be used, another type of procedure can be attempted in certain cases. If a stopping place is known to be close to another one that was geocoded, then the places located within a certain distance from that recognised place can be selected as geographical candidates. Their validation is more problematic. Validation strategy uses many criteria. By order of importance, they are:

- consistency with the region or Nuts 3 zone;
- plausibility of average speed obtained from distance as the crow flies and duration of stage (it should vary between 5 and 120 km/h);
- analysis of phonetical resemblance between the geographical candidates and the survey data, such analysis is difficult to implement in a software but is often conclusive;
- population of the geographical candidates, the larger being the most probable.

If additional geographical information (e.g. region) is not consistent with the geographical candidates, then a searching strategy is used again. It is first oriented on the additional geographical information. For instance, the geocoding can be validated if the place-name from the survey matches the name of the geographical candidate and if the Nuts 3 zone indicated by the respondent is close to the actual Nuts 3 of the geographical candidate. It can be close by the letters (e.g. Loire, F, and Loiret, F) or geographically (e.g. Savoie, F, and Isère, F) or both (e.g. Savoie, F, and Haute-Savoie, F). If the inconsistency remains, the searching strategy can eventually be applied to the place-name.

A prototype tool was made to progress the analysis of the problem and to work on small samples. Basic functions that were implemented were:

- reading the survey datase;
- querying the place-names dataset to find geographical candidates, at two

---

settlements are, the more diverse are their names, because languages have evolved a great deal. As towns in Europe are often very old settlements, the diversity of their names is very large. Many villages were founded in the same periods in Europe, by waves of colonisation (clearing forests, dyking up polders, etc.) to exploit neglected lands by new techniques. Such places often acquired similar names scattered in different regions. As local parlances have become more homogeneous, differentiation has diminished. Thus, risks of homonyms between place-names depends on rural and urban character and on population size.

levels of searching strategy;
- display geographical candidates in a table and on a GIS map, with attributes such as:

Figure 16.3   Principle for geocoding place-names

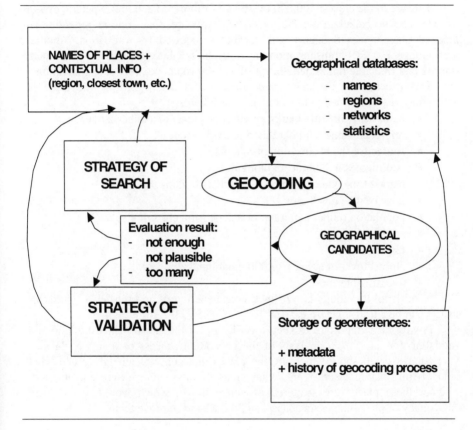

- o   distance to any other stopping place and average speed;
- o   region;
- o   route calculation;
- o   storage of results.

The GIS is required only for displaying the map and for storage. These operations use procedures of Mapinfo™ Integrated mapping with Microsoft Visual Basic™, based on OLE link. This technology has been also used at Inrets for the European project *Commute* (CSST, ENEA and Inrets, 2000). Other functions are implemented apart from the GIS, so that they can be optimised and adapted to a non-graphical environment. This implies that GIS data about places and networks have to be extracted into ASCII or DBF files to become input data for these modules. GIS is used upstream of geocoding for the organisation and maintenance of the geographical databases, and downstream for the storage of results and cartographic analysis. Updating and enriching the geographical datasets with new data require lots of specific GIS operations: conversion of coordinates, minor modifications on positions and geometry (e.g. if a town "falls" into the sea because of biases in the coordinates), enrichment of tables with contextual information (e.g. distance to the closest 100,000 inhabitant or more urban area). Specific export routines can be called inside the geocoding software. One routine generates an indexed place-names database with attributes required for validation. Another routine exports GIS transportation network layers into graphs matrices, with starting and finishing nodes, length, speed, type of road, etc., for route generation.

The structure of the place-name database is determined by the logic of geocoding. A minimum structure contains these fields:

- name with diacritic marks, or alternate name in another language;
- reference name, without diacritic marks (index);
- source for the localisation of this place;
- coordinates in latitude and longitude;
- name of the Nuts 5 territorial unit that contains this place;
- code of the Nuts 5 unit;
- population (either a number or a code for a class of size);
- country;
- region;
- closest town of at least 10,000 inhabitants;
- touristic interest.

Note: if all the points are distinct, concatenation of coordinates as character strings can be a useful key (e.g. " E2°20'58"N48°51'53" " for Paris).

Finally, it is important to keep log files of all the steps of investigation and validation for an *ex post* analysis of the geocoding process of a survey dataset. Such analysis will show which are the places that generate ambiguity and what kind of information clears it up; what kinds of misspellings were encountered; whether these places are scattered or concentrated, which would reveal local inadequacy of place-names databases, and the way to improve them.

16.5 SPECIFIC PROBLEMS OF EUROPEAN SURVEYS

The European context raises specific problems due to the historical multiplicity of geodetic systems, linguistic diversity, and multiplicity of national territorial policies which have induced a great heterogeneity in territorial administration units. Mastering this heterogeneity is necessary when carrying out a survey at the European scale.

16.5.1 Different mathematical coordinate systems

Each European country has its own national geodetic system and its own set of projections for maps, national, cartesian, and legal coordinates, that are not compatible, so that geographical objects of two neighbouring countries cannot be mapped without homogenising coordinates and projections. Most GIS software does that easily, but statistical software packages cannot. What common coordinate system should be used? Geographical coordinates, latitude/longitude noted (L,M) are homogeneous[6] for all the countries and simplify the storage of position. If it proves necessary to make computations in place coordinates in a neighbourhood of a specific place, it is convenient to use a Cassini projection (Figure 16.4). No reference to any national geodetic system is required.

However, the distance between two points is a little more complicated to compute out of a GIS because it is no longer cartesian, but spherical. This is not too serious a difficulty, because a very good approximation of distance is given by the formula of the length of a great circle on a sphere:

Given $P_1(L_1,M_1)$ and $P_2(L_2,M_2)$, the angle α of the great circle arc joining P_1 and P_2 is given by the fundamental formulas:

$$Cos\ \alpha = Sin\ L_1 . Sin\ L_2 + Cos\ L_1 . Cos\ L_2 . Cos\ (M_1-M_2)$$
$$Distance = Radius . ArcCos(Sin\ L_1 . Sin\ L_2 + Cos\ L_1 . Cos\ L_2 . Cos\ (M_1-M_2)).$$

Figure 16.4   Cassini projection

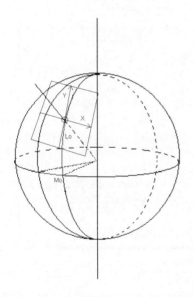

Close to the point of geographical coordinates (L_0,M_0), plane coordinates (X,Y) of other places are given by the formulas of the Cassini projection :

$$X=ArcSin(Cos\ (L-L_0) . Sin\ (M-M_0))$$
$$Y=ArcTg\ (\tau\ (L-L_0) / Cos\ (M-M_0))$$

---

[6] With the accuracy required by long-distance transport survey, a spherical model of the planet, with a radius of 6,366 km (average between the big and small axis of the ellipsoid or approximately $40,000 /2.\pi$) is sufficient.

16.5.2 Heterogeneity of Nuts 5 and Nuts 3 zoning systems in the different European countries

Territorial integration is very different according to national political systems and the size of the national territories. The local level is logically the most homogeneous since European local communities may be considered to be culturally similar. But municipalities are still very heterogeneous throughout Europe (Figure 16.5) (Le Bras, 1996). Average areas and populations vary from 52 km^2 and 17,740 inhabitants (1996) in Belgian municipalities; 59 km^2 and 27,200 inhabitants (1997) in Dutch municipalities; 38 km^2 and 7,000 inhabitants (1991) in Italy; 22 km^2 and 1,700 (1991) in Greece; 15 km^2 and 1,500 inhabitants in 1990 in France.

Nuts 5 centres and boundaries can be purchased from national geographical institutes. Creation and merging of municipalities changes this database every year, sometimes drastically (e.g. the UK in 1974). National geographical institutes have joined forces in the Megrin consortium, to publish an official Nuts 5 coverage, but without any demographic information (Hubert and Moriconi, 1999).

Figure 16.5   Example of Nuts 5 coverage heterogeneity between four countries

---

Comparison of Nuts 5 distributions in Belgium, France, Grand Duché de Luxembourg, Rheinland Pfalz, Saarland. Municipal boundaries are represented by schematic voronoi polygons

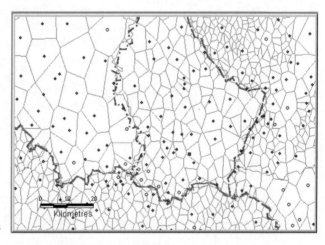

Nuts 5 names, actual or past, for each European country must be the core of the place-name dataset in order to merge transportation data with local statistics. However, Nuts 5 units may not be a relevant set of place-names for geocoding in some countries which have a very small number of municipalities: Sweden has only 289 units for 450,000 km^2 and 8.8 million people (1994), but there are more than 2,000 "parishes"; Portugal has 274 *conselhos* but more than 3,800 *freguesias* (70 of them in Lisbon and Porto alone); the 589 Belgian *communes* can be complemented by the names of 2,400 places which were municipalities before the administrative reform in 1977, similar for most *Länder* of Germany. In the Netherlands and UK, administrative denominations may differ a lot from commonly used place-names[7]. The place database of the US National Imaging and Mapping Agency (NIMA) can give an idea of the adequate number of places for the different countries of the European Union (Table 16-2).

Table 16-2   Number of Nuts 5 units compared to population and number of place-names gathered by US NIMA

Country	Number of Nuts 5 in 1991	Number of inhabited place-names in NIMA sets (year)	Average municipal population after 1990	Places in NIMA sets per municipality
Portugal	270	16 480 (1961)	36 410	61
Sweden	290	26 240 (1989)	30 320	90.5
Netherlands	630	7 950 (1990)	24 410	12.6
Denmark	280	7 050 (1990)	18 590	25.2
Belgium	590	15 370 (1963)	17 090	26.1
Poland	2 320	42 500 (1988)	16 610	18.3
Finland	450	11 210 (1962)	11 320	24.9
Norway	440	9 730 (1996)	9 830	22.1
Italy	8 100	17 720 (1996)	7 060	2.2
Germany	14 850	77 080 (1960)	5 480	5.2
UK	11 500	14 650 (1950)	5 050	1.3
Spain	8 080	27 820 (1961)	4 850	3.4
Czech Republic	3 000	16 270 (1955)	3 440	5.4
Austria	2 370	14 500 (1963)	3 390	6.1
Luxembourg	120	620 (1950)	3 340	5.2
Hungary	3 070	9 950 (1993)	3 340	3.2
Switzerland	2 920	3 040 (1950)	2 400	1
Greece	5 920	11 340 (1960)	1 760	1.9
France	36 660	57 820 (1964)	1 520	1.6
Eire/Ireland	3 440	10 400 (1950)	1 040	3

For Nuts 5, national statistical institutes, country population: Bartholomew, figures rounded. San Marino, Andorra, Gibraltar, Vatican City, Channel Islands, Malta, Cyprus etc. are not present for simplification purpose)

---

[7]   An example is given by British wards where we can find in Cheshire: "Macclesfield Central, "Macclesfield East", "...North East", "...North West", "...South", and "...West". There are 14,000 wards but less than 8,000 names when these adjectives are suppressed.

In EU countries, upper territorial levels (sub-regional - Nuts 3- and regional - Nuts 2 -) which are possible aggregation level for the construction of OD matrices are stable in their limits but still very heterogeneous in size, population and numbers (around 50 Nuts 3 for Spain and UK, ten more than Belgium and the Netherlands, half as many as France or Italy, while Germany counts more than 400 *Kreise*). Conceptions of urban areas and towns also differ (Pumain *et al.*, 1991). Countries preparing their entry into the EU, such as Poland, have conducted wide administrative reforms at these levels. Heterogeneity of municipal coverage is an historical and political result, and is not unique to Europe. The colonisation process of northern America has also produced a very heterogeneous set from one coast to the other.

For this project, Inrets had to gather several geographical databases:

- Nuts 5 basemap was assembled from various national lists of municipalities or smaller territorial units, with recent populations and coordinates of their centres (such file is now available from the Megrin basemap);
- two geographical indexes complete the Nuts 5 layer: Bartholomew Euromaps gazetteers and NIMA datasets for European countries (see Table 15.2);
- transportation networks are taken from Bartholomews Euromaps;
- administrative boundaries of Nuts 3 and Nuts 2 basemap from Eurostat;
- urban areas of more than 100,000 inhabitants from Geopolis database (Moriconi,1994).

16.5.3 Multiplicity of languages and regulations

Most European countries have one national language. But some, such as Belgium, Spain or Switzerland, have two or more. History has often bequeathed to towns and villages several spellings in different languages, especially for renowned cities (e.g. Köln [Nordrhein-Westphalen, D], Cologne; Paris [F] Parigi, Parijs; Venezia [ITA], Venedig, Venice, Venise; Lisbõa [PRT], Lisbon, Lisbonne; Lille [Nord, F], Rijsel, etc.). Furthermore, some towns spelt in the foreign language may become homonyms of towns from other countries: Wien [AU], in French is identical to Vienne [Isère, F]; Valencia [ESP], in French is identical to Valence [Drôme, F], etc.

If places have only one official spelling with diacritic marks - their toponym - several spellings without diacritic marks are worth considering. In most Latin countries, accented letters are simply replaced by letters without accent: Lisbõa [PRT] and LISBOA; A Coruña [Galicia, ESP] and A CORUNA in Galician, and La Coroña in Castilian; Almería [Andalucia, ESP] and ALMERIA; Orléans [Loiret, F] and ORLEANS...; but, in Italian, accented letters are replaced by the letter plus an apostrophe: Viganó [Lombardia] and VIGANO'. In Germanic languages, accented letters are transliterated: München [Bayern, D] MUENCHEN; Malmö [Skåne, SWE] MALMOE, Århus [Jylland, DK] AARHUS... Things become more complicated for Cyrillic and Greek names where we can find English, German or French transliterations. These different spellings should be included in the place-name database structure. Attention has also to be focused on the most common locutions, which are often abbreviated (Saint, Sainte, Santo, Sankt, becoming St, Ste, Sto...) or added to the place-name, such as ending "*stadt*" for most German towns in Nuts 5 lists (Karlsruhe Stadt [Baden-Württemberg, D]), since a town as a *Gemeinde* does not have the same administrative name as a town as a *Kreis*. Place-names often have articles in Latin countries, but some national administrations make their lists with the article at the beginning, as people use it (e.g. Belgium) while other countries put them at the end (France, Spain).

Finally, European countries still have various policies concerning copyrights, publication and marketing of geographical data (GISDATA, 1995-97). There are no equivalent products to the "Tiger" data, which include places, administrative divisions and networks, and which have been freely distributed for several years by the US Census Bureau (see http://www.census.gov and Muscará and Zamparutti, 1994). This may explain why a unified Nuts 5 coverage, such as Megrin product, was so late to arrive or why an extensive network database, such as teleatlas, was so expensive. Then most research institutes had to constitute their geographical data set by gathering data which were, according to the countries, more or less expensive and subject to strict copyrights. The legal frameworks are presently changing considerably because of the development of GIS and the Internet, but it seems that geographical coordinates integrated into a travel dataset are not directly involved with such regulation. Indeed, such geographical data are not accurate (100 m to 1 km), they are not necessarily measured in any legal projection system, and the general set that they can constitute altogether is only a small part of the place-names of a country. Therefore, such a set cannot have any other use than the analysis of the transportation data.

16.6 CONCLUSION

A survey implies a chain of information where data are produced, analysed and published. In the case of long-distance travel diary surveys, early integration of geographical information by geocoding of activities consolidates the data, because of better estimations of distances and better intersections with information about transport supply. Travel diary datasets enriched with such geographical information can be integrated in a GIS for thorough analysis of geography effects on travel, in terms of distance and accessibility, with a cartographic representation. Geocoding entails some problems, however, because geographical information is difficult to collect in a travel diary survey, particularly in the case of long-distance mobility studies, when respondent's destinations are scattered in a large territory and maps or electronic positioning devices are not easy to use.

We have mentioned the difficulties raised by the lexicon of toponyms: place-names are more difficult to remember and to recognise automatically because of alternate names in other languages and of the absence of general orthographic rules. Nevertheless, analyses made on the French surveys show that the geographical set of stopping places is very much concentrated in space. This implies that most of the problems of geocoding activities will be associated with small places visited by few people in the surveys. These results indicate that it is useful, in the context of long-distance travel surveys, to add further items to the question about the destination, which help to locate these smaller places. It also implies that place-name lists from earlier surveys can be reused successfully. The point where the place rank-population distribution of the old survey ceases to coincide with the known distribution from official statistics can be taken as a low estimate of the share of place-names in any new survey which can be geocoded with the old list of place-names.

The existence of comprehensive and accurate databases of place-names is a precondition for any automatic geocoding. We have also stressed the fact that the spatial set of European municipalities can be considered as the finest level for statistical analysis for our scientific purpose, but not as the most relevant set of place-names for geocoding. It raises substantial problems in its accuracy and its comprehensiveness, in particular with regard to leisure-related places (hotel complexes, sports facilities etc.) and small settlements. This last problem is especially acute in countries with a highly aggregated administrative structure, such as the UK or Netherlands. Geographical databases, such as common place-names, simple but updated networks, and Nuts 5 centres are a basic but valuable capital of information to enrich and maintain. Coding places is indeed a learning process generated by the constitution of large databases and the analysis of errors.

16.7 REFERENCES

Battelle Transportation Division (1997) - Global Positioning Systems for Personal Travel Surveys, Lexington Area Travel Data Collection Test, Final Report. *US DOT*, Washington.

CSST, ENEA and Inrets (2000) - Commute tools, Commute project (CEC DG TREN). *Presented at Commute/Internat workshop*, Brussels, 20/3/2000.

Didier, M., C. Bouveyron and C.N.I.G. (1993) - Guide économique et méthodologique des SIG. Hermes, Paris.

Flavigny, P.-O. and C. Bouvier (2000) - Using RDS identification for localisation. *Paper presented at the 9th IATBR conference*, Goldcoast, July 2000.

Flavigny, P.-O. and J.-L. Madre (1994) - How to get the geographical data in the households surveys? *Proceedings of IATBR 94*, **2**, 619-630, Valle Nevado, Santiago, Chile.

GISDATA (1995-7) - *GISDATA Newsletter*, Strasbourg, European Science Foundation.

Hubert, J.-P., P.-O. Flavigny and J.-L. Madre (1999) - Tools to enrich travel diary data sets. *Deliverable 4 of 4th framework project TEST (CEC/DG VII)*, Arcueil, Inrets.

Hubert, J.-P. and F. Moriconi-Ebrard (1999) - Terrae statisticae. Il database sui comuni d'Europa. *Sistema Terra*, **8** (1-3) 120-125.

Le Bras, H. (1996) - Le peuplement de l'Europe. *DATAR La documentation française*, Paris.

Madre, J.-L. and J. Maffre (1997) - La mobilité régulière et la mobilité locale en 1982 et 1994. *Insee*, Paris.

Muscarà, P. and E. Zamparutti (1994) - The last frontier in GIS, The role of rapidly decreasing data costs and business mapping in launching the US Market. *Sistema Terra*, 3.

Pumain, D., T. Saint-Julien, N. Cattan and C. Rozenblat (1991) - Le concept statistique de la ville en Europe. *Eurostat*, Luxembourg.

Thill, J.-C. (2000) - Geographical information systems in transportation research, Special Issue. *Transportation Research*.

Zito, R., G. D'Este and M.A.P. Taylor (1994) - Global positioning system in the time domain: how useful a tool for intelligent vehicle-highway systems? *TransportationRresearch*, **3** (4), 193-209.

16.8 Numerical databases for Europe:

Bartholomew Euro Maps on CD-ROM, London, Bartholomew Digital Data, 1996.

L'Europe des populations, Tours, Articque, 2000.

Seamless Administration Boundary of Europe, Bruxelles, Megrin consortium, 2000.

NIMA Geonet server, through http://nima.mil, Washington, National Imaging and Mapping Agency.

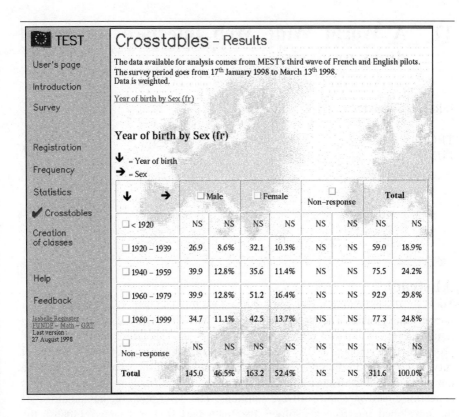

Chapter 17
A World Wide Web interface for travel diary analysis

I. Reginster and Ph. L. Toint

17 A World Wide Web interface for travel diary analysis[1]

I. Reginster and Ph. L. Toint

TRG
FUNDP
B – 5000 Namur

Abstract

Tools for disseminating travel diary data are essential so that collected data do not remain unexploited. The World Wide Web (WWW) offers a medium allowing remote access to and also remote analysis of the data. Therefore, during the TEST project, we developed a WWW interface to the database containing the travel surveys collected in the course of the MEST project. In this chapter, we describe our objectives and discuss the design issues and the implementation decisions concerning hardware and software solutions. The description of the actual use of the developed interface constitutes the main part of this chapter. Finally, the management of the server is also sketched.

Keywords

WWW, on-line statistical analysis, travel diary, long-distance travel, MEST, TEST.

---

[1] Preferred citation: Reginster, I. and Ph. L. Toint (2003) A World Wide Web interface for travel diary analysis, in K. W. Axhausen, J.-L. Madre, J. W. Polak and Ph. L. Toint (eds.) *Capturing Long-Distance Travel*, 277 - 296, Research Studies Press, Baldock

17.1   INTRODUCTION

In Europe, like everywhere in the world, the cost-effective collection of long-distance travel behaviour data is crucial for the formulation of the transport policy, especially at a level that crosses national boundaries. But the collection of this data is essentially useless if techniques to analyse it and to disseminate the results of this analysis are not made available at the same time. While many analyses and dissemination tools are indeed available, we concentrate in this chapter on a single medium, whose ubiquity and importance become more obvious every day: the World Wide Web[2] (WWW).

Why is the WWW of interest for the dissemination of travel data?

Several reasons may be considered. The first, and maybe the most immediately critical, is because a WWW interface to travel data makes this (or indeed any other) data accessible simultaneously to a larger number of analysts. In particular, it is often not convenient, even if it is possible, to transfer the large datafiles corresponding to one or several travel surveys from the computer of one transportation analyst to that of another. The sheer size of the dataset is one of the problems, but not the only one: one should also mention the questions of data integrity and coherence (making sure that different copies of the files do indeed contain the same data) and documentation. Furthermore, it is not unusual for the owner of the data to take measures to protect its ownership and, for instance, allow analysis of the data, but not actual copying.

A second reason to favour a WWW interface is to overcome incompatibilities between various computer systems. While one may think that this should be mostly irrelevant in a computer-based society, the mutually incompatible formats used by various operating systems or different statistical packages often require tedious and error-prone conversions. Conversely, the format of WWW sites is sufficiently standardised to make their access easy from most platforms, which is one reason why the WWW has become so pervasive so quickly. If travel survey datafiles can be accessed via the Web, then the incompatibilities mentioned above can be easily overcome. Furthermore, the technology behind this important function is not *ad hoc*, and is therefore likely to evolve irrespective of the amount of effort that can be put in by the transportation research community.

Thirdly, this technology allows easy access not only for researchers, but also for a much wider public. If the main use of transport statistics today is in administration and research, the public is more and more interested to obtain access to data on which public policies are based. This trend is noticeable not only from the action of ever more numerous and well-informed opinion groups, but also from the growing demand for personal access to data collected on public resources (Axhausen and Yousefzadeh, 1998). Again, disseminating data through the WWW appears to be the most elegant and durable manner of providing such an access while preserving the potential for some screening of the users, according to the policy set up by data owners.

---

[2] We often simply mention "the web".

Finally, the design and implementation of a WWW interface is made possible not only because of the increasingly pervasive nature of the Web, but also because the associated software tools are becoming increasingly rich in terms of functionality and content.

All these reasons were at the origins of the proposal made to develop, in the TEST project, a WWW interface for the database containing the travel surveys collected in the course of the MEST project. In what follows, we discuss the context, design issues, implementation decisions and, most importantly, actual use of the interface that resulted from this proposal. The chapter is structured as follows. We first describe our objectives and briefly survey the sites that existed at the beginning of our development and which presented some functionalities that we had in mind (Section 2). In Section 3, we review the decisions that we made in terms of software implementation. Section 4 contains a discussion of the general structure of the interface, a brief introduction to the structure of the data contained in the relevant databases and an illustrated example of use. The management of the server is covered in Section 5. Some conclusions and perspectives are proposed in a final section.

17.2   OBJECTIVES AND CONTEXT

17.2.1   The functionalities of the interface

In line with the motivations outlined in the introduction and after consulting our partners in the MEST and TEST consortia on their requirements, our ambition, at the beginning of the project, was to build a WWW interface to the MEST travel surveys that would offer the following features to the user:

- The most obvious function is to allow the user to obtain basic statistics for the data collected. One of the main objectives was *to allow the user to define his or her own requests on the data*, such as requests for means, variances and other simple statistics on selected subsets of the data.
- We also were keen to allow the user to obtain not only simple statistics but also various *cross-tabulations*, again defined on user selected data subsets.
- We were also interested in offering to users the possibility of obtaining *simple graphics*, such as bar-charts, from the data.
- The possibility for the user to abandon a particular analysis and to return to it later, without loosing the work done during the first session, was also considered important.
- Finally, the possibility for the user to *download the results* of his or her analysis on the data in a commonly available spreadsheet file format was considered to be an objective.

The WWW interface, hereafter called "the TEST website" is the result of our attempts to fulfil all these goals (see http://www.fundp.ac.be/~grt/test for the current implementation).

17.2.2 Comparable efforts

Other initiatives along the lines described above did exist when the project started. We were of course interested in assessing the usability of the corresponding sites, which depends on a number of issues. In particular, we wished to consider the following questions:

- Is the access to the site free (in the sense of not being financially charged)? Does the site allow interactive tabulations and/or graphics?
- Does the site impose some screening on access, in that its access is conditional to obtaining a password ?

Finally, for reasons that will become apparent below, we were also interested in the question: are the software tools underpinning the site in the public domain?

We now provide a brief summary of our analysis of the main sites of interest.

- The *Nationwide Personal Transportation Survey (NPTS)* website for the 1990 and 1995 USA surveys (http://www-cta.oml.gov/npts) provides a comprehensive look at personal travel in the US. The surveys address general travel behaviour in the American population. Data on the relationship between social and demographic change, land development patterns and transportation is provided. Among the functionalities of the site, we note an excellent documentation and the possibility to obtain statistics and graphics on user-defined data subsets. It is possible to download the data, although only in the ASCII (simple text) format, which is somewhat inconvenient. The site statistical engine is SAS (see http://www.sas.com) and its graphics interface is based on "Visualise" (see http://www.visualizetech.com), two commercially available packages. The main difficulty in using the site is that of selecting a variable (for building statistics), which requires browsing across a relatively large number of pages.
- The *Bureau of Transportation Statistics (BTS)* web site (http://www.bts.gov) is operated by the US Department of Transportation, and makes accessible a large amount of information on the US transportation system. It also collects data on intermodal transportation. It provides some graphical output and allows for data download. On the other hand, it does not allow user-defined requests.
- The *Tourmis* web site at the Wirtschaftsuniversität Wien (http://tourmis.wu-wien.ac.at) provides access to a range of tourism surveys and statistics, including the European Travel Monitor. Data download is possible, but at a price. It does not allow for user-defined requests.
- The *Ten-io* web site (http://ten-io.com/transportation.html) is of a somewhat different nature, as it gives access to online airline booking, airline statistics (using BTS "US Bureau of Transportation Statistics - Office of Airline Information") as well as coach and train information.

It does not support user-defined requests nor data download.

- The *DST* web site (http://www.mtc.dst.ca.us) is a comprehensive system to gather, organise and disseminate timely information on the San Francisco area traffic and road conditions, public transit routes and schedules, carpooling, highway construction and other road closures and other travel services. Like Ten-io, this is a "consult only" site, with no user interaction such as data download or special requests.

A feature of all these sites is that they are based on commercial software tools.

17.3   SOFTWARE ISSUES

Seen from the software tools point of view, the World Wide Web is a collection of applications called *clients* and associated *servers* that support a unified communication protocol, HTTP, across the Internet. Briefly, a client is a program that wants something and a server is a program that provides something. A client can send requests to many different servers and a server can send results (in the form of *web pages*) to many different clients (Spainhour and Queria, 1996). In general, it is the client that usually initiates this conversation or session with a server (Matthews *et al.*, 1996). The client is typically a *browser*, that is an application allowing the visualisation of web pages, running on the computer of the Internet user. The mechanism of this client(browser)-server interaction is shown in, and typically contains, three stages. In a first stage, the user makes contact with the interface by requesting the server to show the main TEST web page. He or she then uses this page to submit his or her requests. In the second stage, these requests are sent from his or her computer to the server (2). The third stage is realised by the server, which returns the desired pages (1) or handles the received requests. This last process either directly accesses the data files (the travel survey, in our case), or calls the statistical engine when the user request implies a statistical treatment of the data (2b). The server then formats the results as a web page and sends this page back to the client (3). These server actions are performed by running, on the server, the so-called *cgi-scripts*[3], which therefore constitute the core of the interface. In accordance with widespread practice in this area, we have chosen to write these scripts in the Perl language (Schartz, 1995; Wall *et al.*, 1997). In addition, some access statistics are also maintained on the server. One clearly sees that the user in fact uses two computers: his or her own, running the browser client, and the computer that the HTTP server runs.

Having now briefly outlined the mechanism of communication over the web, we are in position to consider the choice of the various components of this architecture. In particular, the initial choice of hardware and software tools is of paramount importance.

---

[3] CGI stands for Common Gateway Interface.

Figure 17.1   General diagram of the server

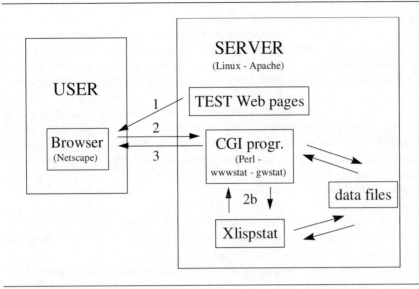

17.3.1   Hardware platform

On the hardware side, we thought we would simply use the most ubiquitous type of machine available, therefore also maximising the probability of an easy upgrade mechanism along the technology path.   We therefore chose to develop our interface and the web server that supports it on a PC Pentium Pro 200, at the time a recent member of the PC family. We have since transferred the server to newer PC models without trouble.

17.3.2   Software tools

When considering the options in choosing software tools, it is worth noticing immediately that we do not have to make any specific choice for the browser-client. Indeed, all such tools support the same HTTP protocol, which ensures their universal functionality while leaving the freedom of choice (taste and, potentially, price) to the user. We chose to use Netscape (see http://www.netscape.com/) as our own browser, but did not assume that all users of our interface would make the same choice.

Regarding the server software, two constraints of the project turned out to play a very important role. The first constraint was a budgetary one. Although we knew of commercial software products whose use was possible in our context, not many of the necessary tools were consistent with our means. For instance, we were first interested in using the SAS statistical package, but we soon realised that the cost of a server licence would be beyond the project budget. Thus, we investigated whether our objectives could be met with less expensive software, which immediately lead us to the question of whether our goals were accessible if we restricted our choice to *public domain software tools*.

This option was also consistent with our second constraint, which was to use tools whose lifespan – that is average time between substantially different (and often incompatible) releases – would be as long as possible. Indeed, not only was our development investment limited, but we also anticipated that users of our tools, such as transportation departments or other administrative bodies, would appreciate not having to update or completely revamp the tool too often. As it turned out later, they were also extremely keen on using free software tools, which made transfer and installation of the web interface on their machine not only easy but independent of obtaining licensing agreements for half a dozen different software packages.

Thus we resolved to base our design on:

- the Linux (see www.linux.com/) operating system;
- the Apache HTTP Server (see www.apache.org/), for providing the environment to run the cgi-scripts;
- the Perl (see www.perl.com/) scripting language for writing these scripts;
- the HTML markup language for the resulting web pages; (see www.w3.org/hypertext:WWW/MarkUp/MarkUp.html/)
- the Xlispstat (see http:www.stat.ucla.edu/) statistical package (at least in a first approach) for processing the user requests for travel data statistics[4]; and
- the wwwstat and gwstat server management tools.
- All these tools were chosen because they were (and still are) powerful, widespread and freely available.

17.4   THE TEST INTERFACE

17.4.1   General structure

The architecture of the TEST server (the support of our web interface) is based on its use by a client. As with most web sites, the TEST site may be explored by using successive menus. Ten different pages or menus are available, allowing access to the results of the MEST's third wave[5] of pilots in France and the United Kingdom.

---

[4] We also considered, and abandoned, CSA , R, S-Plus , Vista , SPSS , SPAD and SUDAAN.

[5] The survey period ranges from January 17th 1998 to March 13th 1998.

The introduction page greets the user and gives a brief overview of the TEST project's objectives.

The survey menu next provides a complete on-line description of the available surveys, such as sample size, sample type, period and place of the survey, and a description of each data file corresponding to these surveys. The type of information (variable) available in each file is also described.

The registration page allows new users to specify their name and to request a password, which is necessary for accessing the data.

The frequency page allows the user to request cumulative counts on the values of specified variables, i.e. to count the number of occurrences in the data files for each value of the selected variables and to compute the associated percentages. Bar-charts are available to visualise the results.

The statistics page allows the user to request basic statistics on the variables (mean, variance, median standard deviation, etc.) of the selected survey.

The cross-tabulation page provides the possibility of requesting cross-tabulations involving the survey variables, i.e. tables reporting the number of records combining selected values of two different variables.

The "creation of classes" page allows the user to define his or her own classes of categories, which is important for meaningful analysis. For example, the years of birth from 1950 to 1970, and to 1971 to 1990 may be grouped into two distinct classes, or, alternatively, merged into a single one.

The help menu provides a complete on-line documentation of the TEST web site, including a description of the possible requests and how to use them, as well as a list of 'frequently asked questions' (and corresponding answers).

The feedback page allows the user to send comments to the webmaster.

The user's page provides links to the last results obtained by the user, which may be preserved on the server for later access.

The selection amongst the accessible travel surveys takes place in the "frequency", "statistics" and "cross-tabulation" pages.

In addition to the functionalities provided by these pages and menus, the user is also allowed to specify *filters* on the data, that is an *a priori* selection of the data on which counts, statistics or cross-tabulations are then built. For instance, a user might be interested in analyzing a subclass of respondents consisting only of people in the 50–65 years age range. Filters are constructed by the users from the "frequency", "statistics" and "cross-tabulation" pages.

17.4.2 A brief description of the MEST survey data

Before entering into a more explicit description of the functionalities that we have outlined, it is necessary to briefly review the survey data, and, more specifically, the data associated with the third wave of MEST pilots. We refer the reader to Chapter 2 for a detailed discussion of the vocabulary used, and in particular for the precise distinctions between journeys and trips.

Variables, classes and weights

Like most travel diaries, these contains two types of variables: discrete and continuous. *Discrete variables* are those whose values are limited to a finite set (for example, the "sex" variable has only three possible values: male, female and non-response). On the other hand, *continuous variables* are numerical variables that may assume real value (for example, the "current mileage" variable associated to a vehicle). Most continuous variables have upper and lower bounds: the "year of birth" variable must, for example, lie between 1900 and 2001. These bounds can be used to specify *classes* by selecting a ranges for a continuous variable. Considering the "year of birth" again, we may define a first class consisting of the years between 1900 and 1950 and a second class for the years 1951 to 2001. Note that one may also specify classes for discrete variables by explicitly selecting a list of accepted values instead of a range. Note also that classes can be predefined (at the level of the server) or user-defined.

In addition, four *aggregate variables* are also provided (and calculated *a priori* without any special action from the user). These are the number of vehicles per household, the number of journeys per household, the number of trips per household and the number of trips per journey.

A *weight* may be associated with each value of a variable in the data, in order to reflect its relative importance or quality. Weights typically result from statistical treatment where the population of respondents is "reweighted" better to resemble (at least in terms of relevant statistics) the given target population. Because of this feature, we have chosen to assign a double weight to 15% of the households and the sum of the weights being equal to the total number of households living in the survey area. It is important to note that the statistics that are computed at the user request by the server take these weights into account.

The data files

The data for each of the surveys is distributed in four different, logically coherent files:

- The *people* file describes the personal situation of each household member, regarding his or her age, marital status, sex, education, working status, etc. It also contains information about ownership of public transport passes.
- The *vehicle* file contains a description of the household's vehicles in terms of model, type, year of production, presence of catalytic converter, mileage and main users.
- The *journey* file contains the description of the journeys reported by the respondents. As already discussed in Chapter 2, a journey starts and ends at the same place, which is typically the respondent's home but can also be anywhere he or she stayed more than two consecutive days. Each description reports the places of origin and destination, the time of departure and return, the identifier corresponding to the household

member reporting the journey and the number of trips within a journey.

- The *trips* file contains the description of the reported trips in terms of departure and arrival times, origin and destination, purpose, transportation mode, and travelling party. Each stage is a leg of a journey to a destination. A journey consists of at least one outward and one return trip.

17.4.3   An example

In order to give the reader of this book (as opposed to an Internet user) a feeling for the functionalities and look of the interface (Figure 17.2), we present next a (very simple) example of its use. The purpose of the section will be to obtain a rough analysis of the age-sex structure of the population of respondents for the French survey. We now follow the pages as seen by a registered user within his or her browser.

After connecting to the TEST site, the welcome page shown in appears.

Figure 17.2   Welcome page

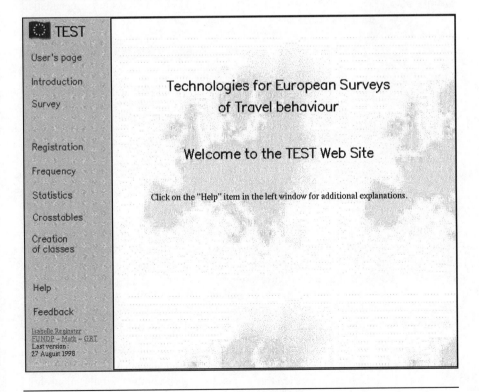

288

A click on the **Crosstables** link then produces the page displayed in Figure 17.3.

Figure 17.3   The first part of the crosstable page

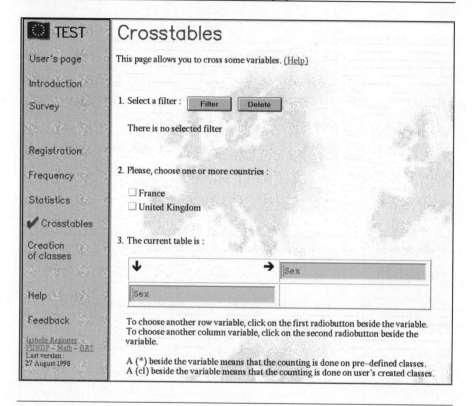

Notice that the user is first prompted to select a filter on the data. In order to keep our guided tour reasonably short, we assume at this stage that no particular filter is required, i.e. that the user wishes to perform the analysis on the complete sample. A click on the button corresponding to **France** then selects the French survey, while the third part of the page indicates the current status of the desired crosstable (the "sex" variable is selected by default both for rows and columns). Scrolling down a page displays the content, where the selection of variables (other than "sex") is possible.

Figure 17.4   The second part of the crosstable page

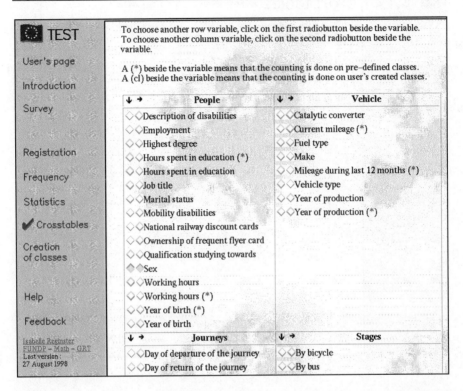

After clicking on the left button associated with **Year of birth**[6] to choose the column variable and sending the request (a suitable button is available at the bottom of the web page, but not visible on the picture), the server returns the user to the page shown in Figures 17.4 and 17.5. The first of these figures gives the desired crosstable, in which the symbol NS stands for "non-significant". The second figure shows a second (smaller) table giving the explicit definition of the classes, which are fairly obvious in this case. A button immediately below this table allows the user to download the table in Excel format.

---

[6] Observe that the (*) symbol indicates that this selection corresponds to a set of predefined classes (ranges).

290

Figure 17.5   A result crosstable

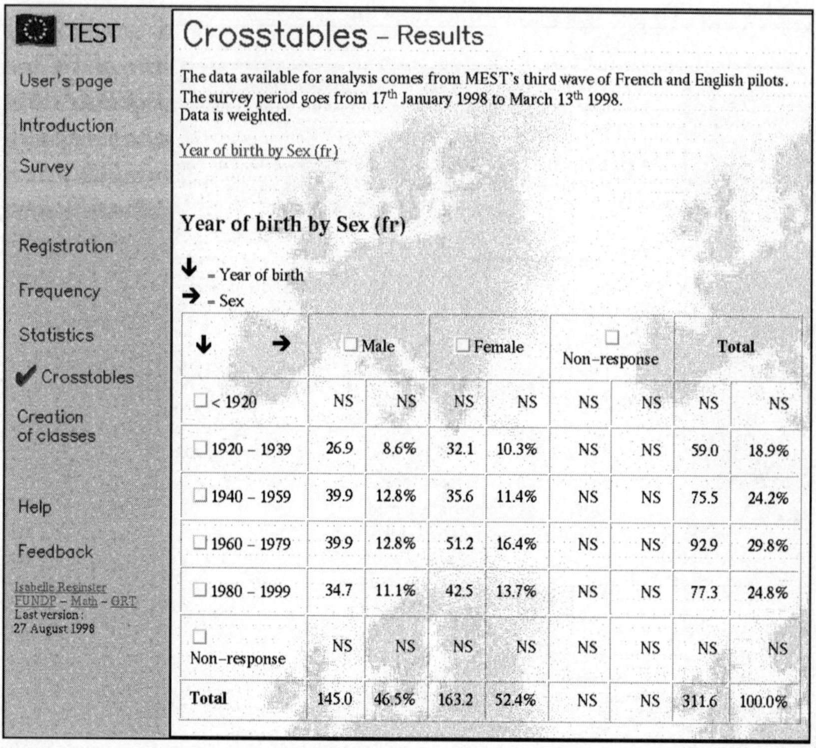

TEST

Crosstables – Results

The data available for analysis comes from MEST's third wave of French and English pilots.
The survey period goes from 17th January 1998 to March 13th 1998.
Data is weighted.

Year of birth by Sex (fr)

Year of birth by Sex (fr)

↓ – Year of birth
→ – Sex

↓ →	☐ Male		☐ Female		☐ Non-response		Total	
☐ < 1920	NS	NS	NS	NS	NS	NS	NS	NS
☐ 1920 – 1939	26.9	8.6%	32.1	10.3%	NS	NS	59.0	18.9%
☐ 1940 – 1959	39.9	12.8%	35.6	11.4%	NS	NS	75.5	24.2%
☐ 1960 – 1979	39.9	12.8%	51.2	16.4%	NS	NS	92.9	29.8%
☐ 1980 – 1999	34.7	11.1%	42.5	13.7%	NS	NS	77.3	24.8%
☐ Non-response	NS	NS	NS	NS	NS	NS	NS	NS
Total	145.0	46.5%	163.2	52.4%	NS	NS	311.6	100.0%

User's page
Introduction
Survey
Registration
Frequency
Statistics
✓ Crosstables
Creation
of classes
Help
Feedback
Isabelle Reginster
FUNDP – Math – GRT
Last version:
27 August 1998

The presence of the NS symbol is important not only for purely statistical purposes, but also as a means to enforce minimal standards in privacy protection. Indeed, it is imaginable that a suitable filter and variable selection could reduce the sample to a very small, or even a single, data item(s). In this case, identification of the respondent would become possible in some cases, which would clearly not be allowable. The server software therefore provides a configurable parameter to set the minimum number of records that have to be aggregated for the result to be significant and sufficiently anonymous.

Also observe, in the centre of Figure 17.6, that merging row or columns variables in user-defined classes is also possible after the initial table has been computed and displayed. For instance, the result of such a merger is shown in Figure 17.7, where the definitions of the specified mergers is displayed together with the results in terms of the new merged variables.

Figure 17.6   The second part of the result crosstable

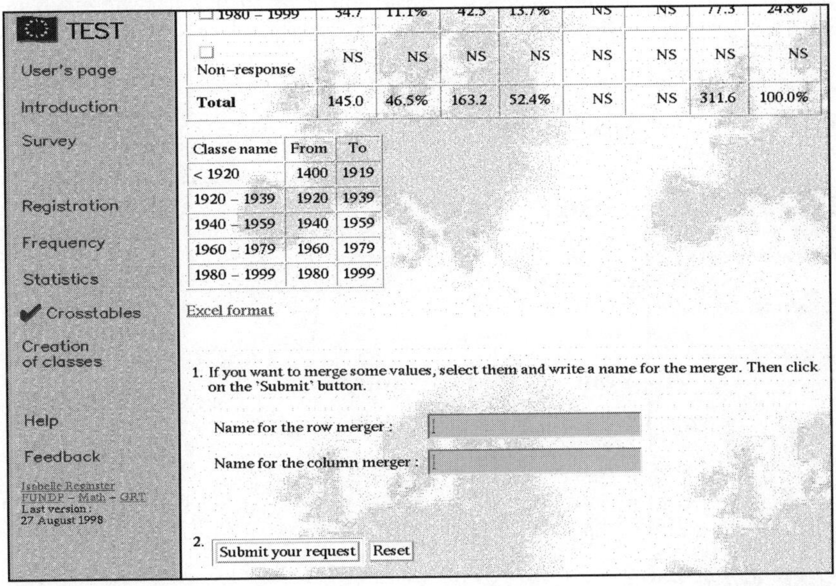

Figure 17.7   A crosstable after merging

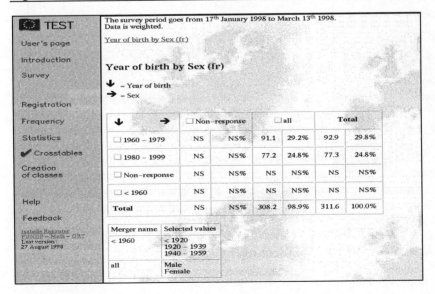

As indicated above, the results obtained are stored in a user's page which can be retrieved later for further analysis. An example of such a page is given in Figure 17.8.

Figure 17.8   An example of a user's page

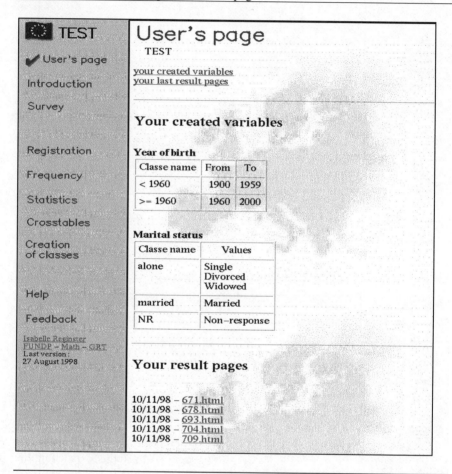

17.5   MANAGING THE SERVER

The management of the server may be divided into two different aspects: installation and maintenance.

17.5.1 Installation

Care was taken to make the server software as portable as possible. In particular, we made sure that the relevant software may be installed on a new machine without difficulties by clearly identifying the requested software tools as well as the web sites from which these tools can be freely downloaded. Once the tools are downloaded and installed, it is enough to transfer a single *tar* file on the machine and to "detar" it in a suitable directory (the TEST home directory) to obtain an operational version of the server. The sub-directory structure associated with the server is shown in Figure 17.9.

Figure 17.9   The files structure of the TEST web site

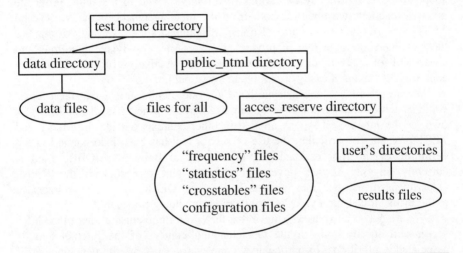

Of course, the server manager may wish to adapt his or her version of the server to a specific set of travel diaries. This can be achieved by manually editing two simple configuration files. The first contains a description of each variable in each survey file, while the second contains additional information about the structure of the server, like the paths to the data files and other information of this nature. These procedure has been tested and validated on several occasions.

Uninstalling the software, if necessary, is simply done by deleting the directory structure illustrated in Figure 17.9.

17.5.2 Maintenance

The regular management of the server involves a few easy tasks. The first is to grant access to new users by issuing passwords upon request, and after a possible verification of the new user's rights to access the data. The second is to retrieve statistics of access regularly, and purge unused users' directories. Note that mechanisms are included within the software to make these tasks essentially trivial, including the production of graphics reporting the main usage variables, such as traffic by archive, traffic by country or domain or time distribution of accesses. We may also hope that a typical server manager will spend some time answering user feedback.

17.6 CONCLUSIONS

We have discussed both the options and some of the implementation details of an interactive WWW interface to travel diary data. This interface allows for users specified statistical requests of various types, including filtering and specification of user-defined classes. The interface is capable of producing simple graphics and allows the user to download the results of his or her investigations in a widespread spreadsheet format. It is entirely based on free software, and is easy to install, to adapt to the data structure of various travel surveys and to maintain. From the positive reactions we obtained both from the other members of the MEST and TEST consortia and from national transport administrations, we believe that we have attained our objective of producing a versatile, convivial, ubiquitous and cheap tool for analysis, therefore prolonging the effective useful life of a survey exercise and making it easily accessible to a vast public.

We are pleased to say that we have not only demonstrated that these goals could be achieved at reasonable cost, but also that the project has taken a life of its own, as the interface has been applied in other contexts outside the MEST and TEST projects. In particular, the use of such a tool has been incorporated in the definition of the first national mobility survey in Belgium (MOBEL) and is currently ongoing further development in a joint project with the British Department of Energy, Transport and the Regions (DETR) to provide an interface to the British travel survey. Other applications are being considered.

We are not so naive as to believe that the current implementation of the TEST server will survive long in the fast changing context of the Internet and its associated applications. In particular, we are well aware that the development of software tools whose specific purpose is to interface databases with web access may make re-definition or re-implementation necessary. However, we believe that tools like the one we have discussed are inevitable components of the future environment of transport analysts, administrative decision makers and even the general public.

17.7 REFERENCES

17.7.1 Publications and web-based documents

Aubert, O. (1996) - Introduction à Perl, olivier.aubert@enst-bretagne.fr

Axhausen, K.W. and M. Youssefzadeh (1998) - Towards a new European Long Distance Diary: Analysis of MEST pilots wave III. *MEST Deliverable*, **D3 and D4,** Innsbruck.

Boivin, D.J. and L. Gauthier (1996) - Un manuel illustré de programmation en HTML, www.image.fr/Multimedia/miroirs/manuelhtml/manuelhtml.html.

Boutell, T. (1996) - CGI Programming in C & Perl. Addison Wesley, New York.

de Leeuw, J. (1994) - An introduction to xlisp-stat. UCLA, Los-Angeles.

Gross, C. (1997) - Configuration du logiciel Apache, aspects sécurité. *CNRS*, Grenoble.

Hekman, J.P. (1997) - Linux in a nutshell: A Desktop Quick Reference. O'Reilly, Sebastopol.

Johnson, B. (1996) - Perl Tutorial. www.ncsa.uiuc.edu/General/Training/PerlIntro/

Levine, J.R. and C. Baroudi (1994) - Internet pour les nuls. Sybex, Paris.

Maires, G. (1996) - UNGI, un nouveau guide Internet, www.imaginet.fr/ime/.

Matthews, R.D., P. Jones, J. Magid, D.A. Ball Jr and M.J. Hammel (1996) - The Unix Web Server: Tools and Techniques for building your own Internet Information Site. Vantana, Research Triangle Park.

Musciano, C. and B. Kennedy (1996) - HTML: The Definitive Guide. O'Reilly, Sebastopol.

Neuss, C. and J. Vromans (1996) - Applications CGI en Perl pour les Webmasters. International Thomson Publishing, Paris

Reginster, I. (1997) - A www interface to travel diary results. *TEST Deliverable,* **D6,** FUNDP, Namur.

Scales, J.A. and M.L. Smith (1996) - A whirlwind Tour of Lisp-Stat. landau.mines.edu/~samizdat/

Schartz, R.L. (1995) - Introduction à Perl. O'Reilly, Sebastopol.

Spainhour, S. and V. Queria (1996) - Webmaster in a Nutshell. O'Reilly, Sebastopol.

Tackett Jr., J. and D. Gunter (1997) - LINUX Le MacMillan. S & SM, Paris.

Tierney, L. (1988) - Xlispstat, A Statistical Environment Based on the Xlisp language. University of Minnesota, Minneapolis.

Tierney, L. (1990) - Lisp-Stat: An Object-Oriented Environment for Statistical Computing and Dynamic Graphics. John Wiley and Sons Inc., New York.

Tierney, L. (1992) - Statistical Computing and Dynamic Graphics Using Lisp-stat. University of Minnesota, Minneapolis.

Tierney, L. (1996) - Xlispstat 2.1. Release 3, Beta release notes. University of Minnesota, Minneapolis.

Tittel, E., M. Gaither, S. Hassinger and M. Erwin (1996) - Web Programming: Secrets with HTML, CGI and Perl. IDG Books, Foster City.

Vanderdonckt, J. (1998a) - Conception ergonomique de page web, course notes. *FUNDP*, Namur.

Vanderdonckt, J. (1998b) - Conception ergonomique de transparents et diapositives. *FUNDP*, Namur.

Vanderdonckt, J. (1998c) - Conception ergonomique d'une présentation assistée par ordinateur. *FUNDP*, Namur.

Vromans, J. and S. Design (1996) - Quick Reference Guide, programming Perl. ftp.kulnet.kuleuven.ac.be/pub/mirror/CPAN/authors/Johan_Vromans/

Wall, L., T. Christiansen and R.L. Schwartz (1997) - Programmation en Perl. O'Reilly, Sebastopol.

Werbach, K. (1996) - Le guide rapide du langage HTML. werbach.com/barezones.

17.7.2   Web-sites used

The Netscape Site: www.netscape.com

The CGI web site: www.w3.org/hypertext/WWW/CGI/Overview.html

Introduction to CGI Programming: www.usi.utah.edu

HTML Guide: www.cnw.com/~drclue

Web Site of Xlipstat: www.stat.ucla.edu

The home page of Linux: www.linux.com

The Apache Site: www.apache.org

The web site of HTML Language: www.w3.org/hypertext/WWW/MarkUp.html

The home page of Perl Language: www.perl.com

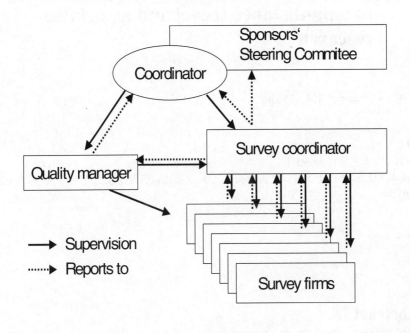

Chapter 18
Recommendations for a European survey of long-distance travel and associated research

K. W. Axhausen, J.-L. Madre, J. W. Polak and Ph. L. Toint

18 Recommendations for a European survey of long-distance travel and associated research[1]

K. W. Axhausen   J.-L. Madre   J. W. Polak   Ph. L. Toint

IVT   DEST   CTS   TRG
ETH   INRETS   Imperial College   FUNDP
CH–8093   F–94110 Arcueil   UK–London SW 2BU   B – 5000 Namur
Zürich

Abstract

This chapter discusses recommendations for the implementation of European surveys of long-distance travel and for future methodological and technological research. It is based on experiences and discussions reported in the other chapters of the book, drawing therefore on the results of the Eurostat long-distance pilot surveys, the 4th Framework projects MEST and TEST and of the Eurostat Working Group on Passenger Mobility.

Keywords

4th Framework Programme, EU, Eurostat, MEST, TEST, long-distance travel, survey design, survey protocol , survey technology, recommendations.

---

[1] Preferred citation: K. W. Axhausen, J.-L. Madre, J. W. Polak and Ph. L. Toint (2003) Recommendations for a European survey of long-distance travel and associated research, in K. W. Axhausen, J.-L. Madre, J. W. Polak and Ph. L. Toint (eds.) *Capturing Long-Distance Travel*, 297-318, Research Studies Press, Baldock.

18.1 INTRODUCTION

The task of this final chapter is to bring the results presented above together and to discuss our recommendations and conclusions for long-distance surveys and for future work in the area. It reflects not only the results presented above, but also the results of the parallel streams of work which were undertaken during the project period, e.g. the Eurostat long-distance pilot surveys (Axhausen, 1998 or Weckström-Eno, 1999).

The recommendations are structured into four parts; the design of protocol; the design of the contents; the implementation of the survey in an administrative sense; and, finally, a discussion of future technological and research needs.

18.2 RECOMMENDATIONS FOR THE PROTOCOL

The pilot surveys of MEST and during the Eurostat Pilots, by and large, tested protocols which mixed postal and telephone elements to overcome the respective weaknesses of the two methods in terms of sampling biases: costs and level of detail achievable. These mixed method formats have proved very successful in daily mobility surveys (see Erl, 1998 or for a recent application in the Belgian National travel survey (www.mobel.be) and led to their adoption in those exercises. The experience of the consortium's fieldwork was mixed. The total response of 60–70% during MEST was satisfactory, but the large reliance on the telephone element to obtain this response is worrying for a method largely based on paper forms (see Axhausen and Youssefzadeh, 1999 and Chapter 6).

The protocol of the last wave of MEST surveys included a telephone call just after the arrival of the survey materials with the respondents. This had the aim of motivating the respondents to co-operate with the postal survey. It was not intended to collect data. This was scheduled for possible later phone contacts. This worked very well in Sweden, with the National Statistical Office acting as the fieldwork firm, but many UK respondents used the opportunity to refuse further co-operation. In Portugal there was the feeling that the extensive survey pack had upset respondents, particularly in the third wave. Still, overall the postal element increased total response. These mixed experiences have to be compared with positive reports from German, Austrian and Dutch surveys of daily mobility, which use a similar format. While overall the limited evidence available is not negative enough to warrant the recommendation of a different protocol at this point, future developments might change this assessment. Within the protocol it may be worthwhile delaying the motivation call until a week after the mailing and to offer a full CATI interview at this point. This may help speed up response.[2]

As mentioned above, MEST did not have the opportunity to run a full pilot project using a CATI-only approach. The experiences in Portugal and Sweden in the first wave were positive, as were the experiences in Sweden and Denmark during the Eurostat pilots. At this point complete reliance on a CATI approach does not seem possible, because of:

---

[2] The DATELINE project, which will be conducting the full scale long-distance survey during 2001/2002, has adopted a similar mixed method.

- *quality concerns about the sampling frame*: e.g. unlisted numbers and rapid increase in mobile phone ownership, which are often unlisted and only a way to contact persons and not households (Mediatrie, 2000); exclusion of office numbers;
- *capture of highly mobile persons,* unless there is a provision for a sufficient number of contact attempts at all times of the day over an extended period;
- *omission of persons with a longer absence,* unless there is a provision of a sufficient period for the contact attempts;
- *number of non-phone owners,* unless there is a provision of a non-phone based method of contact with non-phone owners.

The treatment of non-response is essential for the overall quality of the protocol. The treatment has to encompass three elements: non-response conversion efforts; scheduled non-response interviews with all non-responders (i.e. interviews covering the core topics of the survey); and finally a sub-sample of the original sample for a high quality validation survey conducted with a different protocol (control of the quality of the normal survey response and full non-response survey of non-respondents).

The following protocol is recommended:

- *Sampling frame:* Official population registers or the official address lists of the postal authorities.
- *Sampling unit:* For financial reasons, a two-phase sample of people (suitable random selection, weighted by the probability of the number of long distance journeys, when only household addresses are available) for ages six and over with proxy reporting by parents for respondents aged between 6 and 14 years.
- Contacts:
  1) initial letter announcing the survey (Day 1);
  2) distribution of survey materials (Day 4);
  3) reminder postcard, if required (Day 11);
  4) telephone call for motivation and, if desired, CATI retrieval of survey information (Day 11) (7 contact attempts over 3 days);
  5) reminder postcard, if required (Day 18);
  6) telephone call for motivation and, if desired CATI retrieval of survey information (with changed reporting period) (Day 25) (7 contact attempts over 3 days);
  7) reminder postcard, if required (Day 32);
  8) CATI retrieval of survey information (with changed reporting period) (Day 39) (10 contact attempts over 7 days);
  9) "Thank you" postcard to all respondents.

The reminders should be continued, even if there is an initial refusal to participate.

- Incentives: None[3]

Respondent errors should be addressed in the follow ways:

- Written replies: Immediate coding and error checking; telephone interview within 3 (7) working days (10 attempts) to obtain corrections and to probe for further suspected unreported journeys (even if no omission is visible)[4].
- CATI replies: Extensive error checking in the CATI routine, semi-automatic geocoding of place names; probing for suspected but not reported trips or journeys.
- Unresolved missing items: Documented imputation of missing items using documented imputation software.
- Unresolved unit non-response: Documented weighting using the results of the non-response surveys at the level of person, journey and trip.

The sampling strategy should focus on highly mobile persons, respectively regions to optimise the precision of the estimates of the flows.

For the purposes of non-response analysis, validation and correction, a special survey of a minimum 5% sample of sampling units drawn at Day 1 of the survey should be considered. This survey should be conducted as a face-to-face interview covering the same contents as the main survey (10 contact attempt over 14 days from Day 28). It serves as a quality control survey for responding units and as a survey of non-response for non-responding units (for details see Armoogum, Madre, Han and Polak, 1998 and 1999).

This protocol provides an intensity of contact which allows achievement of a sufficient response rate for the collection of enough journeys for the intended analysis and, in combination with the specified non-response treatment, a proper way to correct most of the remaining non-response biases. The protocol specifies a complex and comprehensive treatment of respondent errors, which is needed to maintain a high quality database of long-distance travel, as well as to open up research opportunities for the proper correction and weighting of travel diary data.

18.3 DESIGN OF THE CONTENTS

The MEST project and the parallel Eurostat pilots tested a wide variety of different definitions of the survey scope as well as written designs. In terms of design it was

---

[3] If incentives were to be distributed, then it has been demonstrated that a small gift (cash or stamps) in the survey pack works best.

[4] Typical problems concern the starting point of the journey (home, office, elsewhere), which can be addressed during the interview or by an appropriate question of the detailed movement form. Equally problematic are the access- and egress stage of a journey, which might need to be given special attention.

possible to conclude that (Axhausen, 1998; Axhausen and Youssefzadeh, 1999):

- *retrospective* surveys increase response as the respondents have a limited and known workload, but they reduce the number of journeys reported;
- *non retrospective* surveys reverse the pattern, but there is doubt that respondents use the opportunity to record their journeys on an ongoing basis, which reduces the larger number of reported journeys to a commitment and sample selection effect;
- *complexity*, as indicated by the number of items and the detail of the coding, improves within limits both response and the number of journeys reported. Too little complexity can actually reduce response;
- *reporting periods* of up to eight weeks seem quality neutral but problems of memory recall can be observed for the earlier weeks in longer reporting periods, in particular for business journeys;
- *generous* page layouts, e.g. one trip per page, using large fonts and some colour, are preferred.

The final test in the third wave of MEST showed that it is possible to obtain approximate stage information by asking for the route taken by the respondent (points of interchange, main points along the route) within a trip context. The experiences with a journey roster with a very limited set of items are generally positive and allow the request for detailed data to be limited without sacrificing information about the overall level of movement.

Based on the discussions above, the following design and survey scope are recommended:

- *Survey scope*: All journeys during the reporting period to destinations longer than the minimum distance.[5]
- *Resolution:* Trip-based, requesting information about all movements between major activities including a description of the route taken between the activities
- *Minimum distance*: 100 km crow-fly distance from the current base of the respondent; the survey form should specify a lower threshold, such as 75 km, to minimise boundary problems.
- *Minimum duration*: None
- *Current base of respondent*: Any location where the respondents spends two consecutive nights, as a rule the home, but also any second residence or the holiday accommodation.

---

[5] A movement can be defined to consist of: journeys – a sequence of trips starting and ending at home; trips – a sequence of stages between two activities; stages – an uninterrupted movement with one mode or means of transport (including any pure waiting time before and during the movement); activity – a purposeful and substantial action within a constant social and spatial context and with an unchanging purpose, meaning and type.

- *Resolution of destination area*: the municipality level or equivalent distinct place (holiday resort, name of firm, etc.) for prompting. Within the European Economic Area (EEA) coding at minimum to Nuts 5 or a more detailed level, if available, especially in those member states with geographically large Nuts 5 units. Outside the EEA coding to at least an equivalent of Nuts 2, i.e. the secondary administrative level of province, federal state or similar.
- *Geographical range of exclusion:* journeys within the destination area and non-qualifying journeys from the current base.
- *Temporal range of exclusion*: None, other than those periods covered by geographically excluded journeys.
- *Treatment of regular journeys:* No special treatment, but see below.
- *Treatment of frequent travellers*: None, but see below.
- *Temporal orientation*: Retrospective.
- *Duration of reporting period*: Eight weeks.
- *Structure of the survey pack:* The following elements should be included:
  - o *announcement letter* explaining the selection criteria, the rules for selecting the respondent from among the household members, the data protection policy and a request for co-operation;
  - o brief *explanatory flyer* detailing the purpose of the study;
  - o *household, person and vehicle* form covering all members of the household and their vehicles. Examples on the form;
  - o *movement form* covering the following sets of items:
    - ▪ most recent long distance journey (roster style, see below)[6].
    - ▪ roster of all other long-distance journeys within the reporting period.
    - ▪ booklet to report journeys in detail (trip level with route description; one trip per page). The booklet should accommodate three journeys. The respondent should report in detail three journeys or, if the number is smaller, all journeys of the reporting period. The reporting should start from the most recent one;
  - o *map* showing a circle of 75km around the residence of the sampling unit;
  - o *explanatory booklet* is a modified movement form explaining a set of example journeys.

---

[6] The journey can be within or outside the reporting period.

- *Physical design*: all forms should either be A4 portrait or A3 landscape orientation, as required.

The proposed structure of the movement form stresses the roster by adding a question about the most recent journey either inside or outside of the survey period. This question is added to ensure that virtually everyone will have a journey to report. The roster provides information about the frequency of travel, the main purpose, main destination and main mode and the size of the travelling party. For many modelling purposes it is desirable, but not necessary, to have detailed descriptions of all journeys undertaken. Details of the three most recent journeys should prove sufficient for this purpose and limiting response in this way should increase the quality of the reported detail by reducing the workload of highly mobile travellers and by shortening the recall period on average. As the survey should be carried out across a whole year, no biases in the timing of these reported journeys should exist.

Tables 18-1 to 18-5 list the proposed set of question items and their proposed precoded categories. This proposal is essentially identical to the set used in the final MEST surveys. The inclusion of an assessment of the quality of trip in its description has proved to be helpful in motivating respondents, even though there is no need to use this variable in the analyses. The coding of the modes used has been further simplified, as it clear that respondents often do not have the ability to distinguish between busses and coaches, regular air service and charter service or between the different sorts of train service (e.g. local, inter-regional, intercity or high speed rail). The detail about the types of service has to be added in the post-processing, if desired.

It is recommended that items that are very country-specific in their coding – for example type of accommodation, ownership of accommodation, vehicle categories, driving licences, education levels, etc. – should be country-specific with suitable post-processing. If income is to be estimated with externally-derived approaches, then further items should be added to match the variable set of the respective imputation approach.

The route question allows the extraction of the most important stages of the trip. Further detail can be obtained in the telephone error checking/probing interviews with the respondents, if desired. This applies also to other items of potential interest, such as class of ticket, costs of travel, further detail of the trip purpose and the activities undertaken. The design proposed is intended to reduce the apparent complexity of the forms to avoid discouraging those with literacy problems and busy respondents, while still covering all major items for retrieval from a respondent willing to reply in writing. It is clear that any postal element will discourage some respondents to the extent that they may not respond positively to the subsequent phone calls. However, this loss is justified as long as it is more than compensated for by the written responses from respondents who would have not answered by phone. Obviously, this is a choice of the lesser of two evils, based on current evidence. This indicates that CATI surveys could have larger biases because they tend to exclude the highly mobile, a key group. Respondents with literacy problems, discouraged by the paper forms, are likely to be relatively immobile due to their limited earnings potentials. If response behaviour changes, this trade-off will also change. Only ongoing research into non-response mechanisms can monitor this problem.

Table 18-1 Proposed set of items: Household

Item	Categories offered	Coding
Location of residence	Open	NUTS5 or finer
Type of accommodation	Country specific	
Ownership of accommodation	Country specific	
Number of phones	0, 1, 2, 3, 4, 5+	
Number of mobile phones	0, 1, 2, 3, 4, 5+	
Number of faxes	0, 1, 2, 3, 4, 5+	
Internet access at home	No, Yes	
Number of motorcycles	0, 1, 2, 3, 4, 5+	
Number of cars and vans owned	0, 1, 2, 3, 4, 5+	Local definitions of the vehicle
Number of further vehicles (e.g. trucks, mobile homes etc.)	0, 1, 2, 3, 4, 5+	types are required

Table 18-2 Draft set of items: Vehicle

Item	Categories offered	Coding
Owner	Open	Given name
Main user	Open	Given name
Type	Car/van, motorcycle, truck, other (Open)	
Make	Open	
Type of fuel	Petrol, diesel, other	
Current odometer reading	Open	
Year of production	Open	
Kilometrage in the last 12 months	Open	
Other household members driving the vehicle	Open	Given name

Table 18-3　　　　Proposed set of items: Person

Item	Categories offered	Coding
First name	Open	
Year of birth	Open	
Gender	Female, Male	
Motorcycle driving licence	Yes, No	
Car driving licence	Yes, No	
Marital status	Single, Divorced, Widowed, Married/with partner	
Presence of a disability affecting travel	No, Yes	
Type of disability	Open	Suitable derived codes
Highest education level	Country specific	
Employment status	Employed, self employed, not employed (not seeking work), in education, homemaker, retired, unemployed (less than a year), unemployed (more than a year), none of these	
Number of paid working hours/week	Open	
Job title	Open	Socio-professional categories
Hours in class per week	Open	
Location of any workplace more than 75 km from home	Open	Nuts 5 or finer
Qualification aimed for	Country specific	
Existence and locations of		
Student's residence	No, Yes and open	Nuts 5 or finer
Parent's home	No, Yes and open	Nuts 5 or finer
Holiday home	No, Yes and open	Nuts 5 or finer
Other type	No, Yes and open	Nuts 5 or finer
Number of visits to other residences	N.A., less than once a month, once a month, twice a month, more than twice a month	
Personal kilometrage in the last 12 months	Open	
Ownership of frequent flyer card of an airline	No, Yes	
Ownership of a public transport season tickets	No, Yes	Local and national separate
Ownership of a railway discount card	No, Yes	

Table 18-4   Proposed set of items: Journey roster and most recent journey

Item	Categories offered	Coding
Journey name	Open	Standing in for purpose
Date of departure	Open	
Date of return	Open	
Origin	Open	Nuts 5 or finer
Main destination	Open	Nuts 5 or finer
Main mode	Open	
Size of party	Open	

Table 18-5   Proposed set of items: Trip

Item	Categories offered	Coding
Journey name		As in Journey roster
Main purpose	Return home, work, education, shopping, visiting friends/relatives, leisure/holiday, picking up/dropping someone/ delivery, accompanying someone, other (Open)	Categories and suitable coding of open element
Origin	Open	Nuts 5 or finer
Destination	Open	Nuts 5 or finer
Number of overnight stays	Open	
Kind of accommodation	N.A., private, hotel or other rented	
Size of party	Open	
Departure date and time	Open	
Arrival date and time	Open	
All modes used	Car, rental car, taxi, motorcycle, bus, train, aeroplane, ship, bicycle, other (open)	Categories and suitable coding of open element
Role	Car driver, passenger, both	
Route taken	Open (major roads and junctions, stations where you changed modes, airports ...)	Extract stages, Nuts 5 or finer
Handicaps	None, more than hand luggage, travelling with young children, physical disabilities, other (Open)	Categories and suitable coding of open element
Assessment of trip	Pleasant, too long, uncomfortable, too expensive, other (Open)	Categories and suitable coding of open element
Payment of travel costs	Self, household member, employer, other (open)	Categories
Payment of accommodation costs	N.A., self, household member, employer, other(open)	Categories

18.4   RECOMMENDATIONS FOR IMPLEMENTATION
The experiences with the results of the MEST pilot surveys and with Eurostat pilots have highlighted the need for suitable organisational structures, because otherwise such an international survey will suffer grievously from a number of problems. The main problems are:

- *maintenance of a uniform protocol*: It is very easy for local firms to drift towards their preferred practices, even if a clear written description of the protocol is available. This may be due to local difficulties, lack of training, lack of commitment to the survey or further subcontracting with the associated information loss, etc.;
- *maintenance of a uniform question set*: The translation requires great care due to differences between the design language and the respective local language;
- *maintenance of uniform coding*: Unless a single uniform coding program is used, it is very difficult to maintain uniform coding standards due to local drift and local decision making, even if clear instructions are provided.

These problems require an organisational structure, which allocates clear responsibility for the maintenance of the uniform protocol and design to a central contractor. The organisation of the fieldwork is the contractor's task and it should be irrelevant to the sponsor, however many fieldwork firms are actually involved. Experience suggests though, that the fieldwork firms should not be reduced to data collection only, but they should also be involved within limits in the design process to increase their understanding of the study and their commitment to it. The survey firms should also accept the quality standards of the European market research societies.

In the design of the survey, the main contractor has to make sure that he integrates the experiences of all institutions with relevant experience, in particular national governments, national statistical offices or the relevant academics and consultants. However, it has to be clear that the timetable for such a benchmark survey makes it impossible to achieve perfect consensus.

Again, the constraints of a survey timetable and of the uniformity of the design and the protocol, plus the commercial risks involved, make a system of joint responsibility between a group of contractors cumbersome, expensive and potentially counter productive. Joint responsibility without central managerial control is fraught with difficulties.

In addition to the managerial tasks, the main contractor should be responsible for the following procedures:

- *Translation and retranslation*: The forms should be translated from the design language into the target languages and the translated versions should be retranslated into the design language to check the consistency of the terms and concepts. This approach is standard practice for any text of importance, as it is a very efficient means to find errors in understanding. Difficulties and local adaptations (e.g. specification of education levels) should be resolved at this point.

- *Production of forms, letters and support materials in all languages* to maintain the consistency of style. Extensive error checking is required for the language of the forms (errors, omissions, additions, etc.).
- *Writing of CATI software in all languages* to maintain the consistency of the questions, their order and of the coding. Proper checking of the language is essential. If the available CATI environment is not uniform among the fieldwork firms, then special attention has to be given to the verification of the uniformity of the language and of the coding.
- *Writing of coding software in all languages* to maintain the consistency of the questions, their order and of the codes. Proper checking of the translations is essential. This should include various error checking routines. The software should implement the automatic storage of the different generations of the data. It has to provide a suitable interface to the CATI software used. It should also include a routine for the semi-automatic geocoding of locations.
- *Provision of training materials* and participation in the training of the interviewers and line managers. The training of the telephone interviewers is essential, especially those used for the motivation calls.

The quality control of the whole survey process should be the responsibility of a separate firm, the task of which is to control adherence to the contract, implementation of the training schemes, and to ensure quality of the data capture and of data coding.

The contractor should have a single contact institution, which is also acting as the moderator of the sponsors' co-ordinating committee. In particular, individual sponsors should not be allowed to influence the fieldwork directly to avoid unnecessary friction and/or deviation from the agreed contents. The agency acting as the moderator has to make enough staff time available to perform this essential task properly. If such work is funded by the EU, the European Commission should undertake the task of organising the sponsors itself.

The complete recommended organisational structure, showing links between the various shared responsibilities, is shown in Figure 18.1.

Independent of the framework discussed above, is the question, if the survey should be organised as a one-off exercise, lasting a couple of months, or a truly continuous survey, such as the British, Swedish, Danish or Dutch national travel surveys. Wherever financially and organisationally possible, a continuous survey has to be recommended. It allows for the ongoing improvement of the survey, but more importantly it allows the ongoing monitoring of the changing travel markets and of the behaviour of the travellers in them.

310

Figure 18.1   Recommended organisational structure

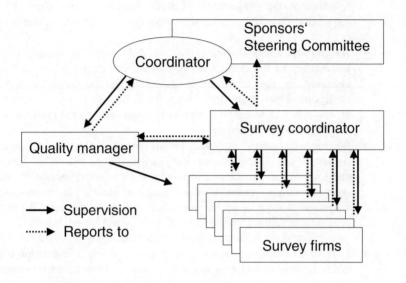

18.5   IN CONCLUSION, TECHNOLOGY AND RESEARCH ISSUES

It is clear that a European survey of long-distance travel is needed to fill the gaps in our knowledge of this important element in the travel behaviour of Europeans. These recommendations here cannot be supported by empirical evidence in all their aspects, because the research undertaken so far is inconclusive in certain respects or the work so far could not fill all the gaps due to time and resource limitations. Even so, the recommendations are a promising starting point for the further work. This future work might consist of three streams, with one stream focussing on *fieldwork* using the recommendations as the starting point, but continuously updating and revising it, based on the experience gained with its use and with alternative approaches, such as those discussed below. A second stream could address the many open *methodological research* questions and new issues and possibilities, in particular those raised by new technologies. Finally, there could be a stream *integrating survey data* into the European transport policy and research through archiving, web-based access tools and use of the data for modelling and monitoring.

18.5.1 Fieldwork

Ongoing fieldwork, as implied by the recommended continuous survey, offers the opportunity for further improvement of the survey approach. It is good practice in survey research to test new alternatives suggested either by theoretical considerations or by practical experience with the instrument and protocol.

Uniformity over time is of limited value, especially if problems are beginning to emerge in the survey approach. This permanent search for improvement overlaps with methodological research, which can benefit from the economies of scale offered by linkage with an ongoing survey.

The main issues for continuing research are, among others:

- *wording* of the forms;
- *design* of the forms and their structure;
- *wording* of the associated materials and reminders;
- *wording and sequencing* of the CATI interviews and the motivation discussions;
- *sequencing of contacts*, i.e. the timing, type and order of the different contacts.

Overlapping with the methodological research are studies of the following issues, which are urgent:

The proposed *size of item set* is the result of the development of the various pilot waves and the core requirements of transport modelling. It was not possible to undertake further detailed testing of whether this set has the optimal level of complexity. Further tests should be conducted to see if further detail can be obtained from the respondents without an undue decrease in response rate or data quality or if, alternatively, the detail should be reduced to achieve further gains in both respects. The detail could be increased in terms of the number of items or the number of journeys to be described. Alternatively, one could try separate journey rosters for different types of journeys. These tests should differentiate between the different elements of the survey (household, person, vehicle, journey and trip).[7]

The suggested *allocation and division of the items* between a household (background) and a movement form reflects the traditions of travel diary research. It would be worthwhile testing what effect it would have if the journey roster were moved to the background form to obtain a specialised trip description form.

The proposed protocol assumes that the respondent should be able to provide all information required on the form. Many travel diary surveys use their survey form as a memory jogger and not as a data capture form. The actual data retrieval, often covering more items than on the form, takes place during a telephone interview. It would be worthwhile testing such different *allocations of tasks between the paper and the telephone elements*, especially with regard to the trip or stage details, which create an impression of high complexity on the paper form for many potential respondents.

The proposed protocol assumes that two main phases are available for the contact with the respondents. In principle, further phases could be added. For example, the trip form could be separated and become a further follow-up phase in the survey protocol.[8] Experiments with such *multi-phase approaches* would be useful.

---

[7] This idea of separate journey rosters is being implemented in DATELINE.

[8] This approach is used in the DATELINE survey.

The *use of passive tracking* technologies, such as the use of GPS sensors or suitably adapted mobile phones, is rapidly moving into the mainstream (see e.g. Batelle, 1997; Garben *et al.*, 1999; or Flavigny *et al.*, 2000). Their use could be integrated into ongoing fieldwork.

18.5.2 Methodological research

It is clear that it is impossible in survey design to answer all questions due to the large number of variables which influence the success of a survey, whether measured in terms of response rate, data yield or data quality or as a mixture of these dimensions. In addition to these variables under the control of the researchers, there are numerous variables outside their control whose impacts can only be alleviated, never completely removed (e.g. total amount of survey and market research activity, political sensitivities, etc.)

The recommendations reflect current possibilities, in particular with respect to the availability of the phone and the Internet. It is clear that any survey has to be developed further in response to experience with it and the technological and social developments surrounding it. Even now, the evidence above suggests that a pure CATI or CAPI survey could be considered a viable alternative.

Clearly, further methodological research is not only needed in the area of survey administration, protocol and design, but also in the areas of sampling, imputation and weighting. The successful work of MEST in these areas has shown the potential for further work. Detailed recommendations for further research are discussed in Armoogum *et al.* (1999).

In addition to those issues mentioned above, in the short term, further research might focus on the following topics:

- *Household sampling*: The protocol proposed a person-based sample to reduce costs, to avoid proxy reporting and to reduce the required co-ordination within the household and between the household members and the survey firm. A further argument was the partial lack of independence of the observations given the significant degree of joint travel in the long-distance context. Reversing this assessment, it would be worthwhile to test a joint household journey roster and movement form to see how much additional information could be gained in this way.
- *Allocation of the sample* between different classes of regions, areas, household and person types to optimise the data yield and precision of the estimates.

In the longer term a number of further topics could be pursued, with the following ones being most relevant.

Development and field tests of travel diary *surveys on handheld devices* of the organiser or palmtop class. The work in the project TEST has demonstrated the feasibility of this approach. This work could be continued, in particular with respect to the integration of web-based information or web-based survey administration.

Development and field tests of *web-based travel diary surveys* expanding the successful work of TEST with respect to survey design and the integration of databases and graphical interfaces for route capture.

Further field-testing the acceptability of *passive data collection* technologies such as voluntary GPS-, GSM or RDS-TMC-based tracing or schedule reconstruction from credit card bills and current account details (see for example Batelle, 1997; Garben *et al.*, 1999; Flavigny *et al.*, 2000) (see below for a more detailed discussion).Further *refinement of sampling schemes* using the additional information about regions, areas, residential areas, household and person types made available by both official statistics and commercial market research firms.

18.5.3 Technological issues

The project TEST encompassed a series of work packages which looked at different technologies, all aimed at improving the quality of the data obtained from travel surveys, in particular long-distance travel surveys. All work packages demonstrated not only feasibility of the approaches chosen but also their long-term potential:

- a handheld HPC-based *travel diary application (TDA)* was shown to be acceptable under the conditions of small scale field tests to respondents in four countries;
- a WWW-based *iTDA* (Internet TDA) was also successful in two countries, in spite of the current slowness of the Internet. The overall system architecture with its specialised HTML tags opens new avenues for travel behaviour research;
- the structure and size of place-name databases and their sources provided a semi-automatic tool for the geocoding of place-names and the incorporation of shortest paths between places visited;
- an *AI-based data parsing system* made the classical techniques of imputation available to transport research enriched by logical checks for the standard variables and the provision of an audit trail for the data correction process;
- the *neural net*-based work showed that self-organising maps (SOM) can be a valid alternative to many classical imputation techniques while also offering the identification of suspect data;
- the *WWW-based interface* to travel diary data demonstrated the usefulness of this open approach to data publication with a sophisticated website built with free software tools, making it transferable to all interested parties.

The TDA and iTDA work show that the optimal design of the survey interface depends very much on the technological environment. On the small screen HPC, respondents preferred a single page of questions, requiring scrolling, to give them an idea of the complexity of the task. In contrast, on the large PC screen, *iTDA* respondents preferred a dedicated one-page-one-question format, which minimises data transfer across slow Internet connections. The design has to be determined afresh for each new survey medium. The success of both approaches opens the way for truly near real time data collection of travel behaviour, as both allow respondents to be prompted at regular intervals in a non-threatening way.

The work on geocoding, parsing and imputation of travel surveys, imputation and error detection using neural networks has shown how current computing technologies and algorithms can support the survey manager and designer by providing very powerful tools to enrich and correct the data received by the respondents. The main conclusion derived from these efforts is the need to learn continuously from past surveys, either in the form of improved and expanded lists of place names, but also in the form of imputation methods properly calibrated. These should be integrated into ongoing surveys, at the earliest possible moment, preferably while the survey is still in contact with the respondent: the CATI system, which prompts for the clarification of place names or the SOM, which queries outliers defined in terms of speed, mode and distance simultaneously.

The web-based interface to travel data, successfully implemented here, and the parsing work has drawn our attention to the need for a specification language for surveys in general and travel surveys in particular, both with regard to the content and the logic of the data storage. The investment in a website, which should be a core component of both the general executive information system for decision makers and professional users as well as a citizens information system, will only show large dividends, if a wide variety of surveys can easily be defined in the system without the need for extensive reformatting and change.

The experience gained indicates a variety of new and interesting research directions, some specific to the technologies used and others directed at the integration of the approaches. This integration will be crucial for speedy take up in ongoing survey work. It is also clear that the methodological developments need to be seen in parallel with ongoing fieldwork, as only the dialectic between large scale application and ongoing technological work can yield the desired results in terms of improved data for European transport policy.

The HPC class of devices is evolving rapidly to include mobile telephones as a standard feature, while their market is attacked by the even smaller palm-top class of devices. In addition, WAP-enabled phones could be used. GPS receivers are becoming available as PCMIA cards. Important research possibilities therefore are:

- using the *iTDA* approach on WAP phones speeding up data retrieval;
- integration of GSM, GPS or RDS/TMC based tracking and establishing its acceptability to survey respondents;
- a large scale field test with the approaches to establish their potential as new survey tools for large scale survey work.

Besides the important possibilities opened up in the integration of geocoding into other software, especially CATI and data coding software, automatic geocoding requires further work in its own right:

- improvement and maintenance of official and public place-name databases;
- development of comprehensive public map files of Europe, cross referenced against the place-name data bases (the GISCO database of Eurostat is a start);
- integration of public and private databases, especially for leisure

and tourism locations;

- improvement of automatic geocoding search strategies to reduce the number of possible candidates in the case of ambiguities.

The increasing computing power available at home and/or on the road, the rapid development of geographical databases and electronic maps and the work on error detection in TEST indicates that the following approaches are fruitful avenues for further work:

- integration of automatic geocoding into survey software either in the framework of a standard commercial CATI systems, the web-based system developed here or – in reduced form – into the TDA software;
- integration of automatic detection of suspect data into either standard commercial CATI systems, the web-based system developed here or the TDA software;
- integration of further external databases, such as timetable databases, gazetteers of places and attractions and similar travel-relevant data, preferably via the Internet.

The work on imputation in MEST and TEST has demonstrated the usefulness of a standard suite of such tools, as well as the potential of some new approaches. It is clear, that integration of the new approaches into the suite of imputation tools would be an important contribution to professional practice, in particular in conjunction with tools for the automatic selection of SOM for imputation and identification of suspect data

In summary, the TEST project demonstrated the contribution that a selected set of computing technologies and approaches can make to the improvement of travel data quality. As well as further development, fieldwork with the techniques developed is needed to advance the state of the art in this field.

18.5.4 Integration of the survey data

Databases which are not linked into a coherent information system cannot be fully utilised. From the general experience of the last years, but in particular on the experiences with the project TEST (TEST Consortium, 1999), such an information system should include, *inter alia*, the following elements:

- A *European Transport Data and Network Archive*: The systematic archiving of survey and observational data is an essential element of data quality in the social sciences which has not been adopted in the transport sector (Axhausen, forthcoming). There is little value in discussing the reasons for this, but large clients, such as the Commission or the national governments, should use their market power to make it happen, as they would be the main users and beneficiaries of such an archive. This archive would support the work of the information system and of the various research projects. It would protect the investment in the data and network information collected through professional storage and provide the data for re-analysis and re-use.
- A *web-based data interface* to display and query the data stored in

the data and network archive, which should be based on the successful initial implementation of this approach reported above. This implementation and the results of other 4th Framework projects are part of the basis of the further work required, especially for the integration of the mapping and analysis elements of such an interface.

- A *continuous programme of model implementation and development* which assures the exploitation of the data collected and provides for the updating of the survey contents in the light of modelling and monitoring needs. This modelling programme cannot be specified in detail here, but it could include among other tasks the following:
  o maintenance of European wide logical transport networks at different level of spatial resolution for passenger and freight transport;
  o continuous improvement of geographical databases of place-names, activity centres (leisure, shopping, freight facilities, etc.) and boundaries;
  o regular estimation of central behavioural parameters, such as values of time, values of reliability or values of life, for suitably defined regions and market segments; development and maintenance of origin-destination matrices at appropriate levels of spatial resolution for both passenger and freight broken down for different market segments; integration of the data with approaches based on traffic counts or intercept surveys.

The discussion above has shown that a European benchmark survey of long-distance travel is only one part, albeit an important part, of a coherent European Transport Policy Information System. This system requires continuous attention and development to serve the needs of European policy makers and of the European general and scientific public.

18.6   REFERENCES

Ampt, E. (1997) - Respondent burden: Understanding the people we survey. *Transportation Research Circular*, **E-C008**, II-G/1, TRB, Washington D.C.

Armoogum, J., J.-L. Madre, X.L. Han and J.W. Polak (1998) - Improved methods for weighting and correcting of travel diaries. *Report to the CEC, DG VII, MEST Deliverable*, **D8**, Fakultät für Bauingenieurwesen und Architektur, Leopold-Franzens-Universität, Innsbruck.

Armoogum, J., J.-L. Madre, X.L. Han and J.W. Polak (1999) - Suggested administration and evaluation methods for travel diaries: a manual. *Report to the CEC, DG VII, MEST Deliverable*, **D9**, Fakultät für Bauingenieurwesen und Architektur, INRETS, Arcueil.

Axhausen, K.W. (1998) - The EUROSTAT pilots of long distance travel diaries. *Report to the Österreichischem Statistischen Zentralamt*, Wien and Eurostat, Luxembourg, Innsbruck.

Axhausen, K.W. (Forthcoming) - Presenting and preserving travel data. *In P.M. Jones and P. Stopher (eds.) Raising the Standards: Proceedings from the International Conference*, Transportation Research Board, Washington, D.C.

Axhausen, K.W. and M. Youssefzadeh (1999) - Towards an European Survey of Long Distance Travel Incorporating A new European Long Distance Diary: Second draft of content and structure and A new European long distance diary: Final draft of content and structure. *Report to the CEC, DG VII, MEST Deliverables,* **D3 and D4**, Fakultät für Bauingenieurwesen und Architektur, Leopold-Franzens-Universität, Innsbruck.

Batelle (1997) - Global positioning systems for personal travel surveys: Lexington area travel data collection test. *Report to the Office of Highway Information Management, Office of Technology Application and the Federal Highway Administration*, Battelle Transport Division, Columbus.

Erl, E. (1998) - The new KONTIV-design. *Presentation at the 3rd MEST/TEST workshop*, Pörtschach, September 1998.

Flavigny, P.O., C Bovier, W. Ochieng and J.W. Polak (2000) - Conceptual and empirical issues in the use of positioning technologies for collecting travel. *Paper presented at the 9th International Conference on Travel Behaviour Research*, Goaldcoast, July 2000.

Garben, M., J. Janecke and M. Wermuth (1999) - Tele Travel System TTS – Telematiksystem zur automatischen Erfassung des Verkehrsverhaltens. *In Heureka '99 Optimierung in Transport und Verkehr*, 47-58, FGSV, Köln.

MEST Consortium (1999) - A suggested European long distance travel diary. *Report to the CEC, DG VII, MEST Deliverable,* **D5**, Fakultät für Bauingenieurwesen und Architektur, Leopold-Franzens-Universität, Innsbruck.

TEST Consortium (1999) - Final recommendation. *Report to the CEC, DG VII, TEST Deliverable,* **D8,** Fakultät für Bauingenieurwesen und Architektur, Leopold-Franzens-Universität, Innsbruck.

318

Summary of References

Summary of references

Ampt, E. (1997) - Respondent burden: Understanding the people we survey. *In P.M. Jones and P. Stopher (eds.) Transportation Research Cicular*, **E-C008**, II-G/1, TRB, Washington D.C.

Ampt, E., L. Buchanan, I. Chatfield, and A. Rooney (1998) - Reducing the impact of the car – creating the conditions for individual change. *Paper presented at the ETC*, Loughborough.

Ampt, E.S. and A.J. Richardson (1994) - The validity of self-completion surveys for collecting travel behaviour data. *Proceedings 22nd European Transport Forum*, PTRC, London.

Armoogum, J. and J.-L. Madre (1996) - Accuracy of Data and Memory Effects. *In Home Based Surveys on Travel Behaviour*, MEST working paper.

Armoogum, J. (1996) - La pondération de l'enquête Transports et communications 1993-94. *Note de l'Insee N°1068/F410*, December 1996.

Armoogum, J. (1997) - Correction of a non-response due to the potential response: Case of the French N.P.T.S. *8th IATBR Conference*, Austin, September 1997.

Armoogum, J. and J.-L. Madre (1996) - Non-response correction in the 1993-94 NPTS, the example of daily trips. *Proc. 4th International Conference on Survey Methods in Transport*, 342-361, Steeple Aston, September 1996.

Armoogum, J. and J.-L. Madre (1997) - Accuracy of data and memory effects in home based surveys on travel behaviour. *Paper presented at the 76th Annual Meeting of the Transport Research Board*, Washington D.C., January 1997.

Armoogum, J. and J.-L. Madre (1997) - De l'opimisation du plan de sondage au redressement d'une enquête: l'exemple des voyages à longue distance dans l'enquête. *Transports et Communications*, Rennes, June 1997.

Armoogum, J. and J.-L. Madre (1997) - Interview et présence au domicile. *Symposium of Statistic Canada*, Ottawa, November 1997.

Armoogum, J. and J.-L. Madre (1998) - Weighting or imputations? The example of non-responses for daily trips in the French NPTS. *Journal of Transportation and Statistics*, **1** (3), 53-64.

Armoogum, J. and J.-L. Madre (2000) - Item non-response, sampling and weighting. In P.M. Jones and P. Stopher (eds.) *Transport Surveys: Raising the Standards*, Transportation Research Cicular, **E-C008**, II-D-1-II-D-19, TRB, Washington D.C.

Armoogum, J., Y. Bussière and J.-L. Madre (1995) - Demographic dynamics of mobility in urban areas: The Paris and Grenoble case. *World Conference on Transport Research Society*, 1995.

Armoogum, J., J.-L. Madre, J.W. Polak, X.L. Han and M. Herry (1996) - Sampling and weighting schemes for travel diaries: review of issues and possibilities. *MEST Deliverable*, **D6**, INRETS, Arcueil.

Armoogum, J., J.-L. Madre, X.L. Han and J.W. Polak (1998) - Improved methods for weighting and correcting of travel diaries, report to the CEC, DG VII. *MEST Deliverable*, **D8**, Fakultät für Bauingenieurwesen und Architektur, Leopold-Franzens-Universität, Innsbruck.

Armoogum, J., J.-L. Madre, X.L. Han and J.W. Polak (1999) - Suggested administration and evaluation methods for travel diaries: a manual, report to the CEC, DG VII. *MEST Deliverable,* **D9,** Fakultät für Bauingenieurwesen und Architektur, INRETS, Arcueil.

Armoogun, J., M. Herry, J. Polak and J.-L. Madre (1996) - Sampling and Weighting Schemes for Travel Diaries: Review of issues and Possibilities. *Report to the CEC, DG VII, MEST Deliverable*, **D6,** Fakultät für Bauingenieurwessen und Architektur, Leopold-Franzens-Universität, Innsbruck.

Ås, D. (1978) - Studies of time-use: problems and prospects. *Acta Sociologica*, **21** (1), 125-141.

Aubert, O. (1996) - Introduction à Perl, olivier.aubert@enst-bretagne.fr

Axhausen, K.W. (1995) - Travel diaries: An annotated catalogue, 2nd edition. *Working Paper*, Institut für Straßenbau und Verkehrsplanung, Leopold-Franzens-Universität, Innsbruck.

Axhausen, K.W. (1996) - Possible contents and formats for long-distance-travel-diaries: Proposals for the first wave of MEST-pilots. *MEST Deliverable*, **D2**, MEST-Project, Fakultät für Bauingenieurwesen und Architektur, Leopold-Franzens-Universität, Innsbruck.

Axhausen, K.W. (1997) - The Eurostat pilots of long-distance travel diaries: summary of intermediate reports. *Report to the Österreichisches Statistischs Zentralamt, Wien and EUROSTAT*, Luxembourg, Institut für Straßenbau und Verkehrsplannung, Leopold-Franzens-Universitat, Innsbruck.

Axhausen, K.W. (1998) - The EUROSTAT pilots of long distance travel diaries. *Report to the Österreichischem Statistischen Zentralamt*, Wien and Eurostat, Luxembourg, Innsbruck.

Axhausen, K.W. (1999a) - Surveying long-distance travel: effects of survey contexts and protocols. In Statistics Sweden (ed.), Official Statistics in a Changing World, Proceedings of the 3rd International Conference on Methodological Issues in Official Statistics, 141-149, Statistics Sweden, Stockholm.

Axhausen, K.W. (1999b) - Non-response and data yield: Experiences from Austria and France, paper presented at ICNS 1999, Portland, October 1999, *Arbeitsberichte Verkehrs- und Raumplanung*, **8,** Institut für Verkehrsplanung, Transporttechnik, Strassen- und Eisenbahnbau, ETH, Zürich.

Axhausen, K.W. (2000a) - Definition of movement and activity for transport modelling. In D. Hensher and K. Button (eds.) *Handbooks in Transport: Transport Modelling*, Elsevier, Oxford.

322

Axhausen, K.W. (2000b) - The Eurostat pilots of long-distance travel diaries: Summary of the final report. *Report to the Österreichisches Statistisches Zentralamt*, Wien and Eurostat, Luxembourg.

Axhausen, K.W. (2001) - Methodological Research for a European Survey of Long-Distance Travel. *Transportation Research Circular*, **E-C026**, 322-342, TRB, Washington D.C.

Axhausen, K.W. (Forthcoming) - Presenting and preserving travel data. In P.M. Jones and P. Stopher (eds.) *Raising the Standards: Proceedings from the International Conference*, Transportation Research Board, Washington, D.C.

Axhausen, K.W. and M. Youssefzadeh (1997) - Tender documents: Second MEST pilots. Report to the CEC, DG VII, *MEST Internal Working Paper,* **IWP03 and IWP04,** Fakultät für Bauingenieurwessen und Architektur, Leopold-Franzens-Universität, Innsbruck.

Axhausen, K.W. and M. Youssefzadeh (1998) - Towards a new European Long Distance Diary: Analysis of MEST pilots wave III. *MEST Deliverable*, **D3 and D4,** Innsbruck.

Axhausen, K.W. and M. Youssefzadeh (1999) - Towards an European Survey of Long Distance Travel (a new European long distance diary: Second draft of content and structure and a new European long distance diary: Final draft of content and structure. Report to the CEC, DG VII - Transport, *MEST Deliverables*, **D3 and D4**, Fakultät für Bauingenieurwesen und Architektur, Leopold-Franzens-Universität, Innsbruck.

Axhausen, K.W., A. Zimmermann, S. Schönfelder, G. Rindsfüser and T. Haupt (2000) - Observing the rhythms of life: a six-week travel diary. *Arbeitsbericht Verkehrs- und Raumplanung*, **25**, Institut für Verkehrsplanung, Transporttechnik, Strassen- und Eisenbahnbau, ETH Zürich.

Axhausen, K.W., H. Köll, M. Bader and M. Herry (1997) - Workload, data yield and data quality: experiments with long-distance travel diaries. *Transportation Research Record*, **1593**, 29-40.

Babbie, E. (1990) - Survey Research Methods. Wadsworth Publishing Company, Belmont.

Bankier, M.D. (1986) - Estimator based of several stratified samples with applications to multiple frame surveys. *Journal of the American Statistical Association*, **81**, 1074-1079.

Batelle Transport Division (1997) - Global positioning systems for personal travel surveys: Lexington area travel data collection test. *Report to the Office of Highway Information Management, Office of Technology Application and the Federal Highway Administration*, Battelle Transport Division, Columbus.

Bishop, C. (1995) - Neural Network for Pattern Recognition. Clarendon Press, Oxford.

Boivin, D.J. and L. Gauthier (1996) - Un manuel illustré de programmation en HTML. www.image.fr/Multimedia/miroirs/manuelhtml/manuelhtml.html

Boutell, T. (1996) - CGI Programming in C & Perl. Addison Wesley, New York.

Box, G.E.P., W.G. Hunter and J.S. Hunter (1978) - Statistics for Experimenters. John Wiley and Sons Inc., New York.

Brög, W. (2000) - The New KONTIV design: A total survey design for surveys on mobility behaviour. *Paper presented at the ICES – II International Conference on Establishment Surveys – II*, Buffalo, New York.

Brög, W. and A. Meyburg (1980) - The non-response problem in travel surveys - an empirical investigation. *Transportation Research Record,* **775**, 34-38.

Brög, W. and A. Meyburg (1981) - Considerations of non-response effects on large scale mobility surveys. *Transportation Research Record,* **807**, 39-46.

Brög, W., E. Erl, A. Meyburg and W. Wermuth (1982) - Problems of non-reported trips in surveys of nonhome activity patterns. *Transportation Research Record,* **891**, 1-5.

BTS (1997) - 1995 American travel survey profile. US Department of Transportation, Washington D.C.

Bundesministerium für öffentliche Wirtschaft und Verkehr (1992) - Österreichisches Gesamtverkehrskonzept, BMöWV, Vienna.

Bundesministerium für Wissenschaft und Verkehr (1998) - Der Masterplan des österreichischen Bundesverkehrswegeplans, BMWV, Vienna.

Bushnell, D. (1994) - The National Travel Survey; Report on the 1991 Census-Linked Study of Survey Non-response. Office of National Statistics, London.

Celeux, G. and J. Diebolt (1985) - The SEM algorithm: a probabilistic teacher algorithm derived from the EM algorithm for the mixture problem. *Comp. Statist. Quart.,* **2** 73-82.

Cockerell, N., N. Barrie, M. Manente, V. Minghetti, E. Celotto, M.C. Furlan, G.R.M. Jansen, M.J.W.A. Vanderschuren, F. Potier, Y. Israeli, S. Blais, G. Röschel, A. Troitiño and R. Vickerman (2000) - Artist Agenda for Research on Tourism by Integration of Statistics/strategies. *Deliverable,* **5**, ARTIST Project, Brussels.

Cornelis, E. (1997) - PACSIM users' manual. *FUNDP - Transportation Research Group*, Namur.

COST 305 (1988) - Data system for the study of demand for interregional passenger transport. *Final Paper*, Brussels, Luxembourg.

Cruddas, M., J. Thomas and R. Chambers (1997) - Investigating Neural Networks as a Possible Means of Imputation for the 2001 UK Census. *Proc. Symposium of Statistics Canada: New directions in Surveys and Census*, 153-158, Quebec, November 1997.

CSST, ENEA and Inrets (2000) - *Commute tools,* Commute project (CEC DG TREN). *Presented at Commute/Internat workshop*, Brussels 20/3/2000.

324

Dagnelie, P. (1992) - Statistique théorique et appliquée. Les presses agronomiques de Gembloux, A.S.B.L, Gembloux.

DATELINE Project (2000) - Sampling Methodology. *Deliverable, 3*, Socialdata, München.

de Heer, W. and G. Moritz (1997) - Respondent sampling weighting and non-response. *Paper presented to the International Conference on Transport Survey Quality and Innovation*, Grainau, Germany, May 1997.

de Heer, W. and G. Moritz (1997) - Respondent sampling weighting and non-response. *Transportation Research Circular*, **E-C008**, II-C/1, TRB, Washington D.C.

de Leeuw, E.D. (1992) - Data Quality in Mail, Telephone and Face to Face Interviews. PhD thesis, Universiteit Amsterdam.

de Leeuw, J. (1994) - An introduction to xlisp-stat. UCLA, Los-Angeles.

Dempster, A.P., N.M. Laird and D.B. Rubin (1977) - Maximum likelihood estimation from incomplete data via the EM algorithm (with discussion). *Journal of the Royal Statistical Society Series B, 39*, 1-38.

Denstadli, J.-M. (1999) - Travel behaviour 1998 - journeys of 100 km or more. *Summary of TOI Report 466/1999*, TOI, Oslo.

Denstadli, J.-M. and J.-I. Lian (1998) - Memory effects in long distance travel surveys. *TEST Working Paper*, TOI, Oslo.

DETR (1999) - Transport Statistics Bulletin, National Travel Survey 1996-1998 update. DETR, London.

Deussner, R., G. Eisenkölb, A. Hendrich and E. Lichtenberger (1996) - Österreich-Matrizen: Urlauberreise- und Urlauberlokalverkehr. *Report to the Austrian Ministry of Science, Transport and Arts*, Vienna, Österreiches Institut für Raumplanung, Vienna.

Deville, J.-C. (1998) - La correction de la non-réponse par calage ou par échantillonage équillibré. *Paper presented at the 25th annual meeting of the Statistical Society of Canada*, Sherbrook, Canada, May 1998.

Deville, J.-C. and C.E. Särndal (1992) - Calibration estimators and generalised raking techniques in survey sampling. *Journal of the American Statistical Association*, **87** (418), 376-382.

Deville, J.-C. and C.E. Särndal (1994) - Variance estimation for the regression imputed Horvitz-Thompson estimator. *Journal of Official Statistics*, **10** (4), 381-394.

Deville, J.-C., C.E. Särndal and O. Sautory (1993) - Generalised raking procedures in survey sampling. *Journal of the American Statistical Association*, **88** (423), 1013-1020.

Didier, M., C. Bouveyron and C.N.I.G. (1993) - Guide économique et méthodologique des SIG. Hermes, Paris.

Diebolt, J. and E.H.S. Ip (1996) - Stochastic EM: Method and application. In W.R. Gilks, S.Richardson and D.J. Spiegelhalter (eds.) *Markov Chain Monte Carlo in Practice*, 259-273, Chapman and Hall, London.

Dillman, D.A. (1978) - Mail and Telephone Surveys: The Total Design Method. John Wiley and Sons Inc., New York.

Eriksson, S. (1999) - Proceedings from the methodological workshop on the implementation of the Council Directive 95/57/EC on Tourism Statistics. 4/2000/D/no.1, Luxembourg.

Erl, E. (1998) - The new KONTIV-design. *Presentation at the 3rd MEST/TEST workshop*, Pörtschach, September 1998.

Ettema, D., H. Timmermanns and L. van Veghel (1996) - Effects of Data Collection Methods in Travel and Activity Research. *European Institute of Retailing and Service Studies*, Technical University of Eindhoven.

Eurostat (1995) - Implementation of the EUROSTAT methodology on basic tourism statistics: A practical manual, 2nd draft, EUROSTAT, Luxembourg[1].

Eurostat (1995a) - Definitions and variables of a household survey for mobility, Passenger transport statistics and mobility. *Document T7/95-2/5/EN*, Luxembourg.

Eurostat (1995b) - Council Directive 95/57/EC of 23 Nov. 1995 on the collection of statistical information in the field of tourism. Brussels.

Eurostat (1998) - Community methodology on Tourism statistics. Eurostat, Luxembourg.

Eurostat (1999) - Progress report on methodological developments in the EEA Countries of Tourism Statistics following the implementation of the Council Directive 95/57/EC. *Document TOUR/99/32/EN*, Luxembourg.

Fabre, F., A. Klose and G. Somer (Eds.) (1988) - Data system for the study of demand for interregional passenger transport, final report. *COST*, **305**, Commission of the European Communities, Brussels.

Federal Highway Administration (1998) - Personal travel: the long and the short of it. *Working Paper published by the Office of Highway Information Management* , Washington D.C.

Fessant, F. and S. Midenet (1998) - Imputation of partial non-responses in surveys with a self-organizing map based model. *Paper presented in ACSEG'98 Fifth International Meeting on Connectionist Approaches in Economics and Management Sciences*, November, Louvain-la-Jeune.

---

[1] This report was included as item TF/95/9/EN for the "*Joint meeting of the task force on Passenger Transport Statistics and on Tourism Statistics*", 31.1. and 1.2.1995 in Luxembourg.

Fessant, F. and S. Midenet (1999) - A knowledge-based parser : neural network based approaches ; development of a neural network based imputation system for travel diary data. *TEST European Project, 4th Framework CEC/DGVII, Deliverable D5-B*, INRETS, Arcueil.

Fessel+GfK and IFES (1996) – Feldbericht. Report to the Ministry of Stated Owned Industries and Transportation, Vienna.

Flavigny, P.-O. and C. Bouvier (2000) - Using RDS identification for localization. *Paper presented at the 9th IATBR conference*, Goldcoast, July 2000.

Flavigny, P.-O. and J.-L. Madre (1994) - How to get the geographical data in the households surveys? *Proceedings of IATBR 94*, **2**, 619-630, Valle Nevada, Santiago, Chile.

Flavigny, P.O., C Bovier, W. Ochieng and J.W. Polak (2000) - Conceptual and empirical issues in the use of positioning technologies for collecting travel. *Paper presented at the 9th International Conference on Travel Behaviour Research*, Goaldcoast, July 2000.

Gamerman, D. (1997) - Markov Chain Monte Carlo: Stochastic Simulation for Bayesian Inference. Chapman and Hall, London.

Garben, M., J. Janecke and M. Wermuth (1999) - Tele Travel System TTS – Telematiksystem zur automatischen Erfassung des Verkehrsverhaltens. *In Heureka '99 Optimierung in Transport und Verkehr*, 47-58, FGSV, Köln.

Geman, S. and D. Geman (1984) - Stochastic relaxation, Gibbs distributions, and the Bayesian restoration of images. *IEEE Proc. Pattern Analysis and Machine Intelligence*, **6**, 721-741.

Gerber, E.R., M.L. Crowley and S.R. Trencher (1999) - Identity thieves, warrantee cards and government surveys: The ethnography of personal information management. *Paper presented at the International Conference on Survey Non-Response*, Portland, October 1999.

Gidas, B. (1985) - Nonstationary Markov Chains and convergence of the Annealing Algorithm. *J.Statis. Phys.*, **39**, 73-131.

Gingras, F. and Y. Bengio (1996) - Recurrent neural networks for missing or asynchronous dat., *In Proc. NIPS 8 Advances in Neural Information Processing Systems*, 395-401, MIT Press, Cambridge, USA.

GISDATA (1995-7) - GISDATA Newsletter. Strasbourg, European Science Foundation.

Grabowski, M. (1998) - Application of self organizing maps to outlier identification and estimation of missing data. Proc. *IFCS'98 Sixth Conference of the International Federation of Classification Societies*, 279-286, Roma, July 1998.

Greene, W.H. (1995) - Limdep Version 7.0. Econometric Software, Bellport.

Greene, W.H. (1997) - Econometric Analysis. Prentice Hall, Upper Saddle River.

Gross, C. (1997) - Configuration du logiciel Apache, aspects sécurité. *CNRS*, Grenoble.

Groves, R. (1989) - Survey Errors and Survey Costs. John Wiley and Sons Inc., New York.

Haccou, P. and E. Meelis (1994) - Statistical Analysis of Behavioural Data - An Approach Based on Time-Structured Models. Oxford University Press, Oxford.

Han, X-L. (1993) - Markov Chain Monte Carlo and Sampling Efficiency. PhD thesis, University of Bristol, Bristol.

Hassounah, M., L.S. Cheah and G. Steuart (1993) - Underreporting of trips in telephone interview surveys. *Transportation Research Record*, **1412**, 90-94.

Hastings, W.K. (1970) - Monte Carlo sampling methods using Markov chains and their applications. *Biometrika*, **57**, 97-109.

Haubold, I., K.W. Axhausen, P. Jackson and J.W. Polak (1997) - Technology Assessment, report to the CEC, DG VII. *Transport Research Programme of the 4th Framework Programme, TEST Deliverable*, **D1**, Fakultät für Bauingenieurwesen und Architektur, Leopold-Franzens-Universität, Innsbruck.

Hekman, J.P. (1997) - Linux in a nutshell: A Desktop Quick Reference. O'Reilly, Sebastopol.

Herry, M. and G. Sammer (1996) - Österreichischer Bundesverkehrswegeplan: Gewichtung, Hochrechnung und Zusatzerhebung zur KONTIV Österreich. *Report to the BMöWV*, Vienna.

Herry, M. and G. Sammer (1999) - Mobilitätserhebung österreichischer Haushalte, Österreichischer Bundesverkehrswegeplan. *Forschungsarbeiten aus dem Verkehrswesen*, **87**, Vienna.

Hertz, J., A. Krogh and R.G. Palmer (1991) - Introduction to the Theory of Neural Computation. Addison-Wesley, Redwood City.

Hubert, J.-P. and F. Moriconi-Ebrard (1999) - Terrae statisticae. Il database sui comuni d'Europa. *Sistema Terra*, **8** (1-3), 120-125.

Hubert, J.-P., P.-O. Flavigny and J.-L. Madre (1999) - Tools to enrich travel diary data sets. *Deliverable 4 of 4th framework project TEST (CEC/DG VII)*, Arcueil, Inrets.

Ibbou, S. (1998) - Classification, analyse des correspondances et méthodes neuronales. Thèse de l'Université Paris 1 Panthéon Sorbonne, Paris.

Idan, Y. and R. Chevallier (1991) - Handwritten digits recognition by a supervised Kohonen-like learning algorithm. *Proceedings of IJCNN '91 International Joint Conference on Neural Networks*, 2576-2581, IEEE, Piscataway.

INE (2000) - Destaque do INE, Viagens turisticas dos residentes (1999-2000). *INE*, Lisboa.

INRETS (1989) - Un milliard de déplacements par semaine. La mobilité des Français. La Documentation française, Paris.

INRETS (1996) - Correction de l'enquête transports et mobilite 1993-1994. *Working papers*, **1/42 - 40/42**, INRETS, Arcueil.

INSEE (1998) - La mobilité à longue distance des ménages en 1994. Enquête transport et communication 1993-1994. *Insee Résultat, collection Démographie-Société*, n°72-73-74,1998, INSEE, Paris.

Ip, E.H.S. (1994) - A stochastic EM estimator in the presence of missing data-theory and applications. *Technical report*, Department of Statistics, Stanford University, Palo Alto.

IPSOS Region (1997) - Survey on long-distance mobility, report to the French Ministry of Transport. *IPSOS Region*, Lyon.

ISTAT (1997) - I viaggi in Italia e all'estero nel 1997. ISTAT, Roma.

Jensen, K and N. Wirth (1997) - PASCAL, manuel de l'utilisateur et rapport de définition. Eyrolles, Paris.

Jochems, P. (1998) - German long-distance travel: Results of the on-going 'Mobility' survey. *Presentation at the 3rd MEST Workshop*, Pörtschach.

Johnson, B. (1996) - Perl Tutorial www.ncsa.uiuc.edu/General/Training/PerlIntro/

Kalfs, N. and W.E. Saris (1996) - New data collection methods in travel surveys. *Paper presented at the Fourth International Conference on Survey Methods in Transport*, Steeple Aston, September 1996.

Kalton, G. (1983) - Compensating for Missing Survey Data. *Institute for Social Research*, University of Michigan, Ann Arbor.

Kim, H., J. Li, S. Roodman, A. Sen, S. Sööt, and E. Christopher (1993) - Factoring household travel surveys. *Transportation Research Record*, **1412**, 17-22.

Kitamura, R. and P.H.L. Bovy (1987) - Analysis of attrition biases and trip reporting errors for panel data. *Transportation Research*, **21A** (4/5), 287-302.

Kohonen, T. (1995) - Self-Organizing Maps. Springer, Heidelberg.

Laarhoven, P.J.M. van and E.H.L. Aarts (1987) - Simulated Annealing: Theory and Applications. R.Reidel Publishing Company, Dordrecht.

Le Bras, H. (1996) - Le peuplement de l'Europe. DATAR La documentation française, Paris.

Lehtonen, R. and E.J. Pahkinen (1996) - Practical Methods for Design and analysis of Complex Surveys (Revised Edition). John Wiley and Sons, Chichester.

Lessler, J.T. and W.D. Karlsbeek (1992) - Nonsampling Errors in Surveys. John Wiley Inc., New York.

Levine, J.R. and C. Baroudi (1994) - Internet pour les nuls, Sybex, Paris.

Little, R.J.A. and D.B. Rubin (1987) - Statistical Analysis with Missing Data. John Wiley and Sons, Chichester.

Lopez-Vazquez, C. (1997) - Application of ANN to the prediction of missing daily precipitation records and comparison against linear methodologies. *Proc. EANN'97 International Conference on Engineering Applications of Neural Networks*, 337-340, Stockholm, June 1997.

Lothaire, O. (1999) - A Knowledge-based Parser: Implementation of a Tool-box. *Report to the CEC, DGVII, TEST Deliverable*, **D5A,** Groupe de Recherche sur les Transports, Facultés Universitaires Notre-Dame de la Paix, Namur.

Lyons, G. (1998) - A case study of teh development of car dependence in teenagers. *Paper presented at the ETC*, Loughborough, UK.

Madow, W.G., I. Olkin and D.B. Rubin (eds.) (1983) - Incomplete Data in Sample Surveys, Theory And Bibliographies. **2**, Academic Press, New York.

Madre, J.-L. and J. Maffre (1997) - La mobilite des residants francais: Panorama general et evolution. *Revue Transport and Securite*, **56**.

Madre, J.L. and J. Maffre (1999) - Is it necessary to collect data on daily mobility and on long distance travel in the same survey? *Transportation Research Circular*, **E-C026**, 343-364, TRB, Washington D.C.

Madre, J.-L. and J. Zmud (1997) - Transport surveys, raising the standards: workshop 3: item (sampling, weighting, non-response). *Presented at the International Conference on Transport Survey Quality and Innovation*, May 24-30, Grainau, Germany.

Maires, G. (1996) - UNGI, un nouveau guide Internet. www.imaginet.fr/ime/.

Mason, T. and D. Brown (1990) - Lex and Yacc. O'Reilly, Sebastopol.

Matthews, R.D., P. Jones, J. Magid, D.A. Ball Jr and M.J. Hammel (1996) - The Unix Web Server: Tools and Techniques for building your own Internet Information Site. Vantana, Research Triangle Park.

MEST (1996) - Methods of European Surveys of Behaviour: Technical Annex. *Transport Research Programme of the 4th Framework Programme*, Fakultät für Bauingenieurwesen und Architektur, Leopold-Franzens-Universität, Innsbruck.

MEST Consortium (1995) - Methods for European Surveys of Travel Behaviour: Technical Annex, contract with the CEC, DG VII – Transport. *4th Framework Programme*, Brussels.

MEST Consortium (1999) - A suggested European long distance travel diary, report to the CEC, DG VII. *MEST Deliverable*, **D5**, Fakultät für Bauingenieurwesen und Architektur, Leopold-Franzens-Universität, Innsbruck.

MEST Consortium (1999) - Methods for European Surveys of Travel Behaviour, final report to the CEC, DG 7 – Transport. *MEST Consortium*, Innsbruck.

Metropolis, N., A.W. Rosenbluth, M.N. Rosenbluth, A.H. Teller and E. Teller (1953) - Equations of state calculations by fast computing machines. *The Journal of Chemical Physics*, **21**, 1087-1092.

Meyburg, A.H. (1997) - Question formulation and instrument design. *Transportation Research Circular*, **E-C008**, II-H/1, TRB, Washington D.C.

Midenet, S. and A. Grumbach (1994) - Learning Associations by Self-Organization: the LASSO model. *NeuroComputing*, **6**, 343-361.

Mitra, S. and K. Pal (1995) - Fuzzy multilayer perceptron, Inferencing and generalization. *IEEE Trans. on Neural networks*, **6**, 51-63.

Muller, S., P. Garda and J.D. Muller (1998) - Un codage neuro flou pour le traitement de données incomplètes par réseaux connexionnistes. *Proc. IPMU'98 Seventh Conference on Information Processing and Management of Uncertainty in Knowledge-based Systems*, EDK Editions Médicales et Scientifiques, 973-980, Paris, July 1998.

Murtagh, F., G. Zheng, J. Campbell, A. Aussem, M. Ouberdous, E. Demirov, W. Eifler and M. Crepon (1998) - Data imputation and nowcasting in the environmental sciences using clustering and connectionist modeling. *Proc. CompStat 98 International Conference on Computational Statistics*, 401-406, Bristol, August 1998.

Muscarà, P. and E. Zamparutti (1994) - The last frontier in GIS, The role of rapidly decreasing data costs and business mapping in launching the US Market. *Sistema Terra, 3.*

Musciano, C. and B. Kennedy (1996) - HTML: The definitive guide. O'Reilly, Sebastopol.

Neuss, C. and J. Vromans (1996) - Applications CGI en Perl pour les Webmasters. International Thomson Publishing, Paris.

Nordbotten, S. (1996) - Neural network imputation applied to the Norwegian 1990 population census data. *Journal of Official Statistics*, **12-4**, 385-401.

OECD and Statistics Canada (1995) - Literacy, Economy and Society: Results of the First International Adult Literacy Survey. OECD, Paris.

Ortuzar, J. de Dios and L. Willumsen (1994) - Modelling Transport. John Wiley and Sons, Chichester.

Polak, J.W. and E.S. Ampt (1996) - An analysis of wave response and non-response effects in travel diary surveys *Proceedings 4th International Conference on Survey Methods in Transport*, Steeple Aston, 9-11 September 1996.

Potier, F., N. Cockerell, G.R.M. Jansen, M.J.W.A. Vanderschuren, M. Manente, V. Minghetti, E. Celotto, M.C. Furlan, O. Heddebaud, G. Röschel (2000) - Analysis of tourism and transport flows and overview of recent trends. *Deliverable, 1*, ARTIST Project, Brussels.

Potier, F. (2000) - Trends in Tourism and international flows in Europe. *In ECMT (ed.) Transport and leisure, Report of the 111th Round Table of Transport Economics,* ECMT, Paris.

Pumain, D., T. Saint-Julien, N. Cattan and C. Rozenblat (1991) - Le concept statistique de la ville en Europe. Eurostat, Luxembourg.

Reginster, I. (1997) - A www interface to travel diary results. *TEST Deliverable,* **D6**, FUNDP, Namur.

Richardson, A.J. and E.S. Ampt (1993) - The Victoria Integrated Travel, Activities and Land-Use Toolkit: *VITAL. Working Paper,* **VWP93/1,** Transport Research Centre, University of Melbourne.

Richardson, A.J. and E.S. Ampt (1994) - Non-response effects in mail-back travel surveys. *Paper presented at the 7th Conference of the International Association for Travel Behaviour Research,* Valle Nevada, 1994

Richardson, A.J. and R.K. Seethaler (1999) - Estimating Long-Distance Travel Behaviour from the Most Recent Trip *Paper presented at the TRB Conference on Personal Travel: The Long and Short of It,* Washington D.C.

Richardson, A.J., E.S. Ampt and A.H. Meyburg (1995) - Survey Methods for Transport Planning. Eucalyptus Press, Melbourne.

Riede, T. (1993) - Zur Einsetzbarkeit von Laptops in Haushaltsbefragungen in der Bundesrepublik Deutschland, Schlußbericht SAEG-Studie. *Ausgewählte Arbeitsunterlagen zur Bundesstatistik,* **20,** Statistisches Bundesamt, Wiesbaden.

Ritter, H., T. Martinetz and K. Schulten (1989) - Topology conserving maps for learning visuo motor coordination. *Neural Networks,* **2,** 159-168.

Rouquette, C. (2000) - Chaque anée, quatre Français sur dix ne partent pas en vacances. *INSEE première, No. 734,* INSEE, Paris.

Rubin, D.B. (1976) - Inference and missing data. *Biometrika ,* **63,** 581-592.

Rubin, D.B. (1983) - Conceptual issues in the presence of nonresponse. In W.G. Madow, I Olkin and D.B. Rubin (eds.) *Incomplete Data in Sample Surveys, Vol II : Theory and Bibliographies,* 125-142. Academic Press, New York.

Rubin, D.B. (1987) - Multiple Inputation for Non-response in Surveys. John Wiley and Sons Inc., New York.

Rumelhart, D., G. Hinton and R. Williams (1986) - Learning internal representations by error propagation. *In Parallel Distributed Processing : Explorations in the Microstructure of Cognition, Volume 1: Foundations,* Rumelhart D. and McClelland J.(eds.), 318-362, MIT press, Cambridge, USA.

Samad, T. and S. Harp (1992) - Self organization with partial data. *Network,* **3,** 205-212.

Särndal, C-E. and B. Swensson (1987) - A general view of estimation for two phases of selection with applications to two-phase sampling and nonresponse. *International Statistical Review,* **55** (3), 279-294.

Särndal, C.-E., B. Swensson, B. and J. Wretman. (1992) - Model Assisted Survey Sampling. Springer, Heidelberg.

Sautory, O. (1993) - Redressement d'un échantillon par calage sur marges. *INSEE Document de travail, N° F9310,* INSEE, Paris.

Sautory, O. (1995) La statistique descriptive avec le système SAS, INSEE - Guides N°1-2. *INSEE,* Paris.

Scales, J.A. and M.L. Smith (1996) - A whirlwind Tour of Lisp-Stat. landau.mines.edu/~samizdat/

Schafter, J.L. (1997) - Analysis of Incomplete Multivariate Data. Chapman and Hall, London.

Schartz, R.L. (1995) - Introduction à Perl. O'Reilly, Sebastopol.

Schnabel, C. (2000) - DATELINE up-dating review of existing long-distance surveys.

Schnabel, W. and D. Lohse (1997) - Grundlagen der Strassenverkehrstechnik und der Verkehrsplanung. Verlag für Bauwesen, Berlin.

Semmence, J. (1997) - Family resources surveys: a practical example of imputation. *Proc. Symposium of Statistics Canada: New directions in Surveys and Census*, 149-152, Quebec, November 1997.

SES/ESA (1998) - Actes du colloque déplacements à longue distance. Mesures et Analyses. *Département des études économiques du Service Economique et Statistique (SES)*, Paris and ESA Consultants, Strasbourg.

Sharpe, P. and R. Solly (1995) - Dealing with missing values in neural network based diagnostic systems. *Neural Computing and Applications*, **3**, 73-77.

SIKA (2000) - RES 1999 Den nationella reseundersöknigen. *Sveriges oficiella statistik*, IKA, Stockholm.

Simpson, S. and D. Dorling (1994) - Those missing millions: implications for social statistics of non-response in the 1991 Census. *Journal of Social Policy,* **23** (4), 543-67.

Skinner, C.J., D. Holt and T.M.F. Smith (1996) - Analysis of Complex Surveys. John Wiley and Sons, Chichester.

Spainhour, S. and V. Queria (1996) - Webmaster in a nutshell. O'Reilly, Sebastopol.

Statistics Sweden (2000) - National Travel Survey, NTS 1999, Official Statistics of Sweden. *Swedish Institute for Transport and Communications Analysis.*

Stecher, C.C., S. Bricka and L. Goldenberg (1996) - Travel behaviour survey data collection instruments. *Paper presented at the Fourth International Conference on Survey Methods in Transport*, Steeple Aston, September 1996.

Stopher, P. and C. Stecher (1993) - Blow up: Expanding a complex random sample travel survey. *Transportation Research Record*, **1412**, 10-16.

Sudman, S. and N.M. Bradburn (1983) - Asking Questions. Jossey-Bass, San Francisco.

Sudman, S., N.M Bradburn and N. Schwarz (1996) - Thinking about Answers. Jossey-Bass, San Francisco.

Szalai, A. (ed.) (1972) - The Use of Time. Mouton, The Hague.

Tackett Jr., J. and D. Gunter (1997) - LINUX Le MacMillan. S & SM, Paris.

Tanur, J.M. and S.E. Fienberg (1992) - Cognitive aspects in surveys: Yesterday, today and tomorrow. *Journal of Official Statistics,* **8** (1), 5-17.

TEST (1996) - Technologies for European surveys of Travel Behaviour: Technical Annex. *Transport Research Programme of the 4th Framework Programme,* Fakultät für Bauingenieurwesen und Architektur, Leopold-Franzens-Universität, Innsbruck.

TEST (1997) - Technologies for European Surveys of Travel Behaviour: Detailed work package descriptions. *Report to the CEC, DG VII, Transport Research Programme of the 4th Framework Programme,* Fakultät für Bauingenieurwesen und Architektur, Leopold-Franzens-Universität, Innsbruck.

TEST Consortium (1999) - Final recommendation, report to the CEC, DG VII. *TEST Deliverable,* **D8,** Fakultät für Bauingenieurwesen und Architektur, Leopold-Franzens-Universität, Innsbruck.

Thakuriah, P., A. Sen, S. Sööt, and E. Christopher (1993) - Non-response bias and trip generation models. *Transportation Research Record,* **1412,** 64-70.

Thill, J.-C. (2000) - Geographical information systems in transportation research: Special Issue. *Transportation Research.*

Tierney, L. (1988) - Xlispstat, A Statistical Environment Based on the Xlisp language. University of Minnesota, Minneapolis.

Tierney, L. (1990) - Lisp-Stat: An object-oriented environment for statistical computing and dynamic graphics. John Wiley and Sons Inc., New York.

Tierney, L. (1992) - Statistical Computing and Dynamic Graphics Using Lisp-stat. University of Minnesota, Minneapolis.

Tierney, L. (1996) - Xlispstat 2.1. Release 3, Beta release notes. University of Minnesota, Minneapolis.

Tittel, E., M. Gaither, S. Hassinger and M. Erwin (1996) - Web Programming: Secrets with HTML, CGI and Perl. IDG Books, Foster City.

Toint, Ph.L., E. Cornélis, C. Cirillo, Ph. Barette, A. Dessy, T. Jacobs., R. Verfaillie, J.-M. Museux, E. Waeytens, S. Saelens, C. Durand, V. André, K. Van Hoof, E. Heylen and I. Pollet (2001) - Enquête nationale sur la mobilité des ménages. Réalization et résultats. Rapport final. *SSTC,* Brussels.

Vamplew, P., D. Clark and A. Adams (1996) - Techniques for dealing with missing values in feedforward networks. *Proc. of Australian Conference on Neural Networks,* 251-254, Camberra.

Vanderdonckt, J. (1998a) - Conception ergonomique de page web. *Course notes,* FUNDP, Namur.

Vanderdonckt, J. (1998b) - Conception ergonomique de transparents et diapositives. FUNDP, Namur.

Vanderdonckt, J. (1998c) - Conception ergonomique d'une présentation assistée par ordinateur. FUNDP, Namur.

Vromans, J. and S. Design (1996) - Quick Reference Guide, programming Perl. ftp.kulnet.kuleuven.ac.be/pub/mirror/CPAN/authors/Johan_Vromans/

Wall, L., T. Christiansen and R.L. Schwartz (1997) - Programmation en Perl. O'Reilly, Sebastopol.

Weckström-Eno, K. (1999) - Long distance passenger travel. *Statistics in focus, Transport*, **Theme 7, Volume 4,** Eurostat, Luxembourg.

Werbach, K. (1996) - Le guide rapide du langage HTML. werbach.com/barezones.

Wermuth, M. (1985) - Non-sampling errors due to non-response in written household travel surveys. In E.S. Ampt, A.J. Richardson and W. Brög (eds.) *New Survey Methods in Transport*, 349-365, VNU Science, Utrecht, Holland.

Wermuth, M. (1985) - Errors arising from incorrect and incomplete information in surveys of non-home activity patterns. In E.S. Ampt, A.J. Richardson and W. Brög (Eds.), *New Survey Methods in Transport,* 333-347, VNU Science Press, Utrecht, Holland.

Wofinden, D. and M. Scott (1997) - Report on the cognitive-laboratory pre-test surveys for the MEST-project. STRS, Twickenham.

Youssefzadeh, M. (forthcoming) - Long Distance Diaries today: A Collection of Recent Surveys. *Arbeitsberichte Verkehrs. und Raumplanung*, 55, Institut für Verkehrsplanung, Transporttechnik, Strassen- und Eisenbahnbau, ETH, Zürich.

Youssefzadeh, M. and K.W. Axhausen (1996) - Tender documents: First MEST pilots. *Report to the CEC, DG VII, MEST Internal Working Paper,* **IWP01 and IWP02,** Fakultät für Bauingenieurwessen und Architektur, Leopold-Franzens-Universität, Innsbruck.

Youssefzadeh, M. and K.W. Axhausen (1998) - Tender documents: Third MEST pilots. *Report to the CEC, DG VII, MEST Internal Working Paper,* **IWP05 and IWP06,** Fakultät für Bauingenieurwessen und Architektur, Leopold-Franzens-Universität, Innsbruck.

Youssefzadeh, M. and K.W. Axhausen (1996) - Long distance diaries today: Review and critique, *Deliverable*, **D1**, MEST-Project, Fakultät für Bauingenieur-wesen und Architektur, Leopold-Franzens-Universität, Innsbruck.

Youssefzadeh, M. and K.W. Axhausen (1996) - Long distance diaries today: Review and critique. *Deliverable*, **D1**, MEST-Project, Fakultät für Bauingenieurwesen und Architektur, Leopold-Franzens-Universität, Innsbruck.

Youssefzadeh, M. and K.W. Axhausen (1996) - Long-distance diaries today: Initial review and critique. *Report to the CEC, DGVII, Transport Research Programme of the 4th Framework Programme, MEST Deliverable,* **D2**, Fakultät für Bauingenieurwesen und Architektur, Leopold-Franzens-Universität, Innsbruck.

Zito, R., G. D'Este and M.A.P. Taylor (1994) - Global Positioning system in the time domain: how useful a tool for intelligent vehicle-highway systems? *Transportation Research*, **3** (4), 193-209.

Zmud, J. and C. Arce (1997) - Item non-response in travel surveys: causes and solutions. *Transportation Research Circular*, **E-C008**, II-D/20, TRB, Washington D.C.

Index

Index